Praise for the *New York Times* bestseller
SMALL SACRIFICES

"Rule has an instinct for suspense, knowing just what information to leak to the reader and when." —*The Washington Post Book World*

"A detailed, probing inquiry. . . . From start to finish, Rule's account informatively unweaves the sad features of Downs's life and gives a moving description of the human side of law enforcement." —*Boston Herald*

"A raw docudrama of almost unbelievable intensity." —*Booklist*

"Excellent. . . . One of the most detailed studies of a sociopath to dignify the true-crime circuit." —*The San Francisco Chronicle*

"A fascinating and grisly story. . . . Unputdownable." —*New York Daily News*

"A good read. . . . Rule springs surprises and revelations with a novelist's skill." —*The Seattle Times*

"A riveting, engrossing account." —*The Portland Oregonian*

"Fascinating." —*Seattle Post Intelligencer*

"Superb. . . . [A] riveting detective story. . . . As good a page-turner as any fictional murder mystery." —*Indianapolis Star*

"Fascinating. . . . Rule does a marvelous job!" —*Palm Springs Desert Sun*

"Chilling. . . . A good whodunit made better—and more horrible—by the fact that it's true." —*Rapid City Journal*

"Fascinating and well-documented!" —*Fort Worth Star-Telegram*

"A page-turner. . . . Superb. . . . Riveting." —*Panama City News-Herald*

"An utterly mesmerizing true story, told in intricate detail." —*Newark Advocate*

SMALL SACRIFICES

ANN RULE

BERKLEY

NEW YORK

BERKLEY
An imprint of Penguin Random House LLC
penguinrandomhouse.com

ISBN: 9780593335178

Signet mass-market edition / July 1988
Berkley mass-market edition / June 2019
Berkley trade paperback edition / March 2021

Printed in the United States of America
1   3   5   7   9   10   8   6   4   2

Cover design by Jason Booher

For Christine and Danny . . . and Cheryl Downs.

The fairest things have fleetest end,
Their scent survives their close:
But the rose's scent is bitterness
To him that loved the rose.

—Francis Thompson

PROLOGUE

There is no more idyllic spot in May than the Willamette Valley that cradles Eugene and Springfield, Oregon. Sheltered by the Cascade Range to the east and the steel-blue and purple ridges of the coastal mountains on the western horizon, the valley was an oasis for pioneers more than a century ago. It remains an oasis today. Rivers thread their way through Eugene and Springfield: the Willamette, the McKenzie, the Mohawk, the Little Mohawk—nourishing the land.

Eugene and Springfield are sister cities—but far from twins. Eugene, with a population of 100,000, is bigger, brighter, and far more sophisticated. Eugene has the University of Oregon and the prestigious Hult Center for the Performing Arts. Eugene is the runners' mecca of the world—spawner of champion after champion; it has been estimated that one out of three of its citizens run regularly. Not jog—*run*. Eugene is fitness personified, with bicyclists' paths emblazoned along the edges of even the busiest downtown street, sacrosanct. Eugene is the successful sister of the paired cities, cool and slender, professional. Her restaurants serve artichoke and ricotta pie, salads with raspberry vinegar, Brie and paté and wild mushroom and sorrel soup, and vie with one another to discover ever more obscure spices.

Springfield, half Eugene's size, is the sister who never graduated from high school, who works for Weyerhaeuser or Georgia–Pacific, and no longer notices the acrid smell. People in Springfield work a forty- or fifty-, or sixty-, hour week, and if they still need exercise, they go bowling or to a country-western dancing tavern. The appetizers in a good Springfield restaurant are carrot sticks, celery, pickled beets and soda crackers; the entree is excellent chicken-fried steak or prime rib. The main street is called Main Street and it wears its neon signs in proud proliferation. Excepting Portland, Springfield is the largest industrial region in Oregon, and yet pioneers' descendants cling to tradition even as factories threaten to obliterate the old days. It is a city unpretentious and homey.

A long time back, Clint Eastwood lived in Springfield for a while.

The dipping, curving Belt Line freeway connects Eugene and Spring-field, and their boundaries merge into one another. Some citizens live in Eugene and work in Springfield—or commute to Eugene from neat ranch houses in Springfield. Both cities have wonderful parks and spectacular scenery. Between the two, everything that anyone might seek—barring tropical temperatures—is available.

Willamette Valley winters are long and dismal for rain-haters, clouds hanging so low that they obscure even the huge buttes looming north and south of Eugene. In May when the sun glows and the rivers have absorbed the rainstorms, it is as if the gray days never were. Oaks and maples leaf out, brilliant against the darker green of fir and pine. The air is drenched with the sweetness of fresh-cut rye grass, wild roses, strawberries, and a million bearded irises. Beneath this sweetness: the pungent lacing of on-ions, sawdust, cedar, and the fecund smell of good red earth, furrowed and waiting for seed.

MAY, 1984

It was ironic that it should be May again. Four seasons had come and gone since it happened. May to May. Neat. Some slight sense of order fi-nally after months of chaos and uncertainty.

Oregon has good springs and bad springs, depending on the point of view. This May was not good. The wind that whipped around the Hilton Hotel and the Lane County Courthouse was as sodden as a handkerchief drenched with tears. Rain pelted and slashed and dripped, finally trap-ping itself in small torrents in the gutters at Oak and Eighth Streets. The first day of the trial so many had waited for was a day to stay at home, light a fire, and read a good book.

And still the parking lot across the street from the courthouse was full, and the Hilton had dozens of rooms reserved for out-of-town media.

The carnival began where the elevator doors opened onto the court-house's third-floor lobby. Cameras and lights and reporters and micro-phones. Technicians laying cable along the floor, covering it carefully with silver duct tape. Photographers leaning precariously over the "No pictures beyond here" barrier, pressing their luck for a forbidden candid shot. The hall was filled—not with sadness but with excited expectancy.

The would-be gallery lined up—a hundred, two hundred people, shivering and drenched, women mostly, hoping to be admitted to the inner sanctum of Courtroom Number Three, to pass beyond the double oak doors whose two tiny windows were covered with butcher paper blocking even so much as a peek inside. Uniformed deputies and a thick rope attached to a heavy steel stanchion held them back. The women, and a sprinkling of embarrassed-looking men, carried raincoats and lunches in precisely creased brown bags. Those first in line had been there for hours. Occasionally, necessities of nature forced one or another to dash around the corner to the restrooms, a neatly folded raincoat left to save a place in line. The fabric marker was always honored.

Oregonians, all Northwesterners, are a civilized breed. Even so, when the doors finally opened, there was a stampede. Two little old ladies were carried along in the surging tide of human bodies, their black laced shoes inches above the floor. Unruffled, they sailed in, and found two narrow spots on the long benches, hats still firmly planted on their heads.

The long wait promised to be worthwhile. Advocacy both for and against the defendant was passionate. The gallery murmured and twittered; spectators half-rose to crane their necks for a closer look at the principals—mostly at the defendant.

Few eyes lingered long on Fred Hugi, the lone assistant district attorney who would be prosecuting this case for the State. Thirty-nine years old, his dark hair already salt-and-peppered, Hugi had shouldered the final responsibility for bringing the defendant to trial. Tall, lean (or downright skinny, depending . . .), tough as whipcord, he wore a moustache that gave him the look of a man from another, earlier century—some frontier lawman or judge, maybe, peering solemnly from a browning tintype.

From time to time, Hugi's brown eyes swept over the courtroom. They seemed to fix on no one, and they revealed nothing. He glanced over his notes on the long yellow legal pad. Behind his tightly capped facade, he was champing at the bit, eager to get on with it. He was neither pessimistic nor elated; he was immensely relieved to find himself at last in court. By avocation a long-distance runner, Hugi saw the weeks ahead as a marathon—steady, determined pacing after meticulous training. Brilliant and stubborn—no, *tenacious*—Fred Hugi never gave up on anything he set out to do, even though his single-mindedness had been known to irritate the hell out of people around him.

The words before him blurred. No matter. He was ready. He knew it all by heart; he could make his opening statement in his sleep. He'd lain awake too many long nights, worrying this case—seeing it from one angle, and then reversing it, turning it in his mind like a Rubik's Cube. Sometimes he suspected he knew more about the defendant than he did about his own wife after almost two decades of marriage. It was a good thing Joanne understood him, accepted that her husband had to do what he had to do, and left him alone, unquestioning; he'd been obsessed with this case for a year.

The defendant sat so close to him now that with the slightest extension of his right elbow, their arms would touch. Hugi caught the scent of jail soap and a faint whiff of acrid perspiration. He was accustomed to the peculiar economy of space in Lane County courtrooms. The prosecutor, the defendant, and the defense attorney sat adjacent to one another along one nest of tables. Normally, the State and the Defense in a major trial have their own space, but these battle lines were only imaginary, drawn in the air—as thick and impenetrable as iron walls. Fred Hugi sat on the far left, the defendant sat in the middle, and Jim Jagger, attorney for the defense, sat on the far right. They composed the triangle around which everything else would revolve.

Hugi saw that the accused seemed confident, rolling—as always—with any punch, leaning over often to whisper and laugh in Jagger's ear, ignoring the prosecutor. That was fine with him. He had taken infinite pains to be seen as only "a dopey guy," an unknown factor. The defendant clearly viewed him as negligible. No threat. That was exactly the way Hugi wanted it.

He, on the other hand, had tremendous respect for his opponent. Smarter than hell, a quick study, and, through the defense's rights of discovery, aware of *his* whole case going in. The worthiest of adversaries, armed with a clever attorney, and backed, seemingly, by a huge fan club.

It was bizarre that the crimes the defendant was accused of defied credulity. Their very nature threatened to turn the tide against the State. Too cruel to believe.

Fred Hugi had waited so long for this moment. Days had become weeks, and weeks months—months that had promised to stretch into a lifetime. This was the case that appeared initially to be simple—even or-

dinary in a macabre way—and easy to adjudicate. He'd been hopi[ng]
entrusted with a murder case that might demand much more of h[im]
Something interesting. Something that would challenge him, push hi[m]
to the wall, and hone his trial expertise. When the Downs case came
along, he had made the erroneous assumption that it would be over in a
day or so, that it would take just long enough to clear to make him lose
his place in the long line of assistant DA's waiting for a "good" homicide.

Easy. It had been hell. There was every indication that it would continue to be hell. There had never been a single moment when this somber,
intense prosecutor had shouted "Aha! Now we've got it! From here on, it's
a shoo-in."

A year in Vietnam had tested Fred Hugi severely; a year jousting with
this media-savvy defendant, and with at least half the population of Eugene and vicinity, had been worse. Prosecuting a defendant like this—for
particularly heinous crimes—scraped roughly across the grain of middle-
American mores. Fred Hugi knew he was sniping at traditions as en-
trenched as Mom and apple pie. His eyes slid again over the packed
gallery, and he winced at the row upon row of "concerned" citizens.

He figured they sure as hell weren't there for him. Solid support for the
accused. If *he* recognized this outpouring of sympathy, he knew the jury
would see it too. It did not occur to him that some of the spectators might
be there simply to hear the juicy details of the defendant's purportedly
promiscuous sex life, or even that some of them might be *his* cheering
section.

He felt quite isolated. That was OK; he was accustomed to it.

Fred Hugi believed absolutely that what he was doing was right—that
he had no other way to go. He had someone to answer to and if he lost, he
would lose big.

And so would they.

He looked at the jury. Twelve jurors; three alternates. Hugi had rather
unorthodox theories about juries. He considered the ceremony of voir dire
to pick unprejudiced jurors basically bullshit, easily abused, and a vehicle
for influencing likely jurors to take a position before they heard any evidence at all. He was no good at it; he knew he had neither charm nor
charisma, and he detested having to play the game.

Now Jim Jagger *was* good at it. Jagger and the prospective jurors had

:d. Hugi had been content to play off Jagger. As long
ln't attempted to slant facts that might come out in
i kept his mouth shut. But he tensed when he heard
/ ask about religious affiliations and insinuate refer-
iurch work. Still, Hugi was relieved that it was Jim
not Melvin Belli, who had been scheduled to head the
defense team. Belli would surely have held press parties on the top of the
Eugene Hilton every night, effectively turning this bleakest of tragedies
into a media circus.

Hugi had just about had it with the press; he glanced at them, packed
into the first row behind the rail. He suspected for most of them this was
all headlines only—not pain and blood and tears. They were as bad as the
gallery—worse, really; many of them had pandered to the suspect, dancing obligingly to whichever tune was called. Well, now they'd get their
headlines all right. He couldn't stop that, but they might be in for a surprise or two.

Hugi hadn't changed anything about himself for this trial. Balking at
the advice of his courtroom expert—DA's investigator, Ray Broderick—
he'd refused to grow his hair longer so he'd look less rigid. Nor would Hugi
consider modifying his apparel. In court he always wore a conservative,
off-the-rack suit with baggy trousers, or a blazer and slacks, a regimen-
tally striped tie, and heavy, polished, wing-tipped shoes. He rarely smiled.

Hugi's strategy in this trial was to be a teacher. He was going to show
the jury exactly what had happened, presenting some extremely technical evidence and testimony. Would the jurors understand it? Would they
even *try* to understand it—or would it strike them as repetitive and boring? And one of his witnesses was very fragile, in danger of being broken
beyond repair.

The trial would be like walking on the cutting edge of a knife.

With it all, he was as ready as he would ever be. He would demonstrate
what he believed devoutly to be the truth. That was what justice was
about. *The truth.* No frills. No high jinks. No pratfalls.

Hugi expected that he would have to play catch-up after voir dire. He
assumed he wasn't likeable, so why should the jurors warm to him? He
knew some people—particularly the cops—delighted in calling him an

asshole. Hell, sometimes his own investigators called him worse. When he was working on a case, he could be a juggernaut—and Lord help anyone who got in the way or failed to complete an assignment. But he never asked anyone to do more than he himself did.

The voir dire hadn't been as bad as Hugi expected. He'd used all his challenges, and he still had some reservations about the final twelve, but basically it was a crapshoot. He would have been just as happy to pick the first twelve people who came out of the jury pool. Same difference.

All he asked were a dozen intelligent human beings with common sense, salt-of-the-earth people who couldn't be flimflammed. He knew that most people are frightened of making a decision. Americans have become so used to "seeing" the crime committed on television that anything else—including real life—becomes fraught with "reasonable doubt."

He looked at his jury now, sitting up there, getting used to their new roles. How many of them had guts enough to look someone in the eye and say straight out, You're a murderer! All he needed was one bozo who had already made up his mind and four to six weeks of trial would be down the tubes.

Fred Hugi was asking for a conviction on murder. He needed all twelve of those jurors. He couldn't afford to lose even one of them.

The defendant only needed one to beat the murder charge. Everybody on the West Coast had heard the story by now, and half seemed to suspect a "railroad." Hugi thought of the stacks of letters in his files, calling him and the cops everything from cruel fascists to crooked grandstanders. Was one of those fifty percent sitting up there at this very moment, smiling guilelessly down at him? If someone wanted on a jury bad enough, it wasn't that hard to come up with the right answers on voir dire.

Fred Hugi bit down hard, unconsciously grinding his teeth. The weeks ahead were so important to him. This was more than just a trial. For him, it was as simple as good against evil; the verdict waiting down the road might help him allay his growing feeling that the system wasn't working.

He rose to make his opening statement. The accused listened, bored at first, and then with an incredulous expression. For the first time, Fred Hugi was a recognizable enemy. A dangerous enemy. The defendant bent

over a yellow legal pad, furiously scrawling huge letters, and then holding
it up for Hugi to see. He read it without missing a beat in his presentation
to the jury.

The tablet read, LIE!

Jim Jagger reached for the pad and shook his head slightly. The pad hit
the oak table with a slap; the defendant was seething.

Someone was lying. Maybe when they emerged from this courtroom
a month or two down the road, the question of who it was would be put
to rest forever. . . .

CHAPTER 1

It had been, if not a quiet night, at least a normal night for the Springfield Police Department. Cops know that hot weather encourages impromptu parties and triggers family beefs. The SPD log for that twenty-four-hour period lists the expected ration of trouble between a quarter after ten and twenty minutes to eleven Thursday night.

An anonymous caller complained at 10:16 P.M. about a party on North First Street. "RP [reporting party] called to report a loud party in the above area. Unit dispatched. Responsibles contacted. Noise abated. Subjects to depart the area."

"Suspicious conditions" were reported—again anonymously—at 10:22 P.M. "RP reported hearing a small child crying. Unit dispatched. Involved parties contacted, found to be a dispute between children. No crime involved."

At 10:32 the call was a bit more serious. "RP called to report a male/female verbal dispute in the apartment complex on North Seventeenth. Male half reported to be carrying rifle. Units dispatched. Charged with menacing. Lodged Lane County Jail."

At the headquarters of the Lane County Sheriff's Office in Eugene, Sheriff Dave Burks's officers were also pulling a fairly quiet shift. Rob Rutherford was the graveyard shift sergeant; Detective Lieutenant Louis Hince would be on call for anything that might require his detectives; thirty-one-year-old Doug Welch was at home in Springfield with his wife, Tamara, and two young sons. Richard Blaine Tracy (of *course*, "Dick Tracy") was a year away from retirement after twenty-six years as a cop, and he would be just as happy if nothing heavy came down before he left. Divorced, Tracy was getting ready for bed alone in his Eugene apartment. Kurt Wuest was away at a training seminar that Thursday night. Roy Pond was working days.

Assistant DA Fred Hugi, radio and television turned off, was reveling in the quiet of a perfect spring evening at his lodgelike home set far back in the forest along the McKenzie River. It was a different life out there in the woods, and he was a different man. He wore frayed jeans and battered logging boots as he planted seedlings to thicken even more the forest outside his windows.

Joanne Hugi, co-director of the computer center at the University of Oregon, was lost in concentration in her computer room. It made her husband smile; he, who had degrees in forestry, finance, and law, had been baffled by the single computer course he'd attempted, and he'd challenged Joanne to try it. She had proved to be a natural, understanding terms and concepts that eluded him. Hugi gave up on computers, but Joanne flew with them, higher and higher. He was extremely proud of her. She'd worked her way up at the university from an entrance level job to the top.

The sun set long before 10 P.M., and Hugi paused to look at the filigree of tree branches silhouetted against the last bit of sky before he took his dirt-caked boots off and went inside. The Hugis' two cats sat on the deck, alert, staring at the glowing eyes of something—probably a deer or raccoon—out there in the woods.

The Hugis had come to this perfect spot along the McKenzie after years of living in the kind of apartments students could afford in the city. It was well worth the half-hour commute into Eugene. Sometimes, they could hear logging trucks zooming by far away on the road, but usually they heard only the wind in the trees, or rain, or the cry of a nighthawk.

The bad call came into the Springfield Police Department at 10:40 P.M.: "Employee of McKenzie–Willamette Hospital advises of gunshot victims at that location. Officers dispatched. Arrived 10:48 P.M."

Rosie Martin, RN; Shelby Day, LPN; Judy Patterson, the night receptionist; and Dr. John Mackey, physician in charge, comprised the evening shift in the emergency room at the McKenzie–Willamette Hospital in Springfield.

The McKenzie–Willamette ER as it existed in the late spring of 1983 was a little cramped, a little out of date. Paint on walls and baseboards had been scrubbed dull and drab; the waiting room furniture was chrome and peeling vinyl.

Facing the two sets of doors that led to the circular driveway off Mohawk Boulevard, the three treatment rooms were to the right: Day Surgery nearest the street, Minor Treatment in the middle, and the Trauma Room at the back. On the left, Judy Patterson's desk was just behind a small waiting area near the street doors. Five feet or so behind her desk there was a small bathroom and beyond that a larger waiting room.

The floors were hospital-waxed shiny—the forest-green-and-white-swirl asphalt tile popular in the 1950s, patched here and there with odd squares. The rooms smelled old. Old wax, old dust, old disinfectant. Old sorrows, it would seem, with the sharpness of immediate grief dulled by time. The old ER had known decades of pain.

That velvet black spring night Dr. Mackey and his staff, working in an almost obsolete ER, would be the first to encounter what was unthinkable for Springfield, what would be unthinkable for even a big city. None of them would have much time to think during the hours they fought to save the injured, their white shoes sliding on floors slick with fresh blood. Only later would terrible musings rush in to destroy all hope of sleep.

Shelby Day is a slender, soft-spoken woman near forty, with six years' experience in the McKenzie–Willamette ER. She wears white slacks and pastel, patterned smocks. When she remembers the night of May 19, 1983, tears well unbidden in her eyes.

"We were working the 4 P.M. to midnight shift. We had the usual kind of 'nice day' injuries—lacerations, bumped heads, sprains, and broken bones. We were busy steadily, but there were no real emergencies. Dr. Mackey was finishing up with a patient at a quarter after ten, and Rosie and I were in that little back room doing paperwork. There's always paperwork to catch up with. Judy was out at her desk in the corridor . . ."

Judy Patterson, a smiling strawberry blonde, works two jobs to support her son Brandon, who was nine in 1983. She is the receptionist in Pediatrics at Eugene's Sacred Heart Hospital on the day shift; after five, she puts in another five or six hours as the ER receptionist at McKenzie–Willamette.

Rosie Martin was pregnant in the spring of 1983, into her second trimester. Already her belly had begun to get in her way as she moved swiftly to care for patients. She was tired, but she didn't complain to her co-workers. She and Shelby worked together quietly in the back room.

When Dr. John Austin Mackey had a full beard, his nurses wondered if he ever smiled. When he shaved it off, they saw that he had been smiling all along behind his hirsute facade. Tall, balding, and broad-shouldered, a bear of a man, Mackey inspires confidence. The perfect emergency room doctor; his assessment of patients' needs is deft. In his late thirties, married, and the father of young children, he had worked full-time in the ER for eight years.

Because they were winding down, the others told Judy she could go home a few minutes early. She was scheduled to leave anyway at 10:30, but she grinned gratefully and grabbed her sweater and purse. As she walked toward the ambulance doors, a woman in the hall, a relative waiting for a patient, called to her.

"There's someone out there honking their horn and yelling for help. You'd better check."

Judy whirled and walked back to where Shelby Day and Rosie Martin were shuffling paperwork.

"Someone needs help out there. They're laying on the horn."

Judy ran back then to the ambulance entrance. Rapidly, she propped open both sets of doors to the drive-through.

Rosie Martin grabbed an air-way and an oxygen mask and headed toward the drive-through. Their most common crisis was cardiac arrest; that's what she and Shelby Day expected to find. It was strange, though, that they had had no prior warning. Invariably, paramedics and police called to warn that they were coming in with a critical case so that the ER crew could gear up.

The two nurses hurried through the double entry doors into the emergency drive-through. A shiny red foreign car was parked under the rain roof. The fluorescent lighting bounced off the car's glittering paint, casting eerie elongated shadows. It was almost impossible for them to see *inside* the car.

"What's going on here?" Rosie Martin asked.

"Somebody just shot my kids!"

A slender blonde woman in jeans and a plaid shirt stood next to the car. She was pale, but she was in control. She wasn't crying and she didn't appear to be hysterical. Desperately she implored them to do something. The two nurses and the young woman gazed at each other for a fraction of a second, and then the emergency personnel went into action.

Rosie Martin had reached the car just ahead of Shelby Day. She ducked through the passenger door; she'd seen a child lying across the right rear seat. Rosie emerged, carrying a girl with long brown hair. The child had to be heavy. Dead weight, Shelby Day thought, and then bit her lip. Rosie carried the little girl in maroon corduroy slacks and a bloody multicolored T-shirt as if she had no weight at all, draping the child carefully around her pregnant abdomen.

As Rosie rushed past Judy Patterson's desk, she turned her head slightly. "Judy! Call a code! It's bad!"

A "code" meant Code 4, a page to summon all available personnel to the ER. Judy Patterson called the hospital operator and told her to activate a code.

Back in the drive-through, Shelby Day saw there was another child on the back seat, behind the driver's seat—a yellow-haired little boy, hardly more than a toddler. She ran around the front of the car and leaned over to release the back of the driver's seat. Her fingers numb with shock, she couldn't find the right lever. She heard Dr. Mackey's voice behind her.

"What's going on, Shelby?" he asked.

"These kids have been shot," she said softly.

"Oh, Jesus Christ," the doctor murmured.

It was not an oath; it was a prayer. Only two words had registered in Mackey's mind: "kids" and "shot." He could see over Shelby's shoulder to the tiny child who was gasping for air and crying weakly.

The blonde woman murmured that the seat lever was on the side. Shelby's hand reached the right spot, clicked the catch free. Before she could straighten up, Dr. Mackey had reached past her, scooped the little boy up in powerful arms, and disappeared into the hospital. He had seen what the nurses hadn't noticed yet. When he leaned in to get the little boy, he'd glimpsed yet another figure crumpled on the floor in front, and thought, My God! There's a third one! What are we going to do?

Mackey was sure Shelby Day had seen the third child a moment after he had. But in the shadows, in her shock, she hadn't.

The quick look he'd had at the first two injured youngsters told Mackey they were dealing with chest wounds. Short of a direct head shot, there is nothing more cataclysmic than gunshot wounds into the chests of little children. Mackey too shouted at Judy Patterson. The command was short, but Judy understood.

"Find Wilhite!"

Dr. Steven Wilhite is a thoracic surgeon. To crack a chest, to break the sternum and reach with gloved, artist's hands into the heart and lungs of a human being, takes skill that few surgeons possess. Wilhite is one of the few board-certified thoracic surgeons in the Springfield–Eugene area. His presence in the ER was something devoutly to be wished.

Wilhite was just pulling into his own driveway when his beeper picked up the code call at the hospital, followed by a specific request for his presence. Children had been shot. He shifted into reverse and turned back toward McKenzie–Willamette. The drive normally took him twenty minutes. Driving eighty miles an hour, he cut his time to eight minutes.

Shelby Day turned to follow Mackey into the ER.

"No—" the blonde woman said urgently. "Cher . . . Cheri!"

Shelby stopped, puzzled. "What?"

The woman pointed toward the floor area of the passenger seat in front. "Cheryl's on the floor. She hasn't moved at all."

Shelby peered into the shadowy car. *There was another child!* A dark sweater had been draped over a little girl who lay facedown on the carpet. The slender nurse had to sit the youngster up to get a good grip on her. Then, with one fluid movement, she had her free of the car and was running toward the ER. This child was as heavy as a stone in her arms. When she felt not even a faint independent support of muscle from her burden, Shelby feared that this victim was gone. Still, she ran. Shelby felt a heartbeat bumping crazily, but it was only her own.

She laid her burden gently on the bed at the left rear of the trauma room. She could see doctors and nurses working frantically on the other two youngsters. She could hear the hospital's PA system droning out the Code 4 over and over. Already, the ER was beginning to fill with personnel, all of them working efficiently with at least surface calm.

Jan Goldberg Temple, a registered nurse assigned to the intensive care unit, hurried to the ER. She joined Shelby Day at the bedside of the third child. Carleen Elbridge, an X-ray technician, was there and Ruth Freeman, the supervising nurse on duty, and Sue Sogn, an RN from the third floor. Two respiratory therapists—Bob Gulley and Demetria "D.J." Forester—rushed in. Joe "Tony" Curtis, the maintenance man, worked along with the medical team, running for blood units, propping doors open, doing whatever was needed.

It was sheer luck that so many physicians were available to help this late on a weekday evening.

Dr. David Scott Miller is a pediatrician, a fine-boned man with a moustache and glasses, a gentle man meant to be a children's specialist. Ordinarily, his hospital rounds would have ended hours before, but on this night one delay after another had kept him at McKenzie–Willamette Hospital. He was walking toward the hospital parking lot when he heard a commotion and deciphered electrifying phrases in the words cutting through the night air. He heard "children" and "shooting."

He turned and sprinted for the ER, all his fatigue forgotten.

Judy Patterson reached Dr. George Foster, a pediatric surgeon on staff at Sacred Heart Hospital in Eugene, and he too raced to McKenzie–Willamette.

Four of them had arrived in the red Nissan Pulsar. Shelby Day had noted how the young woman—the mother?—had stood so woodenly next to the car. Shock. The layman is never prepared for the gore and suddenness of traumatic injury. Shelby turned to see that the blonde woman had followed her into the trauma room. Stark white but dry-eyed, she stood mutely and glanced from bed to bed to bed.

She shouldn't be here, Shelby thought. No mother could deal with such a sight. All three of her children were probably dying. Shelby spotted Judy Patterson standing quietly outside the doorway to the treatment room and called softly, "Judy! Take her out of here!"

The woman went obediently with Judy. "OK. I'll just sit here on the stretcher." She waited there, perched on the wheeled gurney across from Judy's desk.

Shelby Day forgot about the blonde woman as she fought to save the child she'd found crumpled on the front floorboards. She suctioned the youngster's throat to clear blood clots that were blocking air. But the clots were as thick as liver, hemorrhagic blood in the throat so long that it had coagulated. Odd. It was rare for the ER crew to see coagulated blood. Patients were usually brought in while they were still actively bleeding. Each time Shelby removed a blood clot, she found another beneath it.

As Shelby struggled with her hopeless task, Jan Temple stripped off the child's clothing, leaving her naked save for a pair of green shorts she wore in place of panties. Jan attached the Life-Pak leads to the patient's chest. The heart monitor required human electrical impulses to react. There was nothing there. Only a straight line; she might as well have hooked up the monitor to the bed or a chair.

Dr. Mackey broke off for a moment from his ministrations to the two children who still breathed, however tenuously. He too attempted to intubate the last victim discovered, but only elicited blood. Puzzled, he lifted the child gently and found two bullet holes in the little girl's back—one over the right shoulder blade, and one just below the left shoulder blade. He stared at the heart monitor and slowly shook his head.

"There's nothing we can do for this child," he said flatly.

Shelby was angry, unwilling to accept the death of this child, whose butterscotch hair lay so brilliantly alive against the white sheet. "What do you mean you're not going to do anything for her?" she demanded of Mackey.

"Shelby," Mackey said gently. "She's gone. There's nothing we *can* do. She was dead when you carried her in. I'm sorry."

She knew he was right; she put aside the suction device, and stared down at the little girl, her skin as waxy yellow and translucent as a crushed gardenia. So young—not more than six or seven. She'd worn a pair of brown cord jeans with a blue Levi belt, and a faded purple and white striped T-shirt. The sweater that had hidden the youngster from the view of the rescuers was far too big for a child. It was blue gray, U.S. government issue for postal workers. There was a U.S. Mail patch on the left sleeve. Shelby folded the clothing and put the garments in the clothes basket at the end of the bed.

The other two children were barely alive. The blonde boy whimpered softly, panicked by his inability to draw air into his lungs. Jan Temple moved away from the dead child and pitched in to help with the boy.

The other girl was motionless. David Miller worked feverishly over her. She looked to be a year or so older than the dead child. She had two small-caliber bullet wounds in the left chest. One slug had entered near the left nipple, traveling completely through her chest, exiting at the scapula in her back. The second bullet had entered two or three centimeters from the first, leaving a much larger wound, and was still in her body. There was a third through-and-through wound near the base of her left thumb.

She was as close to death as a human can be, actually in the beginning processes of dying. She registered no blood pressure, and she was not breathing beyond a few agonal gasps for air. Her pupils had reacted to light when she arrived, but even as David Miller watched, he could see the life fading from her eyes. Damn it! They would not lose this child too.

On Miller's orders, respiratory therapist Gulley inserted an endotracheal tube into her throat, and tried to force air into her lungs. There was some blockage preventing the oxygen from expanding her chest. A portable chest X ray pinpointed the problem. In the left lung a massive hemorrhage left no room for air.

Moreover, the patient's right lung was collapsing. She was rapidly bleeding out, in imminent danger of dying from exsanguination. Her blood tests indicated barely enough oxygen-carrying hemoglobin to sustain life.

She was drifting away from them. Her skin was cold, shaded the dread blue of cyanosis, and her heartbeat was faltering and sporadic on the monitor. All signs were incompatible with life. She had nothing going for her beyond the adamant refusal of her physicians to let her slip away.

The patient's heart stopped beating.

Miller "pushed" (rapid, forceful injection) thirty milligrams of sodium bicarb to urge it to beat, then glanced up to see Steve Wilhite rush into the room.

The chest surgeon looked at the patient. She *looked dead* and he cursed himself for being too late. There was no blood pressure now. No pulse. Her pupils were fixed and dilated.

Wilhite and Miller simply refused to give up.

Steve Wilhite grabbed a chest tube and plunged it directly through her skin and chest well into the left lung. There was no need for anesthetic; the child could feel nothing. He recovered 300 ccs of bright red blood.

Swiftly, he plunged another chest tube into her right lung. No blood appeared in the tube and there was very little, if any, air. That lung had folded in on itself, flat as an empty bellows. In the other lung, she was drowning in her own blood.

Wilhite rapidly inserted a CVP line and hit an artery with the first try—the first bit of good news: the patient's veins and arteries had not collapsed. O-negative blood was rapidly infused.

And then . . . miraculously, the heartbeat, tentative as the fluttering of a butterfly's wings, began again. Somewhere along the sure passage toward death, this little girl had turned around.

Wilhite, Miller, and Mackey dared to hope that she might come all the way back to them when they saw that her pupils had begun to react, and that she now had a systolic blood pressure of sixty!

New chest X rays showed that her right lung had expanded, but the left lung was still filling relentlessly with fresh blood. Her chance for survival remained as frail as a strand of spider webbing. As rapidly as blood was infused into her veins, it leaked away through her left lung.

It would be 11:45 P.M. before she was stable enough to be transported to surgery. Even then Bob Gulley would still have to breathe for her through the trach tube, as her stretcher was walked to the operating room with Drs. Wilhite and Miller trotting alongside.

Dr. Mackey and Dr. Foster stayed with the little boy. Jan Temple worked beside them, trying to comfort the toddler. She removed his clothing—a green and white Hockey Puck shirt with the number forty on the front, a pair of faded OshKosh B'Gosh jeans, and size two jockey shorts—and put them in the clothing basket attached to the gurney.

He looked to be about three. John Mackey had begun resuscitation from the moment he'd first carried him into the trauma room. He'd inserted a CVP line into the right jugular vein and started the flow of a solution to keep the veins open and ready for medication or a transfusion.

There was a small bullet wound of entry a fraction of an inch to the right of the spinal column. It was a near-contact wound. Mackey could see black powder from a gun's barrel around the bullet hole.

The tiny boy was washed of color and terrified, his heart racing one hundred and fifty beats a minute. He couldn't draw a good breath. Mackey found markedly diminished breath sounds in his left lung. He inserted a chest tube; blood and trapped air gushed out. The small lung expanded, and the towheaded boy began to breathe easily, but he continued to sob, a steady keening wail.

He was out of immediate danger, but the bullet had come so close to his spinal cord. Injuries to this vital nerve center are unpredictable. If all went well, he might recover completely. If the spinal cord, insulted, should swell. . . .

The bullet had slammed into his back close to T-6 and T-7. His arms would be all right. Everything below midchest was threatened; there was a possibility that he might never walk again.

Steve Wilhite performed an exploratory thoracotomy on the surviving girl. He found the ragged exit wound in the upper lobe of the left lung, cut away the ravaged tissue that was steadily oozing blood, and joined the now-clean edges with sutures. There was no more seepage, but so much of her blood had had to be replaced. With complete blood replacement, there can be a profound loss in clotting capability, as well as diminished hemoglobin. Blood chemistry, out of balance, may behave chaotically.

But she *lived*.

At the completion of surgery, she had a normal blood pressure reading. She woke up quickly, fighting the endotracheal tube, pulling at the proliferation of tubes that were connected to her body. She was very, very, frightened, but she responded to the nurses' voices.

One child was dead. One child had defied the odds and lived through profound blood loss, heart stoppage, and delicate surgery. One child seemed stable, but was at risk of paralysis. Who in the name of God could have aimed a pistol at three small children and pulled the trigger five times?

CHAPTER 2

Call the cops! He shot my kids!

—Diane Downs, May 19, 1983

It fell to Judy Patterson to comfort the young woman who had brought the wounded children to the hospital—and to try to find out what had happened to them.

She told Judy that her name was Elizabeth Downs, but that she went by Diane, her middle name. The injured children were her own: Christie Ann, eight, Cheryl Lynn, seven, and Stephen "Danny" Downs, three.

Diane Downs remained in a shocklike state; she spoke with a certain flatness of expression, holding her emotions in.

She wore a pale blue T-shirt that spelled out "Nantucket" across her ample breasts. Over that, she wore a blue plaid shirt. There was a small red stain on one sleeve. Diane's blue jeans were well-worn, even baggy, but she had a near-perfect figure. She looked young, probably in her mid-twenties. She was quite tan, although now the golden tan was a thin veneer of false color over chalky skin beneath.

Diane was not pretty; depending on the angle, Judy thought, she was either plain or beautiful. She had the facial bone structure that models have: high cheekbones, an expanse of delicately rounded brow. There was a Dresden-doll quality about the round curves of Diane's face, and yet it was far from a perfect face, marred—ever so slightly—by a jaw a trace too prominent, lips a shade too thin over long teeth. When Diane looked away, her profile *was* perfect.

Her eyes . . . Diane's eyes dominated her face: somehow devoid of depth, and yet almost hypnotic in intensity. They were huge, pretty eyes; there was no fault there to jar the viewer. Diane's pupils were gray or green or yellow, depending on how the light caught itself in them, and they *resembled* something. What? Green grapes, maybe . . . or cat's eyes.

Something. Judy felt as if she were gazing into those sunglasses that bounce back only the observer's own image, giving no clue to the identity of the watcher behind the mirrored lenses.

Diane's pupils floated toward the top of her eyes, with an unusually wide expanse of white beneath. Her brows were plucked into two pencil-thin lines, exposing her eyes even more.

Judy caught herself staring and dragged her gaze away. She tried to organize her thoughts. She had called all the emergency medical personnel; the children were in good hands.

But Diane was insisting there was still a man out there with a gun . . .

There was so much more to be done. Judy called the Springfield Police Department. She wasn't sure just where the shooting had taken place; the city limits were not that far from the hospital. The gunman might even be on his way here.

"I figured that it had to be some kind of domestic dispute," she later recalled. "If a man had been crazy enough and cruel enough to shoot three children, I thought he might follow them into the ER and shoot everybody here. I wanted to get the police here. I don't mind saying I was scared."

"I want to call my parents," Diane murmured. "I need to call them."

Judy nodded and covered the phone. "I'm talking to the police. Just a moment. Could you tell me what happened again, so that I can tell them?"

"Somebody shot my kids . . ."

Judy repeated information as Diane related it to her. Diane didn't know just where the shooting had occurred, but she thought she could find it again. She mentioned "Mohawk" and "Marcola." Mohawk *Boulevard* ran directly in front of the hospital, but then there was Old Mohawk *Road* just outside of Springfield. Marcola was a crossroads town northeast of Springfield. It was difficult to tell exactly which area Diane was talking about.

As Judy talked to the dispatcher, Diane went into the small restroom just behind her desk area. The door remained open; Judy could hear running water.

As she hung up the phone, she saw Diane head again toward the trauma room. She hurried after her to stop her. Judy glanced into the trauma room. Someone had drawn the drapes around the bed where Cheryl's body rested; there was a gap in the cloth, though, and one chalky arm was partially visible.

Judy quickly tugged Diane away, into the minor surgery room. In the bright light, Judy saw that Diane had apparently been injured too. Beneath the plaid shirt, her left arm was wrapped from elbow to wrist in a brightly colored beach towel. Unwrapping the towel, Judy found an ovoid, nasty-looking wound on the outer surface of Diane's arm, almost exactly halfway between her wrist and her elbow. There were two smaller wounds.

Judy wasn't a nurse, but she was the only one available. She put Betadine on the three bloody lesions to disinfect them, wiping away the black particles around the first hole. Then she bandaged the arm. The wounds weren't life threatening, although they looked painful.

"What happened?" Judy asked Diane again. "Where were you when he shot the children?"

"We went out toward Marcola to see a friend. We were headed back, driving along Old Mohawk Road. My kids were laughing and talking. I was laughing at something Danny said, and talking to Christie. . . . There was this man, standing there in the middle of the road. He looked like he needed help. I stopped the car, and got out. He wanted my keys. He just reached in through the window and shot my kids. It's a terrible thing to be laughing one minute, and then have something like this happen to you."

Judy touched Diane's good arm. There were no words to say. "You can call your father now. Come on back to the desk."

Wordlessly, Diane followed her. Her face was a mask. She dialed a number, waited for someone to answer, and then blurted into the phone, "He shot the kids. He shot me too."

She hung up and turned to Judy. "They're on their way."

Wes and Willadene Frederickson, Diane's parents, the grandparents of Christie, Cheryl, and Danny Downs, had retired for the night in the white ranch house where they lived, less than two miles from McKenzie–Willamette Hospital. Elizabeth Diane was the oldest of their five grown children. She had moved from Arizona to be near them only weeks before. Now, just when their lives seemed to be moving along with some serenity, a ringing phone in the night had signaled disaster.

Willadene was particularly afraid of hospitals; she could not imagine that anything good could come of a call from a hospital. Wes had lost both his parents in a terrible car accident a decade earlier; Willadene had never again been able to hear a phone ring in the night without a stab of anxiety.

She threw on clothes, not noticing what she wore, and joined her husband. The Fredericksons raced for the hospital. Wes realized just as he drove up to the emergency entrance that he had forgotten his false teeth.

Wes Frederickson is an ascetically handsome man in his early fifties, who resembles Palmer Cortlandt, the millionaire-in-residence on the soap opera "All My Children." He was an important man in Springfield, the number-one man in the local branch of the U.S. Post Office: the postmaster himself. It seemed inappropriate for him to appear in public without his teeth. He stopped the car, let Willadene out, and raced home to get his dentures.

Willadene Frederickson was forty-six but she looked a decade older. Fortune's assaults had humbled her, making her bend nervously into the wind as if braced for her next catastrophe. She seemed a woman who expected trouble at any moment. Her lovely thick chestnut hair—still styled as it had been back in the fifties when she married Wes—was shot with gray. Willadene looked like what she once had been: a good, solid Arizona farmwoman.

She stood alone and indecisive in the empty parking lot outside the emergency room. She sought a way into the waiting room, considered using the double doors, but was afraid they might be only for ambulance crews. She found a single door and walked into the corridor. Diane stood in front of the window to the nurses' station.

"What *happened*?" Willadene gasped.

Diane stared back at her mother, seemingly unable to respond.

Judy Patterson spoke up. "The children have been shot."

"*Shot?*" Willadene echoed incredulously. "*Shot?*"

"Yes," Judy said softly. "Right out in the middle of the road."

"Where?"

"Marcola."

"*Marcola?*"

Willadene Frederickson could not comprehend what had happened.

She had seen Diane and the children only that afternoon. She'd looked after Danny all day as always, and the girls too when they came home from school. Usually, they all ate supper together at her house, but she and Wes had had a meeting. Diane had picked the children up after she finished work and had taken them home for supper. Everything had been fine then. Why on earth would Diane and the children have been in Marcola?

Diane spoke up. "We were out to Mark and Heather's . . ."

Willadene could not remember who Mark and Heather were, or if she'd ever known them. That didn't matter at this point. She reached an arm out to her daughter.

Willadene and Diane walked into the large waiting room.

"Mom, I can't live without my kids."

Willadene Frederickson did what she has always done; she tried to smooth things over. "Don't worry. They'll be all right." She patted Diane. "The children will be fine. They have very good doctors."

That seemed to calm Diane a little. The two of them filled out forms that Judy Patterson gave them. Why were there always forms? What did it matter at a time like this?

No one told Diane or Willadene that Cheryl was dead. Nor would they let Diane see her children again. Neither woman could, of course, see the desperate struggle going on in the trauma room, but they were angry at being shunted aside. Diane had apparently blanked out the sight of her younger daughter lying as still as a broken doll behind the drapes because she said nothing about that to Willadene. Surely, she must *know*, the nurses thought. How could she not know? Afterward, Diane said she had no memory of seeing Cheryl in the hospital. "I never saw Cheryl until I saw her in her coffin."

When a nurse or aide raced past for more blood or on some other errand, they called out to Diane and Willadene that the children were "serious," but alive. They meant Christie and Danny.

Wes Frederickson hurried into the waiting room. He was the parent that Diane resembled the most physically. His face was taut and impassive as he joined the women. Less than a half hour had passed since the first call for help in the parking lot.

Springfield's "Morning Watch" begins at 11:00 P.M. The shift's briefing takes place from 10:30 to 11:00 P.M. Officer Rich Charboneau had been summoned out of that "show-up" and dispatched to the hospital.

When Charboneau walked in, Diane looked up at him and cried angrily, "It's about time you got here! There's some maniac out there shooting people."

It was now 10:48 P.M. Eight minutes since Judy Patterson's call.

Diane told Charboneau basically the same story she'd told Judy Patterson. A stranger had demanded her car and then shot her children when she refused to give it to him. No, the children hadn't been awake; she recalled now that they had all been sleeping.

"I wasn't going to let him have my new car!" she murmured angrily. "I just bought it."

Diane appeared frantic with worry over her children. To compound matters, the wrong department had responded to the call for police assistance in the confusion over the location of the incident. When Diane recalled landmarks she had observed, Charboneau realized that the shooting had taken place outside the Springfield city limits. He called the Lane County Sheriff's Office. Sergeant Robin Rutherford responded.

Rutherford and Charboneau were horrified as Diane outlined her encounter with the gunman. The trouble might not be over. Old Mohawk Road was only a few miles long, a curving, two-laned road that paralleled the main road between Marcola and Springfield. The river edged most of its west boundary, and there were vast fields, but near Springfield a score of homes huddled along the road. If a maniac was out there with a gun, they had to find him. Rural Springfield residents would open their doors to a stranger in need of "help." They had to be warned.

Someone had to verify that Old Mohawk Road *was* indeed where the gunman had last been seen. No one but Diane could do that. Rutherford asked her if she would come with him back to the shooting scene.

It was a lot to ask. Diane explained that her arm was injured, and that she hadn't much more than a Band-Aid for it. Rutherford asked one of the nurses to evaluate Diane's wounds.

"I'm sorry," she called as she ran past. "I have no time. Take her to Sacred Heart."

Finally, Judy Patterson wrapped the arm again, but she wasn't confident about it. Rosie Martin stopped, looked askance at the arm, and unwrapped the gauze. She quickly put a less flexible bandage on it.

"How are my kids?" Diane asked.

Rosie answered that everyone was working on them—that they were
still very serious. "We have four doctors doing their best for them."

That much was true. Neither Rosie nor anyone else had time yet to
come out and tell the family just how bad things were.

Diane and her parents conferred with the deputies. They decided that
Wes and Diane would go with Rutherford to show him where the shooting
had occurred.

Shelby Day knelt down in front of Diane and said softly, "One of your
girls is really bad. She may not be alive when you come back."

Diane nodded. She drew a deep breath and turned to Rob Rutherford.
She would go with him. She couldn't save her children just sitting there in
the waiting room anyway. Judy heard Diane murmur something else, but
she couldn't understand it, the words didn't make sense; she turned back
toward her post at the front desk.

When Diane and her father walked out of the emergency room with Rob
Rutherford, the sheriff's sergeant noted that though Diane was clearly in
pain, she seemed to have tremendous willpower. She appeared calmer
now that she had something to do, something that might help find the
gunman.

They walked past Diane's red Nissan, guarded by Rich Charboneau.
She looked it over. "I hope my car's OK. Does it have any bullet holes in it?"

"I don't know," Charboneau said. "Nobody's checked it over yet."

Sergeant Rutherford headed away from Springfield, along Mohawk
Boulevard, following Diane's directions. At the intersection of Nineteenth
and Marcola Road, he turned right. They moved away from the sprinkling
of city lights, past empty houses with lawns that had long since become
do-it-yourself junkyards, past the man-made mountain of sawdust that
loomed through the night at the Kingsford Charcoal Briquet plant. Beyond the grubby northeast outskirts of Springfield, the innate beauty of
the land took over, although it was shrouded now in the black of night.

The squad car rumbled across Hayden Bridge. Beneath them, the

McKenzie River narrowed itself into a chute of turbulent froth as it raced by the power plant.

"This is where Christie stopped choking," Diane remembered. "Right here on the bridge . . ."

Rutherford shivered involuntarily.

They came off the bridge to a crossroads of sorts. To the right, Camp Creek Road, barricaded for resurfacing, meandered off, forking again and again into a series of dead ends; to the left, two-laned Old Mohawk Road cut away from the main road to attach itself again to Marcola Road a few miles north. It was only a local access road, well off the regular route between Springfield and Marcola.

Rutherford looked questioningly at Diane, and she nodded. Old Mohawk was the road where it had happened. She had driven across the railroad tracks and then over Hayden Bridge as she raced to the hospital with her children.

"I never should have bought the unicorn," she murmured softly, almost to herself.

"What did you say?" Rutherford asked.

"The unicorn," she answered. "I bought the kids a beautiful brass unicorn, and I had their names engraved on it—just a couple of days ago. It was . . . you know . . . It meant we had a new life. I shouldn't have bought it."

They passed by the patrol units that were stopping all cars entering or leaving Old Mohawk—not a busy job, since the road was sparsely traveled late at night. Rutherford drove slowly past darkened homes. It was very quiet; the Little Mohawk flowed more gently than her big sisters. Occasionally there was the sound of a dog barking, or the soft whinny of horses behind the barbed-wire fences along the road. The air smelled sweet—cottonwood trees just budding out. Old Mohawk seemed the most peaceful of country roads. It was hard to believe that four people had been shot here less than two hours earlier.

As they approached the far end of Old Mohawk just before it reconnected with Marcola Road, the road narrowed, with no shoulders or turning-off places. Every so often, a thin white milepost protruded through the black beside the road.

"Here," Diane said. "We're getting close. It happened just about here."

They were hard by the river. The current had nibbled at the bank so hungrily that it fell away only a few feet beyond the fog line at the edge of the road. The underbrush was thick, clotted with blackberry vines; firs and bulky dark maples loomed over the road.

What a lonely place it was, Rutherford thought, and how frightening it must have been for a young woman and her three children to come upon a maniac with a gun out here. It was the most isolated spot along Old Mohawk. The river pushed by in the dark on one side; on the other, a field of wild phlox trembled in the wind as if the blossoms were woven into a solid sheet of white.

Diane and Wes Frederickson stared out of the squad car's windows, and Rutherford followed their gaze. He saw nobody human out there in the darkness.

Of course there wouldn't be. The gunman had had ample time to get away by now, and good reason to be long gone. Still, the trio peered into the night, searching for some quick movement in the fields, some separation of shadows within a clump of evergreens as a figure moved to break and run.

No one.

The river gurgled and tumbled, heedless of the watchers on her banks. Rutherford felt a cop's familiar tightening of the muscles at the base of his neck. *Was* the gunman waiting somewhere out in the black? He cut the lights on his vehicle.

Officers from the Springfield Police Department were already working the road and the fields with a search dog. More men were on the way from Lane County, from Springfield, and from the Oregon State Police.

Diane asked why there was only one tracking dog.

"That's the only dog available now," Rutherford explained. "But these fields are full of horses. If there was a stranger out there in the dark, the horses would let us know."

"Oh," she said, "I didn't know that."

"They're almost as good as dogs when something alien gets into their fields."

That sounded reasonable; Diane had always loved horses, and she had great respect for their sensitivity.

Suddenly, she remembered something she'd forgotten in all the panic at the hospital. The yellow car. She could see it in her mind, she told Rutherford. An "icky yellow car" parked somewhere along this road. It hadn't seemed important before. They looked for it, but the yellow car was gone.

As the squad car cruised slowly back toward the south end of Old Mohawk Road, they passed a huge old farmhouse. Diane saw a light on upstairs and nudged her father. They peered up at the looming structure. Wes saw the light; then it went out. Rutherford, too, saw the light but doubted that anyone waited high up in the dark window of a farmhouse, taking a careful bead on them. That made little sense; why would a gunman choose to draw further attention to himself when the area was alive with cops?

Diane's injured arm was beginning to throb, and she complained to Rutherford. She was frightened too, she said.

The sheriff's sergeant picked up his radio mike and asked for someone to meet them and transport Diane and Wes back to the hospital. He would remain at the scene to help man the roadblocks.

One of the most massive criminal investigations in the state of Oregon had begun.

It was a quarter after eleven on that Thursday night when Lane County detectives Dick Tracy, Doug Welch, and Roy Pond were called at home and told to report to the McKenzie–Willamette Hospital. That was procedure: the cops were called first, then the DA's office if they needed a search warrant or other legal backup.

Unaware, Fred Hugi slept the last good night's sleep he would have for a long time. As the crow flies, the site of the shooting was no more than six miles away on the other side of the forest land behind his house, much too far for him to have heard the shots.

From the brief information the sheriff's detectives got from Lt. Louis Hince, they expected to find kids with minor injuries, children caught in the cross fire of a family fight escalated out of control. Photographs would be required, close-ups of the kids' wounds, something to hand to the district attorney's office. It was a chore Pond and Welch dreaded—directing hurt kids to sit frozen under bright lights at midnight so that the lurid topography of the damage done to them could be preserved for legal posterity.

Welch checked on his own two sons before he left the house. He tried not to identify, but child abuse got to him. Some kids drew the short straw in life, and it wasn't fair.

Doug Welch, oldest son of a Detroit Tigers catcher-turned-Montana-Levi-jeans salesman, sometimes wondered how he'd ended up a cop. "I never thought of being a cop. A ballplayer maybe, like my dad. He played pro ball, and then semi-pro when I was a kid. I remember going to the games. I always fell asleep before the seventh inning; even so, ball players were my heroes. Or fighter pilots. Not cops. No way."

Welch had been about to graduate from the University of Oregon, six months away from a second lieutenant's commission *and* pilots' training, when the government ordered a reduction in force. They had enough pilots. "I had a wife, and a baby on the way. I looked on law enforcement as an interim career at best. I'd always been a little intimidated by cops, and I sure couldn't imagine myself actually *arresting* anyone."

But Welch did make arrests, and they soon became routine. The sandy-haired, freckled, would-be pilot turned out to be a sensitive, intuitive cop. After several years on patrol, Doug Welch had become a detective less than three months before Diane Downs and her children were shot.

Welch reached the ER parking area in five minutes. He nodded to Rich Charboneau standing guard over a red Nissan Pulsar and walked to the trauma room. Three children lay on treatment tables, hardly what he'd expected. One child had been dead for at least an hour, her skin mottling with the purplish striations of lividity—blood reacting to gravity when the heart no longer pumps. Welch noted a gunshot wound in her left shoulder. Someone murmured that there was a similar wound in the other shoulder. He nodded; there was a roaring in his head.

Sergeant Jon Peckels photographed the body. Welch focused on the other side of the room. Doctors were working feverishly over a second little girl; he could barely see her beyond them. Within a minute or two, she was rushed—table and all—out of the room. He had no idea where they were taking her.

The little boy was crying. The three detectives watched as the doctors rolled the toddler over onto his side so they could treat his back. Welch recognized the single bullet hole, located almost dead center down his spine. He saw the black sprinkling—powder and debris from the gun barrel—stippling.

Contact wound. Or almost.

The doctors closed in again around the little boy. The ER crew had domain here.

Jon Peckels was in charge of physical evidence for the county. He moved around the gurney where the dead child lay, taking more photographs. She looked so exposed that Welch had the impulse to tug the blanket over her so she wouldn't get cold. He looked away.

Roy Pond gathered the bloodstained clothing and the purplish-orange towel from the baskets at the end of the gurneys and bagged them for evidence. Labels with names, dates, locations. A .22 slug was still caught in one of the shirts. Pond slipped it into a clear envelope.

Dick Tracy had almost two decades on the other detectives in Lane County. "Silver Fox" attractive—white hair, ice-blue eyes—Tracy could be dapper and shrewd or play the country hick to perfection. A long time back, when he played football in Warwood, West Virginia, Tracy was All-City, All-State, All–Ohio Valley. He won a scholarship to the University of Iowa, but with the Korean War he joined the Marines. Like everyone else on this case, he hadn't planned on being a policeman either. He hadn't even liked cops. But here he was, with a quarter century of law enforcement behind him.

Dick Tracy had cleared every homicide he'd ever worked; Welch had never worked a homicide as a detective. Off-duty, Doug Welch researched the stock market; Tracy was an avid student of metaphysics. Fellow cops tormented Welch by telling him he looked like Howdy Doody. Tracy had his name to contend with. They would be only the first of a number of "odd couple" partners in a case just beginning to unfold. Dick Tracy turned into the emergency drive-through. Louis Hince waved him down, leaned into the car window. "The family's waiting for you to pick them up at the E-Z Mart. The mother's evidently been shot too and she needs treatment. Bring them back here."

"How about the children?" Tracy asked.

Hince shook his head. "One little girl is gone. The others are critical."

Tracy sighed and turned his car northeasterly. He expected to find a hysterical mother waiting for him in Rutherford's police cruiser. Instead, he encountered a woman still in control: "very rational, considering what she had undergone." Tracy had seen all manner of emotional responses to disaster. He didn't know the woman or her father, who seemed as stoic as she was; he wouldn't presume to predict how they might react when the numbness wore off. Anxious to get his passengers back to the hospital, he pressed down on the accelerator.

Back at McKenzie–Willamette, Hince motioned to Doug Welch. "Dick's coming in with the mother now. I want you to work with him in questioning her."

It was two minutes to midnight when Diane Downs and her father once again entered the McKenzie–Willamette emergency room. Dr. Mackey leaned protectively toward Diane, quietly telling her that Cheryl Lynn had died, that she had been dead on arrival. Welch watched Diane's face as she heard the news. Her expression was impossible to read, a faint flickering of emotion, and then a closing in. Stoic.

Diane followed Tracy into a small treatment room. Welch joined them. The woman was young, slender, and quite pretty. Her face was a papier-mâché mask.

Welch found Diane's demeanor flat, almost brittle. She laughed inappropriately; her mind didn't appear to be tracking. It seemed to him that she simply would not accept that her little girl had died.

Tracy and Welch accompanied Diane into the X-ray room. Dr. Mackey came to tell Diane that Christie was critical and in surgery. She thanked him for letting her know.

Dr. Miller came to treatment room number eight and told her that they were cautiously optimistic about Danny. He described the bullet's pathway in Danny's body.

"You mean it missed his heart?" Diane asked.

"Yes."

There was too much for the family to absorb that night. Diane was confused over which of her daughters had died. Wes made the final identification. Shelby Day remembers him as he stood, impassive, in the center of the trauma room, gazing at the body of his younger granddaughter, nodding slightly as he said, Yes, that is Cheryl.

While the doctors worked over Christie and Danny, Diane talked with

Dick Tracy and Doug Welch. She spoke rapidly in a breathy teenage voice, her sentences running on with no discernible ending. They scribbled frantically to keep up with the fountain of words.

She said she had had no alcohol that evening and no drugs or medication. She did not smell of liquor; her pupils looked normal. (Indeed, blood tests would bear this out.) She was coherent and sober. Her brittle shell of vivacious cooperation remained intact. It was as if she felt compelled to keep talking; if she stopped, she might have to remember.

Doug Welch studied her. "Her words were like . . . the only way I can describe them . . . like verbal vomit. They just kept flowing."

"You have a tremendous amount of recall," Dick Tracy commented at one point. "You must be fairly intelligent."

"There are eight levels of intelligence," Diane explained. "And I'm at the seventh level."

They had never heard of the "eight level IQ theory," but Diane Downs was undoubtedly very intelligent; her vocabulary, syntax, and ability to answer their questions indicated that. And yet she was like a robot programmed to respond. She had taken on a mantle of words to protect herself, talking faster and faster and faster.

It almost made them dizzy.

Shortly after 1:00 A.M., Springfield Police Detective Sergeant Jerry Smith and Detective Robert Antoine came into the room. Diane held her hands out while Antoine swabbed them with a five percent solution of nitric acid—a routine test to discern the presence of trace metals that might have been left had she fired a gun. The next of kin must always be eliminated first. A positive reaction to the test (GSR-Gunshot residue) wasn't that precise. Especially with .22's. Rimfire .22's have a very low antimony-debris factor. Smoking a cigarette, urinating, or using toilet tissue can leave similar residue.

The tests on Diane's hands were negative for the presence of barium or antimony. Antoine sprayed her hands to test for other trace metals. Iron would turn her hands reddish; copper dusting would elicit a green tinge.

Negative.

Tracy and Welch started with the easiest of questions. How many policemen, doctors, and nurses begin by asking legal names and birthdates—

as if putting the dead in some kind of order will numb the pain? And how many laymen answer with eager efficiency? Those who still have first and middle names and birthdates cannot possibly be dead or dying.

Diane gave her own full name: Elizabeth Diane Frederickson Downs, born August 7, 1955; she would be twenty-eight in two months. Christie's birthdate was October 7, 1974; Christie had been seated in the right rear seat of the red car. Stephen Daniel's birthday was December 29, 1979; he'd been in the back seat with Christie, on the left. Cheryl was born January 10, 1976; she had been on the floor in front, sleeping under a sweater.

"The car is yours?" Tracy asked.

"Yes," Diane nodded. "I bought it in February—a red Nissan Pulsar MX with silver streaks on the side."

It was time for the harder questions. Diane explained quickly the horror along the dark road, the stranger with the gun, her flight to save her children. They had gone to see a friend of hers that evening: Heather Plourd, who lived northeast of Springfield on Sunderman Road. Diane knew Heather wanted a horse, and she had found an article about horses that could be adopted for free. Heather had no phone so Diane had taken the clipping out to her. After a visit of fifteen or twenty minutes, they'd headed home. Diane said she had detoured impulsively to do a little sight-seeing, but when she realized her children had fallen asleep, she turned around and headed toward Springfield.

Again with no particular plan, she'd turned off Marcola Road onto Old Mohawk and gone only a short way when she saw the man standing in the road, waving his arm for her to stop. Fearing an accident, she had pulled over.

"Can you describe him?" Welch asked.

"He was white . . . in his late twenties . . . about five feet nine, 150 to 170. He had dark hair, a shag-wavy cut, and a stubble of a beard—maybe one or two days' growth. Levis, a Levi jacket, a dirty . . . maybe off-color, light T-shirt."

The man had been right in the center of the road.

"I stopped my car," Diane continued, "and I got out, and I said, 'What's the problem?' He jogged over to me and said, 'I want your car,' and I said, 'You've got to be kidding!' and then he shoved me to the back of the car."

And then, inexplicably, the man had stood outside the driver's door and put his hand inside the car. Diane heard loud "pops" and realized with despair that the man was firing a gun at her children! First Christie, and then Danny—and finally Cheryl, who lay asleep under Diane's postal sweater on the floor of the front seat.

"What did you do?" Welch asked, shaken by the picture of the three children trapped in a dark car.

"I pretended to throw my car keys. That made him angry. I wanted him to think I'd thrown the keys into the brush. He was about four or five feet away from me. He turned in my direction and fired twice, hitting me once. I pushed him or kicked him—maybe both—in the leg. I jumped into the car and took off for the hospital as fast as I could."

"Did you see the gun?"

"No . . . Wait . . . Yes . . ."

"Can you describe it?"

"That's difficult."

"Do you have any weapons?"

"A .22 rifle that's on the shelf in my closet at home. You could go and get it if you wanted."

"We'd have to have you sign a consent-to-search form to do that," Tracy advised.

"That's OK. I'll sign that."

She was very cooperative. If Diane voluntarily signed the form, there would be no need for a search warrant. Tracy handed her the consent form. Diane perused it, and then read it aloud. She came to a paragraph stating, "I understand this contraband or evidence may be used against me in a court of law." She paused and looked at the detectives. "Does this have to do with someone who's a suspect?"

Tracy nodded.

Diane said that, of course, she had no objection to their searching her car or the duplex at 1352 Q Street in Springfield where she and the children lived. Anything that might help find the gunman quickly. She signed the form.

But there was a stilted—forced—quality in Diane's speech, hiding some fear they didn't understand.

The detectives were beginning to tumble the crime more slowly around in their minds. They didn't really know if the shooting had happened in Springfield or in the country, even after Diane had shown them the river site. They wondered if she might possibly have recognized the person who had shot them but be under some constraint not to tell. Was the killer holding a worse sword over her head? Had he let her go to get treatment for her kids on the condition that she return, having told the cops nothing? The most unlikely chance meeting on a lonely road made the investigators think that the killer *had* to be acquainted, or have some specific connection, with Diane Downs.

It was an emergency situation. They had to check out her home, and they also had to get to Heather Plourd's to see if anyone waited there with a loaded gun, possibly with hostages, for Diane to come back. Officers were dispatched to both addresses.

Dick Tracy left the ER briefly and joined Jon Peckels as he photographed the red car, his strobe light illuminating the interior. Something glinted in the intermittent flashes. Bullet casings. They looked like two .22 caliber casings. Both men saw them, but they didn't touch them. The car was sealed, ready to be towed to the Lane County shops for processing by the Oregon State Police Crime Lab.

As Tracy strode back to the ER, he saw Diane's parents in the waiting area. The father looked grim; the mother's face was swollen from crying. Wes Frederickson verified that Diane owned a rifle, which she kept stored in its case, as well as—he thought—a revolver. "She had those weapons because her ex-husband beat her up in the past."

When Tracy asked Diane if she owned, or possessed, any other weapons, she remembered that she had an old .38 pistol, a Saturday Night Special. It was a cheap gun and unpredictable; she kept it locked in the trunk of her car away from her children.

Tracy and Welch had walked into Diane's life at a crisis point; it was akin to walking into a movie in the middle. They had to play catch-up in a hurry.

Diane said that she had come to the Eugene-Springfield area only seven or eight weeks earlier. She had lived all her life in Arizona, working as a letter carrier in Chandler for the previous two years. Her parents had urged her to move to Oregon, and she'd done so—mostly to please them—to give them more of a chance to be with their grandchildren. Since her father was the postmaster of Springfield, he had helped her transfer and she was presently working as a letter carrier in the Cottage Grove post office. She was divorced from her first and only husband, Stephen Duane Downs, twenty-eight, who was still living in the Chandler/Mesa, Arizona, area. She gave them his phone number.

They talked for more than two hours, and the clock on the wall inched its way toward 3:00 A.M. The circles under Diane's eyes purpled. Still her voice held strong, and her words tumbled out, bumping into each other.

It was after 3:00 A.M. when the two detectives left Diane and headed out to join the men at her townhouse on Q Street.

Dr. Terrance Carter, an orthopedic surgeon, treated Diane's wounds. Her left arm was broken, but there was no nerve or tendon damage. Fortunately, she had still been able to open and close her fingers—and drive—despite the pain. In a week or so she would need surgery to strengthen the arm. Carter excised tissue around all three wounds to ensure drainage.

He took Diane's blood pressure and pulse. Both readings were normal.

Carter also found Diane quite flat emotionally, her words so alive and rapid while her eyes looked somehow dead. She didn't want to stay in the hospital, although he told her that she must—at least for a few days. She made him promise not to tell her father about the tattoo on her back. It was not an ordinary tattoo; it was a huge rose etched in scarlet on her left shoulder.

Beneath it was a single word: Lew.

CHAPTER 3

MSG ID 3293 SENT 5/19/83 2340 FROM TID 42 (AI) AM.EGS.
*EGO. * * * ATTEMPT TO LOCATE ARMED SUBJECT * * WHITE*
MALE ADULT POSSIBLY ARMED WITH .22 SEMI-AUTOMATIC
WEAPON. DESCRIBED AS WMA 5'9" 150–170 LBS DARK BROWN
SHAGGY HAIR, STUBBLE BEARD, WEARING DIRTY T-SHIRT,
LEVI JACKET, BLUE JEANS. POSSIBLE VEHICLE INVOLVED '60
TO '70 YELLOW CHEVROLET CHEVELLE, BEAT-UP, NO LIC.
KNOWN. SUBJ. WANTED IN CONNECTION WITH SHOOTING
IN MARCOLA AREA. OCA 83-3268.
LANE CO. S.O., EUGENE, 687-4150 VLB.
—First teletype sent by Lane County

Steve Downs had spent a pleasant Thursday evening in Mesa, Arizona. He and his date had gone for a walk around the reservoir in the cool of the evening and then returned to her apartment. Although he and Diane had been divorced for two years, their lives had remained entwined—often abrasively—until she'd left for Oregon. With his family gone almost eight weeks, Downs was finally beginning to feel single, although he missed the kids. He missed Diane, too, in a way. Their relationship had derived from the can't-live-with-her/him; can't-live-without-her/him school—full of passion, jealousy, estrangements, and reconciliations.

The desert sky over the Superstition Mountains had faded from the peach and yellow striations of sunset to deep black by the time Steve's roommate—advised of the tragedy in a phone call from Wes—located him. The man blurted out that all three of Steve's kids had been shot. Steve's new girlfriend drove him to Sky Harbor Airport in Phoenix to catch the first plane out to Oregon.

Steve Downs had no idea how it could have happened. He berated himself silently for letting his kids go away as he sat, wide awake, amid his dozing fellow passengers.

Roy Pond and Springfield Detective Al Hartman had been dispatched to Heather Plourd's trailer. They drove north on Marcola Road and turned right onto Sunderman Road, a weathered asphalt path through the woods. Gnarled maples and oaks leaned over the road, giving the sensation of driving through a tunnel. The air was damper here, and colder.

As they approached the far end of Sunderman, which—like Old Mohawk—hooked into Marcola Road at each end, the road broke out of the woods. There were cleared fields here and a small cluster of mobile homes on the left side of the road. Pond shone his flashlight on the mailboxes and read "Plourd."

The trailers were dark. Pond had a discomfiting feeling. This road was so like Old Mohawk; he wondered if Diane *might* have been holding back for some reason nobody knew yet. The shooting might have taken place here. The detectives walked cautiously up to the porch of the mobile home and knocked, waited, and knocked again. Finally they heard movement inside.

A sleepy young couple opened the door. Heather Plourd verified that Diane Downs had come to visit her earlier.

"She came driving up in her red car around eight thirty or nine. I was shocked to see her because she had only been here once before, about three weeks ago. She drove over then to ask me to work a shift for her so she could fly to Arizona. She had the three kids with her tonight. I went outside to talk to her. She told me she had found an ad in the paper about adopting a horse. I said we'd just bought a horse, and we couldn't handle another one. Her kids played with our new horse for a few minutes while I talked with Diane."

Diane hadn't seemed upset and she wasn't in a hurry when she left, although Heather had the impression that she had somewhere else to go. Heather was sure Diane hadn't been drinking and wasn't under the influence of drugs.

"Why are you asking me all these questions?" she asked Pond. "Has there been an accident?"

Pond hesitated; the woman's story certainly sounded straight. "It's a very serious matter," he answered cryptically. "You'll probably find out about it later on today. Do you own any firearms?"

"No."

The Plourds said they had two children, who were asleep. Pond asked to see them. Puzzled, Heather led the detectives through the trailer and showed them a little boy and girl. The investigators were relieved. It was apparent that nothing violent had happened here. Whoever the Downs family had encountered had come upon them after they left the Plourds' trailer.

Pond headed to join Welch, Tracy, and several Springfield officers at the Downses' duplex on Q Street. Diane had given them the key to the unit. She'd carried no purse—just her house and car keys on a ring she'd fished out of her jeans pocket.

The apartments were bland two-storied boxes, built for economy. The double units hulked around a cul-de-sac, and faced the I-105 freeway. In the dark, they were no-color; in the daylight they were all the same dull brown. There were a few desultory rhododendrons edging the communal lawn. Somewhere in the shadows beyond the porch lights, a dog barked frantically.

But the investigators had found no one inside—nothing to indicate someone had been waiting there for Diane to come back, no ground-out cigarette butts or empty beer bottles. The television sets were cold.

Tracy and Welch had surveyed the downstairs first—a living-room/ dining-room and a kitchen. The place was almost empty; it looked as if someone had moved in only a day or so before, leaving boxes to be unpacked after a good night's sleep.

Tracy shook his head, puzzled. "Didn't she say they moved up here at Eastertime?"

"Yeah," Welch nodded. "Pretty bare bones here, isn't it?"

There was no furniture downstairs except for a chair and a console television set. They peered at the cluttered top of the TV. There were four framed photos. Two were of Diane herself, and they could see that she *was* a beautiful woman in happier circumstances. She smiled at them from both slots of a double eleven-by-fourteen-inch frame. One picture was a head shot, and the other a three-quarter body view of Diane in a blouse and tight jeans, leaning against a wall. There were two smaller pictures of a dark bearded man with a high forehead who grinned at the camera.

"Lew maybe?" Tracy asked, recalling the tattoo.

"Could be."

There were no pictures of the children on the TV. There was a box of Kleenex and a cluster of crepe-paper flowers attached to pipe cleaners—obviously a school art project—bearing a tag that read "Christie." There was the control panel for the cable television hookup, and a small orange figure: Garfield the Cat grinning a plastic smile.

But the object that drew the eye was the gleaming brass statuette, a unicorn pawing the air. The mythical creature was nine inches tall, its mane flaring, its single horn set at a phallic angle. Welch and Tracy leaned closer and winced as they read the engraving on its base.

CHRISTIE, CHERYL, AND DANNY

I LOVE YOU!

MOM

MAY 13, 1983

"That's only six days ago," Tracy mused. "Rutherford said she kept saying she shouldn't have bought the unicorn. I wonder what she meant . . ."

Welch shrugged. "There're some myths about unicorns, but I don't know what they are."

They were searching for tangible evidence, not myths, and they forgot the shiny statuette for the moment.

There was an air of impermanence, as if no one really lived here—no couch, no table or dinette set, no kitchen chairs. Most of the kitchen utensils and staples were still packed.

Welch opened the refrigerator and saw only a few open cans. He picked one up and grimaced; the contents were scummed over with mold. All the cans were that way.

"There's not enough here to cook even one meal."

"Maybe they eat out a lot."

"Yeah."

They moved up the beige-carpeted stairs. Here, too, there were unpacked cartons. The master bedroom—Diane's room—had a king-sized waterbed with a green-, pink-, and brown-flowered spread. There were matching pillow shams, and the bed was made up neatly.

Tracy reached up to the closet shelf. His hand touched what he sought, and he gingerly lifted down a long, sheathed object. It was a .22 Glenfield rifle in its scabbard, stored just where Diane had said it would be. It was loaded, but it had not been fired recently; its barrel was full of dust and lint.

Tracy pulled back the action and a single live round popped out. He eased the action forward very slowly and took the cap off the tubular magazine. Seven rounds slipped out onto the bed. Carefully, so that his own prints wouldn't be on the bullets, he slipped the rounds into an evidence envelope. He pulled the gun's action back once more and a last round popped out. Nine .22 rounds—some of them silver, some a bronzy-copper color. But Tracy's weary eyes had missed one round; a copper-washed cartridge had rolled onto the flowered spread and blended with the protective coloration of the pattern there. Of the eight rounds he'd picked up, six were copper-washed with a "C" stamped on the end (head-stamped "C"). The other two were lead bullets and headstamped "U."

They searched the other two bedrooms silently, trying to ignore the empty beds where children should have been safe in dreams.

Diane had given carte blanche permission for the detectives to take away anything that might help them find the shooter.

Springfield Sergeant Jerry Smith searched for a particular item at Diane Downs's request. She had asked him to bring her her diary, written in an ordinary spiral notebook. He found it, flipped through it, and saw that it was written as a series of letters, letters that had apparently never been mailed. The first entry was dated weeks before in April, and with one exception, all the salutations were to someone named Lew.

The diary too became evidence. Smith duplicated it before he took it to Diane at the hospital.

At dawn, the search far from completed, the investigators left the Q Street residence cordoned off and under guard. They would be back.

The weary men who worked through that first long night knew nothing about Diane Downs except her age, her marital status, the fact that she was a letter carrier, new to Oregon from Arizona. They had met her parents, seen her shattered children. They did not know what it might take to make her break down and cry, or what hopes and dreams might have mattered to her when she woke up only a day earlier. If the shooting had not been a random thing, if Diane had been a preselected target, they wondered what she could have done to make someone hate her enough to attempt to obliterate her and her children.

They planned to find out, and the sooner the better. Any detective knows a murder that doesn't result in arrest in the first twenty-four to forty-eight hours often goes unsolved. Chances decrease with each passing day. Now, the detectives were still filled with the flush of the chase, not even twelve hours into the probe.

Diane had not slept at all that first long night; she'd waited wide-eyed in her hospital bed for the first glow of dawn. A deputy was posted outside her room to protect her— just as deputies guarded her two surviving children—in case the gunman should come back.

At seven, Diane reached for the phone beside her hospital bed and dialed a number she knew by heart. It would be eight o'clock in Arizona. She waited, tense, as the rings br-r-red far away. She could picture the building where the phone was, could see everything in her mind, even feel the heat of the sun reflecting from its rock facade.

"Chandler Post Office, Karen speaking."

"Karen? It's Diane."

They were good friends, and Diane had called often from Oregon. Karen Batton, who was twenty-five, had taken Diane in to live with her once when Diane's trailer had burned. Karen noted something different in Diane's voice. She didn't sound upset, and she wasn't crying, but she sounded . . . *hollow.* Their conversation was prosaic though, as always—until Diane suddenly blurted, "Somebody shot my kids! Cheryl's dead . . . I'm shot too."

Karen gasped and began to cry. She turned with the phone in her hand and watched the tall, bearded man who stood nearby. He could hear her conversation, but his face was averted and he continued to sort mail for his route. He knew she was talking to Diane, and he had given everybody in the Chandler post office explicit orders that he would not talk to Diane. Diane had called him regular as clockwork for weeks—every morning at 7:00 A.M. But Lew had suddenly stopped accepting her calls. And he'd stamped "Return to sender" on all her letters and packages.

This news was too shocking not to share. Karen covered the phone and whispered urgently.

"Lew, I think this is a call you should take. Please talk to her."

Grimacing, he reached for the phone. He heard her voice across the miles, the voice he'd heard a hundred times, a thousand times. She sounded just the same.

"Hello, Lew," she said softly. "How's it going? How's everything in Chandler? Are you doing all right? Are you happy, babe?"

He mumbled replies, anxious to hang up. Her words had mesmerized him before, tumbling him around until he no longer knew if his desires were his own or what *she* wanted. He hadn't heard from her in weeks, and he'd hoped maybe it was really over, that his life had finally settled back to normal. No more hassles. Only his wife and his job. What the hell did she want now?

"What's going on, Diane? What happened? Karen's crying."

She hesitated. He could hear her draw in a shuddering breath at the other end of the long wire between Oregon and Arizona.

"What's going on, Diane?" he pressed.

She told him.

"What *happened*?"

"I don't know."

"What do you mean you don't know? The kids are shot. You're shot. What happened? Who did it?"

"Lew, I don't know. We were on a dirt road about eleven last night . . . out in the country and we left my friend's house . . . and there was this man standing in the middle of the road waving his arms . . . he wanted my car and he just started shooting at the car . . ."

Lew sank back against the wall. What did she expect him to do? What *could* he do for her now? He began to shake. She wanted too much from him. If he gave her his blood, she'd want his breath. If he gave her the oxygen from his lungs, she'd ask for the marrow from his bones. Nothing was ever enough. She was reaching back for him, trying to draw him to her with her mad stories of murder.

"Give me your room number, and the hospital phone, Diane," he said. "I'm writing it down. I'm giving this to Karen. But Diane—if you're coming to Chandler, any time at all, don't come and see me."

"I love you, Lew," she said softly.

"I have to get back to work, Diane."

"Can I talk to Karen, then?"

"Karen's already left on the route."

He hung up the phone and turned into the bright sunlight. He spoke to no one in particular: "I don't know what to think. I just don't know what to think."

He shouldered his mailbag and walked slowly out into the heat of the morning.

She had expected that coldness from Lew. He was scared. She knew him as well as—no, *better*—than anyone. Lew hated kinks, hassles. Maybe that was why she loved him so; he just wanted to live and not have problems, just be happy. Naturally, he would back away from her now; it was too awful for anyone to deal with, at first. But he'd come back and help her get over it. She hoped the police wouldn't bother Lew. He'd consider that a definite kink.

CHAPTER 4

Even before Diane called Lew, Fred Hugi had already awakened on that Friday morning, May 20, 1983. He didn't turn on the radio as he dressed, gulped a cup of coffee, and headed down the long private lane from his house to the main road. He didn't turn on his car radio; the Belt Line freeway bypassing Springfield into Eugene was packed with commuters and demanded a driver's full attention.

Passing the Weyerhaeuser plant, its soaring chimneys belching acrid fumes, he held his breath unconsciously for thirty seconds or so. The sky grew blue again as he turned toward downtown Eugene and his office in the courthouse.

It was a day like any other day—or so it seemed.

Well before eight, Fred Hugi reached his office, the very last cubicle along a corridor flanked by door after door. Like those of the other deputy prosecutors, Hugi's office was eight feet by eight feet. Behind his neat desk, there was a single window next to a translucent rectangle of solid glass blocks. The branches of a huge pine tree, four stories tall, tapped at the window.

Hugi's office was a mixture of whimsy, black humor, and paperwork—all but the paperwork *just there* because stuff tended to pile up. A hangman's noose swung from a wooden sconce, but the macabre effect was mitigated by a silly hat with a stuffed white teddy bear sitting on the cap's bill. There was a handful of framed certificates: college degrees, a law degree, and documents certifying that Hugi was an Oregon Guide and Packer and a McKenzie River Guide. Photographs showed a relaxed Hugi, grubby in fishing clothes, holding a three-foot steelhead. There was an antique photo—a pastoral scene along some now-unidentifiable stretch of the McKenzie River a hundred years ago—and a huge map of Oregon. A lone Wandering Jew—virtually impossible to kill with neglect—hung yellow and limp from a planter.

Other offices were empty, but the corridor was alive with members of DA Pat Horton's staff. There had been a multiple shooting during the night. Hugi paused to listen at the edge of one group, catching scraps of detail. There wasn't much information yet, only a great deal of speculation. He heard one of the DA's investigators, Howard Williams, say, "And guess where Mama's bullet wound's going to be?"

Hugi was puzzled. "Where?"

Williams held up his arm and pointed at the lower part. "Right there—where it won't kill you, and it won't even hurt much."

"That's where it *is*?"

Williams shrugged. "We don't have the reports yet. I'm laying odds though."

Williams's remark didn't make much of an impression on Hugi. It was the kind of banter that proliferated in cops and DA's offices. He moved to another desk and listened to that first sketchy story of the shootings: a mother and three kids. He knew he was next up.

District Attorney Horton assigned homicide cases on a rotating basis. Hugi had been slated to prosecute the first murder case in Lane County as April ran into May. On May 1, a thirty-two-year-old California man was shot to death outside a Eugene tavern. The defense indicated it would employ a "Vietnam delayed-stress syndrome" tactic. That would have been "Fred Hugi's murder," but Dave Nissman, another assistant DA, had evinced interest in prosecuting a delayed-stress case. He asked Hugi to trade, and Hugi had stepped aside gladly. He'd seen and heard enough of Vietnam firsthand to last him a lifetime. And he thought delayed-stress reaction was a cop-out. Let Nissman have it.

That meant that this shooting was sure to be his, and Hugi wasn't particularly fired up about it from what he'd heard so far. Every attorney has his own set of criteria of what makes a "good homicide," pragmatic standards set apart from emotion. The least sought-after cases involved bar fights and bum knifings. It was hard to wring sympathy out of a jury for victims who hadn't seemed to care much about themselves or anybody else.

Hugi kept a mental list of pluses and minuses to rate homicide cases. Pluses were: respected and innocent victims; victims and suspects who didn't know each other; multiple victims; lengthy, difficult investigations; suspects who tried to evade conviction rather than confessing. Few assistant district attorneys yearn to prosecute a case where the killer is found standing over the body with a smoking gun. The challenging cases polish skill and set adrenaline flowing. Hugi found circumstantial cases preferable to eyewitness cases; physical and scientific evidence were a lot better than eyewitnesses or confessions. A defendant "innocent by reason of insanity" was to be avoided if at all possible.

Other DAs had their own guidelines; this was Fred Hugi's mental list. He was a prosecutor who wanted to feel he'd made a difference in the lives of those he represented. Overwhelming evidence mattered to him only when *he* was the reason for obtaining that evidence. He didn't want convictions handed to him on a platter.

DA Pat Horton buzzed Hugi's phone and summoned him.

"Remember I promised you the next homicide case?" Horton asked.

"Yeah." Hugi answered with moderate enthusiasm.

"Well, you got it."

Hugi nodded. He didn't even know the names of the victims. He would find out, and then try to piece the case together. If Williams wasn't just blowing smoke—if the mother had shot herself too—it would be over quickly. Mental. Mother goes crazy. Shoots kids. The biggest decision Hugi would have to work out would be which institution to send her to. If it turned out to be a ringer, he'd simply have to get in line again and wait for a better one next time around.

On the other hand, there were aspects of this case that interested Fred Hugi. It was too early to tell.

Fred Hugi went back to his office, pulled out a fresh yellow legal pad, and started a list: MAY 20, 1983—THINGS TO DO, and QUESTIONS? Good or bad, if this was his case—and it was—he was going to do it right. He hoped the press wasn't going to build it into a huge sob story, hampering his work, maybe even distorting facts.

Why did Fred Hugi, a private man, a loner, choose to be a courtroom lawyer in the first place? He detested publicity. Unlike many prosecuting attorneys who use publicity as a stepping-stone to build a private practice, Hugi had come *from* a successful private practice because he was intrigued with the system and the way it *should* work.

His goal was quite simple. He wanted only to be the kind of prosecutor a victim would choose to handle *their* case, to be "someone who will make the system work and do *whatever* it takes to see that it does work." That he could occasionally be a rescuer or an avenger was the part of his profession that gave him the most satisfaction. Talking with the press gave him the least.

Born in the Bronx three months before VE Day, Fred Hugi is third generation American: German-Hungarian (Swiss really), the son and grandson of meatcutters. His grandfather was instrumental in starting the first labor organization for meatcutters. His father moved his family out of the Bronx to Woodbridge, New Jersey, so that Fred and his sister, three years younger, wouldn't have to grow up in the city. And then the elder Hugi rose at four in the morning to commute seventy miles roundtrip to New York. His wife ran a little store in Woodbridge.

Hugi began pre-med studies at Rutgers University. He hated it, but he did like botany and earned a degree in, of all things, forestry. On June 1, 1966, commissioned a second lieutenant in the U.S. Army, Fred graduated, married Joanne on June 4, and left at once for Fort Belvoir, Virginia, to train with the Army Corps of Engineers. He had aspired to helicopter pilot training at Rutgers, but it didn't seem fair to pursue such a dangerous avocation now that he had a wife. They were sent next to Fort Lewis south of Tacoma, Washington. It rained constantly. They loved it.

Fred and Joanne knew it was only a matter of time before he was sent to Vietnam, a conspicuous consumer of second lieutenants. He left in May of 1967 and returned exactly a year later. It was not the last time that the parameters of a searing experience in Fred Hugi's life would be marked by the coming and going of the month of May. Hugi will not speak of Vietnam, except to say that he came back wondering why any man could not be happy as long as he had enough to eat, a roof over his head, and no one shooting at him.

Qualifying for his private pilot's license, Hugi took a job with the Simpson Timber Company in Shelton, Washington. The forestry graduate roved the Olympic Peninsula—not in a plane but in a company jeep—locating scattered plots of timber, measuring trees, and predicting growth. He liked the outdoors, and he liked trees—but he saw the job as a dead end. Hugi soon perceived that it was not the foresters but the financial people who made all the decisions in the timber business.

He went back to college at the University of Oregon on the G I. Bill, eventually earning both a master's in business *and* a law degree. His interest in law had always revolved around defending the innocent. He believed then that the system worked, that the defense attorney did protect the innocent who had been falsely accused.

By 1973, Fred Hugi was making a comfortable living in private practice as a defense attorney. He often ate lunch with the assistant DAs in the courthouse across the street, and he listened, fascinated, as they discussed their cases.

"Once I realized how the system worked, I saw that the glamorous law school notion of defending the innocent could best be accomplished from the *State's* side of the case," Hugi later remarked. "Defendants were *not* wrongfully accused. It was the innocent victims of crime that needed the protection."

On November 12, 1975, Fred Hugi joined the Lane County District Attorney's Office. A neophyte, he was assigned to prosecute misdemeanors
in district court. At first, there was no pressure. He *couldn't* worry about
how a case was going to turn out if he wanted to because his cases were
assigned each evening. When the day was over, that day's cases were over.
The next morning, there would be others. Gradually, his caseload included a general assortment of offenses from juveniles to manslaughter
with an automobile. Eventually, after he paid his dues with misdemeanors, he would work up to felonies. But in the heirarchy of the DA's office in
1976, Fred Hugi was a long, long way from representing the state in a
major murder case.

When he walked away from the Lane County Courthouse, he could
forget it—head up home and be on the river in his drift boat, fishing for
steelhead, in half an hour. Sitting in that craft that blends so subtly with
the water's own color, he viewed a McKenzie River shoreline much like
the nineteenth-century photograph in his office.

Still, Fred Hugi was by nature a workaholic. So was Joanne. They had
no children. They had weighed parenthood seriously. But, should they
have children, they would want to give them time and attention. Each of
them was entirely involved in a career. When Fred was in trial and Joanne
had a particularly difficult problem at the university, they scarcely had
time to talk to each other. That was their choice; they were adults. But
children deserved more. He had grown too used to staying on the job
until midnight if he thought he needed to. When he was worrying a problem, he closed the rest of the world out. Years passed and once in a while
he and Joanne talked about having kids, but they'd never changed their
minds. As each took on more and more career responsibility, they figured
it had been the best decision.

On the morning of May 20, 1983, Hugi started to fill in the Things-to-Do
list on the neat yellow pad, but something tugged at him, a strangely compelling urgency. He had to get to the hospital, and he couldn't really explain why. Hugi and Paul Alton, one of the DA's investigators, arrived at
McKenzie–Willamette Hospital at 10:00 A.M.

They found Christie and Danny Downs in the ICU, their beds arranged
at the top of a lightbulb-shaped room so that the medics could monitor

their vital functions at a glance. It was apparent to Hugi and Alton that the kids were desperately injured.

The two men stood quietly at the end of Christie Downs's bed. It was well nigh impossible to see Christie herself through all the tubes, monitor leads, and bandages. A clear oxygen mask was clamped over the lower half of her face; only her thick gold-brown hair, her eyes, and her eyebrows were visible. Her left hand was heavily bandaged, and so was her chest. Above the transparent mask, she watched them. They could see that she was conscious and alert.

But she looked very small and lost, as if the odds were all against her survival. She was alone, except for doctors and nurses; there were no family members waiting to see her.

And then Christie's eyes caught Fred Hugi's and locked there.

Paul Alton glanced over at Hugi, started to say something, and paused, astounded. He had never seen Hugi show any emotion beyond irritation and impatience. There were tears rolling down Hugi's cheeks.

Alton looked twice to be sure. He was not mistaken.

"It was that simple," Alton remembered. "In that moment, Fred 'adopted' Christie. Nobody was going to hurt her anymore—not unless they went through Fred first."

The bonding was as immediate as it was surprising. Fred Hugi—the man who gave too much of himself to his career to have anything left for kids—was caught unawares. Christie and Danny Downs became, in a heartbeat, his to protect. His to avenge.

He knew full well that there was nothing tangible he could do to stop them from hurting, or dying. And yet he felt compelled to stay with them. As Alton watched, bemused, Hugi pulled up a chair and sat down just outside the globe of the ICU where he could see both youngsters.

He sat there for a long time, and he could hear the machines that kept them alive clicking, blipping, chkting-chkting. Christie and Danny breathed so quietly that he had to check occasionally to be sure that they did, indeed, breathe.

Fred Hugi watched over them—as if by sheer force of will, he could hold death away from them.

On the back of a hospital form headed "24 Hour IV Therapy and Fluid Balance Record," he scribbled notes.

Fri-5/20/83

10:05 McKenzie–Willamette.
w/8 year-old & Stephen Daniel
Mother due down soon.

Things to Do—Check clothing for stippling.

Go to scene—
 Metal detectors.
 Beer cans?
 I.D. weapon that fired rounds.

When will she leave hospital? Need someone else to talk w/
 her—PK? Get tape recorder.

Lew—33? Cheryl—The child that died.

Check on stippling on Diane.

Diary

He was starting from scratch. The cops were starting from scratch.
None of them even knew yet what kind of gun had fired the shots into the
kids. Fred Hugi was just learning their names. It was no longer "kids"; it
was "Christie" and "Danny" lying there, breathing so laboriously.

This case wasn't going to be so easy after all.

Given his choice, Hugi wouldn't have left the children at all, but there
was so much to do. The list got longer and longer.

Each time he was away from Christie and Danny that first Friday,
Hugi hurried back to check on their conditions and to sit with them for a
while. They were still alone, although their father was said to be on his
way from Arizona. Their mother apparently was not well enough yet to
leave her own room in the same hospital.

Hugi talked with John Mackey and to the nurses on duty the night
before in the ER, gathering their impressions. Mackey felt that the shooter
had probably stood near the driver's door—as Diane had described—
because of the angle of the children's wounds.

Hugi's notes were almost indiscernible hen-scratchings. The river had to be searched; the scene had to be searched. The townhouse on Q Street had to be gone over in daylight. He wanted to confer with Doug Welch and Dick Tracy, and with Sergeant Jerry Smith and Bob Antoine from the Springfield Police Department.

There was so much to catch up with.

Jim Pex had been up since 2:00 A.M. Pex—formally James O. Pex—was a Criminalist III with the Oregon State Police Crime Detection Laboratory in Eugene, an expert in forensic science. In demand by dozens of departments in Oregon, he was trying to juggle the forensic work in too many investigations.

The principle put forth by the great French criminalist Edmund Locard—that the criminal always leaves something of himself (no matter how minute) at the scene of his crime, and always carries something of the scene away with him (again, no matter how infinitesimal)—has not changed in seventy-five years; the tools of the criminalist have simply become more sophisticated.

With a resume pages thick, Jim Pex posed only one problem as a witness: his skills are so esoteric that jurors sometimes have difficulty understanding him. Few laymen can decipher his language without a crash course in forensic science. One of Pex's articles appeared in the *Journal of Forensic Science*: "Phenotyping Phosphoglucose Isomerase in West Coast Cervids for Species Identification and Individualization." Translated for the man on the street: "How to classify deer out west through factors in their blood."

Jim Pex can determine the time of death in certain animal species. From animals to humans is not that long a jump. Forensic science has become the backbone of a solid homicide case, and Fred Hugi suspected Pex might come up with answers to questions just beginning to form.

A drop of blood may look like any other drop of blood, and one strand of hair may seem indistinguishable from another. A stain may be saliva or semen or egg white. Threads and tool marks and dried leaves and pebbles and broken buttons seem alike. But not to Jim Pex. He is particularly adept in analyzing firearms and tool marks, and in serology (the study of body fluids). He can discern many things from blood—both from its serological components and from the way it has been shed. Pooled blood is different from dripped blood. Victims who have been shot will lose blood in a "high velocity" manner. There is, indeed, a subscience of forensics that listens to the silent testimony of our life's fluid—blood-spatter pattern interpretation. Not only does Jim Pex understand blood spatter; he teaches the art to lawmen and other criminalists.

Pex reviewed what he had found during the past several hours with Fred Hugi. Pex and Jon Peckels had processed the Downs car at the Lane County shops, looking for tangible evidence that the killer had left.

The Arizona plates read BJY-787; the odometer had only 5,948 miles on it. First, they had observed the exterior. Peckels pointed out the casings he and Tracy had spotted earlier. They found no gunpowder particles visible on or around the doors or windows. There was no damage to the car.

The interior was upholstered in scarlet plush; it was hard to differentiate the blood from the rich shade of the fabric. The hollow in the console was filled with pennies and nickels; the top of the dash and the carpet was sprinkled with beach sand and seashells.

There was a large semiliquid pool of blood on the floor below the passenger seat. Cheryl had lain there, covered with the postal sweater. A tube of Avon cuticle conditioner and an empty paper Pepsi cup were retained from the floor near the blood.

Pex had gently loosened the red carpet under the glove compartment. When he reached beneath it, he'd found a chunk of metal—a .22 caliber lead bullet, which would prove to weigh 39 grains.

Blood smears and large drops were visible on the inside of the door next to the passenger, probably left—Pex speculated—when medical personnel lifted a child out of the car.

"How about the driver's side?" Hugi asked.

Pex shook his head. "No blood at all on the driver's side, no smears on the steering wheel."

When a gun is fired, some of the smokeless powder fails to ignite, but is blown out the end of the barrel. The criminalists found gunpowder particles on each quadrant of the car, save the driver's seat.

Photographs taken of the back seat showed a blue nylon postal-issue jacket with a few bloodstains, a pair of rubber thongs beneath it, and a single .22 rimfire cartridge casing, headstamped "U."

Each item had been bagged and initialed by Jon Peckels. The chain of evidence from the car to some courtroom someday could not be broken. Peckels would have to swear he had the evidence in his possession—or knew exactly where it was—from the moment he took it out of the red Nissan.

One picture showed a pair of children's athletic shoes with polka-dotted pink laces and an oxygen mask left behind, incongruously juxta-posed on the floor of the back seat.

The rear bench seat where Christie and Danny had lain bore mute testimony. Pex had found pooled fresh blood and vomitus on the seat where Christie had been, and blood on the seat back too. Two .22 casings, headstamped "U," lay in the blood.

Blood had also sprayed onto the headliner over the rear seat, the rear side windows, the side panel, the rear window. Early assessment of the blood patterns suggested that the shooter had leaned into the car at the driver's seat, just as Diane had described.

Pex and Peckels had checked the trunk. No blood there at all. A U.S. postal cap, a Eugene–Springfield phone book, a tennis racket, a tape re-corder, and a gaily wrapped box filled—oddly—with dead flowers.

"We found a gun . . ."

Hugi looked up sharply. But Pex shook his head.

"It wasn't a .22. It was a Rohm model 63 revolver—a .38 Smith and Wesson Special. Mass produced, in poor shape, and rusted. We found a box of .38 Smith and Wesson Special ammo in the trunk too, but that gun hasn't been fired for a long, long time."

Pex and Peckels had photographed everything inside the car as they worked through it. Then they shot pictures of its exterior. They'd vacu-umed the car and retained all the debris in special bags. They had no way of knowing which—if any—of the evidence they'd gleaned might be im-portant to the investigation. The rule of thumb was to take it all; better too much than too little. The scene of a crime can blow away in the wind.

There had been more prosaic items in the glove box. A half-dollar, minted in 1949, a note on pink memo paper with directions for an engrav-ing to be done on a brass unicorn. Another note reading: "Welcome Home Cheryl, Daniel, Christie . . . Aunt Kathy and Israel." A grocery list: "TV Guide, Nox [Noxema?], Fish Sticks, Tater Tots, Catsup." Manuals for the vehicle and its air-conditioner. They removed a Duran Duran cassette ("Rio") from the tape deck.

The Nissan had been secured in the county shops at 5:15 A.M., and Pex had headed out to Old Mohawk Road as daylight broke through.

Later, Jim Pex observed Dr. Ed Wilson's postmortem examination of Cheryl Lynn Downs. It was necessary to find answers to questions that might seem moot. How close had the gun been to Cheryl's flesh when it was fired? Had Cheryl lived at all after the first shot?

Clad in her little green shorts, Cheryl looked as if she had fallen asleep after a hard day of tumbling play. Except for the blood. She had been a pretty little girl.

Wilson found that Cheryl had been shot twice; both wounds were fatal. The first shot had been near-contact and had entered just below the left shoulder blade, damaging a rib, her left lung, her aorta, her trachea. The second entrance wound was also close up, just over the right shoulder blade. The bullet had gone through a rib, her right lung, her aorta, her trachea and still rested just beneath the skin of her left shoulder.

After the first shot, Cheryl wouldn't have lived long enough to react in anything more than a reflexive manner. She might have had time to fling her arms out instinctively, perhaps even hit the door handle, in her futile flight from death—so close behind her that it could whisper in her ear.

Cheryl's body had been released to a local funeral home: Major-Frederickson's. Jim Pex and Detective Kurt Wuest retained the spent bullet (.22 caliber lead, weighing 38 grains); two sealed paperfolds containing gunpowder debris; three paper packets containing swabbings for the presence of semen from Cheryl's mouth, vagina, and rectum (all would prove negative); and a yellow envelope that held a gold chain with a solid heart entwined in an open heart, the locket they had gently untangled from Cheryl's long, thick hair.

CHAPTER 5

At McKenzie–Willamette Hospital, Diane and her surviving children remained under tight guard. They had been shot for a reason—albeit a reason that no one had yet discerned—and there was a chance the shooter might return to try again.

While Fred Hugi had been with Christie and Danny much of the day, Doug Welch spent most of Friday outside Diane's hospital room. He had been up all night, and it would be another dozen hours before he could think about sleep. He propped his chair against the corridor wall and propped his eyes open by willpower. No one would enter Diane's room without his scrutiny.

Heather Plourd, who now knew why the detectives had come to her trailer, was one of Diane's first visitors. The pretty brunette's face was drained of color and she had obviously been crying. Welch passed her into the room.

A few minutes later, Diane called to Welch to ask him a question.

"We've been sitting here trying to figure out how on earth it happened," she said. "And where the gun could be."

"Put yourself in the suspect's place, Diane," Welch suggested. "What would *you* have done with the gun?"

She was silent for a moment, concentrating.

"I would have taken it to the top of the hill and buried it. Or I would have thrown it in the river."

Her guess was as good as theirs. Divers were in the Little Mohawk already.

Doug Welch met the children's father the afternoon after the shooting. Steve Downs was ashen faced, exhausted, thoroughly shaken. Doug Welch knew little about Steve Downs; he had heard a great deal more about the guy named Lew, and Downs seemed to be history.

Steve Downs said he still lived in Chandler, and that he owned his own electrical contracting business—DOWCO—there.

"You talk to your ex-wife lately?"

"Since Diane moved to Oregon—about two months ago—I've probably talked to her on the phone seven or eight times. She's called me at home a coupla times, and I've called her at her folks' house five or six times."

"What did you talk about?"

Downs shrugged. "Nothing special. The kids. General conversation."

Downs described his current relationship with Diane as "stable—we're still friends." He knew all about Lew—"Lew" Lewiston. His ex-wife had fallen hard for Lew. Downs said that Lewiston was a married man and that, in his opinion, Lew had been leading Diane on.

"They had an on-again/off-again relationship for the past six months. She flew down to see him a while back, and she told me that they had all their problems worked out."

"You saw her then?" Welch asked, a little startled by the Downses' civilized attitude in what might still be a classic triangle.

"Sure. She stayed at my place that night."

Downs discussed the men in his ex-wife's life with some degree of equanimity. "She's slept with six or seven different guys, but she's not loose or anything; she would never go to bed with a guy unless she really cared for him—or at least thought she did."

"Did you and Diane own any guns—or do you know if she presently owns any?"

"Diane's got three guns: a .22 rifle, a .38 revolver, and a .22 Ruger Mark IV nine-shot semi-automatic pistol."

Welch carefully kept his face bland, but he felt his muscles tense. Diane had listed the first two guns when she'd talked to him and Tracy the night before, but she had failed to mention having owned a .22 pistol. Steve Downs had mentioned this .22 to Paul Alton too, and Alton had suggested that Welch try to find out more about it.

Welch waited, afraid his fatigue might make him falter and say the wrong thing. A fly buzzed over a vase of flowers somebody had put in the ICU waiting room; footsteps padded down the hallway; the elevator bell dinged.

"OK," Welch began. "If we could start from the top. Where did she obtain those guns?"

"Let's see ... Diane bought the rifle and the .38 for me for Christmas. I got the .22 Ruger about a year and a half ago in exchange for some work I did for a customer."

"When did you see the Ruger last?"

"Maybe six months ago, in my bedroom. See, Diane's borrowed it from me before, and I just figure she has it now, because it's gone. She doesn't know a lot about guns, but I showed her how to operate those three."

"She can shoot the .22 pistol?"

"Oh yeah. I showed her how to chamber a round by pulling the slide back, and I told her that she should be certain the clip is sticking halfway down to keep a round from being accidentally chambered."

Welch took a deep breath. The next question was one that had to be asked diplomatically. It was such a far-out supposition.

"Would your wife—ex-wife—Diane ... would she ... *might* she ever put Lew Lewiston before her children?"

Downs was dumbfounded at the suggestion. "No way. She loves those kids. She'd never put Lew before them!"

Physically, Diane was doing well. Danny was critical but stable. He lay with drainage tubes in his chest, nasal prongs in place for oxygen, a Foley catheter in his penis. He would not—perhaps could not—talk to the nurses who attended him. His toes curled back when the nurses tickled the bottom of his feet. That was a hopeful sign. That might mean that he wouldn't be paralyzed.

Christie had quite literally come back from the dead. But she was alive. Pediatrician David Miller had been gratified to see that when he hurried into the intensive care unit on Friday. Christie still had the tube in her throat to help her breathe, but her eyes followed him alertly and he was sure she understood what he said.

After checking off a number of items on his Things-to-Do list, Fred Hugi hurried back to the ICU at McKenzie–Willamette Friday afternoon. It was hard to believe that the case was less than twenty-four hours old. Hugi's tension eased when he saw both Christie and Danny in their beds, still surrounded by monitoring equipment. But a nurse motioned him aside. Christie had had a critical complication.

Dr. Bruce Becker was on duty. He'd kept a close watch over Christie. Becker said he'd noted an alarming change in Christie's condition. She was having clonic movements on the right side of her body and face. It was some manner of seizure, small spasms and twitches that signaled trouble inside the brain itself. As far as they knew, Christie had suffered no head injuries. But she had "bled out." Such massive blood loss wreaks havoc with the body's chemistry. Moreover, she hadn't breathed at all for some time. By 1:30 on the afternoon of this first day, Christie had no longer been able to respond consistently to verbal commands no matter how hard she tried. Something was terribly wrong, something more than the bullet wounds in her chest. Becker told Hugi that Christie had had a stroke in the left side of her brain. No one could say yet what that might mean to her eventual recovery.

Reluctantly, Hugi left the ICU once more. They needed him in the continuing search of the Downs duplex.

Dick Tracy and Doug Welch were still on duty, but they were too exhausted after being up thirty-six hours to be effective searchers at Diane's home. They stayed downstairs and logged items carefully into evidence as Hugi, Paul Alton, and other members of the DA's staff brought them downstairs.

Had there been something in Diane Downs's life before the evening of May 19 that set her up as a target? And would they find some lead to it here?

They found stacks of letters, cards (almost all of them addressed to Lew), newspaper clips, instructions on how to file for bankruptcy, and, surprisingly, a number of articles and papers on surrogate parenting. Diane had evidently been very interested in the process in which a woman can bear a baby for a childless couple through artificial insemination. Hugi found several documents bearing the letterhead of a psychologist in Arizona. Those might help them understand Diane Downs's world up to now. Maybe. Maybe not.

Alton found a Montgomery Ward receipt for $21.09. It was dated a week earlier—payment in full for a brass unicorn.

Curious about Welch's report that there was no edible food in the house, Hugi poked into the garbage can in the storage shed and found a large ravioli can. The tomato sauce hadn't yet dried; this must have been what Diane and her kids had had for supper just before they left for the drive out to Heather Plourd's.

Looking through the downstairs coat closet, he pulled out a red chiffon "baby-doll" nightgown with diamond-shaped sections cut away from strategic areas over the breasts and navel. Hugi wondered idly why it was downstairs instead of in a lingerie drawer.

Alton shouted from upstairs. He had found the .22 round that Tracy had taken from Diane's rifle and then overlooked in the wee hours of the previous morning— a copper-wash cartridge nestled in the folds of Diane's bedspread. It was head stamped "U"—just like some of the spent casings found at the shooting scene.

There were thousands of .22 rounds with the same headstamp in the state of Oregon. Still, it was a coincidence.

They left the Downs duplex after 7:00 P.M., turning small mountains of possible evidence over to Jon Peckels for transport to the safety of the locked property room. It was only when they finally finished the search that Fred Hugi glanced at his list again to see what was next.

"Call Joanne."

It was a good thing he'd written it down. And a good thing that she understood the moment she heard his voice how obsessed he already was with this case. He picked her up, explaining that they were on their way to meet with Paula Krogdahl, and then he needed to go back to the hospital just once more that night.

Paula Krogdahl was the "PK" on Fred Hugi's original list of things to do. He had a deal to offer Paula that she might well refuse.

Paula, an attractive dark-haired law student, had once worked for the Children's Services Division of the State of Oregon. Smiling, soft-spoken Paula *spoke* to children. She knew instinctively how to hug and cuddle and make a frightened youngster feel safe. Danny and Christie had every reason not to feel safe, and Hugi wanted someone who might change that.

Knowing he had no funds to pay her, and that Paula probably needed her time away from her law studies to earn a living, Hugi plunged in anyway.

"Paula, I've got a case I really need your help with, a case involving the shooting of three children. One child is dead; one child is going to live, but he's too little to help; the other child might know who shot them. But she needs someone she can learn to trust. Ideally, I need you to be with them for an hour in the morning and an hour in the afternoon. There isn't any money in the DA's budget to pay you. It would have to be a volunteer job..."

She stopped him, nodding. The three of them—Joanne Hugi, Fred, and Paula—went back to the hospital together.

Steve Downs was there, sleeping in a chair between his two surviving children.

Diane wasn't there, nor were her parents.

Joanne and Fred Hugi and Paula Krogdahl sat for hours, watching Christie and Danny sleep. Long after midnight they pulled themselves away.

Hugi didn't sleep. He tossed all night, thinking, worrying.

Paul Alton didn't sleep either. He kept remembering something he'd observed during the afternoon when he was spelling Hugi beside Christie's bed. Alton was there the first time Diane came to visit her daughter. He expected a tearful reunion.

Instead, it had been a strange, tense tableau. Diane had entered the ICU quietly and stared down at Christie. Then with her uninjured hand she had reached for Christie's right hand—her good hand—and squeezed hard. She stared fixedly into Christie's eyes. She wasn't smiling. She spoke through clenched teeth, and she repeated the same phrase over and over again: "Christie, I *love* you ... I *love* you."

"I happened to glance at the heart-rate monitor—the pulse—when Diane came in," Alton recalled. "The scope showed Christie's heart was beating 104 times a minute [80 is normal]. When Diane took hold of her and kept telling her that—that scope jumped to 147! It took a long time for it to drop back down after her mother went back to her own room."

Christie and her mother had been through a ghastly experience together, but Alton could not put a name to the emotion he saw in Christie's eyes as she'd looked up at her mother's face.

Fear, he thought finally.

CHAPTER 6

*Elizabeth Downs and her three children had been in the Marcola
area visiting with a friend and were in the process of returning to
Springfield when she was flagged down by a stranger who demanded her car. Suspect then began shooting into her car, killing
one child and wounding the other two. He then shot Elizabeth
Downs, wounding her in the arm. Suspect then left the area, and
she drove her vehicle to McKenzie–Willamette Hospital . . . The
case is being investigated by the Lane County Sheriff's Office with
the assistance of the Springfield Police Department.*
— Lt. Louis Hince, first news release, 5-20-1983

Hince had released that succinct paragraph to the media early Friday
morning. Even with the paucity of details, the story and its sidebars filled
most of the front page of the Eugene *Register-Guard.* There was a color
photo of Rob Rutherford and Deputy George Poling pointing to the spot
where they'd found two .22 caliber casings on the macadam of Old Mohawk. A bright yellow map with fuchsia arrows indicated the alleged
shooting site and route to McKenzie–Willamette. And there were the
usual filler quotes from locals voicing outraged shock; the same three
people appeared on Eugene's three television stations, peering nervously
into the cameras' lenses and declaring over and over that things like that
just don't happen out here.

The door-to-door canvass of the night before spread in scope. The entire area between Hayden Bridge and Marcola was alive with cops and
dogs and search-and-rescue Boy Scouts. Helicopters fluttered over the
river and the narrow road beside it—giant dragonflies shimmering in the
sunshine. If the killer was still out there someplace, his belly pressed to
the red Oregon dirt, the searchers and their dogs would find him. If the
shaggy-haired man had tossed the gun into the river or stashed it in a tree
trunk, they'd find that too.

Jim Pex had joined the crew at the scene at 8:30 A.M. Beyond the two bullet casings, there wasn't much in the way of physical evidence. Some footprints were photographed along the side of the road away from the riverbank. Some Blitz-Weinhard beer cans—empty—and some Dubble-Bubble gum—chewed—were bagged and saved on the off chance the killer had consumed them. There were tire tracks, but they were from a tractor, not a car.

The gun was what they needed. Pex was almost positive that they were looking for a semi-automatic .22 pistol or rifle with a clip-style magazine. If they only had the weapon and its serial number, ownership could be traced back from hand to hand through a ballistic family tree.

Lieutenant Howard Kershner, twenty-four-year veteran of the Lane County Sheriff's Office—tall and ramrod-straight as a Marine drill sergeant—directed the search. His men and the scouts had been at the site since dawn. Working with machetes and brush hooks, they pulled at the blackberry thickets, and then chopped wild foliage down to six inches from the ground. They nudged deadfall logs aside with boots, exposing only grubs and snakes. They walked arm's length abreast into the field of pale flowers, staring down, until they were so deep into the field that no major league pitcher could have flung a gun so far. When they finished each search sector, they tied bright plastic ribbons to mark where they had been, mocking snippets of color in the wind.

When the land gave them nothing, Kershner and his two divers—Ned Heasty and Earl McMullen—slipped into the Mohawk itself, the icy chill quickly penetrating their black rubber suits. The water was clear near the banks, but midstream current churned up the bottom. Light and shadow mixed together as the disturbed silt exploded like dust. It was an eerie quest. The root balls beneath the water were as gnarled as a witch's grasping fingers, waterlogged sirens waiting to snare and hold a diver fast until his lungs emptied of air.

They found no gun. This should have been the most likely spot to dispose of it; the casings had been at the one spot along Old Mohawk where the road came nearest to the river. When they didn't find it there, they knew they would have to go in the river at Hayden Bridge.

Even for experienced divers, there are few more treacherous sites than "The Chute" under the bridge.

"It's fast water," Kershner explained. "Half the water goes downstream, and half goes upriver."

The current is so swift there—there under the bridge where Christie Downs "stopped choking"—that it rips off face masks, dislodging muscular men off ropes like leaves snatched from a thin branch in a windstorm. It is forty-five feet deep, and there are boulders twenty feet high beneath the surface.

"You can only release yourself and fly through the water . . . and it seems like you're going a hundred miles an hour as you go past the boulders. If you don't gauge exactly, you'll get trapped. Once you're caught under the water there, no one can get you out."

Kershner and his fellow divers found a number of things—including a motorcycle—but they did not find a gun. In the end, they would have put in 1,149 man-hours.

For nothing.

Reporters scattered throughout Lane County to get quotes from people who had known Diane Downs *before*.

"You could tell she really loves those kids, just by the way she used to talk about them," Floyd Gohn, the Cottage Grove postmaster, told them. "I think she is probably as good a mother as an employee, and she's a number-one worker as far as I'm concerned!"

Superintendent of the Cottage Grove post office, Ron Sartin, was furious. "When the hell are the law enforcement agencies or the people going to do something about all the dopeheads in this country?" he fumed to reporters. "Here's a gal with three kids and something like this happens out of the blue. You can't even drive your car down the streets at night!"

Sartin pretty much spoke for the citizens of Lane County, appalled that such a tragedy could happen to a young mother and three little kids.

Diane's room at McKenzie–Willamette Hospital had begun to fill up with floral offerings and cards; cut flowers, potted plants, and tastefully subdued sympathy cards covered every available surface. Room 322 had a funereal odor, a too-heavy clotting of fragrance. Although Diane had lived in Oregon for such a short time, she had her parents there, and she'd made friends at the post office where she worked. She'd trained with Heather Plourd at the main branch.

Post office officials said Diane had transferred to Cottage Grove because she wanted a smaller facility where she could learn all aspects of the postal business. She had shown great ambition.

Cottage Grove, Oregon, is twenty miles south of Eugene and Springfield. Fewer than 5,000 people live there, and all of them seemed to have heard about the Downs shooting. Diane's fellow postal workers were particularly distressed.

Diane had no great love for cooking. She and the children ate dinner at Willadene's table almost every night, or picked up fast food. But she often brought home-baked cake-mix goodies to the Cottage Grove post office to share. On one occasion, she'd even come in on her day off to bring them a cake, and the children were with her. Everybody there had been taken with her kids. Now, they chipped in and sent a huge bunch of flowers to Diane at the hospital.

The Page Elementary School PTA mothers were in the midst of setting up a garage sale when they got the news. They felt the stab of horror first, and then grave concern about how their children would handle it. Cheryl Lynn's teacher, Sharon Walker, arranged for Ellie Smith, the school counselor, to come in for an hour and help the children spill out their feelings.

"They talked about feeling sad, and some of them shared experiences of losing grandparents or pets. They also expressed fear. I led them into a discussion about how a person lives on in our memories, even when they're taken from us."

In Christie's third grade class, teacher Beverly Lindley kept her students busy making get-well cards.

The public was squarely behind Diane Downs, aware that she was going to need all the emotional support she could get in the weeks ahead. Total strangers sat down to write cards or letters to help her through her grief.

Doug Welch rolled into his own driveway very late Friday evening. He was very troubled at a thought that refused to go away.

"I sat down in my chair, over by the bookcases, and I probably popped a beer. To tell you the truth, I was so tired I can't remember. My wife, Tamara, came over and sat down beside me and she said, 'Well?' and I said,

'Well, what?' She hadn't heard a word from me for over twenty-four hours and she kept asking, 'Well?'

"You won't believe it."

"Well, tell me."

"I think she did it."

"Who?"

"Diane."

"...No-o-o! She's their *mother*..."

"I know."

"No mother could ever do that to her children. I'm a mother and I know women better than you do."

"They'd have to pump drugs into you or me right and left to keep us sane if that happened to our kids," Welch mused. "Diane—she never shed one tear."

"I still don't want to believe that."

"Neither do I. Tracy and I are going to talk to her again in the morning. Maybe I'll feel different after."

Fred Hugi was back at his post between Christie and Danny early Saturday morning. Nobody bothered him; he had become a familiar fixture, this brooding guardian angel who watched over two children he barely knew.

Late in the morning, Hugi spotted a smiling middle-aged couple hurry in and head toward Danny and Christie. Instantly, he was on his feet and blocking their way. He asked who they were.

Wes and Willadene Frederickson identified themselves: "We're their grandparents."

The Fredericksons stayed at the children's bedsides for a short time. When they walked out, Hugi was puzzled by their demeanor. They seemed so happy, so cheerful. They noticed he was looking at the name tags on their shoulders and they explained merrily that they had come from a service club's "Fun Run."

To Hugi's amazement, Wes laughed. "We had to supervise," he explained. "You know how social obligations are—you can't break 'em."

Fred Hugi stared at him, speechless.

At 2:00 P.M. that Saturday, Doug Welch and Dick Tracy talked to Diane in her hospital room. They had finally had a night's sleep and presumably so had Diane. Welch tried to keep an open mind, wondering if his gut feelings of the night before might have been the result of too little sleep.

Diane was ivory-pale, her heavily bandaged left arm resting on a pillow. She was willing to talk to them but was a little put off when she saw the tape recorder Tracy held. Finally, she sighed and said she guessed it wouldn't hurt to record their conversation.

And so the trio sat, amid the thickening profusion of floral offerings, talking of sudden inexplicable death.

Tracy took the lead, his voice as lazy as an old cowpoke's. He sensed that Diane considered him a harmless country rube, a dumb old cop.

"Why don't you take it from the top? I guess we could start back on the nineteenth," he suggested. "That's Thursday."

From time to time, their conversation was interrupted by nurses bringing more flowers and cards, by phone calls from out-of-town friends. To be strictly accurate, it was not a conversation at all; it was a monologue. Once Diane opened her mouth, she continued nonstop, seemingly without oxygen to sustain her, feeling relief, perhaps, at the catharsis.

Thursday. The last day. Diane had gotten up at 5:15, awakened the kids a half hour later, and delivered them to Willadene's house at 6:15. The girls would have breakfast there and then walk to school, while Danny stayed with his grandma. Diane had carried along a Bundt cake she'd made for the gang at the post office.

"We had the cake at break and all that, and then I got off at 3:30, but I hung around and talked to the guys for a while."

Later, she had picked up the kids and visited with Willadene.

"Cheryl went out and cut me a couple of roses, and she cut one for Christie too."

Usually, they ate at her folks' house, but Wes and Willadene were going out. It had been just Diane and her kids for supper at home.

Diane recalled that Cheryl had been begging for a kitten. Diane told her she could have one, and she'd galloped happily to the neighbors to bring the cat and litter box home.

Diane said she'd talked on the phone after dinner to a girlfriend in Arizona. Then she'd remembered the clipping she'd found, the one about adopting a horse. Heather hadn't had a phone when Diane trained with her in Eugene so after she'd finished the dishes, she and the kids had driven out to the Plourds' trailer, leaving around 9:15. It wasn't full dark when they left Q Street.

It turned out that Heather already had a horse. The kids had shrieked with delight as they ran back and forth from her car to the horse, feeding it grass, petting it.

"And then we left, and we went back out Sunderman Road, and, like I said, we like to just cruise around and see stuff. The kids love the scenery and the trees, and they like to watch the rapids in the water at the river and stuff like that . . . so we just went out cruising."

When she realized the kids had fallen asleep, Diane had turned her car toward home, picking Old Mohawk Road on a whim.

"There was a guy standing in the road waving his arm. He was not like on the white line, but he was in the center of my lane. So I stopped and got out and asked him what was the problem. 'Cause it looked, you know . . . like he needed something. He was frantic! And so he came over to where I was and he said, 'I want your car,' and I said, 'You've got to be kidding!' I mean, how many people do that in real life?"

Welch opened his mouth to speak, but Diane was already beyond him.

"They don't. And he pushed me back and he fired into my car so many times. My God. It was horrible, and my little girl raised up in the back seat . . ."

"Which one was that?" Tracy darted a question into the stream of words.

"It's Christie . . . and she raised up and she had such a look of terror . . . or confusion, or something. That's just a look I'll never forget, but I can't describe. And then she fell back on the seat and grabbed her chest. God! It was just so bad . . . and then he goes, 'I want your car,' and I was just aghast. I had to do something. So I faked throwing the keys to distract him . . . I knew I couldn't beat him up in a fistfight, and he had a gun anyway . . . so I kicked him with my knee sort of and shoved him . . . as he was swinging around when I threw the keys. He shot a couple of times and one of them caught me in the arm and it didn't even hurt."

Diane said she'd managed to shove the man aside, jump back in her car, put her key in the ignition, and drive off. She didn't know if the man had fired after her.

"Christie was laying in the back seat, just choking on her own blood, and I kept telling her to roll over on her stomach ... She was just drowning in it. God. Cheryl was on the floor, not making a movement or a sound, and Danny was in the back seat just crying so soft, going *'Mommie'* so soft, and God, I just kept on ... I couldn't stop. If I'd stopped to roll Christie over on her stomach ... she would of just, in a panic, rolled back, and I would have lost five seconds and five seconds was a lot ..."

Desperate, Diane had carried on a running conversation with God, she said. "God, do what's best. If they've got to die, let them die, but don't let them suffer. I just kept driving ... kept driving ... kept driving."

She recalled that her arm had started to hurt a little bit, that she'd grabbed a towel from somewhere in the car, and wrapped it around her arm. It might have been a beach towel left from the trip they'd taken to the ocean the week before. She had no idea when she'd done this. She'd made it to the hospital and laid on the horn.

"I wanted to grab my kids up and run in; but I couldn't, my arm was starting to hurt ... and I told a lady to call the cops right away and she ... she called a couple of other people first ... but I kept sitting there, saying 'Call them! Call them!'"

The detectives had no need to ask questions; Diane anticipated them, leaping ahead with her words, explaining, explicating, describing. She was wound so tightly, her words welling up as if they had been under intense pressure somewhere deep in her core. At the very moment a word was released into the antiseptic air of Room 322, ten more formed, a swarm of words fighting their way to sound-life.

Tracy was not interrogating Diane. He considered himself fortunate if he could throw out a one-word question from time to time. He was like a man in a steel mill directing the flow of hot metal with a careful shifting of channels.

Diane's skin pinkened. Her voice grew less breathy.

She went over the whole night for them, in detail. It was as if it would all be erased if she could tell it often enough, as if she believed she could talk it away.

Diane began to talk about Cheryl, and for the first time, her voice faltered. She hadn't known at first which of her children was dead.

"I finally accepted it was Cheryl who had died. I know she didn't suffer in the least and that's good, because now the rest of us, you know, we're going to go on . . . My mom wanted to know Cheryl's favorite color, and she's going to buy her a dress. We're going to have a small service for her . . . Cheryl loved new dresses. And so I told her red. But I've been thinking I want it to be white. I mean she's such a good kid and it should be white. She's an angel now . . ."

Tears blurred the tape. Instantly, Diane choked them back, deeply embarrassed that she had broken down.

Dick Tracy asked her carefully if it was possible that she could have been under the influence of drugs that night, if her memory might be flawed. She shook her head.

"The reason that I drink and the reason that I . . . occasionally . . . smoke marijuana is when I feel lonely and depressed. It was like on Friday night when Mom would take the kids and I would be alone in the house . . . wondering why the hell Lew wasn't here . . . because he had promised we were going to be mates and we were going to raise the kids and everything was going to be just fine. And I couldn't understand why all that was different and that's when I would drink—when the kids weren't around—'cause I'm a real conscientious mother and I despise people that are lax in raising their kids . . . that can allow themselves to get drunk . . . You can't tell when an emergency is going to arise and the kids will need care . . . That's very immature, so I didn't do that around my kids."

She had been so careful with her children that the tragedy seemed doubly ironic. She never took a chance on her kids' safety. Life with them had been so fulfilling lately, Diane told them, that she hadn't even had the urge to drink or smoke pot.

"Even in my book [diary] I told Lew, 'I think I love the kids more than you . . .'"

Tracy cut in. He had learned that when he heard the name Lew, he was in imminent danger of losing control of the questioning. Diane seemed to use her memories of her Arizona lover to block out pain.

"What about the area out there? How many times have you driven it?" Tracy asked quickly.

"Never. Never on Old Mohawk. Once to Marcola. Twice to Heather's."
They had only been exploring, sightseeing, in the hour after sunset on a
May night.

CHAPTER 7

We've got a BHS here. She calls him "shaggy-haired." Same thing.
The infamous Bushy-Haired Stranger.
                                                    —Fred Hugi

The forty-eight-hour cut-off point had come and gone with no arrest.
Maybe it was only superstition, but missing the deadline cast a pall over
the group that met each morning at eight. Hugi, his investigators, and
Sheriff Burks's detectives met first in Louis Hince's office and then in
Fred's. It was the only time they could halfway count on. They hadn't the
luxury of putting all other business aside to concentrate on the Downs
probe; each of them had between thirty and a hundred *other* cases of
greater or lesser importance to juggle. Before they were through, thousands of phone messages would be left, scores of meetings rescheduled. If
a killer had deliberately set out to choose the optimum county in which
to commit murder, he could not have picked better than Lane County,
Oregon, in the spring of 1983. Underfunded, understaffed—and now facing a tax vote that might well make it worse—both the DA's office and the
sheriff's department always seemed to be running to catch up.

Only days had passed. Diane was still in the hospital when the whole
complexion of the case began to change. Almost to a man, the investigators had begun to suspect that the shooter was someone closer to the
family than the ephemeral shaggy-haired stranger Diane had described.

The "BHS" (bushy-haired stranger) is an integral part of forensic folk-
lore. The BHS is the guy who isn't there, the man the defendant claims is
really responsible. The suspect is merely an innocent person who hap-

pened to be in the wrong place at the wrong time. Of course, the BHS can never be produced in court.

"We estimate that if the BHS is ever caught, the prison doors will have to be opened to let out all the wrongly convicted defendants," Hugi mused.

The BHS allegedly holds the answer to many unsolved crimes, but an essential part of the BHS defense is that he can never be precisely identified or produced in court.

"Dead people with criminal records make the best BHS's," Hugi said wryly. "They are unable to deny their guilt."

Diane's description of her attacker had raised the hairs on the back of the detectives' necks. The term in police parlance is "hinky."

"Hinky" cannot be literally defined; it is something that doesn't ring true, that is off-center, suspicious—something that nags at the mind, that comes in the night and interrupts the sleep of even an exhausted detective.

If Diane Downs had blamed a creature from another planet for the shootings, she could not have raised more doubts in the minds of the men who questioned her. Once she'd opened that Pandora's box, there were other problems with her story.

"I don't buy it," Paul Alton said flatly. "How would the shooter know which road Diane was going to take that night? She goes out Sunderman to see Heather Plourd, she decides to go sightseeing and heads toward Marcola. She finds the kids have fallen asleep, so she turns around and she heads back toward Springfield. The normal route would be straight down Marcola and then onto Q Street. But suddenly she decides she'll veer off on the Old Mohawk Road. Say we buy the story that she's sightseeing. Even if it's almost pitch dark, she's sightseeing. She says the kids liked to watch the moonlight on the river, or whatever. Anyway, we believe that story for now. How do we explain that the shooter knew she was going to be there? If he's following her in his own car—say the old yellow car—he could trail her onto old Mohawk. But she tells us that the stranger's *in front of her, standing in the road* waving her down. How does he get there?"

The detectives in Lewis Hince's office shrugged. It *was* unexplainable. And if there had been a shaggy-haired man who needed a car badly enough to flag a stranger down on a lonely road, and then demand that car at gunpoint, why hadn't he shot Diane first? She was the adult who could have resisted him physically, who could have identified him.

Why would the stranger have reacted to Diane's "You've got to be kidding!" by immediately aiming his gun into her car and shooting her children? How would he have even known there were children there? Christie and Danny were supposedly asleep on the back seat, their heads below the shooter's line of sight through the windows. And Cheryl. Diane said that Cheryl had been sound asleep on the floor in front of the passenger seat, covered with a gray postal sweater, virtually invisible even to someone who *knew* she was there.

Suppose the shaggy-haired killer *had* shot Diane first? Suppose *she* had lain dead on the macadam of the Old Mohawk Road with a .22 caliber bullet in her breast? The investigators took that a step further, and considered what the gunman might have done once he had the vehicle, only to discover that there were three children asleep inside. Three children could certainly slow down someone who was trying to make a getaway, but it was doubtful they could identify him. And the killer would have known that.

Would the gunman not have lifted those three children out—perhaps even pulled them out roughly—tossed them onto the shoulder of the road and driven off?

Of course.

It didn't wash at all. *Hinky.*

They looked at it from another angle. Suppose, just for the sake of conjecture, that someone had a reason to assassinate the entire Downs family: a hired killer, maybe—or two—sent out to gun down Diane and her kids, or a disappointed lover who was jealous enough to want to kill the kids along with Diane?

That was a good theory, but theories were the icing on the case. First, they had to construct a corpus delecti—not the corpse of the victim, as is generally believed, but the "body of the crime itself." This includes everything that has gone into the commission of a particular crime, everything that has resulted, the complete faceting of an almost physical entity—not unlike the mirrored balls that revolve continually over dance floors, casting floating circlets of reflected light on floor, ceiling, walls, and the dancers below. The body of the crime of murder is as complex as these glittering globes of mirror tiles; different angles produce different shadows of light, different clues produce different theories.

Investigators are always looking for motive, opportunity, means. The familiar MO (modus operandi) beloved of fiction and television writers means quite simply, "In what manner did the killer carry out his crime?"

Real detectives look for circumstantial evidence, precious nuggets of information or coincidence that make someone *look* like a good suspect. But they are not nearly as entranced with it as television detectives are. The working cop wants good, hard physical evidence: something that a jury can see or hear or touch or smell, something tangible and so incontrovertible that *its very existence links the killer with the victims at the moment of the crime.*

The Lane County team had only battered bullets and cartridges with no gun to match them. And they had blood—of all types and enzyme characteristics, dripped, spattered, pooled. It wasn't enough.

"Suppose, just suppose," Alton began again. "Suppose there *were* two of them. Two people waiting out there?"

Welch snorted. "OK. Two assassins. They'd have to have had a two-way radio. One follows Diane and signals to the other that she's turning onto Old Mohawk. The second one parks his car, messes up his hair, and runs out to flag her down."

"Great," Tracy answered. "He's just far enough ahead so that he can get back down Old Mohawk in time to trick her into stopping. She's never talked about anyone passing her before she saw the man."

"You have to twist it to make it work, mold it to fit," Welch said. "I'm having a lot of trouble with her story."

There were little inconsistencies that troubled all of them. Minor changes. Diane had told Judy Patterson that the man had leaned in the window to shoot her children. She had told the detectives that she had watched the man stick his arm inside the car while he stood outside. She sometimes said the killer had been standing in the road, and at other times that he'd jogged up to her car. Sometimes she remembered that her children were awake and laughing; sometimes they were asleep.

Minor discrepancies.

They were getting tips from the public about suspects. The Lane

County Sheriff's Office was deluged with leads, and a lot of them sounded entirely plausible on paper. But when Paul Alton or Roy Pond or Kurt Wuest went out to do follow-up interviews with the informants, things fell apart. Either the timing was off—even by a week or two. Or the weather was wrong—some citizens described seeing the stranger in jeans walking in a pouring rain; the vital night had been clear and dry.

Fred Hugi had little doubt that there *had* been a stranger out along Old Mohawk Road—and probably an old yellow car too—but he wondered if either had anything to do with the shooting. Diane might merely have incorporated them into her recollection of what had happened.

Hugi, like Welch, wondered if they might already have met the killer, or the instigator.

Diane.

But then he kept coming back to "Why?" What could she have to gain from shooting her own children? There was no insurance on them. No monetary motivation. He could not conceive that she might simply have wanted to be rid of them and chosen such a brutal solution. It had to be more than that—if Diane were behind it. And anyway, that was an assumption Hugi wanted to reject as much as the rest of them.

They had to know more about her. Hugi recognized Diane's confidence as facade. Innocent or guilty, she had to be at her lowest ebb during these first days in the hospital. Hugi talked daily with the detectives who guarded her and interviewed her. If she was the shooter—or an accessory— she would be terrified that she would be found out. She could be so frightened, perhaps, that she might blurt out a confession. No one was leaning on her. To a burdened conscience, silence and solicitude can be more threatening than interrogation.

To Hugi's surprise, nothing happened. Diane seemed more well each day, more in control of her emotions.

He watched Diane covertly as she made her way down to see her living children. At first she had seemed full of anxiety; now she seemed . . . what? *Resigned.* Was she working up her nerve to confess? Hugi didn't think so. Watching Diane recover was like watching a snake shed its skin; underneath, she was all shiny-new, blooming with health and assurance.

Diane scarcely glanced at Hugi, apparently assuming that he was just another plainclothes policeman. She visited her children—yes—but she seemed unable to talk to them, like someone who had never been around youngsters. She stood awkwardly at the end of their beds, her movements stilted and self-conscious. After shifting from one foot to the other for a while, she would leave, often without saying a word. She never spoke to Fred Hugi, hurrying past him as he sat there watching over Christie and Danny. He was part of the furniture.

Hugi asked Dr. Terrance Carter about Diane's injuries.

"The receptionist treated her first, put Betadine on the wounds to sterilize them . . ." Carter began.

"Did she notice any stippling—powder burns?" Hugi asked.

"Yes. Judy Patterson said she wiped away some black specks."

"And what did you find?"

"A single bullet entered her left forearm on the . . . dorsal, er . . . the thumb side. It split in two as it shattered the radius, and then exited, leaving two smaller wounds."

As Carter explained the trauma Diane had suffered, Hugi felt a sense of déjà vu, remembering Howard Williams's half-joking prediction that first morning. The surgeon's hand pointed to his left forearm in the exact gesture Williams had used.

Hugi paused for a moment. "Let me ask you something . . . and it might sound strange. If you were going to shoot yourself, deliberately, but you didn't want to do any *real* damage, where would you shoot?"

Carter looked straight into Hugi's eyes. "*There.* Right there. Right or left forearm, depending on which handed you were."

Maybe. But if she'd held up her arm, warding off a bullet, she might have the same injuries.

The early-morning meetings continued. Hugi scribbled quotes from the detectives concerning Diane's attitude in the left margin of his yellow tablet.

"Mother acted . . . like maybe her parakeet died. Joking." One detective had summed up Diane's reaction with a crude phrase: "Mother's attitude totally fucked."

"Many statements—fairly consistent," Hugi wrote.

The case built only in their minds. Diane could act "totally fucked" but they had no case without the gun. Although fingerprints are the best physical evidence available, ballistics is only a shade less precise. Criminalists can determine with microscopic certainty that a bullet has been fired from one and only one weapon. Every gun (except a shotgun or other smooth-bore barrel) has had rifling machined into the barrel to make the bullet's path truer, lands and grooves resembling a bas relief candy cane, circling spirals. The high points, or "lands," mark the bullet as it passes through the barrel. Some manufacturers' lands and grooves are so familiar to firearms examiners that they can identify the manufacturer by the marks on the bullets. (A Colt has six lands and grooves and a left-hand twist; a Smith and Wesson has five lands and grooves and a right-hand twist.)

"Tool marks" are left on bullet casings by a gun's extractor and ejector, by the firing pin. Even if a bullet has not been *fired* from a gun, but has merely been worked through the magazine, there will be distinctive tool marks left on the slug's casing.

But there was no gun. Pex told them that tool mark comparisons and the lands and grooves on the .22 caliber bullets retrieved from the victims were consistent with a semi-automatic pistol or rifle using a clip-style magazine.

All the diving and searching hadn't turned up a gun. Every letter box along the route from Marcola to the shooting site to McKenzie–Willamette Hospital had been checked. Someone directly—or peripherally—connected to the postal system might have mailed a gun to a fake address in a previously prepared envelope, aware that it would eventually end up in a dead-letter office far away from Springfield, Oregon. But none of the boxes between the river and the hospital had slots big enough for anything but letters.

Fred Hugi and Paul Alton decided to go out and look for the gun themselves.

Alton had been a detective in the biggest county in California (San Bernardino County) for twenty-two years. Desert country. He suspected that *whoever* the shooter had been, he or she had come to Oregon from Arizona.

"We're creatures of habit," Alton argued. "If you're from Arizona, you don't throw something in the river, because there are no rivers to speak of there, or they're dried up. You dig a hole in the sand and you bury it. Even with the river right next to the road, I figure the shooter stuck to old habits."

Paul Alton and Fred Hugi walked along the river, searching for the weapon. Alton's eyes were drawn to the white milepost stakes. They would have made good markers if someone wanted to go back later and retrieve the weapon. He dug around each one. And found nothing.

Alton contacted a metal detection expert in Sweet Home, Oregon. They moved along Old Mohawk Road; the sun burned down on them as they tested likely spots to have hidden a smoking gun. The metal detector sounded often, and there were moments when they felt close. "We found a bunch of metal," Alton recalls. "We dug up chunks of car parts, tools, everything, all up and down both sides of the road . . . but we didn't dig up a gun."

Fred Hugi walked every foot of road from the Hayden Bridge turnoff to where Old Mohawk Road cuts away from Marcola Road and back to I-105 searching for the glint of a gun.

Remembering the road dust on Diane's car, Hugi's thoughts kept turning to the Camp Creek Road just beyond Hayden Bridge. Road crews had been in the process of widening it along its entire length of six or seven miles. Each day, a portion would be covered with rock and gravel and then paved. Paving had continued on Friday, the day after the shooting. If a gun had been tossed onto the prepared surface late Thursday night, it nestled safely now under layers of macadam, impervious to metal detectors.

What if they never found the gun?

They would be left with two eyewitnesses.

One was Diane. The other was Christie—who could no longer talk.

Each day after her stroke, it became more obvious that Christie had lost much of her ability to speak. The speech cortex—Broca's Area—is located on the left side of the brain, and damage to that hemisphere almost always compromises speech. In adults, insult to the left brain is often irreversible. In children under the age of ten, the prognosis is more optimistic. They can often be "reprogrammed" with speech on the right side of the brain.

But not rapidly. And there are no guarantees.

Whatever light Christie might have been able to shed on the mysterious shooting was dimmed. Christie understood everything. Fred Hugi could see it in the way her eyes followed visitors to her room. But Christie could not talk. Possibly, Christie might never be able to talk. What her eyes had seen—what she feared—was locked now inside her head, the intricate synapses blocked as surely as telephone lines downed in a windstorm.

The stroke had also paralyzed her right arm. Fortunately, she was left handed. But she couldn't use that hand either; the bullet wound in it was far from healed.

For the moment, at least, they might as well forget eyewitnesses.

Round-the-clock, Lane County deputy sheriffs stayed in Christie's room. Large benevolent presences, sitting quietly in the corner of Room Number Five, ICU. The deputies were under orders from Sheriff Burks and Fred Hugi never to leave Christie alone with *anyone* except the medical personnel.

Quick to pick up negative vibrations, Diane sensed that the investigators were no longer as kind as they had been. She thought she heard them out there in the hallway, talking about her. She closed herself off from them and talked into a tape recorder instead, an idea Dick Tracy had given her when he recorded their interview.

This would be a kind of diary. The cops had copied her first diary and left it tainted. A spoken diary was better.

The suspicions of the investigators that took Diane Downs out of the victim category and placed her tentatively as a suspect were kept "in house." In the Eugene–Springfield community, Diane Downs remained a bereaved mother.

The Eugene *Register-Guard* carried another front-page story on the case. There was a color photo of Diane and her three children, a happy picture from the past. Diane, sitting in a high-backed rattan chair, wore her hair in a French roll and was dressed in a demure long-sleeved, high-necked blouse. Madonna-like, she held a laughing Danny in her lap. The children all wore sweatshirts with cartoon characters on their chests and blue jeans. Both Christie's and Cheryl's grins betrayed gaps where they'd lost baby teeth.

Juxtaposed with the family's picture was Dick Tracy's composite drawing of the alleged killer, put together from an Ident-a-Kit with Diane's help. A heavy-jowled man with piercing eyes stared out at the reader. His hair was dark and shaggy, reaching well below his jawline. Citizens were asked to come forward if they saw someone resembling the composite.

Similar stories appeared in the *Springfield News* and the *Cottage Grove Sentinel*. Readers were also asked to be on the lookout for a yellow 1960s or 1970s model Chevrolet, which Diane had seen parked along the road just before she was flagged down.

Each story elicited more reports of sightings of madmen from the public.

By Monday, May 23, the Downs case had slipped off the front page, and the headlines were calmer. The *Register-Guard*'s read, "Police seek more leads in shooting," and quoted Sheriff Dave Burks's rather cryptic comment: "There are no new leads that I care to reveal. We're continuing the investigation."

Kurt Wuest had become one of the lead detectives investigating the shooting, and he was also Diane's principal guard in the hospital since May 20.

Diane much preferred Wuest to the other detectives. She found Welch offensive and Dick Tracy provincial. She dubbed Roy Pond "Cowboy Roy."

"Are you married, Kurt?" she asked Wuest on her last hospital day.

He nodded. "Why?"

She smiled. "Oh . . . I'm going to need somebody to be with when this is all over. I just wondered."

Sandy-haired, with a luxuriant moustache, Kurt Wuest had come to the Lane County Sheriff's Office by a route even more circuitous than his fellow investigators. Born in Switzerland, the first son of a master chef in the hotel business, he'd lived in Montreal; British Columbia; Pocatello, Idaho; and Seattle, where his father was head chef of the Space Needle restaurant.

"Then it was Chicago, and then Honolulu..."

Wuest joined the Honolulu Police Department. From there, he'd transferred to Eugene and Lane County.

Diane confided to Kurt Wuest that she looked upon him as a friend, not a cop.

"Cheryl's better off, you know," she mused. "I feel almost guilty because I'm happy for Cheryl because she's probably in heaven."

Wuest nodded noncommittally.

"I suppose the police have gone through my diary," Diane speculated. "Well, I gave them all permissions to search. I want to cooperate; I have nothing to hide."

Diane still voiced complete cooperation with the police, no matter what her private thoughts might be.

Wuest found Diane pleasant and compliant, but very worried about her injured arm. She was concerned about telling Danny and Christie that Cheryl was dead.

Funeral arrangements for Cheryl were still pending; Danny had been transferred to Sacred Heart Hospital in Eugene to await further surgery. Doctors hoped that they might be able to ease the pressure on his spinal cord. Danny was now paralyzed from the chest down, perhaps permanently.

On May 23, an endless blue Monday, deputies and nurses observed Diane glaring down from the hospital window at the parking lot below where her ex-husband stood. Her eyes were clouded with undisguised hatred. *She* had planned to break the news to Christie and Danny that Cheryl was dead, and she'd just learned that Steve had told them without her permission.

Diane was antsy to get out of the hospital. The investigative team wanted her there so that they could watch her. That was one of the decisions they thrashed out in the morning meetings. Even though she seemed confident, Fred Hugi felt that Diane had to be at the weakest point she'd ever be—probably expected to be arrested, jumping at the sound of each new footfall in the corridor outside her room.

"We all expected her to cave in, to give up," Hugi remarked. "If she ever gave it up, it would be then."

They did not arrest her; they *could not* arrest her with the sparse evidence they had. As a suspect, Diane had far more going for her than she realized. She couldn't know that infighting had begun in the enemy camp.

The pressure began subtly. The sheriff's office wanted action; Hugi wanted to be sure he had a case that would fly in court. That first week their battle lines were drawn, but they remained civil with one another, camouflaging argument with debate.

On a blackboard or in their notebooks, the investigative team kept an ever-changing double list:

Reasons Diane Did It	**Reasons Diane Didn't Do It**

The first reason under the second heading was always: Mothers don't hurt their kids. And the second reason was: If she had something to do with it, why would she drive them to the hospital?

Cops and prosecutors knew all too well that some mothers *did* hurt their kids. They also knew that lay jurors might stubbornly insist that it couldn't be true.

Even the probers were baffled by the second reason. If Diane had anything to do with the shootings, why *would* she drive the victims—who might be able to testify against her—to the hospital?

They were in a bind. Unless they added a string of positives to their first list, she was going to walk away from them. Diane wasn't sick enough to stay in the hospital. If she got out, how the hell were they going to keep track of her?

"Are we gonna arrest her so we can *really* watch her?" Tracy asked.

Hugi shook his head. "Not yet. We can't."

They were twisting in the wind, going on gut feelings, on their perception of how a mother *should* act when her children are attacked. If they arrested her, they damn well better have something less ethereal than intuition.

"OK," Alton sighed. "Let her out of the hospital. Maybe she'll lead us to the gun."

"Yeah," Welch countered. "And maybe she'll go to Mexico or grab the kids out of the hospital, and try again."

What if they should arrest Diane with no evidence? Oregon has a sixty-day maximum delay between arrest and trial that can be stretched to ninety days in a murder case only if a prosecutor can convince a judge he has good cause. If they could not come up with evidence in that period, Diane might very well be acquitted. Then she would get her kids back, go to Mexico, do anything she wanted.

The public wanted the stranger caught, and many of them would have been happy to assist in stringing him up. The sheriff's men wanted to arrest Diane; Fred Hugi planted himself stubbornly in front of the meeting full of angry detectives and kept saying, over and over, "You haven't even scratched the surface yet."

Every time he said it, he knew he grew less popular with the men from the sheriff's office. And with the public.

They spoke—Fred Hugi and Diane Downs—only once. They happened to be walking down the corridor near Christie's room at the same time. Diane had come for a last visit just before her release from the hospital on May 23.

Hugi expected that she would ignore him, as always. And in his mind, as always, he repeated the silent litany that played itself out when he saw Diane. "I'll get you."

Almost as if she'd heard him speak aloud, Diane suddenly turned toward Fred Hugi, apparently acknowledging him as a person for the first time. She cut her huge yellow eyes sideways at him.

"The look on her face was unmistakable," Hugi remembered. "It said, 'I did it. You know I did it. I know you know I did it. But *you* can't prove it.'"

Then she spoke aloud. Diane Downs's voice was very, very deliberate. There was not the slightest hesitancy in Diane's tone as she looked at Hugi with her now-familiar, mocking, half-smile.

"I'm getting stronger ... and ... stronger ... and *stronger*, and I'm going to beat this."

DIANE

When this you see, remember me,
And bear me in your mind.
Let all the world say what they may.
Speak of me as you find . . .

—Elizabeth Diane Downs, 1983

CHAPTER 8

When I left the hospital I was scared. God, I'd go to that front door in the wheelchair . . . I wanted to just grab the wheels and stop the chair. I was terrified. I didn't know if he was waiting outside ready to get rid of me, afraid that I'd said something. Oh . . . I went outside and I had this sick feeling. It's just a cold-sweat-sick-feeling-fear, and I got in the car and I went home. All those flowers! You wouldn't believe all the flowers we brought home today. Goodness gracious. I need to write Thank You cards to everybody.

Anyway, when we got home, my mom brought all the flowers in. I brought in what I could, but I don't know . . . I just—I don't feel. I feel dead. I feel like I'm not here. I found a heart—Cheri made a heart, cut a little piece of paper out and wrote, "I love you, Mom" on it . . .

—Diane Downs, tape-recorded diary, May 23, 1983

Diane dreaded having to move in with her parents; she had struggled for most of her life to be free of them. Now anxiety drove her back to Wes and Willadene's house.

Diane returned only once to the dead quiet of the duplex on Q Street, a brief visit to retrieve some of her belongings. She couldn't live there alone, she told reporters; she was terrified from the moment she walked in, not knowing who might be waiting there to try to kill her again.

She pointed out that she could not protect herself. Her injured arm had rendered her helpless. Because her postal shoes and thongs had been taken into evidence, she had to borrow a pair of tennis shoes from Willadene. Worse, she had to ask her mother to tie them for her.

Diane was back home again, a little girl again.

"I can't even tie my damned shoes!" she cried—to the press, to the nurses at the hospital, to the police. For this woman who craved autonomy, it was the worst thing she could imagine.

Diane, Christie, Cheryl, and Danny had arrived in Oregon at Eastertime just as the earth was covered with the shimmery green of spring in the Northwest. Their first days had been full of showers and the most tentative sunlight. Almost like being underwater.

Diane was out of her element. She who had been born to the hottest sunshine, a woman who coddled her tan and preferred the tall, bronzed men of Arizona—men who wore jeans and Tony Lama boots and stashed their Silver Belly Beaver hats behind the hot bench seats of their pick-up trucks. Everyone in Oregon looked pale to her. An Arizona girl through and through, Diane could thrive in heat that would knock most Oregonians flat. She had lived in Arizona, hard by the desert, since 1955—since the very first day of her life.

1955

Dr. Jonas Salk discovered his vaccine for polio that summer. Carmen Miranda died of a heart attack, and James Dean shattered himself and his sports car on a California road, spawning a macabre cult who would not concede his death. *Confidential* magazine appeared on newsstands. Charles Van Doren and Dr. Joyce Brothers amazed viewers on TV's "$64,000 Question." *The Bad Seed,* a chilling novel about a little girl who seemed to have been born wicked, topped the *New York Times* bestseller list.

Even so, 1955 was the dull midpoint of an intrinsically dull decade. Men worked; wives were expected to look pretty, wax their floors once a week, shop economically, and have babies. Child abuse was not in media vogue. It existed—it always has—but no one thought much about it. It was considered a problem of the poor and uneducated.

In 1955 there were no warnings about population explosion; it was perfectly acceptable, even admirable, to have four or five or more children. All that mattered was that everyone be happy, and families strived to be like television sitcom families.

Willadene Frederickson was pregnant with her first child that summer, due to deliver in the ovenlike days of August in Phoenix. She was seventeen; Wes was twenty-five.

Wes and Willadene came from large families; Wes was the second child of four boys and two girls. Willadene was the oldest sister of three, and she had two younger brothers. They were members of the strong fundamentalist Southern Baptist church, where a proper wife follows meekly behind her husband. Sex was accomplished with the lights out, but nobody *talked* about it.

As a bride, Willadene believed that she should defer to Wes. She always would.

Elizabeth Diane Frederickson was born at Good Samaritan Hospital in Phoenix on August 7, 1955, at 7:35 P.M. It was a stifling hot Sunday evening.

All memory is flawed, weighted and skewed by individual perception. What has happened does not matter as much as what we remember. That mind-mirror freezes its own images. The child in Diane Downs's memory is pathetic—a skinny, wistful little girl, ignored by her mother, tormented by her father, a waif scuffing through the sifting Arizona dust with the wrong shoes as she walks home from school alone.

A child without friends.

Diane longed continually for a closer relationship with her mother. Willadene Frederickson, not yet out of her teens herself, failed to meet Diane's expectations of what a mother should be. She was so busy fulfilling her husband's expectations of what a wife should be. So young when Diane was born, she became pregnant again almost immediately; John was born a year after Diane. Kathy was born three years later, James a year after Kathy, and finally Paul, eight years younger than Diane. By the time Willadene was twenty-five years old, she was the mother of five children, married to a man who was something of a martinet.

"There were more and more kids, and she ran out of time," Diane explained. "Some little kids need mothers more. I used to sit around the house waiting for my mom to come and talk. She cleaned house for my dad and spent time with my dad—not me."

The Fredericksons moved often, sometimes living in towns around Phoenix, more often on farms. Diane resembled Wes physically, but Willadene realized before Diane was five years old that she was not fond of her father. It puzzled Willadene; Wes didn't care, as long as Diane obeyed.

Diane probably received as much attention from Willadene as any young mother with five children could give. Pressed, Diane could recall *some* good times. Her earliest memory is of going trick-or-treating with her mother in Flagstaff when she was four. It was Willadene who took the kids to movies, who taught them to sew and cook. Willadene appears often in Diane's childhood recollections, yet, in the end, she is found lacking in her oldest daughter's eyes.

Willadene sided with Wes in disciplining the children. Wes made the rules, meted out the punishments.

"She never spoke out on anything. He spoke out on all subjects. Everything," Diane remembered. "*Everything.*"

Diane excelled academically; she was very bright, scoring, as an adult—even under pressure—a full-scale IQ of 125 on the Wechsler Intelligence Scale. If not a genius, Diane was just a hair away. She could have mastered any college curriculum and gone on for an advanced degree.

The childhood that Diane remembers is as bleak as the night wind keening across a dark desert. Some memories are crystalline; she also has vast empty areas of recall. For weeks, months, at a time, she might well have dreamed her life, a blurred diorama rushing by to be lost forever.

Outwardly, the Fredericksons epitomized the perfect family of the fifties and sixties. Of Danish and English descent, they were a mother, a father, and five children who attended church twice on Sunday and again on Wednesday evening. But Diane did not view her family as real, because it lacked "interaction."

She denies any bizarre childhood fears or phobias. "Was I ever afraid of things?" she wrote to the author. "I am assuming that you mean obsessively afraid for an extended period of time . . . I must say that I was afraid of 'little green men from outer space' because of a movie I saw on TV when I was about nine. That's why I don't let my kids watch horror shows, no matter how foolish they appear to grown-ups. As far as the real things in everyday life were concerned, I wasn't afraid of anything. I didn't like lots of things, but I wasn't afraid. I was a pretty trusting child. I had no reason to fear . . . no one was really mean to me."

She cannot remember her brothers and sister as children distinctly. She rarely babysat for them because she hated it.

"I wasn't allowed to punish them, and they were unbearable sometimes. I always got blamed for the breakage. If I told my dad, he said, 'Don't be a tattletale.'

"I mostly only remember looking after Paul—putting him to bed when I was ten and he was two. Once Paul swallowed a jack and I got blamed for it."

Socially, Diane Frederickson was a shadow child who stood alone at the edge of any school group, never privy to secrets shared with screaming giggles.

"First grade is vivid. I went to a new school, and I was really scared. The kids picked on the new kid. My folks told me 'Twinkle, Twinkle, Little Star—What You Say Is What You Are,' and 'Sticks and Stones May Break Your Bones' and all . . ."

It didn't help much. The names hurt.

Diane considered herself an ugly duckling. Her eyebrows were thick, overshadowing her forehead and eyes. She was unaware that anything could be done about them; she accepted her fuzzy brows as a permanent defect.

"I didn't mix because, when I tried, I wasn't taken very well. I don't know why I wasn't liked. It started in first grade. I suppose I resented it and became angry. I turned against them and wouldn't play with them.

"The girls ignored me. When I tried the boys, I got thrown in the boys' bathroom. So I stood next to the door waiting for recess to be over."

She could cope very well with books, and she could beat the others by being a brain, but recess was agony. She was never chosen on a team until she was the last one left, standing scarlet with embarrassment.

"I had no confidence. I was very shy, real quiet, passive. I hate to sound like Charlie Brown, but I was the last one to find out about anything or go anywhere. But . . . the teachers loved me."

Wes was strict about homework. When his children had no assignments, he insisted that they read the dictionary.

Being a "brain" didn't compensate for being unpopular. Until she was eighteen, Diane was invited to only two parties other than church functions.

She manufactured magnificent, grandiose dreams to survive her childhood. Her most consistent ambition was to be a doctor. And, always, Diane—grown-up—would be rich and live in a wonderful house.

"When I was a child, I didn't feel like a total misfit. I thought everyone lived the same way I did. I knew there were things I didn't like, but I thought it was normal. I did not rebel for a very long time. I was an introvert, and I did a lot of listening and watching of people. As I grew, I began to make a distinction between what I liked about life and what I didn't like. And even though I never expressed myself (either because I wasn't allowed or I didn't have the confidence), I still adopted ideas that I would apply to *my adult life.*"

So often alone, Diane began to feel invisible, a child caught behind a wall of glass—screaming and screaming for someone to notice her and rescue her. She could see out, but no one could see in. Years later, she would describe how she fashioned her own survival.

"You go inside yourself. That's the same as blanking out. You're screaming—shut up inside."

As she neared puberty, Diane would have much to scream about inwardly.

By the late sixties, teenagers had emerged as a major faction in the marketplace. Records were made for them, clothing fads were aimed toward them. It was so important to fit in.

Diane fell further and further behind socially.

When she was in the sixth grade, mini-skirts and white go-go boots were de rigueur for every schoolgirl over the age of eight. The Beatles had changed music *and* style. Diane Frederickson went to school in plain brown lace-up oxfords, with sturdy white anklets. Her skirts fell far below her knee. When she saw the smirks of classmates dressed in Mary Quant mini-skirts and white boots, she rolled her skirts at the waist so they wouldn't look quite so long. She was scolded when Willadene saw how they were wrinkled and figured out why.

"When I was twelve years old, all of my friends stopped wearing bobby socks. They were allowed to wear footies or peds, and sometimes even nylons. I was not permitted the same liberties. I was the last one to be allowed to shave my legs. It seemed silly to my parents but it was a very sore problem for me.

"Then came the time when nearly all the girls in my grade started wearing brassieres. I still had to wear an undershirt, and I felt like a freak or outcast when we had to dress for PE. I just knew everyone was watching me in the locker room."

When Diane was in the seventh grade, Wes came home one day raving about seeing a "guy with a beautiful head of hair." It inspired Wes to order Diane to have her hair cut short and permed. No one asked why Wes should want his daughter to look like "a guy . . ."

"I cried and cried . . ."

Of course. In 1967, hair was supposed to be long and absolutely straight. Some girls even *ironed* their hair, and Wes had made Diane cut hers off and curl it as tightly as Little Orphan Annie's.

She hated him even more.

Wes Frederickson had begun to work for the U.S. Postal Service when Diane was about five. Although he never carried mail, he worked sooner or later at almost every other job in the system. He progressed steadily up the ladder, headed for the prestigious perch as a supervising postmaster. For a family man, the postal service offered security and a salary that, while not munificent, was steady and dependable.

For the Fredericksons, then, in the sixties, things should have been all right. But Elizabeth Diane was not happy. She still felt invisible. She studied harder, hoping to achieve acceptance with better and better grades. No one seemed to notice her.

She vowed that one day she would show them all.

Child Abuse

Excerpts from an essay, by Elizabeth Diane Downs
Mesa Community College, July, 1982

The gruesome crime of child abuse not only destroys the lives of our children but it usually brings terror into the lives of our grandchildren. . . .

Abused children develope [sic] different personalities, depending on the type of abuse they receive and the amount of abuse they must endure. The personalities developed in abused children stay with them all their lives. They may receive conciling [sic] or some form of help which turns the child around, but no one can take away the scars and pain inflicted on an innocent child forced to submit to mistreatment.... It will ultimately affect that child's life as an adult. Then, when this scarred child, turned adult, has children of his or her own, these children ... are usually abused in some way or another by their parents....

...I wish we could stop this vicious cycle. If we could only take a whole generation and stop child abuse, we could wipe out the plague....

Generation after generation, the abuse continues. If you abuse your child, he or she will no doubt abuse your grandchildren.

CHAPTER 9

I was trapped. The only way out was to leave the house. My dad said if I told—everyone would hate me.

—Diane Downs

When Elizabeth Diane Frederickson was eleven or twelve, and Paul—the baby—was almost four, Willadene went to work for the post office too, as a clerk. Her late shift kept her away from home most of the night. Wes stayed with the children.

Diane learned now that there were many kinds of "love," some of them ugly. She described more than a year of unquenchable terror. Her father never denied her accusations; he has never commented on them at all.

Hovering at the edge of puberty, Diane knew virtually nothing about sex. She had no breasts, her eyebrows still flourished thickly, and she wore plain little girls' dresses. Boys didn't approach her. She listened to other girls discuss S-E-X and deduced that, "If boys fondled and touched you, that meant they loved you."

No one loved *her.* Sex held no interest for her. She was not happy where she was, yet she was a little afraid of growing up. Unlike most pre-nubile girls, Diane wasn't anxious to date.

She was still different.

There was the darker reason that separated her from her peers. She believed that no one else had experienced what was happening to her. She felt guilty and dirty and afraid to tell anyone. Diane was twelve, she remembers, when Wes Frederickson began to molest her sexually. If he had blocked her way before, he surrounded her now.

There was apparently no one with whom to share her night secrets. She couldn't tell Willadene. And she certainly couldn't confide in her other source of comfort—Grandma Frederickson, Wes's mother.

Five times she packed her bags to run away "... but I had a responsibility to my family."

Loquacious on other subjects, Diane speaks haltingly about her premature introduction to sexuality.

"He was forcing me to grow up too soon. I realize now it was much more serious than I did then. I didn't understand sex then."

Diane had her own room. She thinks that her siblings were unaware of her father's stealthy visits and of the rides she took alone with him. She denies actual intercourse, but she remembers "talking . . . touching . . . fondling."

"I blanked it out."

Throughout her life, Diane had withdrawn behind the curtain in her mind—blanking out—when she could not stand the truth. She slipped more and more easily into the blurry place without memory.

When the late afternoon shadows lengthened, Diane's depression and anxiety began to build. Wes arrived home from work at 5:45. "He would turn the TV off and say, 'It's family time.'"

Diane dreaded dusk and her sure progression of terror as the sun went down and her mother left the house. She wore her shirt and jeans to bed and lay rigid, listening and waiting. She slept fitfully, if at all. Long after the other kids stopped giggling and went to sleep, Diane stared wide-eyed into the dark, her ears tuned for the faintest footfall. What was happening to her didn't seem like love, and she balked at being expected to display "love" when she felt only revulsion.

She never cried or fought; it never occurred to her that she could. "He was the authority figure. I couldn't resist him. I couldn't tell. I would just blank out. It just didn't exist. *I* didn't exist. It's like a nightmare—not real."

Near dawn, in spite of herself, Diane usually fell asleep to awaken to bright light. Willadene slept in, and Wes woke the youngsters by flipping light switches and turning radios up full blast.

How Diane hated him. But she hated herself more. Despite her revulsion, the incestuous fondling evoked an instinctual pleasure response. It felt good, even though it was wrong. She could not separate sex from terror and power . . . and pleasure, and she could not understand the sensations she felt.

At the end of a year, she sank into an almost clinical depression. Her life was dichotomized; during the day at school she was supposed to dress and behave like a child. At night, she was caught in aberrant sexual games, expected to respond as a mature woman would.

"There was no place for me in this life. I had no one to talk to, to relate to, or who cared about *me.* There was no need to be here."

Diane cut her wrists when she was thirteen. "I didn't tell anyone about cutting my wrists—really just my left wrist—but my dad knows everything. I don't like to inflict pain on myself—I'm a chicken—and I had only scratches on my left wrist. My dad didn't ask about it. I didn't tell my mom, but she guessed. Nobody talked about it."

Nobody talked about it.

Diane's acting out was smoothed over, but secrets festered. The situation in 1968 had incendiary potential. Diane finally became physically ill from lack of sleep, and Wes took her to the family doctor.

She was evasive when the doctor questioned her. She was only tired, she said; she was having trouble sleeping. An odd symptom for a twelve-year-old, but the doctor didn't investigate further.

Afterward, Wes headed out into the shimmering hot Arizona desert. Diane knew it would be one of their rides.

"My dad told me to take off my shirt. He told me that my bra was really just like a bathing suit top."

She needed a bra now; she could no longer bind her burgeoning breasts with undershirts. Diane shook her head. Her father insisted. Trembling, she took her blouse off.

Then he told her to remove her bra.

She began to scream. Hysterical, with no one but the Saguaro cacti to hear her, she screamed louder and louder. He was killing her. She screamed that at him, but he just kept driving, farther and farther away from town. Diane grabbed at the door handle and managed to get it open, prepared to jump.

Her father's hand reached across and pulled the door shut. She heard it latch and saw him push the lock button down.

Neither Diane nor Wes was aware of the Arizona Highway Patrolman who was just behind them, alert to the activity in Wes's car. He pulled up and signaled Wes over. The trooper looked directly at Diane and asked her what was wrong. She avoided his penetrating stare, buttoning her shirt quickly.

"I couldn't tell him. I had to shield myself—and my mom and my brothers and sister. If my dad went to jail, we'd have no food or house. I told the cop that I'd been to the doctor's and I had a shot, and that's why I was crying. I told him that we had company at home, and that I wasn't supposed to cry in front of other people—so my dad took me for a ride."

"Are you *sure*?" The trooper's eyes bored into her. "You can tell me if you're in trouble."

She only shook her head, and repeated her lie. She couldn't tell him the truth. The officer drew Wes aside. Diane couldn't hear what he was saying, but his gestures were emphatic. Her father seemed uncharacteristically cowed. They drove home in silence.

The sexual abuse stopped as abruptly as it had begun. Whatever the trooper told Wes was apparently effective. The officer didn't write up the incident, and when Oregon detectives tried to find him fifteen years later, they found that the trooper had been dead for years.

Diane detested her father still, but she bided her time. She held tightly to two primary goals—to run away from home to a safe, free, haven with someone who would love her more than anything else in the world. And to become a doctor, and live in a huge house.

Diane's goals weren't so different from those of other teenage girls. But the intensity of her need was; her hunger for perfect love and success was voracious.

She did not feel worthy of love. If she didn't like herself—and she didn't—how could anyone else like her? She felt unattractive and insecure. She had no dates in junior high school, only unrequited crushes.

When Diane was fourteen, Wes and Willadene paid for a charm school course. She learned to pluck her eyebrows and apply makeup. She still felt ugly—as if what she and her father had done in the night marked her face. In reality, she was very pretty.

Some of the boys at church showed an interest in her, but Diane distrusted their intentions. "Any rejection was self-imposed," she admits. "I was kind of a wallflower who was off the wall by then, but I still couldn't bloom."

Diane yearned to be noticed. And almost overnight, a profound change came over her. Where she had been silent, she became a compulsive talker—as if a flood had suddenly burst from a barren plain. This was the beginning of the streams, torrents, gushers of wordswordswords that were forever after an integral part of Diane.

From the moment she woke, she told anyone who would listen about her dreams. When her listener turned away, she found someone else. She jabbered and chattered. Her new volubility drove away as many—more—potential friends than the glum silence of her childhood.

With Wes Frederickson, Diane remained the listener.

"We were robots as kids. We were told what to do and expected to do it."

She was not allowed to cry. When she'd told the trooper that, she told truth. Instead, she laughed, even when it was inappropriate. That certain peculiarity of response would stay with Diane. She had no sense of how she appeared to others. She bounced from elation to depression to bravado to scorn, her emotions sailing as free as a runaway kite and no better grounded.

Through it all, her mask was in place. The laughing mask or the smirking mask; if she had any tears, they were quickly hidden behind it.

Diane was not popular, but she still made good grades.

She found animals more trustworthy than humans. She had all manner of pets: dogs, cats, turtles—even butterflies. When she was fifteen, the Fredericksons acquired their first horse, Blaze. After that, there was Dutch, a big buckskin.

"My horse [Dutch] was freedom, power, a friend—someone I could talk to who wouldn't talk back. He didn't like men either. I was the only one who could make him do anything. He gave me power. He was something I could be part of that no one else could."

Diane still sought love—unconditional love—and now she added power—unconditional power. She did not realize that the two were incompatible.

Diane Frederickson met Steve Downs when she was fifteen. Steve was seven months older; both of them juniors at Moon Valley High School in Phoenix. Technically, Steve was still an adolescent boy—not one of the "men" Diane hated so. Yet Steve Downs walked with a swagger, the pugnacious air so many short muscular men affect. Even at sixteen there was a sensuality about Steve that made women glance twice at him—older women, younger women. Five feet eight, thick-chested, broad-shouldered, Steve Downs was handsome. Not pretty-boy handsome, but rugged-handsome and Indian-tan, with a mat of curly dark hair on his chest. In the eighties, Steve would be described instantly for his similarity to Don Johnson of "Miami Vice." The sexually dangerous man. The barn burner. The man who could steal virgin daughters away with a glance. In the seventies, he was simply a tremendously sexy boy/man. Naturally, he alarmed Wes and Willadene; he was too adult in some ways, too wild and immature in others. They urged Diane to date other boys.

Of course Diane dated no one but Steve. Knowing he set Wes's teeth on edge only made him more desirable. He was the first male who had ever made Diane believe that she was pretty. She was dazzled that anyone should find her so. And Steve lived just across the street, always there for her.

Diane could feel the power in Steve, just as she felt it with Dutch. If she could make Steve love her, she might somehow harness that strength.

Steve was everything Diane wanted then.

"He came to see me. He would support me. He beat people up over me! He made me feel like I was important. . . . He had long hair, and he never wore a shirt and he was rebellious.

"He was everything my parents didn't like. . . . If their life was wrong, then what they hated should be better—so I chose Steve."

And Steve chose Diane.

Within months, they were sleeping together regularly. She was sixteen. She confided then in Steve; finally, she had someone to tell the secret of what her father had done to her. Steve had no idea how to respond, so he mumbled something and changed the subject.

"She told me when we were dating," Downs recalls. "She never got into graphic details, but she told me her dad was responsible."

Diane's intense physical affair with Steve Downs did not blunt her pursuit of excellence at Moon Valley High. Her intelligence was part of her armor against the world. Her name on the honor roll bolstered her still-fragile ego.

When Diane was seventeen, sudden, violent death threatened to snatch away everything she loved most. Wes's mother was sixty, his father seventy-four, when they died together in a head-on collision caused by a drunk driver.

Next, Eric, Diane's beloved cocker spaniel, was crushed beneath a tractor Steve was driving. Diane blamed Wes, not Steve, because her father had called the dog. Eric was paralyzed, and Wes dispatched it quickly with his shotgun while Diane screamed.

"We had a nanny goat and her baby—Nanny and Betty. My father killed the baby and had the nanny goat slaughtered."

Diane's pet cats contracted ringworm. Wes said the kids would catch it. Diane begged him not to dispose of them, but one night as she was washing the dishes, she heard the shotgun's roar again. For the first time, her blanking out drew her in completely, leaving no seam in the curtain.

"I blacked out. I remember the sound of the gun, and the next thing I knew I was in my room putting on a clean blouse. I guess I ran out when I heard the gun—they found me later, walking down the road. My foot was bleeding as if I'd kicked something. I had complete amnesia for an hour."

Diane lost Steve for a time too when she was seventeen; he joined the Navy in June of 1972.

Wes continued his lecturing. Diane had enjoyed playing the flute, but Wes didn't think she practiced enough.

"He lectured me on it for two hours. You'd get backed into a corner. He'd say, 'Look at me. Don't look at the table. Don't look at the ceiling.'

He'd pressure me into scratching my own face . . . I'd been rebelling since I was twelve, and all I could do was scratch my face."

Diane's face-scratching was the outward manifestation of her profound frustration and helplessness in her father's home, always under her father's will. Her rage toward him turned inward, and she raked her nails down her own face, leaving angry red furrows. But it wasn't herself she wanted to hurt; it was Wes—if only she had the power to do it.

"My father said that I was possessed when I was spaced-out for the first time. I was shouting at him. He usually hit me with a belt, but not this time. I looked at him. I told him to leave me alone. Maybe it surprised him. I guess my first anger backed him off."

The daughter of an obeisant wife had never realized that a woman might control a male; the best she had ever hoped for was to align herself with a strong male. Her father's confusion felt good.

It did not last. Diane still believed that a man was the only salvation for a woman. She wanted out of her parents' home, and she vowed to grab the first chance that presented itself.

When she graduated from Moon Valley a semester early, Diane found a gap in the fence around her. She was offered the chance to go to college— Bible College. She was to study to be a Christian missionary. From there, she thought she could switch to pre-med.

Diane lasted only two semesters at the Pacific Coast Baptist Bible College. But it was a revelation.

"I was popular for the first time in my life. In the first two weeks, I had a date with a strict student. He took me to a Valentine's Dance and kissed me. Well, he just went wild after that. He said it was my kiss that drove him wild. Other boys flocked around. Stories grew, and I finally did with a guy what they said I did. Then another girl got in trouble. To save herself, she told on me. I was kicked out of school for promiscuity." Diane relates the story with a mocking smile.

Another version of her expulsion says that Diane and a male student desecrated the church altar itself by having sexual intercourse there— either as a lark or in a moment of unrestrained passion.

By August, Diane was home again in North Phoenix. She took a job as a waitress for a month, and then found an office position. She was marking time until Steve came home.

Diane wondered sometimes if Steve might be too dominating. Her most damning adjectives for males were "evil," "harsh," and "dominating." In her opinion, her father was all three. She hoped Steve would be different.

When Steve finished his Navy tour and was living in Chandler, a Phoenix suburb forty-five minutes from the Frederickson home, he and Diane were together constantly—or as constantly as they could be under Wes's surveillance. Wes waited for Diane after work to see that she went straight home.

Diane felt pressed to make a decision: "I thought Steve might be a miniature of my dad; I didn't know he'd be an *equal*. But I couldn't make it on my own, and I wanted children.

"It came down to whether I wanted to keep on scratching my face or marry Steve—even if he was evil."

It apparently never occurred to Diane that she could have left home, supported herself, and escaped any man's thumb. She was very intelligent. But she was afraid. The only role model Diane had was Willadene, and Willadene had shown her, unknowingly, that a woman could not survive without a man.

A few months after Diane turned eighteen, she didn't come home from a date one night. If her folks didn't want her to marry Steve, she would live with him.

Livid, Wes showed up with his shotgun and told Steve to either marry his daughter or to bring her back home. Steve said he'd be glad to marry Diane.

Willadene nervously tried to prepare Diane for marriage. "She told me men could be hard to live with, that they had lots of little quirks. Steve probably would be different after, she said. I realized some of the problems she had with my father. It was the closest talk we ever had."

There was no birds-and-bees lecture as such. Willadene handed Diane a box of birth control pills and let it go at that.

The couple was married a week later—November 13, 1973—by a justice of the peace. Steve Downs was much more than a bridegroom; he was Diane's ticket out.

Diane says that Steve changed the day of the wedding. "Steve was always on his best behavior. He does the thing that most people do when they're dating, and that's put their best foot forward. They're nice; they're punctual. They're everything they're supposed to be. And then you marry them, and it's 'Hey, Diane—Can you let yourself in? I have to run down and look at a car.'"

One of the reasons Diane had married Steve was to have someone to love and adore her; she found almost at once that she was going to be alone most of the time.

She got herself a puppy.

Two weeks after their wedding, Steve told Diane that he had a date with another girl. He reasoned that he had to keep it because he'd asked the girl out a month before. He asked Diane to press his pants for the date. She did.

The bride waited into the wee hours for her groom to return to their apartment.

"He came home at 3:00 A.M. and said his car had broken down. But his white pants were still clean."

CHAPTER 10

I loved Steve. He didn't love me. For two and a half years, we had dated, and I grew to love him and he said he loved me. Whether he did or did not, I do not know—but I believed him . . . It was during the next year that I learned not to give too much of your heart to grown-ups . . .

—Diane Downs in an interview with Anne Bradley, KEZI,
December, 1983

In letters and interviews, Diane often refers to other adults as "grown-ups" and to herself as "just a little girl." Yet, she and Steve were the same age.

Perhaps suffocated by Diane's need for constant affirmation, or simply because he was an immature eighteen-year-old, Steve Downs preferred the company of his buddies to his wife; he was obsessed with hot rod cars.

And, less intensely, with other women.

From the night Steve came home from his date with another girl with pristinely white trousers, Diane realized she had made a mistake. Clearly, Steve didn't love her any more than her father had. And Steve's interest in her, like her father's, seemed purely sexual. He had changed his mind about children; he wanted to wait a few years before starting a family.

Years!

Diane made a decision. She needed Steve to carry out her plan, and then she would never need him much again. If Steve wasn't going to love her—and only her—she would have to find another way.

She would grow her own source of love.

Diane *craved* love so that her ambition paled beside her emptiness. First she would have a baby, and *then* she would become a doctor.

Without telling Steve, she threw away the birth control pills that Willadene had pressed upon her. She hugged her secret close; let him run around with his hot rod buddies and his girls. Her baby would love her.

With a better love than Steve's. "Pure love." A baby would be another person, but it would also be an extension of herself, a part of Elizabeth Diane Frederickson Downs.

A month later Diane woke up vomiting. She would prove to be the most fecund of women. With Diane, the thought became the deed when it came to conceiving. She viewed this first pregnancy, and all the pregnancies that followed, as near-immaculate conceptions. The male furnished viable semen; that was all. *She* gave life itself.

During the months of her first pregnancy in 1974, Diane says that she was "in love" with the fetus she carried in her womb. Not that she *loved* her baby, but that she was *in love*. Perhaps she was. She had discovered a magical thing she could do to feel whole and serene for the first time in her life.

Pregnancy not only became her, it gave Diane a reason for being.

Steve didn't even notice the first soft swelling of her abdomen. When he did notice, he wasn't happy. His childhood had been scarred by the struggles his parents had trying—and often failing—to provide for their large family. Only eighteen, he was afraid he wouldn't be able to support a baby. As Diane's due date grew closer, Steve changed his mind. "It was exciting," he remembers. "I began to like the thought of having a baby."

Steve might also have been more accepting of a baby because it looked as if he had a shot at fame and decent money for a change. Diane had always been the one with the ambition, but this time the spotlight was on Steve. He had just signed to appear in a Gillette razor blade commercial. A scout had noticed his tan chiseled features, the insouciant maleness. Steve Downs, wrapped in a towel, might just be a natural for the subliminal seduction of a shaving ad.

Just one ad at first—but the Marlboro Man had to start with just one ad. Steve was jubilant.

The young Downs family moved to a farm, and Steve stayed home more. He was in and out of work, picking up jobs here and there while he waited for filming to start. When Steve had no job, he sent Diane to her parents. Diane considered it "shipping her off," and she resented it.

For a time, Steve *couldn't* work. A car he was fixing exploded, and he was critically burned before he could be dragged free. He was hospitalized. The near-tragic fire didn't kill Steve Downs, but it changed his life. The Gillette commercial producers couldn't wait for his blisters and scars to heal up, and there was no guarantee that they *would* heal entirely. They found themselves another young, good-looking unknown, and Steve's modeling aspirations ended.

Modeling had held out the promise of a measure of fame and financial security. Modeling could have led anywhere—TV, movies. And it was a hell of a lot more exciting than eight hours of hard, physical labor day in and day out. Now that was all gone.

As long as Steve was in the hospital, the marriage was uncharacteristically stable. Diane hovered beside his bed, tender and concerned. For Diane, an injured Steve may have been the perfect husband. He was too weak to boss her around, and he certainly couldn't get out of bed to chase other women. He appreciated her concern, and his attention was focused entirely on her.

When Steve's burns healed enough for him to leave the hospital, he and Diane moved in with Wes and Willadene until he could work again.

The marriage slipped back a number of notches. Steve's roving eye returned, according to Diane, along with his health. It didn't really matter; she had her baby to look forward to.

Diane's recollection of Christie's birth is as syrupy as an old-fashioned valentine.

"My goal had been reached," she wrote a decade later. "I finally found true love and peace with another human being: my daughter! . . . While Christie grew inside of me, I knew for the first time in my life what love really was. . . . That was the first time in my life that I was needed . . . really needed. I finally had a reason to exist and I was happy—truly happy. . . . The happiness I felt when my child moved inside of me was intoxicating. It never stopped. And, after my child was born, I was even happier. . . . Because now I wasn't the only one in love. Christie too loved me. When I would peer into her crib, she would reach for me and grin. She was so excited to see me; she would kick her little feet so hard it would shake the whole crib. . . . I loved her!"

Christie's birth did nothing to solidify the marriage. The more Diane loved Christie, the more she found Steve's love vile.

When Diane describes Steve, he sounds like a Wes Frederickson clone. "Steve had no patience. Crying made him angry. If I laughed, he thought I was tormenting him."

Steve Downs was only nineteen and was trying to support his young family. He had a job overseeing irrigation systems in the fields around Chandler, which required that he get up in the middle of the night to divert the waters' course from time to time. Diane complains that he forced her to get up and go with him "just to be mean."

Steve's sins as a husband grew. Diane was annoyed because he wanted a hot supper ready at five. If he was late, he asked her to reheat it.

And he was jealous. "He'd make me get dressed up in nylons, high heels, dresses, and take me out. Then he'd get furious if someone looked at me or made comments. He'd choke me, shake me, throw me down—almost every day."

"Steve sent us to Flagstaff on the bus one time," Diane remembers. "He said he couldn't afford me anymore!"

Despite all the verbal brickbats sailing around her head, Christie Ann was an easygoing, cheerful baby. She ate and slept well. Christie was *exactly* the sort of baby Diane had needed.

Diane worked part-time. She made $2.10 an hour at Lincoln Thrift, a Chandler savings and loan. Hardly enough to pay the sitter. All her real plans were on hold. Even having Christie didn't make her happy. She still longed for an education and a career.

Diane went up to Phoenix one day and joined the Air Force. Christie was not quite six months old. Steve was left to take care of his infant daughter while her mother slept in a barracks full of other female recruits at Lackland Air Force Base in San Antonio, Texas.

Steve remains baffled by Diane's decision to become a career woman in the Air Force.

Diane says that she had no choice. "I thought the Air Force would be . . . stable. It would be a good career for a single parent. I couldn't take her with me to basic training; you can't take a baby in a duffel bag. I left Christie.

"I called him every other day to see about Christie. We didn't have a phone so I had to call at the neighbors. They said Steve left Christie home alone, locked in the house. Then I talked to him and he said she wouldn't eat—and that he'd dropped her on her head!"

Steve says Diane called him continually, yes, but that it was to beg him to get her out of the service. "She said if I didn't get her out, she was going to go AWOL. I called some major and explained that we had a baby at home."

Diane served only three weeks in the Air Force. Her discharge was not because of her family responsibilities, but because she had developed terrible blisters.

A few days after Diane came home, she and Steve were wrestling, playfully, when she hit her head hard enough to sustain a concussion. It may have been mere coincidence that her blanking-out returned now, just as she'd failed once more in her climb toward a white-collar career.

"I blacked out while I was driving, and the doctor told me I should get off my birth control pills."

Diane spent much of 1975 in transit. She recalls that Steve would pack her and Christie off to Wes and Willadene—who sent them back with the message that she was Steve's responsibility. The picture she paints is of a young woman with no control over her own life. Either she *was* powerless over what happened to her, or—perhaps more revealing—she *remembers* that she was totally dependent on either her husband or her parents and that nobody wanted her. If Steve tugged on her leash, she stayed with him; if he shunted her off to her parents, she stayed there. Diane and Christie, heading somewhere they wouldn't be welcome, saw the world through smudged bus windows. They hurtled along Arizona highways, Diane carrying a diaper bag, Christie clutching her favorite doll. The waiting rooms of grubby bus stations became as familiar as home to them.

At this low point in Diane's life and in her marriage, she conceived another child.

"I began to dislike him [Steve] more and more. I could not support myself, let alone a child, so we stayed. But, because of the unhappiness that was starting to cover us, I needed to fight back. So . . . I did the only thing I had ever known in my life to bring about happiness—I got pregnant. The Air Force had been my last chance to get away from Steve. So I'd just get some 'double love' and have two kids. Perhaps it seems juvenile or irresponsible, but it was (and still is) the only way I know to be happy and feel loved . . . I guess I was just trying to build a wall of love that Steve couldn't break."

Diane conceived immediately. When she announced her pregnancy to Steve, he was appalled. Their financial situation was tenuous at best, and he found Diane the most capricious of mothers; now he felt she had tricked him into a second baby.

As her due date neared, Steve softened a little, allegedly telling Diane that he might welcome a boy baby. He couldn't support more than two children and this was his last chance for a son.

Cheryl Lynn Downs seemed to put her foot in it from the moment of birth. She was a female, and she'd waited too long to be born; if only she had arrived before midnight on New Year's Eve, she would have given her parents a much-needed tax exemption. Instead Cheryl came along on January 10, 1976, two days before her father's twenty-first birthday.

Christie had been the perfect, placid child for an emotionally starved mother; Cheryl Lynn screamed from the moment her shoulders passed through the birth canal, and she kept on screaming.

At Diane's insistence, an unprepared Steve had accompanied her into the labor and delivery rooms and, like situation-comedy fathers, he fainted. Later, he went looking for his son, but found he had a second daughter. Diane says he was angry and that the nurses chased him out. The story has a fictional ring to it, but Steve doesn't deny he *was* disappointed at first.

As a newborn, Cheryl Lynn was skinny and homely; her ears stuck out and her pate was as bald as an old man's. Her mouth was too wide, her eyes too small, and her nose too flat. Indeed, she looked like her father, but the features that made Steve Downs model material were not aesthetically pleasing in his baby daughter. She would have to grow into them. As if she sensed that she had somehow failed, Cheryl was colicky and bellowed whether Diane held her or not.

"She cried all day," her mother sighs. "At nighttime, when *I* should have been able to sleep, he [Steve] would have me wake him to change the irrigation water. At 1 . . . 1:15 . . . 1:30 . . . 1:45 . . . until 3:00 A.M."

Through it all, Cheryl screeched; she would not be comforted, stiffening with rage, anxiety, or some innate knowledge that the world would not be a happy place for her. The baby, conceived to fill in the chinks of Diane's "wall of love," was, instead, a fussy, screaming creature who wasn't even cute.

Diane was peeling potatoes one evening when eighteen-month-old Christie ran to her yelling, "Mommy! Mommy! Baby!"

"I went to look and Cheryl was choking. I put my fingers down her throat and I hit her on the back. She spit up and she started breathing. I started crying. Steve walked in a few minutes later and wanted his supper! I told him that Cheryl almost died, and he just stood there and said, 'Well she looks OK now.'"

Steve and Diane agreed that there should be no more babies after Cheryl; one of them would have to get "fixed." Although he wasn't thrilled with the idea, Steve volunteered. A vasectomy cost $35.00 while a tubal ligation for Diane would run several hundred dollars. Steve went to a clinic in Casa Grande, a little town south of Chandler.

He had the vasectomy, but he did not return ten weeks later for a sperm count to be sure that he was, indeed, sterile.

"I got pregnant," Diane recalls ruefully. "The vasectomy didn't work. He just figured the doctors knew what they were doing. I got pregnant and I knew I wasn't messing around with anybody and that if I was pregnant . . . I knew how I got that way."[*]

Steve accused Diane of having a lover, but when Steve returned to Casa Grande for a check, doctors there vindicated her; Steve was still most fertile.

"I was twenty years old. I had two kids," Diane says.

"My parents were pressuring me to potty-train Christie. Cheryl was colicky. My husband was . . . a bastard. I couldn't take one more pressure. I decided to have an abortion. I might have had another Cheryl—the baby wouldn't have been loved."[†]

Steve, his vasectomy redone and adjudged foolproof, would have accepted this third pregnancy, but Diane was adamant. "There was no way she was going to have another child. I didn't think [abortion] was the way to go . . . but it was her body."

Diane had an abortion; she seemed to emerge from the experience with neither psychological nor physical damage. Rather, she remembers a two-year period when she "didn't feel anything." She no longer loved Steve, but she was as dependent as ever on his financial support. Even so, something was beginning to stir in Diane Downs. She had been running away—either in her head or in reality—since she was ten or twelve. The possibility of escape began to intrigue her again. Her dream of success came back, if only tentatively.

They were still living on a little farm in Stanfield then, and Diane cajoled Steve into letting her have a horse. They brought a mare and a filly to the farm. Diane enjoyed taking care of the horses.

Diane sobbed when they moved to Flagstaff, and she had to sell her horses after having them only six months. Moving day was on Christie's second birthday, October 7, 1976. Cheryl was nine months old and beginning to grow out of her colic.

On Halloween, Diane took both babies and left Steve.

"I got home on a Sunday night about one or two in the morning. She

---

* Anne Bradley interview: KEZI
† Bradley interview: KEZI

was gone. She'd packed up the kids and left," Steve remembers. "I really didn't understand that. I was working two jobs, one with Redi-Mix Concrete. We really weren't having any problems. She just left. She ended up in Texas with her father's brother. The only way I found her was by going over our phone bill. I found calls made to Texas for a month. I called and talked to her aunt and asked her to have Diane call me the next day."

One of Diane's cousins in Texas had assured her that she could find a job there, but she stayed only a week. The job wasn't what she expected.

"Steve called me every day and begged me to come home."

"No," Steve shakes his head. "I wasn't going to beg her. I told her, 'You left on your own—you can come back on your own.' She did."

Three weeks later, they moved again. Back to Chandler.

Diane was twenty-one years old. To date, nothing in her life had turned out the way she planned.

1977

Only inertia powered the Downses' marriage.

Diane ran away again when she was twenty-two; she went to live with her younger sister, Kathy, in Flagstaff and took a job as a concrete truck driver. The money was good. Diane was strong, and she wrestled the huge trucks handily, leaving the kids with a sitter all day.

The truck driving job lasted only a month. Her boss raped Diane. She was a decade beyond the bedroom terror of her childhood, an adult—but the memories resurfaced. She ran back to Steve. He had worked for the same man and knew he was quite capable of rape.

Diane detested sexual intercourse, marital or otherwise. If she had any sexual longings, they were repressed. She trusted no man. She made tentative stabs at freedom, but she was a woman on a tether; she always came back.

She longed continually for so much more.

Diane took the kids to Stockton, California, where Wes and Willadene were living, and she looked for work there. Her parents set a six-week deadline. When she didn't find a suitable job by then, she went home to Steve.

He always took her back. She hated him for that too. They moved from one town to the next; Steve's jobs were mostly seasonal.

Although Steve and Diane lived in the same house and slept in the same bed, they scarcely talked. The little girls carried their father's supper to him, and he ate it sitting on the living room couch. He was gone every night. Diane no longer cared if he was unfaithful.

She waited for *something* to happen. Hostile but passive, she was both bored and angry. Life was passing quickly by her; none of the things she'd promised herself had come true.

In the fall, Diane had a revelation that may well have colored the rest of her life. The abortion was two years behind her, and she'd felt no residual guilt. Suddenly, the child she had destroyed returned to haunt her.

"I was at a fair in Arizona, and I walked past the Right-to-Life booth. They told me at the time I aborted that I was six weeks. I figured 'Six weeks . . . that is a condition. You are not pregnant; that is a *condition*—a little ball of slime. No big deal.' A fetus is slime . . . I saw a six-weeks' fetus. That baby had arms, legs, fingers, toes, a head, eyes. That was a *human being* and I *killed* it! I felt so horrible about it—that I'd killed somebody like that. Oh, I didn't do it myself but *I* hired a doctor to do it.'"

Belatedly, Diane gave her lost baby a name: Carrie. She sensed that it had been a girl. The little girl who never was became an obsession. Diane decided to replace Carrie; she would conceive again, and the baby would be Carrie. "She hadn't had a soul—this would give her one."

For Diane, Carrie was somewhere in limbo, waiting to come back into the world.

Diane asked Steve to have his vasectomy reversed, and he looked at her bewildered. She'd been so damn pushy that he go get cut in the first place!

"I asked him for a year, and he kept saying no. Finally, I said, 'Fine. I will find a suitable donor.'"

Steve Downs does not remember that conversation; he does remember what happened next. Diane was in an excellent position to find—quite literally—a stud. By late 1978 the Downses were living in Mesa, Arizona, both employed by the Palm Harbor Mobile Home Company. Company policy vetoed hiring married couples, so Diane and Steve said they were

---

* Bradley interview

divorced. The end of the marriage was looming anyway, delayed only by their lack of money to pay an attorney.

Diane was a good worker, quick to pick up new skills. She wired mobile homes and was one of the best electricians on the line. Her personality underwent a complete metamorphosis the moment she hit the job. Sullen at home, she was vivacious and fun at work. The wallflower was not only free of the wall; she bloomed scarlet and lush.

"I worked around lots and lots of guys. I met men who treated me like a woman."

For the first time in her marriage, Diane had an affair. Indeed, she had three affairs with men at the trailer plant. She wasn't interested in sex for its own sake; she was doing genetic research. "I watched the people I worked with. I picked somebody that was attractive . . . healthy . . . not abusive of drugs and alcohol, strong—bone structure—you know, the whole bit: a *good specimen*. It was really clinical."*

The father of choice was nineteen years old; Diane was twenty-three. Russ Phillips was flattered and bemused.

"I seduced him. And I know my cycle and it only took once—and I got pregnant."†

Steve suspected that Diane was up to something. "She was going to work early kind of often. I didn't trust her . . . I called her foreman one specific morning. Seven was the regular time for her to leave, and she had left at five. I asked him, 'Hey—what time you guys goin' to work?'"

Not that early. The next morning, Steve followed Diane at 5:00 A.M.

"She was over at Russ Phillips's house. She was in bed, making love to the guy! I hit her . . . him . . . and a couple of his roommates. They pulled a gun on me. It was a settle-down-or-blow-it-away type of situation. That's a bad situation. Real bad. I told her to get dressed. She could come home with me . . ."

Diane refused.

"She should have known at that point it wasn't gonna be a peaches-and-pie relationship."

Diane didn't care. It was too late. The date was April 11. A week later,

---

* Bradley interview
† Bradley interview

she told Steve she was pregnant. He didn't believe her at first—how could she know so soon?

Diane had always known *exactly* when she was most fertile. She had begun to grow the "replacement baby."

"I'd had a vasectomy," Downs said, recalling the breakdown of the marriage. "I knew that wasn't *my* child."

Both Steve and Russ Phillips urged Diane to have an abortion, a suggestion she found patently ridiculous. She'd conceived this baby to make amends for her abortion. Russ thought she was refusing the abortion because she loved him. He urged her to divorce Steve and marry him before the baby was born. Diane was genuinely surprised; it had never occurred to her that Russ had any claim to this baby—or her. He was a nice-enough guy, but she had no special feeling for him.

Or for any man.

She waffled, keeping a lid on things, balancing between Steve and Russ. For the first time in her life, Diane Downs had a little bit of power over men.

When she was six weeks pregnant, she found scarlet stains in her panties. For the next week she moved as if on eggshells, terrified that she would lose the baby. The bleeding stopped and she returned to work at the construction site where they were setting up trailers. Suddenly, she hemorrhaged in great gushes.

Diane was desolate. "When I hemorrhaged, the doctor said the baby was already dead, that the only risk was to me. I figured my life wasn't worth anything without a job anyway—so I took the post office job. I liked the job."

The hemorrhaging slowed to sporadic spotting over the next two weeks. There was no cramping and no fetus was expelled.

Six weeks later Diane felt a tentative tapping in her belly. She was still pregnant.

Diane was still living with Steve, but he was only a shadow in the background of her life—expedient. Her strong Baptist roots still decreed that a woman should be married when she gave birth.

Steve accompanied Diane to the Genetics Center in Tempe when she was five months pregnant. He represented himself as the father and held

Diane's hand because she was scared to death that the baby wouldn't be normal due to so much hemorrhaging. An ultrasound test revealed a perfectly normal fetus. Their genetic chart was favorable (Steve didn't say that *his* family tree wouldn't have a lot to do with this baby).

That clinic report ends, "The family appeared relieved and seemed to be comfortable with this pregnancy."

Diane denies receiving any support from Steve.

"He told me, 'If you have a girl baby, I might let you stay. But if you have a boy, I'm kicking you both out on your butt—and you're taking those two with you too, 'cause how do I know if *they're* mine?'" If he could not have his own son, he wanted no other man's male child.

The baby was a beautiful boy with hair like wheat, but Diane was shocked that he was not a girl. She realized then that she had produced a "different human being altogether" and her fantasy about Carrie seemed to fade.

Steve took Danny willingly when the doctor handed him over. Soon Steve adored Danny.

It had never occurred to Diane that Steve Downs might love her enough that he was willing to forgive, forget, and accept this tiny manchild as his own. Steve's feelings for Danny were perhaps the closest thing to the pure love that Diane sought always.

She did not recognize it.

Steven Daniel Downs was born on Saturday, December 29, 1979. Diane left the hospital on Sunday and was back at work at the post office on Monday: New Year's Eve. She'd carried Danny triumphantly through massive hemorrhaging, worked all along, and delivered him easily. If there was one area where she never failed, it was giving birth. Being pregnant figuratively—and literally—replaced the emptiness Diane felt. A baby in her womb anchored the floating hollow core inside.

If she could have chosen it, she would have been pregnant constantly.

Diane nursed Danny for only two weeks; her nipples cracked and bled. She was not nearly as adept at nurturing her young as she was at bearing them. Danny was a frail infant; photos show a little bird of a baby with no fat on his bones. His eyes dominated his face. Diane didn't worry about him, and she proved to be right. Danny became a robust, almost chubby toddler. He was a cheerful baby, like Christie, and his personality shone, attracting everyone who saw him. Russ Phillips was crazy about his son, but Diane only allowed him to see Danny when she needed a babysitter.

Diane had built herself her wall of love.

Diane's and Steve's combined income was $20,000 a year. They had three healthy children, and that was about all. Their home had become an armed camp. Her worst suspicions confirmed, Diane had come to view her husband just as she had her father—as her punisher, her captor. They fought, physically, far into the night.

Her depression returned full force, and she sobbed impotently. One night, she remembers forcing herself to go limp and stop sobbing. "I quit crying. That spoiled things for him. He'd fed on my crying—it gave him strength. I quit crying, and I just lay there, oblivious of everything."

Oblivion had been her safety valve since childhood: the blanking-out preceding the blacking out, a hiding place in the dark of her own mind.

Pushed to the wall, Diane suddenly hit back—hard. She relished punching her husband. The capped volcano of rage, repressed for almost twenty years, spewed forth. She had only skimmed small portions off her anger before, and she had flung them at the most vulnerable of victims: her own children. A pinch on the shoulder that left blue finger marks, hair-pulling, spanking, screaming at frightened little faces. She had borne those babies to provide herself with perfect love, and she was devastated when they failed her.

She forgot that they were only human. They were only babies.

"I'd usually grab them by the shoulders, scream, and make them sit down. They were quiet because they didn't know what Mom would do. I pulled Cheryl's hair . . . I was mad [at Steve] anyway. Cher knocked curtains off the wall in the bedroom. She saw the look on my face. She tried to run past me, and I grabbed for her shoulder . . . got her hair instead, and she fell on her little bottom . . . I was sorry later."

Cheryl always got the worst of it. "If something broke, Cheryl broke it," Diane says. "She was always hanging on something—or falling off something—or jumping on the furniture."

Diane had slipped easily into her father's pattern of discipline. But the kids made so much noise, and they were always in her way, always breaking things. And they didn't love her nearly as much as they should have. She screamed at them until her throat was hoarse. They tried to duck the blows and run away, but Diane was fast. She could snake an arm out and catch them easily.

Christie and Cheryl were confused. Sometimes their mother played with them, got them pets, dressed them up to take their pictures. And then, without warning, she was angry at them. It was hard for them to tell what they were doing wrong.

Steve and Diane were in a tug of war, and Christie and Cheryl and Danny were tender fibers of a rope, pulled tauter and tauter between them, damaged whoever won.

CHAPTER 11

In April of 1980 Diane watched the "Donahue Show"; the subject of the day was surrogate parenting. Enthralled, Diane heard a woman on the panel of guests explain that she was barren, although her husband was fertile. His sperm could be used for artificial insemination. They wanted a child desperately, a baby who would be at least half their own genetically. The woman said she would be more than willing to let another woman bear her husband's baby.

If only such a woman could be found.

Diane watched, cuddling baby Danny in her arms. God, she could empathize. She remembered the years she'd begged Steve to have his vasectomy reversed; she just knew what the woman was going through. And then, she thought of something! Why couldn't *she* carry a baby for that woman on the "Donahue Show"?

Diane jotted down the address of the surrogate parenting clinic in Kentucky as it flashed across the screen. If there had ever been a way for her to gain a handhold out of the pit she was in, this was it. And, of course, she would be doing a kindness too.

Diane wrote to Kentucky the next morning:

April 30, 1980

Dear Doctor:

   I saw your show about surrogate parenting on "Donahue" yes-terday. I am writing this letter to tell you that I would like to be a surrogate mother for a couple who is unable to have a child through natural means.

   I had heard of couples who could not have children for one reason or another and I felt sympathy for them, but I wasn't aware that there was a way a person like myself could help. I think surrogate parenting is a great idea—especially when I see someone like Mrs. Anderson. I have three children of my own and I know the joy that a child brings to a mother. It just seems so unfair that some women will never experience that happiness. So . . . I would like to help by carrying a child for a couple who really wants a completely fulfilled family life.

   My husband and I have discussed this matter and he is in agreement with me.

   I am not exactly sure what you need to know about me, so I will tell you what seems important to me.

   I am 24 years old and I am in good health. I am 5' 5½ inches tall and I weigh 123 pounds. I have blonde hair and green eyes. I have had three children (2 girls and 1 boy). All three pregnancies were normal and all three deliveries were uncomplicated. All three children are physically and mentally normal. I do not smoke ciga-rettes, and I have never abused alchohol. [sic] I have never used illegal drugs (including marijuana). My husband has had a vasec-tomy, because we had decided 3 children are enough to support nowdays. [sic] My blood type is O +. I am of mixed heritage, includ-ing Danish, English, French, and Irish. I know there is much more that you need to know and I hope to hear from you shortly.

She enclosed her address and phone number.

There were little evasions, small omissions—and downright lies. Diane's pregnancy with Danny could hardly be termed normal, not with the massive bleeding. She *had* smoked pot. She'd been known to take a drink. Her marriage was on its last legs; her own children were driving her nuts.

Diane's letter reached Kentucky and was quickly processed. On paper, she sounded like a prime candidate, good maternal soil. The standard Surrogate Parenting Associates, Inc., preliminary form was mailed to Diane on May 6, 1980. She returned it to Louisville on May 23.

She had vacillated over some of her answers. She chose to call "Carrie" a miscarriage. She denied ever having an abortion. She knew all her conception dates, and that baby had been conceived on March 3, 1976. The "miscarriage" had occurred on June 17. Diane had not aborted a six-week-old embryo as she had always claimed; the fetus would have been closer to eleven or twelve weeks, and she might well have felt life. That could explain her obsession to re-create the "murdered" baby.

Diane gave her religion as "Christian (Baptist)." Beneath this entry she printed, "It is important to me that the parents be Christians."

She enclosed some pictures of herself and her children, apologizing because she looked "overweight and tired" in the photo taken a month after Danny's birth. She added another photo just to be sure, "Picture of husband and myself, taken in October, 1979. This is how I really look."

She might have enclosed many other pictures. In each, she looked so different; she might well have been a mirror reflecting the fleeting images of many women. A chameleon.

Question number sixty-seven was the last and most important: Reason for applying for surrogate procedure?

"I look at my own children and they make me so happy, I just think it's unfair that a couple wouldn't experience that joy without this procedure. And the child would be living with its natural father."

Despite Diane's protestations that the pictures didn't flatter her, it was obvious to clinic screeners that she was a most attractive young woman. But there was so much more involved, so many barriers to clear. If natural parents required as much genetic screening, a good percentage of the population would be deemed unfit to have babies.

Breathlessly, Diane waited for the next step in the selection process. Her own life dulled in comparison. She was positive Steve was seeing other women. It barely mattered to her. Russ kept begging her to marry him. Diane left Steve in September 1980 and moved in with Russ. Steve threw up his hands and shouted, "Fine! Go!"

It only lasted a week. Diane felt she needed the stability and status of a married woman to qualify as a surrogate, but the marriage was a balloon where each new breath threatened destruction. Diane and Steve had lived in many little towns clustered around Phoenix; the watershed point of their relationship was destined to take place in Chandler.

Chandler, Arizona, founded 1912, population: 13,763. Except for tropical vegetation, it looks like any small town in America. Like Eugene, Chandler nestles in valley land caught between distant mountain ridges. Old Chandler has neat little houses with yards lushly overgrown with cacti, palm trees, eucalyptus, mimosa.

South of town, on the way to Casa Grande, there are miles of cotton fields, Merino sheep and quarter horse ranches, and the desert. Out there, the shoulders of the road dance with light, the sun reflecting off millions of fragments of beer and whiskey bottles tossed there over time.

Radiating from the core of Chandler, there is near-frenzied construction of houses along new streets with freshly coined fancy southwestern names. Condos, townhouses, apartment buildings, and single-family residences by the thousands—all of them brown or beige or off-white to appease the desert gods. Most of them are empty, waiting for families to spread "lawns" of plum and amethyst crushed stone. Grass costs too much to water.

Diane and Steve purchased a $60,000 rambler on one of the newest streets: Palomino. Even knowing that the marriage was about to blow apart, Diane was determined to have the model home at 813 Palomino. It was nicer than any house she'd ever lived in, with a beige stucco exterior and semimansard roof. It wasn't Diane's dreamhouse yet but it was a definite step up.

Diane worked every Saturday and extra days on call as a substitute letter carrier at the Chandler post office. It eased the $600-a-month mortgage pressure but strained the explosive marriage even further when Steve's best buddy, Stan Post, moved in with them to share expenses.

"We kinda made a bond to make a go of it," Steve Downs recalls of the marriage, once again completely misreading his wife.

If Diane had made a bond, her fingers were crossed. She was merely biding her time. She had discovered that surrogate mothers were paid *$10,000!*

It would not be paid up front. First, she would be required to sign a contract with the natural father and the clinic. Then if she passed all the tests required to certify her as a worthy candidate for impregnation, she would be inseminated. The money would be paid nine months later when she delivered.

Ten thousand dollars would, at last, set her free!

Diane studied the contract. "Whereas, the Natural Father is a married individual over the age of eighteen years who is desirous of fathering a child who is biologically related to him; and whereas, the Surrogate is over the age of eighteen and is desirous of taking part in the surrogate parenting procedure ... the parties mutually agree as follows ..."

And that was only the first clause! The contract was eight pages long and rife with clauses to protect the privacy of both the natural father and the surrogate mother. Every eventuality had been foreseen. In addition to the $10,000 fee, Diane would receive free lodging, transportation, and medical care.

She signed her copy of the contract with a flourish. She and Steve were scheduled to appear in the office of a Kentucky psychiatrist on December 9. Conceiving, carrying, bearing a child—and then walking away, never to see it again—would demand much of any woman.

That first psychiatrist had grave doubts about Diane. "There is considerable neurotic interplay, both in this marriage and in this woman's total adjustment to life," he wrote in his report. "This would not necessarily incapacitate her as a surrogate mother—but I would like to see a psychological report."

Steve and Diane had been unable to hide the widening fissures in their marriage; the psychiatrist saw instantly beyond the loving facade. More than that, he caught a glimpse of something in Diane herself that disturbed him enough to request further testing.

There was a second joint interview with a clinical psychologist, mainly to determine if Diane *really* had her husband's permission for the insemination procedure. Steve appeared sincere in his support of the project, although the marriage again came off a bit strained.

Next came a barrage of psychological tests—some new and some established—designed to probe beneath the surface.

Diane was given ten standard tests: the Wechsler Adult Intelligence Scale (WAIS), the Bender Visual–Motor Gestalt Test, the Background Interference Procedure, the Wide Range Achievement Test (WRAT), the Problem Checklist, the Rotter Incomplete Sentences Blank, the Rorschach Inkblot Technique, and the Minnesota Multiphasic Personality Inventory (MMPI). Most Americans who have been to college or applied for skilled jobs have had one or more of these tests.

Diane sailed through the IQ tests, placing high up in the "superior range of intelligence." However, there were small red flags scattered in other tests. Diane did not do well in areas where she had to demonstrate social cause-and-effect reasoning, attention span, and concept formation.

"These findings were consistent with, but not absolutely diagnostic, of a major psychopathology," the report from the clinical psychologist concluded.

Diane apparently perceived the world around her uniquely. Her test results might have been early warnings of a profound psychosis (insanity) or only of strong personality quirks. Everyone has personality quirks; very few are insane.

After Diane talked about her parents and her siblings, the psychologist wrote: "Parents are described as strict and distant people who devoted little effort to demonstrating affection to their children. Ms. Downs alleged that at the age of twelve she was sexually molested by her father. (She claims virtually no interest in sex since then, an issue which has continued to buffet her marriage.) . . . The couple's last child, reportedly, was the result of Ms. Downs picking five 'ugly' younger men to seduce in order to have a child by one of them. . . . Ms. Downs was well oriented and generally appropriate. Speech was quite pressured, had a controlling quality, and was characterized by an air of forced jocularity. Ms. Downs's conversation was effusive, immature, and frequently self-disparaging."

Why Diane told the psychologist the story about the "five ugly men" is a puzzle. She never told anyone else that. But she had continued her pattern of compulsive talking—spilling the beans about everything she'd so carefully hidden in her written application form. And the doctor was concerned.

He was particularly fascinated with her MMPI (Minnesota Multiphasic Personality Inventory) results. This test consists of several hundred questions that can be answered "yes" or "no." There are many "deliberate-lie" questions for validation, which appear more than once.

Diane's pattern of response indicated gross deficits of ego-functioning. In layman's language, she did not believe that she was very good or very important. *Her ego was almost nonexistent.* At her core, beneath her bravado, Diane saw herself as a cipher.

Her examiner detected significant psychological problems—but, try as he might, he could not isolate them. Diane Downs *was* unique. She could be compared for a time with other subjects she resembled, but then her responses slipped out of synch. She could not be pigeonholed as either normal or abnormal.

"A clear-cut neurotic picture is not present. Similar individuals display frequent self-depreciation and are seen as very unguarded and without normal social defensiveness (they do not, typically, take advantage of normal social feedback). This individual has poor ability to express anger in a modulated fashion and tends to have poor behavioral controls. Despite a somewhat flamboyant facade, this woman tends to be shy, timid and retiring."

The Kentucky psychologist found Diane depressed and worried because she found no enjoyment of sex, and because she never felt that she did anything right. He thought he understood why she wanted to become a surrogate mother:

> For her, the surrogate parenting opportunity calls forth several motives. She looks at the prospect of being a surrogate mother as an opportunity to present her husband with a "gift" which would deflect attention from a highly unstable marriage where Ms. Downs feels she is not, in a broad sense, able to function adequately. She is, in a characteristically histrionic manner, anticipating being relieved of her sexual and social obligations. She fantasizes respite from many areas of her personal and social adjustment which let her feel inadequate, insufficient, anxious, and ineffectual.

Diane needed time out from her life; she wanted to feel safe and serene. She wanted to do something people would praise her for. Common
goals, but, in Diane, blown all out of proportion.

Being pregnant was her means of running away from life, without having to resort to black forgetfulness. There was another goal Diane hid
from her examiner in 1980. Being a surrogate mother was to be her ticket
out of mediocrity.

Diane flunked her first psychological test because the examiner didn't
believe she would surrender a surrogate baby.

Neither Diane nor Steve learned the test results. Diane assumed she'd
cleared the first hurdle. She was confident she'd impressed the psychologist. After a lifetime of feeling ugly, she now believed she was pretty. She'd
smiled and laughed a lot. She'd practically sailed right off the top of the
IQ scale.

What more could they want?

Nobody in Louisville told Diane she'd flunked; the surrogate clinic
delayed. They surely could locate a psychologist who would give her passing marks. They were aware that the first testers had personal prejudices
against surrogate parenting, which might have colored their report on
Diane Downs.

Two weeks later, Diane and Steve celebrated their last Christmas together. Christmas, 1980. "Steve was hard to buy for. I couldn't afford a car,
but I knew he liked guns." The year before, Diane had given Steve a .22
Glenfield rifle. This year, she gave him a .38 revolver.

During the first week of February, 1981, Diane was examined by a Phoenix
psychiatrist at the request of the Louisville clinic. They still had to have a
satisfactory psychological report before they could even consider her first
insemination. The results of that hour-and-a-half exam were much the
same as the report by the Kentucky psychologists. The Arizona psychiatrist had perceived that Diane could shut her emotions down at will, simply shut off feelings like flicking a light switch.

"[Subject is] very attractive . . . very intelligent . . . somewhat
hypertalkative—*very* anxious to get into the program. Nevertheless, one
gets the impression that, particularly from the point of view of her affect,

it is significantly superficial. . . . In reference to her father—she has for-given him and even though they both know about it [the incestuous mo-lestation] they have never said one word to each other in reference to 'their secret.' She definitely uses defense mechanisms of repression and rationalization.

"On occasion, she gives the impression of being able to isolate her af-fect completely."

This doctor was the second to mention a profound defect in Diane's personality: Histrionic personality disorder. (Histrio = actor.) He too thought it was iffy that Diane would be able to give up the baby. On the other hand, he suggested that participation in the surrogate program might give Diane the opportunity to expiate her guilt over her abortion five years earlier.

Not one of the psychologists or psychiatrists detected her black-outs, nor did they recognize her soaring ambition.

Diane passed.

If she barely squeaked through on her emotional stability qualifica-tions, she aced the physical exam. Her blood pressure was 120/78, her pulse 72, her respirations 18 to the minute. Totally normal.

The genetic flowchart of her progenitors was next. Twenty-four rela-tives: Wes's parents and his six siblings, Willadene's parents and her five siblings, Wes and Willadene, Diane's four siblings, and finally Christie, Cheryl, and Danny. The names marched down the chart. No genetic flaws. Violent and accidental deaths, yes, but no diabetes, hypertension, strokes. Most of the entries' names were followed by "Alive and Well."

A cheerful, optimistic flowchart.

Diane was accepted into the surrogate program. She had given birth to three perfect children, all "Alive and Well"—three blonds, one with green eyes, two with brown eyes. Soon, she would conceive again.

And then she would give the child up.

Pure love.

Diane eagerly awaited her summons to Kentucky. She ignored Steve. Christie, Cheryl, and Danny were farmed out to babysitters much of the time. Russ Phillips leapt at the chance to have Danny whenever he could.

Diane laid down some rules. Russ was not to date other women or to drink alcohol. Sweetening her edicts, she hinted that she might change her mind some day and marry him.

Overhearing the "Diane Rules," one of the women who shared a house with Russ grimaced. But she felt sorrier for the children than she did for Russ. Especially for Cheryl.

"Diane put everything before those kids. If Danny wanted attention, she would push him away . . . but the worst thing was—one time, I caught Cheryl jumping on the bed, and I told her that was not permitted. I made her sit on a chair and think about it. Cheryl sat quietly for a while, and then she looked up. 'Do you have a gun here?' 'Of course not. Why?' 'I want to shoot myself. My mom says I'm bad.'"

When there were no willing sitters, Diane left the kids home alone. Christie was six, Cheryl five, and Danny was fifteen months. Christie bore responsibility well. Mature far beyond her years, she was protective of her little sister and baby brother.

At long last the Downses' marriage burst.

"Steve usually just memorized girls' phone numbers," Diane describes the final split. "But one day I was doing his laundry—cleaning out his pockets, looking for bills . . . I pulled out a wadded-up paper with a phone number and an address on it. That night, after work, I just handed it to Steve and said, 'I want my divorce now.'"

"He said, 'OK.'"

Diane was never without a lover. She moved from one man to the next, as smoothly as if she were changing partners at a square dance. She never allowed them to hurt her. They weren't that important to her. No man had ever bothered to find out what made her happy; they had only taken what *they* wanted.

Why Diane sought the company of men is an intriguing question. She had told several psychologists that she detested sex; perhaps she was only ambivalent. Diane may have looked for sensuous pleasure with no emotional involvement. Or she may have liked the sense of power over men that sex gave her.

And then again, her need for men may have been simply pragmatic. Steve told Diane that she would have to buy out his interest in the house—for $5,000. Thirty-four-year-old Mack Richmond, who also carried mail at the Chandler post office, was most taken with the flirtatious, bubbly Diane he knew at work. His marriage was faltering, and he was lonesome. Mack loaned Diane the $5,000. Two weeks after Steve moved out, Mack and daughters—nine and eleven—moved in.

This first liaison lasted only through the summer of 1981. Mack liked Diane's kids, but he was put off by Steve's frequent visits—and by Diane's parental discipline. "Her kids seemed like . . . a pain in the ass to her . . . she felt that kids were inferior, and they weren't even allowed in the living room."

Worse, Diane called Christie, Cheryl, and Danny vulgar, demeaning names. When she started in on *his* daughters, Mack gazed longingly at the door.

The woman frightened him a little. At home, she was nothing like she was at work. He couldn't figure her out. Diane was a paradox who read the Bible every night, quoting scripture at him, and minutes later, in bed, she was a tigress who drew blood. She raked Mack's back painfully on three occasions during intercourse.

Her scratching wasn't reserved for the bedroom. Once they had an argument in a bar and Diane turned on him, her eyes afire. She reached out with her claws and deliberately scratched both his arms, hissing, "*Nobody tells me what to do.*"

Mack left in the fall—without his $5,000. Diane laughs, remembering him: "Mack had a lot of rules . . . I couldn't cut my hair; I couldn't get fat—so that meant I couldn't be a surrogate mother."

Diane had worked the early shift during the summer of 1981 from 5:00 A.M. to 2:00 P.M. The children were left with a sitter or with Russ. When September came, Danny was enrolled in the Merry Moppets nursery. Christie was in school all day. Cheryl was in morning kindergarten, but when she came home from school at 11:30 A.M., she was alone. Diane couldn't afford to send her to Merry Moppets, and since she was delivering mail in the same general area, she figured Cheryl would be all right.

Cheryl would either sit on the porch of the locked house and wait for

Diane to come home hours later or wander off to find someone in the neighborhood who would let her in. In Arizona, she wasn't cold, but she was hungry and she had to go to the bathroom.

Mary Ward lived two houses down the street. She noticed the little girl who seemed to have no supervision. Mary worried; they were only a few houses from Alma School Road, a fast, heavy-traffic street. Cheryl became a regular at Mary's house. Mary fed her lunch and let Cheryl play with her own children until Diane got home. Mary vowed to say something, but she put off a confrontation. She'd never met Diane. During the first week of September, Mary realized that she hadn't seen the blonde letter carrier for several days. The children's father was living in the house down the street now, caring for them. The kids seemed cleaner and better fed.

That September of 1981, Diane was in Kentucky. The time had come at last in Louisville. In Dr. Richard Levin's office, Diane was impregnated with semen from the man known only as "Natural Father."

She did not catch a glimpse of the man whose seed was introduced into her vagina by syringe, although she wondered if she might. She knew that it was fresh—not frozen—semen that would be used. That meant that the natural father would have to deliver it to the clinic just before she was inseminated.

When the father came in to present a few cubic centimeters or so of viable sperm, obtained by the only method possible—masturbation—he was scheduled to arrive a half hour before the surrogate mother-to-be. If he was tense and his part in the procedure took longer than planned for, there was the slight chance that he might be leaving the office as Diane was entering.

Diane says she didn't want that. "I worried about his romanticizing the woman who would carry his child, and ruining his marriage." It is more likely that *she* had been romanticizing the man who would father this baby, dramatically picturing an impossible love between herself and the rich, successful husband of a barren woman, wondering if the man might not love her more because *she* could bear his child.

Things went smoothly. Diane did not cross paths with the natural father.

Louisville charmed Diane. She was waited on, served hot soup, tucked in at night, totally pampered. It was as marvelous as she had hoped. She was part of a wonderful project—the most important part. The whole experience was exhilarating and fun. Dr. Levin even drove a Corvette with personalized license plates: BABY4U. Diane speculated to herself that the surrogate project must have made him very wealthy.

The initial insemination procedure took only twenty minutes. Diane conceived at once. She knew she would. Confident of her own fecundity even as she flew home to Chandler, she was triumphant and elated.

And pregnant.

CHAPTER 12

Diane Downs was probably as happy as it was possible for her to be in the fall of 1981. Carrying the U.S. mail was the best job she'd ever had, even though she considered it a temporary plateau. She knew that she pleased her superiors at work; she wasn't even worried that they would make her take medical leave when her pregnancy became apparent. She was living in a beautiful house. Best of all, Steve wasn't there—only herself, and Christie, Cher, and Danny. No men to boss her around.

Her pregnancy made her feel so good. Her eyes sparkled, her skin glowed. She knew she was more attractive than she had ever been. She flirted with the men she worked with, and they flirted back. The baby was still a minuscule embryo in her womb, too small to show, but she could picture it snuggled in there—not a "little ball of slime" as she'd once thought, but a real living, growing entity.

Somewhere in America, there were two people waiting with her, exulting with her. She could not replace "Carrie," but she was bringing another life to earth. There would be no diapers, no colic, no bottles, no mess.

Only happiness. Only praise.

"I was very idealistic about it," Diane remembers, but gradually she felt a connection growing. "As the months went by, I got attached to it. Could I give it up?"

That attachment was what the psychologists had feared. They had doubted that this emotionally frangible woman could give up the baby.

Diane still thought she could.

The fall of 1981 wasn't all *that* good for Diane. There was Mary Ward, for instance, whose concern for Cheryl finally reached a point where she had to do *something*. Mary didn't call the authorities—she wasn't a snitch—but she wrote a letter to Diane, saying that it was dangerous for Cheryl to be home alone, especially since there had been some break-ins in the neighborhood.

Enraged, Diane stalked over to Mary's house that afternoon. Her mail route was in the neighborhood, she explained, and she stopped in to check on Cheryl. Cheryl wasn't a neglected child.

Cheryl stood silently beside her mother, her thin face set in worried lines. Mary was horrified when Diane turned to Cheryl and said vehemently, "You're such a bad little girl! If you don't obey Mommy, you deserve to be killed."

But as the women continued to talk, Diane calmed down. An agreement was struck. Mary would care for all three of Diane's children. After that first conversation the two neighbors talked often. Diane admitted that she'd once been abusive to her children, but insisted that she'd stopped shaking them and screaming at them. Mary wasn't so sure it was over. Christie was old beyond her years, a little mother herself; Cheryl seemed a love-starved little waif, so depressed for a child. Only Danny was full of laughter.

One evening, Mary was in her front yard with Cheryl and her own children when her husband arrived home. "I saw John turning into the driveway and I held out both my arms to stop the kids from running in front of the car. Cheryl darted out, right in front of the car, and John just missed hitting her. I ran over and grabbed her and I asked her why she had done such a thing. Cheryl said, 'It doesn't matter. Nobody cares.'"

Diane, however, recalls that she and the children were having a marvelous time in the fall of 1981. "I was as much a kid as they were. I carried them, hugged them, took them out for pizza."

Steve Downs was the only blotch on Diane's perfect world. He continued to visit the children, and Diane claims that he threatened her life.

"Steve came over once in November. I was pregnant and lying on the couch with my back turned to him. I heard a click. I turned around and there was a . . . gun, pointed right at my *head*!"

She says that Steve smiled faintly—and pulled the trigger. There was only another hollow click, an empty chamber.

In her early pregnancy, Diane was no delicate flower with morning sickness and fatigue. Instead, she was running her routes so fast at the Chandler post office that some of the male carriers resented her. She was smart and quick and she wasn't averse to crowing a little bit when she made it back to the post office before any of the men. She started with a rural route, but soon earned herself a city route.

Diane's affair with Tim Lowry began sometime that October when she invited him home for lunch.

"I thought we were just going to eat and talk, but she came over to the couch where I was sitting and started kissing me. We ended up in bed."

He was to be the second in a series of lovers, married men she worked with at the Chandler post office.

Tim saw early on that Diane craved attention. "Steve told me once that she was just looking for love—and maybe he was right. . . . A lot of people at the post office thought she was a slut, I don't know "

Diane moved on. Married men were a fix for her; she drained power from them. The knowledge that she could have a man who was forbidden excited her. Men could be mastered.

"I loved them all . . . I just don't go to bed with people; I *love* them. Sex hadn't been rewarding with Steve—although a relationship is not founded merely in sex. I only slept with Tim two times, and I only slept with Walt Neff once. The other guys were my friends."

But that was, of course, before Lew. After Lew, everything was different.

Diane moved from the heady joy of her early surrogate pregnancy into a period of extreme stress. While she was working full-time, carrying a pregnancy for someone else, having affairs with married men, and living for the first time the life of a single mother, her kids were sick all winter.

Cheryl and Danny were chronically ill with one thing or another. Danny had tonsillitis four times in three months; his temperature soared dangerously high. Cheryl had severe nosebleeds.

Mary Ward wasn't the only neighbor who worried about the Downs children. Dan Sullivan, who lived three doors down on Palomino Street, considered them "emotionally starved." Sullivan saw the kids playing outside often in bare feet and without coats—even in November and December.

And they were hungry. "Cheryl would show up at our house in the evening and ask what we'd had for dinner. She hadn't eaten. She was hungry and she wanted a sandwich. I don't know where her mother was." The Sullivans fed Cheryl, and they discussed adopting her themselves.

Diane Downs and her children were living a curious existence. The baby in her womb was inviolate, floating safely in amniotic fluid, lulled by its mother's heartbeat. Diane took her vitamins and visited her doctor regularly, just as she'd promised to do in her contract. She certainly got enough exercise on her postal route.

The children she'd already given birth to were not faring as well. Cheryl's nosebleeds might well have been caused by malnutrition. Danny's strep infections were certainly exacerbated by playing outside with bare feet and no coat in the November chill that crept down from the mountains. They ate fast-food pick-up stuff: pizza, tacos, hamburgers. Or Christie made peanut butter sandwiches for them.

Diane beat Steve by winning custody of the children, but she had no time to spend with them. She was belatedly living out the playful, teenage years she lost when she'd been so anxious to get away from home that she married Steve. She reveled in all the heady flirting, the teasing, the way men responded to her in bed. She didn't have to worry about getting pregnant. She already *was* pregnant!

But she was blind to the way she treated her kids. Her favorite phrase in referring to herself and Christie, Cheryl, and Danny is that they were the Four Musketeers, the four of them against the world. She remembers some wonderful times they had together. She is always the beloved Mommy with her laughing, adoring children gathered around her. It is a picture from a children's storybook.

Karl Gamersfelder—"Gami," her supervisor at the Chandler post office—remembers a discussion with Diane just before Christmas, 1981. She was concerned because she'd "hit the kids the night before harder than she ever had before." He advised her to seek counseling.

Diane didn't go.

In her quest to *be somebody,* Diane was more and more possessed by a kind of manic energy. She often felt she could do anything. She was doing extremely well at the post office; she could aim for an administrative spot one day. But then again . . . she had thought about starting her own surrogate parent program. There was more money in that . . . but it would have to wait until she learned more about the whole procedure. Or she might go to medical school . . . become a doctor as she'd always meant to do.

Diane's surrogate pregnancy was obvious as 1982 started. Some of the people she worked with didn't approve of this "brave new world" concept of being a "baby factory," but they had to agree that the often-sullen, moody Diane they had known before seemed constantly cheerful. It was as if she had suddenly found some elixir of happiness.

She had.

Diane had become part of the lives of her baby's parents, living vicariously their existence, an existence that she perceived as perfect and tranquil. Her own family had always disappointed her. For this time, she was part of another family—an idealized family where people loved each other, where she was a valuable member. Now *she* was the most important member of this family; she was carrying the baby that would make them so happy.

"It was a family thing. I wrote to them all through the pregnancy—cards and letters."

Diane had no idea who the parents of her baby were. One day she would see them, but she was not supposed to know their names. She sent her letters and cards to the surrogate parenting office in Kentucky, signed "Your friend," and they were forwarded on to the expectant parents.

After two and a half decades, Diane finally felt good about herself.

"I had a purpose for being here. And that's been my whole hang-up since I was a little kid. Why *am* I here? Just so my dad can yell at me? Just so my husband can criticize me? Just to take care of my kids? But these people needed me. It made me *somebody*. I told the parents that the baby did more for me than I ever did for them.

"People have wondered why I won't regret this, giving up the baby. And that's very easy to answer. When you kill a child, when you have an abortion, you've terminated something. You've murdered somebody—it's cruel, it's horrible, it's terrible. But when you do something out of love, when you carry a child for somebody else, and turn that life over to them to be cared for, you haven't done anything bad, and it's nothing you can look back on and regret. It's good."

Later, Diane would refer to this nine months of pregnancy as the most stable period of her life. Her thoughts came in an interview that she gave to Elizabeth Beaumiller of the *Washington Post* in March, 1982. Beaumiller had selected three surrogate mothers for a feature article titled "Mothers for Others." Diane was thrilled that it was beginning already. *Fame*. Diane's picture two columns wide in a major newspaper. Dr. Levin had been in *Newsweek* and *Time* and on the "Donahue Show." Diane fully expected to become more and more famous.

The woman presented to the Washington reporter was serene—"The Madonna Diane." The picture that accompanied the piece showed a pretty blonde with a gently swelling belly who gazed back at the camera with the confidence and quiet aplomb of a princess. Beaumiller would recall somewhat ruefully that she gave the most column space in her feature to Diane—who gave her name as "Elizabeth Kane"—because Diane seemed to be the most emotionally mature of the trio of surrogate mothers she interviewed.

The baby was due on May 10, 1982.

As the due date neared, Diane sent the other "mother-to-be" a funny card with a baby swaddled on a backboard. Inside, the papoose baby grinned and said, "HELLO!"

Diane penned in her own hand:

I tried to find a Mother's Day card for the mother-to-be, but I couldn't find one. Then I saw this one, and it was just too cute to

*put down. So, I'll just have to say this with my own words: "Happy
Mother's Day—for the mother-to-be. Hope your day is full of joy
as you are awaiting your new arrival."*

*I am feeling much better now and am getting more anxious
by the day for my trip to Kentucky. I will arrive in Kentucky the
evening of May 10th—so I'll probably see Dr. Levin on the 11th. It's
so hard to believe that the much anticipated day is nearly here.
The time has gone by so quickly.*

*I know you'll be in the delivery room, but perhaps you and
[husband's first name] can stop by the labor room for a short
chat... I wanted you to know that I'm willing if you are! See you
then. Take care.*

*With love,
your friend,
(and wiggly baby)*

Diane was alone in the spring heat of Chandler. She had put Christie
and Cheryl on a plane to Oregon at the end of April. Willadene would care
for her granddaughters for six weeks even though Wes and Willadene
disapproved mightily of what Diane was doing. Steve was taking care of
Danny.

Diane's visits to her Arizona gynecologist indicated that the baby
might arrive early. At twenty-five, she was in her fifth pregnancy. The
baby's head had dropped and was engaged in the pelvic girdle. Labor
could begin at any time. If it did, there was no way Diane could get on a
plane to fly across America even though her contract specified that the
optimum situation was for the delivery to take place in Kentucky, with
the parents at hand.

It was risky for Diane to remain in Chandler any longer. She flew East
in the first week of May—almost two years to the day since she'd first
written to the clinic offering to become a surrogate mother.

The first week of May is the best of all possible times to arrive in Louisville. The Kentucky Derby takes place on the first Saturday in May, the
city and countryside are bright with flowers and the first tender leaves of
oaks and silver maples, the grass is velvety and blue green.

Diane was admitted to the Audubon Hospital on May 7, 1982. It was a new hospital, smaller than the other facilities owned by the huge Humana group, removed from the hullabaloo of the artificial heart implants, designed to be cozy and welcoming. From her room Diane could see the flat, historic city below. The buildings were old and narrow, fancied up with fretwork and cornices—some painted, some brick, and some with cast iron facades bolted on, all in a piece. Far off, down near the Ohio River, the little fish restaurants advertised themselves with thousands of tiny white lightbulbs tracing their rooflines, windows, doorways—shimmering in the night.

It was like a magical carnival; the princess had come here to give birth to a perfect child. Louisville welcomed her with flowers and lights.

Diane's cervix was already one-and-a-half-fingers dilated. Her labor was induced—an elective delivery. A nick in the thinned amniotic sac, and the fluid gushed out. Her contractions began almost at once.

Just before midnight, Diane was rolled into the delivery room. There, holding on to the "other mother's" hand, she gave birth to a baby girl. With tears rolling down her face, Diane held the baby for a moment, and then she placed it in the arms of the real mother who was to raise this child.

"I looked at the baby, between my knees down there, and my first thought was of the mother. There were tears running down her face, and she wouldn't let go of my hand. All she could say was 'Thank you.'

"They put the baby in a little clear cradle, and I looked over at her and thought, 'What if I regret this?' and I said, 'No, that's just not mine. I'm not going to psych myself into believing that I'm giving up a child.'"

For the first time, Diane saw now the face of the man whose sperm had united with her ovum to make a baby. He wasn't movie-star handsome. He was only a man. Diane described him as "... ahhh plain ... not somebody I would ever pick up off the street ... but I have to admit I was very curious."

Diane and the parents talked for hours after the birth. By comparison, Steve had been almost bored at the births of her three children; she'd never known such euphoria as this. At last, she had not one—but two—people to share her feelings with. It was as if she had never had a baby before.

Three days later, Diane asked to see the baby girl one more time before she left the hospital. She walked to the nursery with the slightly apprehensive new parents. Diane gazed silently at her fourth living child, wondering if *this* was the lost Carrie drawn back from the misty place she'd gone to. No. The baby was the image of her father. Her eyes were dark, and her hair was jet-black. She didn't resemble Christie or Cheryl or Danny.

Diane decided she wasn't Carrie.

The RN in charge had been reticent about letting Diane in to see the baby, but she had no legal right to keep her out. She hovered nearby, nervous too, watching Diane cuddle the baby.

"I hadn't terminated my rights as a mother. In Kentucky, it takes five days," Diane smiles. "So the child was still my child."

Would Diane Downs give up this baby? The psychiatrists had given their warnings, concerned that this dramatic, possibly neurotic woman might not, in the end, release the child born of her own womb.

Five days went by . . .

Diane honored her contract. She signed all the papers proffered to her, and received her $10,000 fee. She flew home to Arizona, leaving her raven-haired daughter behind.

Diane immediately broke one of the rules. She bought an expensive layette for the new baby and mailed it to an address she'd ferreted out for the legal parents. The package came back marked: "Moved. No Forwarding Address."

Diane seemed to have no trace of postpartum depression, no grief over giving up her child. She felt only joy and such a sense of well-being.

She could hardly wait to be inseminated again.

CHAPTER 13

... it's never totally successful. In fact there usually is a grief re-
action with the women I'm following. So far, there have been no
severe psychiatric reactions when a woman gives up the baby. I
mean—no one's ended up in a psychiatric hospital. But it's only
a matter of time.

—Philip Parker, M.D., psychiatrist, on surrogate mothers

Diane went back to work in Arizona three weeks after she gave birth. It
was June and full summer. She was slim again and feeling wonderful.
She shouldered her heavy mail bags easily. Willadene was to have kept
Christie and Cheryl while Diane recuperated, but Diane was lonesome.
She sent for the little girls and fetched Danny back from Steve's care.

Diane sold the Palomino Street house back to Steve. She had the
$10,000 payment for the baby, but she still owed Mack $5,000. She used the
rest of the baby money for a vacation and a down payment on a new mobile home. The expandable mobile home had beige siding that blended
into the scrabbly half-desert just beyond the manicured splendor of the
Sunshine Valley Trailer Park at 18250 South Arizona Avenue in Chandler.
When its two halves were joined, her mobile home was as big as a
medium-sized house.

Everything inside was new—most of it on credit. Diane's living-room
furniture was heavy, rough-hewn wood and leather-look vinyl, the cush-
ions of sturdy brown and tan plaid. She hung white organdy curtains in
the kitchen window and planted scarlet bougainvillea so that it would
espalier against the outside walls.

Space 363. The Four Musketeers were locked safe inside. Diane recalls
how they played games in air-conditioned coolness. Outside it was unre-
mittingly hot, and the sky above had no clouds at all.

Nor did Diane seem to have any clouds in her life. The trailer removed the pressure of the hefty mortgage payments. Everything smelled so new and clean it enhanced the illusion of a fresh start. She had never lived here with Steve. At last, they were divorced!

Five years after the fact, Diane had expunged her guilt over the abortion of Carrie. She hadn't accomplished that with Danny's birth, because she'd kept Danny. But she'd given Jennifer—her name for the surrogate baby—away, symbolically undoing any harm she'd done. It was a mystical process, and it had taken her a while to figure it out.

Diane realized that she could trade babies for babies after all!

If there was ever a time when Diane Downs had the opportunity for a new start—her guilt atoned for and all of the negative influences that depressed her relegated to the past—it was the summer of 1982. She was surrounded by choices.

Almost without exception, Diane chose the wrong doors.

"I wanted to study pre-med . . . My dad said I should go to summer school to see if I really liked college. I went two nights a week from seven to nine. Steve took care of the kids."

She took English and math courses first. She had been out of school for a while, and she needed to brush up. Diane's English course was basic composition. She wrote several papers: one on women's liberation, one on her aversion to "dumb rules," and a long essay on child abuse. She was quite good—particularly when her prose was compared with that of other freshmen who were eight years younger.

Diane's essay on "dumb rules" helped her vent her anger when she was not allowed to fence her yard at the trailer park, and when postal employees were forbidden to hang out in the coffee room when they were off duty. Diane had hated rules throughout her childhood; she had somehow expected that adults would be free of them.

She was particularly incensed about the new post office rules:

"The most recent ideas they came up with are the absolute dumbest. Try this one: 'After an employee punches off the clock, he or she must leave the building immediately.' We may not even go to the break room to talk. Now, I abide by the rule of not talking while on the clock, so why do they chase us outside into the heat to talk?"

Diane's social life was entirely dependent on her co-workers, and she looked forward to having coffee and shooting the breeze with the men she worked with. A new rule forced them out into the scorching Arizona sun, and conversations were understandably foreshortened.

Diane was starving for much more intense communication. She grabbed with both hands for new experiences, but especially for some kind of connection with other human beings. She wanted so much. Friends. Fun. Lovers. Money. And her career as a physician. She planned to work her way through pre-med entirely in night school. Then she would go to medical school. She had no college credits to begin with; getting four years of college credits in night school might take years. She would find shortcuts.

Diane wanted her dream house too. And soon. She drew the plans for her perfect house on the back of one of her essays. A huge complex—a square built of four wings surrounding an open courtyard. The smallest room was ten by seventeen ("kids' playroom") while the master bedroom was fifteen by twenty. There were four bathrooms and a sundeck. Interestingly, there was no kitchen. The master bedroom was separated from the children's quarters by a catwalk suspended high above the forty-foot-long living room. Christie, Cheryl, and Danny would be relegated to the farthest corner of the mansion from the master bedroom. Any farther and they would be housed in a separate building entirely.

Diane describes her feelings toward men that summer of '82 as "flirty and playful." In truth, her behavior verged on nymphomania. Diane set out to work her way sexually through the male employees of the Chandler post office.

She went about it very badly, setting herself up in "no win" situations. She attracted her lovers easily by being available, submissive, and gigglingly flirtatious, but her relationships foundered when intimacy began and her compliant exterior cracked and fell away. Men who expected a bubbly cheerleader were understandably turned off when they found themselves alone with the dominatrix who could—and often did—draw blood.

The U.S. Post Office in Chandler, Arizona, is flat roofed and square; constructed of stucco, brick, and rock; and shaded by date palms and jacaranda trees. There are more than a dozen red, white, and blue rigs parked out behind the loading dock early in the morning before the mounted carriers begin their routes. A hundred employees work inside, many of them men between twenty-five and forty-five.

Detectives who have talked at length with the men who moved through Diane's life agree that they were all "nice guys, kind of easy going, friendly guys," tall, mostly bearded, good looking, but not exceptionally handsome. Diane's men were salt-of-the-earth kind of men, dependable and unsophisticated. With one sole exception, they were all married.

One of Diane's short-lived affairs that summer was with twenty-eight-year-old Cal Powell, who had a degree in behavioral science. He transferred into the Chandler post office shortly after Diane had returned from Kentucky. Diane was the aggressor. She went to his apartment and told him that she needed advice on college, confiding too that she was lonely and had no one to talk to. They made a date for Powell to come to Diane's mobile home to discuss her educational options.

Powell was a little surprised to see Christie, Cheryl, and Danny when he arrived—but Diane quickly took them next door.

Diane outlined her plans for med school. She wondered how many courses she could take at a time, how she might work out credit packages so that she could have her degree as soon as possible. She wanted to take twenty-two hours a quarter—an oppressive load even for a solid student who has no outside job. Cal suggested that she take a maximum of twelve to begin with. She sloughed off his suggestions. Didn't he understand she had no *time*?

Diane suddenly became "very sexually aggressive" and Powell responded. They moved to the waterbed in Diane's room. Powell discovered that Diane was wild—dangerous—in bed. She scratched him on his back and buttocks, leaving bloody tracks. He yelped and asked her to stop, and she obliged—but only for a minute or two.

"She started scratching me again, and it made me mad . . . I put my clothes on . . . She just laughed and said, 'Oh, another guy who doesn't like marks?'"

Diane had confided in Powell about the psychiatrist who tested her before she was accepted into the surrogate mother program.

"He told her she was intelligent, but a borderline psycho. She thought it was funny . . . I had the feeling she was angry at men—that she wanted to castrate them."

Diane worked closely with Jack Lenta and Lew Lewiston. The trio prided themselves on being the swiftest mail carriers in the Chandler post office.

At first, Diane was more attracted to Jack Lenta. He went to night summer classes at Mesa Community College too.

Lenta remembers: "I had been working there about four months when she just walked up and said, 'I want to go to bed with you.' I was kind of shocked . . . We got together about a month later."

Beneath Diane's cheerful patter, Lenta found her "very depressed, very lonely," a woman who talked of wanting a husband to come home to. Since he had no plans to leave his wife, he pulled back.

He was also put off by Diane's sexual dominance. "She was the aggressor. She had no inhibitions whatsoever; whatever she wanted, she just asked for it.

"After about three weeks, I told Diane it [our affair] couldn't continue."

"She just said, 'OK. I guess I'll try for Lew.'"

It was July, 1982.

CHAPTER 14

At 8:00 A.M. on Monday, May 23, 1983, an exhausted Fred Hugi sat in Louis Hince's office and read aloud in a flat matter-of-fact voice to a group of detectives, each of them as tired as he was. Even so, the material in Diane's spiral journal fascinated all of them.

> My dear sweet Lew,
>   What happened? I'm so confused. What could she have said
> or done to make you act this way? I spoke to you this morning for

the last time. It broke my heart to hear you say "don't call or
write."... I still think of you as my best friend and my only lover,
and you keep telling me to go away and find someone else. You
have got to be kidding....

"She uses that phrase a lot," Hugi said wryly. He had read Diane's diary—the diary she'd asked Jerry Smith to bring to her on the night of the shooting. On the Sunday after the shooting, he had read it again. A second read was only one of seventeen tasks he'd listed for himself that day. The whole thing in the form of letters. Never sent.

"That's the first entry, and it's dated April 21. Something must have happened to spark all that 'agony.' The thing's got entries every day, right up until—until the nineteenth . . . until the end."

"She keeps saying she expected Lew to be here with her," Dick Tracy mused, ". . . like everything was just dandy with them."

". . . but something happened," Alton said.

"He dumped her, it sounds like," Welch offered. "Sounds like the lady was dumped."

Most of them had already read the diary—or sections of it—and found it gushy and overdone, as if a high school girl had written it, a sixteen-year-old smitten with her first crush, scribbling in her school notebook.

"From what she told us," Welch put in, "Lew was just a step removed from the second coming of the Messiah. She loves him. He loves her. His wife—Nora—is the villainess."

Hugi wrote on the chalkboard: *"Could Lew have shot the kids?"* *"Could Nora have shot the kids?"* *"Steve . . . ?"*

Beyond the phantom gunman, these were the likely suspects. The investigators would have to implicate or eliminate Lew or Nora or Steve. Could they pinpoint where they'd all been four nights earlier? Hugi and the detectives were batting at shadows until they had lab reports back on the casings, the guns, and the blood samples. The state police crime lab was swamped, and the investigators chafed at the delay.

Jim Pex *had* come up with something interesting already. When he'd rolled the red Nissan out of the county shops into the sunlight, he'd seen what could only be detected in daylight. The rocker panel below the passenger door was flecked with a mist of dark red. Testing indicated that it was human blood. Pex recognized it as high-velocity back-spatter, the pattern blood makes as it flies back from a wound toward the barrel of a gun and the hand of the shooter.

High-velocity back-spatter could only mean that someone had been shot *outside* the car, someone who had been almost at ground level. In all of Diane Downs's accounts of the shooting, she had said that the children were shot *inside* her car. Could she have simply forgotten? Perhaps Cheryl had fallen out, and her mother had somehow managed to grab her up and get her back in the car before the shooter fell for Diane's ruse of the thrown keys.

They doubted it. To a man, they thought they had caught Diane in a lie that could not be explained away.

If there was one lie, there would be more.

"Whatever she says, I think Lew's your motive," Welch said. "You get her talking about Lew and forget anything else."

"Maybe," Hugi said. "But why would killing her kids help her get this guy? She's different from any woman I've ever met. She knows we're after her but if she was ever scared, she isn't now. She as much as dared me to try and arrest her."

"Then let's arrest her."

Hugi shook his head. "You bring me your reports—written—and we'll see."

He knew the sheriff's men were irritated. He didn't blame them. But he was counting on the lab reports—on something solid that would let him grab on to Diane Downs and know he could hold her. He barely considered the possibility that lab tests might support Diane as an innocent, the victim of an actual living, breathing bushy-haired stranger.

One thing was clear to Hugi: a team of detectives would have to fly to Arizona to interview Lew and Nora Lewiston and a number of other people mentioned in Diane's diary or in her conversation. If Lew was such a wonderful guy, and if he loved Diane so damned much, why hadn't he flown up here to comfort her? He hadn't sent flowers; he hadn't even called her. They couldn't be sure *where* Lew Lewiston was, or what he had to do with the shootings.

There wasn't enough money in the county budget for two round-trip tickets to Phoenix, much less the expenses a couple of detectives might incur once they got to Arizona. But DA Pat Horton had said to go ahead and do what had to be done and hang the cost.

Sheriff Dave Burks was also giving it full priority. What had been Case #83-3268 would henceforth be called simply Project 100. All the overtime hours were coming in. The budget would somehow be stretched to cover Project 100. They might as well go for it while they could.

The four law-and-order levies on the ballot in the June 28 Lane County elections sought $4.9 million in property taxes to balance a proposed 1983–84 no-frills budget. If they didn't pass, Burks would have to lay off fifty-six of his two hundred forty-eight employees, cancel police patrols, and switch calls to the state police. Horton's staff—which had once numbered eighty-five and was now down to fifty—would be cut in half. Both departments would be crippled without the tax money. A loss at the polls would be disastrous to the Downs investigation. They might as well spend money now, even if it meant putting a murder probe on the tab.

And the other—less overt—problems were exacerbating. Sheriff Burks and DA Horton were political enemies, with a history of chilly relations. Burks had been challenged by one of Horton's investigators in the last election with Horton's full support. In some ways, the cops and Hugi were like a second wife and her predecessor trying to raise the same set of kids. Everybody had good intentions; their methods were entirely different.

The sheriff's detectives still wanted a quick arrest. They feared that Hugi might demand so much information on Diane that it would be too late to catch her before she ran. Fred Hugi knew they hated paperwork and suspected they wanted to rush out and bring Diane in bound and tied to the front bumper of a squad car, tooting their sirens down Oak Street for an admiring crowd.

Hugi planted his feet; he would not be buffaloed or intimidated. The detectives knew that the likelihood of arresting a killer decreases in direct proportion to the delay between the crime and the arrest. And still, they worked together, biting back acrimonious words, trying to ignore frustrations.

It is always that way. Anyplace. Anytime. Not turf wars—turf scuffles. A cop approaches a murder probe differently than a prosecutor does.

They worked it out. Two detectives would go on down to Chandler— one from each office: Doug Welch from the sheriff's office, and Paul Alton as a DA's investigator. They would call in their reports each night—Alton to Fred Hugi, and Welch to Louis Hince or Dave Burks—and the other would listen in on the extension to be sure the reports were identical.

"Go down there," Hugi said. "And see if you can find out who Diane Downs really is."

Six days after the shootings, there were no definitive lab results. Criminalist Chuck Vaughn was working with three or four different Rugers comparing rifling and tool marks, firing them to see if they left residue that would show up on GSR tests. He found nothing that would help one way or another.

To say absolutely that the Downs .22 Ruger had been the death weapon, Vaughn would have to have that gun.

At odd times when Hugi wasn't sitting with Christie and Danny, he walked the route from the river to the bridge and on up to the turnoff to Heather Plourd's road. Possibilities would come to him at night when he couldn't sleep, and he'd check them the next day. Some of the assistant DAs were skin divers, and they put on their gear and joined the sheriff's divers.

Late one night, Hugi, Vaughn, Pex, Alton, Pat Horton, and Chief Criminal Deputy DA Fred Hartstrom had an impromptu meeting at the state police crime lab. Sipping coffee at midnight, they threw out theories about where the gun might have been hidden. Somebody mentioned a grate out by the power plant on the riverbank at Hayden Bridge. Diane had had some snapshots of the river that they figured had been taken from that viewpoint.

Hugi started home, debated with himself, and then he cut his wheel hard and detoured to the Marcola road. It was almost pitch black as he pawed around the grate. Suddenly, he heard something—the scrape of a foot, a soft rustling off to his left. He stood up cautiously, his heart thumping. He could make out a large dark figure a dozen feet away.

Was there a bushy-haired stranger after all, and had he managed to meet up with him, alone, on this slippery bank above the deadly chute?

The figure moved toward him, and Hugi put his hand tentatively on the .45 he carried.

"Hugi!"

It was Fred Hartstrom, late of the same coffee-drinking theorizers. They'd both had the same idea.

And neither found a gun.

In Springfield Wednesday afternoon, May 25, Cheryl Lynn Downs's funeral drew a huge crowd, which included many strangers showing their sympathy for the bereft mother. Diane placed a single red rose in her daughter's coffin and swayed in a near faint. She told her diary later that she had never seen Cheryl so still, not even when she was sleeping.

Diane constantly visited Christie at McKenzie–Willamette Hospital and then Danny at Sacred Heart in Eugene. She had detested Paula Krogdahl on sight. They were close in age, and they were both beautiful and highly intelligent—but there the similarities ended. Paula dressed in classically low-keyed separates and zipped around Eugene in a vintage white sports car. Diane's ambitions had always ended in ashes, and Paula had almost realized hers. Paula was the epitome of the girls Diane had always envied.

Paula spent two hours a day with Christie, morning and afternoon. As Christie grew to trust Paula, Diane deemed Paula "a witch— an *evil* witch." When Paula brought her favorite childhood doll—a rag doll with yellow braids—for Christie, Diane snatched it from the crook of Christie's paralyzed arm and flung it across the waxed floor, where it skidded with a thunk against the wall. Paula watched as Christie struggled to sit up, her eyes misted with terror, choking garbled croaks of protest.

Diane whirled on Paula, spitting out her words flatly, "I don't need somebody interfering in my life with *my* child!"

Christie was no longer in critical condition, but she was confused and frightened by her inability to speak. When she was able to convey to Diane her questions about what had happened to all of them, Diane only murmured, "We've had a tragedy."

The tube in Danny's chest continued to put out fluid, but it was no longer scarlet; packed cells, transfused, had brought his hematocrit within normal range, and he could breathe without distress.

He had not yet discovered that he couldn't walk.

Judy Patterson, who still worked at both hospitals, caught glimpses of Diane as she walked outside Sacred Heart after visiting Danny. "She never seemed to recognize me, or even remember where we'd met before. It's funny. She brought in a big box of chocolates for the staff—the way parents do to say thank you for taking care of their kids—but nobody would touch it. The candy got moldy, and we threw it away."

Fred Hugi learned that Diane was actively seeking the stranger who had shot her and her children, asking questions around Springfield.

Down in Chandler, Arizona, Doug Welch and Paul Alton had figured they'd be back in Oregon in three or four days. "But each person we talked to gave us three or four more names," Welch remembers. "It spider-webbed. We were down there *nine* days."

In Oregon the end of May is a gentle precursor of summer; in Chandler, Arizona, it was brilliantly hot. Paul Alton and Doug Welch felt as if they'd flown into a shimmering oven. Palm trees, cacti, oranges overripe to bursting on the sidewalks and in the gutters, flies droning heavily in the still air—all reminding them that they were far from home, looking for answers to perhaps impossible questions from absolute strangers.

The Oregon detectives walked through the heavy carved door of the Chandler Police Department. The building on Commonwealth Street was off-white, surrounded by palm trees and cedar hedges, its windows recessed inside bunkerlike projections, as cool as a cave against the heat. Lt. Bobby Harris led them to an interview room.

The first interview seemed the most important: Lewis Stanton Lewiston, a good suspect in the shootings either as the actual shooter or as an accomplice. They recognized him; he was the man in the pictures on Diane's television set in Springfield. *Lew.* A tall, wide-shouldered man in his mid-thirties with almost-military short hair, dark brown eyes, a neat beard. When he spoke, he sounded like Texas.

Doug Welch and Paul Alton were eager to hear what Lewiston had to say. They were less anxious to ask their explicit questions when they saw that Nora Lewiston had accompanied her husband to the interview. My God, how do you ask a man intimate details about his lover when his wife is sitting there beside him?

Welch suggested that perhaps Nora might care to wait outside.

Lew shook his head. "She stays. Nora knows *everything.* I want her here."

Nora Lewiston would prove to be the most pragmatic of women. She knew her husband had had an affair with Diane Downs, and she had forgiven everything. She prompted Lew with her own computerlike memory of dates, times, places. The detectives soon learned that they could count on Nora's recall more than on that of almost anyone involved in the case. She was pretty, tiny, and blonde, and scarcely looked the part of a betrayed wife.

Both Lewistons were candid; they seemed very open.

They had been married in September, 1979, in Texas, where Lew carried mail. It was a second marriage for each. Nora was from Chandler and, homesick, she'd persuaded Lew to move to Arizona, where her family lived.

Suddenly, there were stresses on the marriage.

Lew studied the toes of his boots. "I didn't really want to come to Chandler. I liked Texas; I liked my job there. We had a three-bedroom house in Galveston and the payments were only $325 a month. Here, we bought a two-bedroom house and we pay $650! I resented the move, but it was kind of subconscious; I didn't realize quite how much I resented it."

Nora nodded. "Things weren't going great for us. We moved back to Arizona at Thanksgiving, 1981. Lew and I were on shaky ground in our marriage when Diane came along—mostly because of money. The house payments were more, and then Lew found a great piece of land he had to have. It cost $23,000 and that meant I had to go to work full-time, I didn't mind, but our lives changed. I got up at dawn to cook his breakfast before he went out on the route, and then I went to my job. I was ready for bed at seven. We weren't having much fun, or doing any partying at all . . . I was a sitting duck for Diane."

Lew said he'd met Diane at the Chandler post office that November of 1981. He had found her very nice, very gracious in answering his questions. She'd been pregnant with the surrogate baby then, and he noticed she'd mostly hung around with Tim Lowry.

"We were good letter carriers," Lew recalled. "We delivered a lot of mail. We were only friends."

But then, after Diane had her surrogate baby, Lew fell on the loading dock, shattering his elbow. He was confined to jobs he could do inside the post office. That threw him together with Diane constantly.

It was July and hot. Diane wore cut-off T-shirts to work with no bra underneath, and when she reached up to put mail in the high boxes, the lower portion of her full breasts peeked out. It was difficult for Lew to glance away.

Lew and Diane were together day after day.

"We just sort of hit it off," Lew remembered. "I told her from the beginning that all I had in mind was a fling."

Welch glanced at Nora Lewiston. She was not discomfited.

"I'd had affairs before," Lew admitted. "During my first marriage. Not affairs even—just short-term, easygoing things. I guess that's what I expected with Diane."

Lew said he'd found Diane physically attractive, and he admired her brains, her memory. "She had a good memory. She had memorized thirty-six or thirty-seven postal routes."

Lew said he knew that Diane was already planning to be inseminated again as soon as possible. That seemed to be the most important thing in her life—that and becoming a doctor—and he was convinced she wasn't interested in a lasting alliance with a man. She was simply flirting with him, he thought, when she complained she had no boyfriend. He asked her why she didn't have an affair.

"She said she couldn't do that because she'd get pregnant, and I said, 'No. Why don't you have an affair with someone who *won't* get you pregnant?' and she said, 'Like who?'

"And I said, 'Like me.'"

Lewiston, an admitted "hardhead," had actually been on the fence, rankled at being uprooted from Texas. Restless and vaguely unhappy in Arizona, he thought a brief fling—not an affair—with Diane seemed like an answer. He wasn't going to get her pregnant; he told Alton and Welch he'd had a vasectomy when he was twenty-one. He liked kids—he just never wanted to have any of his own.

It was the classic married-man/single-woman situation, one that is played out ten thousand times a day, a pas de deux in the dance/war between men and women.

Lew Lewiston had no inkling of how obsessive Diane could be.

Psychiatrists had warned the surrogate clinic that Diane had problems with understanding "social cause-and-effect reasoning," and that she had poor judgment and poor understanding because she was depressed and anxious. Although she had acquired virtually no protective devices, Diane had continued to polish her cocky, brazen facade.

Diane—who felt she had been given nothing—now wanted EVERYTHING.

It would have taken a professional to see the real woman behind Diane's smiling mask, to winnow the truth from her continual bright patter. Diane made armor out of monologue.

Lew Lewiston wasn't a professional psychologist. He was a man momentarily attracted to a beautiful woman—a man about to buy a ticket to ride where the wheels sped faster and faster, until there was no safe way to jump off.

Diane marked the day she was first intimate with Lew Lewiston, just as she noted all of the important dates of her lifetime: X's on a calendar or lines in a diary to signify romantic encounters, birthdates, even dates she conceived children. Lew warranted a huge red X on one of the calendars detectives removed from her apartment on the night of May 19.

He explained now that Diane had choreographed the affair. She had found ways for them to be together. To begin with, they were restricted to quick kisses in parked cars. They met often after work in Diane's trailer. For weeks there was no communion beyond sex: an hour, a half hour—and Lew was gone. One time only they'd gone to a motel. Lew longed for some discretion, but Diane talked about him constantly in the post office, and the affair was soon common knowledge.

Nora Lewiston had known there was another woman. "Lew's a lousy liar. I knew from almost the beginning. It started the second week of July, 1982."

Nora kept her suspicions to herself, but she kept track of dates and times too—jotting down those periods when she suspected her husband was with someone else.

Lew said he'd seldom seen Christie, Cheryl, and Danny. "I wouldn't be with her if the children were around. It was an affair—it didn't seem right." Diane shuttled the kids around between Steve, Mary Ward, and her Aunt Irene.

Lew had seen Danny, but Danny didn't know who *he* was. "Diane's Aunt Irene had this little secondhand furniture place, and it was on my mail route. She looked after Danny a lot. He'd see me coming and he'd come bounding out, running, yelling, 'Hi, mailman!'"

It became apparent to Lew as the summer of 1982 progressed that Diane was far more serious than he'd intended. She still planned to be a doctor; she still planned to return to Louisville to be inseminated. But she added one more ambition to her already burgeoning roster: she decided to marry him.

She knew he wasn't interested in being a father; she assured him she would just have to find a way that the kids wouldn't bother him. Diane seemed not to hear him when he reminded her that he had no intention of leaving his wife.

Lew had observed that Diane had tired of her lovers after a brief liaison. He assumed he would be like all the rest. Too late Lew realized Diane wanted only him. To possess him utterly.

In August, Steve Downs asked Diane for a trial reconciliation. "I told her to go for it," Lew said. "I told her to try to work out things in her marriage."

It was a most unrealistic reconciliation. Diane stipulated that there was to be no physical contact. Steve moved into her trailer, but he moved out within the week.

Lewiston told the detectives that he'd met Steve face-to-face infrequently. "He came to the trailer one day and he warned me, 'Diane is kind of crazy when it comes to sex. She has some problems—emotional problems—about it.'" Nora described the Chandler post office's annual picnic in August of 1982: "Diane filled her plate at the buffet, and then she very deliberately sat down across the picnic table from us. I looked from her to Lew . . . and it clicked. Wives have antennae; she was the one."

Nora said she'd been disturbed by the odd interplay between Diane and her kids. The kids wore faded clothes, and Diane hadn't bothered to comb their hair—although Diane's outfit was brand new.

"She just plopped herself down across from us. She was wearing a T-shirt without a bra, and short-shorts. It was very strange. She would call her children over—and she'd ask them the same kind of questions over and over. She'd keep asking them, 'Do you *love* Mommy?' and 'You love Mommy more than you love Daddy, don't you?' And the kids were confused and embarrassed."

After the picnic Nora said nothing. She knew that Lew would tell her soon enough.

Paul Alton and Doug Welch listened to the astounding chronology of the summer and fall of 1982. In September, Diane had given Christie, Cheryl, and Danny back to Steve. The youngsters had apparently led a gypsy existence all their lives. They'd lived on farms, in towns, in motels, in the trailer, with their grandparents, and in and out of the Palomino house. They'd been dragged along as their mother rushed willy-nilly through life, like rag dolls bumping along the ground behind a hyperactive child.

Christie and Cheryl had begged to go to the Pomeroy School, and they lived with their father to be in that school district. Diane was allowed to see them whenever she wanted, but she plunged into a punishing school schedule for the fall quarter. She babysat grudgingly for her children occasionally.

Her schedule sounded almost impossible. She worked at the Chandler post office Monday, Wednesday, Friday, and Saturday from six in the morning until two-thirty in the afternoon. She went to school all day Tuesdays and Thursdays and to night school on Mondays and Wednesdays. She also had an appointment in Louisville for her second insemination.

Diane lasted only a few weeks into the fall semester. She found that she had no time for anything but work, classes, and studying. She apparently realized her life would be like that for years and years and years if she wanted to be a doctor. She worried because she didn't have enough time to see Lew.

Doug Welch noticed Lewiston's hands trembled as he told them that the affair had escalated far beyond anything he had envisioned. It weighed like a rock on his conscience. Lew loved his wife, but he couldn't get off the merry-go-round.

"My wife wasn't getting home til five, so I had lots of time in the afternoon. And the affair went on and went on. I lied to Nora all the time and told her nothing was going on, never would admit it. Ahhh . . . but it continued. Finally, in September—exactly September twelfth, my birthday—I told Nora about the affair."

Diane had left three days before to fly to Louisville.

She had noticed a slight vaginal discharge, and she'd accused Lew of giving her a venereal disease. Bewildered, Lew told Diane that he had no symptoms and he hadn't been with anyone but her and Nora.

"I had to tell Nora to protect her," Lew explained to Welch and Alton. "And that meant everything would hit the fan."

And so, just before she flew to Kentucky, Lew broke up with Diane. Predictably, she refused to believe he meant it.

"Lew told me," Nora remembered ruefully. "It was his *birthday* . . . He told me we'd have to go to some clinic and get treated. It was so awful to think about that we had to do *something* and we sure didn't care to celebrate his birthday, so we moved all the furniture in the house that night—until we were exhausted. We did go to the clinic, and we were so humiliated. We had some kind of infection with a long name I can't remember now—but it was something that was transmitted by sexual intercourse."

Diane was the likely source; she had slept with at least four men that summer. Although her contract stipulated that the surrogate mother be free of any disease, she did not cancel her trip.

The detectives were beginning to see that each of Diane Downs's plans hinged on the next. She had apparently needed this next baby and the emotional high that would come with it. She needed the $10,000 fee to help build her huge house so her children wouldn't bother Lew.

At the center of everything was Lew Lewiston. Diane had evidently hoped that Lew's forced confession to Nora would end his marriage. Her strategy didn't work. Nora Lewiston was not about to give her husband up without a fight. She heard his confession, and she forgave him.

As Welch and Alton continued to talk to the Lewistons and to the others who moved in Diane's world in Arizona, they were able to piece together an astounding life. They reported each new chunk of information to Fred Hugi and Dave Burks.

Whether because of the infection, the profound stress she was living under, or some more ephemeral reason, Diane did *not* conceive in Louisville. She could not have known that as she flew home to Chandler, but she was gripped by black depression anyway.

Diane hurried up the off-ramp, scanning the crowd behind the ropes for Lew's face and his wide shoulders towering above the others waiting there in Sky Harbor Airport.

Lew wasn't there. Steve was.

She would sooner have seen the devil himself.

Diane and Steve had had a physical fight two weeks before. Lew said she'd showed up at work the next day with a black eye, a swollen nose, and black-and-blue bruises on her face and neck.

When Steve met her at the airport, he wanted to talk about one more reconciliation. He had come alone to pick her up, leaving the children with a sitter.

Diane was like a strand of elastic tugged so taut that, released, it no longer snapped back. Her behavior on the night of September 13 frightened Steve, he told the Oregon detectives. "I picked her up at the airport and took her back to my home. I felt that she'd wanted Lew Lewiston to be the person to pick her up. We were having some veiled discussions and it wasn't working out very well. She was getting weird. She began scraping her face with her nails. It freaked me out. She began kicking at me."

Before they left Steve's house, he saw her stick something black into her purse. On the way out to the Sunshine Valley Trailer Park, Diane began to mumble about suicide. Steve had heard it before, but she was acting "so weird." At the trailer, Diane ran to the bathroom and locked herself in.

Steve pounded on the door, and Diane called out, "Well, you don't have to worry about it. I'll kill myself..."

He heard the sharp crack of a gun firing, and it scared the hell out of him. Downs put his shoulder to the door and crashed in. Diane sat on the tub inside, uninjured, pointing the .22 pistol at him. "She says, 'I can't kill myself, Steve—but I can kill you!'"

He weighed the possibility of jumping her, but she could fire first, so he tried to dissuade her, "Diane, that's a .22 pistol. You got nine shots in that gun, and you can't kill me."

She hesitated for a moment, and Steve grabbed the gun. Diane wasn't bleeding. Steve saw that she had fired into the trailer floor.

Diane was overtly suicidal, perhaps for the first time since she'd slashed her wrists at thirteen. She had given up medical school for Lew, she had given up other men for Lew, and Lew had abandoned her.

Steve took the gun home with him. They were a family—or rather, an ex-family—where guns were commonplace: rifles, handguns, passing back and forth between them.

Steve said that, as far as he knew, the bullet hole remained in the bathroom floor of Diane's deserted mobile home. The detectives perked up. If there was a bullet hole, there might be a bullet or a casing still there. Alton made a note to tell Fred Hugi about it.

CHAPTER 15

In a second interview with Lew and Nora Lewiston, Doug Welch and Paul Alton learned more about Diane's growing obsession with her married lover. She had prevailed upon Lew to sleep with her again, and her depression lifted. She'd been down, but she'd bounced back. She was so confident that she'd gone to a tattoo parlor and asked the operator to tattoo a huge red rose on her left shoulder.

"She came out on my route and asked me to write my name because she wanted it in my handwriting," Lew recalled. "But I refused—and she got it anyway."

Her tattoo, she explained to him, meant that she was his woman, indelibly marked with a rose and his name to symbolize their pure love. If another man tried to put his hands on her, he would see Lew's mark. When Lew saw the rose, he only felt uncomfortable.

Diane Downs had clearly begun to get lost in tunnels of her own devising, twisting hollow places that demanded too much of her, but her obsession made her a powerful adversary. Doug Welch saw that Lew would be "a rotten liar. He told us he'd been lying to Nora—but she knew he was lying. I don't think he ever even lied to Diane."

His deep voice faltering from time to time, Lew continued the etiology of his affair with Diane Downs, a cyclone sweeping into his life. "The affair continued, and continued, and I was with Diane all day at work, and I'd be with her all night long and it was every day for months. I basically didn't have time to think, you know; I was with Diane all the time."

He was still living with Nora, and Nora could plainly see that it had begun again. She said nothing.

Diane planned a second trip that fall to Kentucky. After the September failure, Clomid—a fertility drug to stimulate the ovaries to release multiple ova—had been prescribed. Should she conceive on this visit, Diane might well bear two, three, even six babies.

She wasn't at all put off by that. If that should happen, she would probably get her picture on the cover of *People* or *Time*!

Diane was due in Louisville on October 9; she attended Christie's eighth birthday party, and then flew east from Phoenix. Later that night, Lew recalled, her trailer burned. The Maricopa County fire marshal found it suspect that a mobile home barely six months old should spontaneously combust. Arson investigators checked the trailer meticulously. They determined the cause was an electrical short in the back wall, a wall constructed of relatively fireproof sheet rock, backed by masonite. There was a single burned spot on the floor inside, but the principal interior damage was from heat. Insulation had melted. So had Diane's stereo and her plastic flowers. Her waterbed was intact.

The mobile home was left marginally habitable. Diane had made only four $300 payments; she collected $7,000 in insurance. Steve agreed to repair the damage for her.

When Paul Alton totaled Diane's income for 1982, he saw that financially, through both design and disaster, it had been a fruitful year. When the insurance payoff was added to the $10,000 she'd received for the first surrogate baby and to her yearly salary, she'd come into almost $40,000 in twelve months. If the trailer had been completely destroyed, there would have been a lot more insurance money.

Lew told Alton and Welch he was curious about the fire. "I asked her how it got started, what the fire department had found. And she said it was either a cigarette burning, or a loose electrical wire . . . it started in the bedroom."

But then Diane had laughed mischievously. "I asked her how it really happened. She said 'I worked it out with Steve. He was supposed to start the trailer on fire. I told him I wanted it completely burned. But Steve messed up—as usual—and left one of the doors shut, and the fire never went any further than the bedroom.'

"She wouldn't tell me if she and Steve agreed to split the money from the insurance, only that they planned the arson . . . I'm not even sure why she wanted the trailer burned—other than that she didn't want it anymore."

Being stuck with a half-burned trailer was the least of Diane's problems. Diane, who had always prided herself on her fecundity, had failed—again—to conceive, even with a boost of fertility drugs. And Lew told Diane frequently that he felt obligated to Nora—that he *loved* her, for God's sake—and would break off the affair.

After the fire, Diane moved in temporarily with Karen Batten. She paid off her Ford Fiesta, gave Steve $100, and purchased some materials needed to fix the mobile home. Steve and his friends said they could make it good as new for $1,000.

They never did though.

Lew acknowledged that he'd never stayed away from Diane for long. The investigators nodded. They had seized Diane's calendars for 1982 and 1983. She'd marked the days they were together, the days they'd broken up; the calendar looked like a patchwork quilt.

Although she was intimate only with Lew, she moved in with Steve and her children in November. Steve reneged on his promise to fix her trailer. He stalled. He had his family back together.

Steve recalled a violent scene. He had been sitting on the tailgate of his truck with Cheryl when he saw Diane's white car racing down Palomino Street. Diane screeched to a stop and held out a black object. "This is what *I've* got!" she'd cried.

It was the gun.

Steve dove through the driver's window toward Diane: she put the car in gear and headed toward the Alma School Road.

"I held on," Steve recalled. "Another car was coming. As we were going toward the other car, I just bailed off. I rolled quite a ways. I could hear the kids then. Cheryl and Danny were running down the street screaming."

Dan Sullivan, from his yard down the street, saw Diane with the gun, and Steve—who appeared to be pinned inside as she revved up the car faster and faster. "He slid on his heels for about twenty feet before he lost his balance and fell."

Steve called the police but he told Diane to stay away when she came back. He had once again softened toward her and didn't want to get her in trouble. He sent the cops away.

Steve recalled that Diane found the incident humorous. "She said it was real hilarious when I let go of the car and rolled down the street."

Christie, Cheryl, and Danny went to bed with their clothes on and fell asleep listening for the sound of their mother's return, covering their ears so they wouldn't hear the screaming.

Nobody remembered to give them supper.

Investigators into murder eventually come to know both the victim and the killer as well—or better than—anyone else. They must turn up hidden things no one was ever meant to see.

Diane Downs had always protested that no one understood her. Fred Hugi, Paul Alton, and Doug Welch were certainly trying to do just that—reconstructing her life from her records, diaries, calendars, and her own voluminous statements. It was a matter of picking up a thread of information, following it back to its end, and then weaving each new thread into a tapestry that steadily revealed a clearer and clearer image.

Welch and Alton talked with a number of Diane's friends—and critics—at the post office, and to several of her discarded lovers. A good percentage turned pale when they learned that their indiscretions had become part of a homicide file.

The investigators also located witnesses who could verify that neither Lew nor Steve Downs could have been in Oregon on the night of May 19. A waitress at the West Chandler Tavern had chatted with Lew and Nora there between nine and midnight. Steve's new girlfriend had walked with him around the Mesa City Canal between 7:30 and 9:00 P.M. She was watching television with him shortly after 1:00 A.M. when his roommate came to tell him about the emergency phone call from Oregon.

A number of the people were asked to take a lie detector test, and all agreed. None of their responses indicated that they had any guilty knowledge about the shooting on Old Mohawk Road.

Diane Downs had never been a contender for Miss Congeniality of Chandler. The lady had made enemies, and the Oregon detectives had to take her abrasive frankness into account. But then homicide investigations are not popularity contests.

Some of the informants described a woman with a single-mindedness, a channeling of ambition, that they had rarely, if ever, encountered. Others disagreed; Diane Downs had been flippy dippy, up and down, mad and sad. A few—a very few—witnesses spoke in her behalf, and then only with faint praise.

"Diane is headstrong; she knows what she wants and will do what she has to to get it."

"Diane didn't care for her kids. Diane's not a good mother. The children were a hindrance to her."

"Diane was moody. One day she would be in a good mood, and the next day she seemed to be mad."

"Diane was looking for love."

"Diane was going to shoot Steve once, but she said she chickened out."

"One time, Danny threw up on the rug. Diane screamed at him and called him a 'fucking bastard.' The kids were hungry. There was never any food in Diane's house."

"Diane took on married men because they are more willing. It was a sexual need that made Diane really come on to men."

"Diane wouldn't hurt her kids."

"She was a very poor mother. Everything came ahead of the children. When she picked the kids up and Danny wanted affection, she pushed him away. She would come to visit and leave the kids home alone—from thirty minutes to two hours. She said they'd be all right."

"Diane was just a sad lady . . ."

"Diane's gone through a lot of people and has no scruples or conscience. She doesn't care who she hurts. That lady is pure poison. The lady is whacked out."

Lew told Welch and Alton that Diane had moved back into her blackened trailer. Her sister Kathy and Kathy's baby, Israel, joined her. Kathy had left her husband too.

Sometimes Diane brought Christie, Cheryl, and Danny to stay at the trailer. The ugly remains of the fire frightened them. Lew hit the roof one night when Diane climbed into bed with him and told him she'd left the kids home alone in the trailer. "I told her that eight wasn't old enough for a little girl to look after two other little kids, and that she had to go home and not come back until Kathy got there to sit with them."

Nora Lewiston bided her time. She never said a word to Lew when he was out late or when she spotted the purple hickeys Diane deliberately planted on Lew.

Just before Thanksgiving, Lew went off by himself to think. When he came back, he told Diane that he was going to leave Nora. Diane found a small apartment on Ray Street and persuaded Lew to sign the lease with her. She furnished the place with a rocking chair and a sleeping bag. Lew never moved in; he only visited there.

Diane gave Lew "messages" that the kids had sent him, which struck him as absurd; he barely knew Diane's children. "They were nice little kids, sweet little kids—but I hardly ever saw them," Lew told the detectives. "And I didn't want to be their daddy.

"Diane kept saying, 'I don't *want* a daddy. I want someone to love *me* and care about *me* and like my kids, but not be part of them.'"

With Lew, Diane had talked about "pure love" and "heart love." But what Diane primly termed "heart love" was something far more earthy in her voluminous diaries and letters. Her confidences to friends were full of sexual references bordering on obscenity.

She had told a number of men that she'd worked a long time to become an expert at making love, that she was very, very, good at it. With other men, Diane's knack with sex was apparently nothing more than a means to an end: seduction . . . gaining control. With Lew, it looked as if Diane was the one in danger of losing control.

Lew was, quite possibly, the only man with whom she was orgasmic.

Lew admitted he'd enjoyed good whiskey before he met Diane, but he'd handled it. Diane had never been much of a drinker—possibly a vestige of her fundamentalist Baptist nurturing. Lew recalled that she hated the taste of whiskey. But they drank together, blurring and softening the cruel edges of his dilemma. They drove through the autumn and winter Arizona nights, sipping Jim Beam or Jack Daniel's. When a glass was emptied, it was placed on the floor of the back seat. When they turned corners, the glasses chinked and clinked together like so many atonal chimes stirred by a desultory wind.

Lew never moved into her apartment. Diane gave it up. Nobody was winning. Nora's patience eroded. Lew asked for a divorce; she refused. Lew spent the night in a motel with a triumphant Diane. But he went home. He couldn't afford a divorce; he moved out of his wife's bed, and he continued to see Diane.

It didn't really matter if Lew was living home or away; Diane flooded him with love poems, cards, letters. He had no place to keep them; he gave them back.

Lew found he could not simply walk away from Diane; he had made a bargain with the devil. Once he chose to cheat on his marriage, there was no turning back.

"No one could believe how that woman could talk, could promise, and coax and argue—unless he'd been involved with her. I was with her *all* the time. She talked and talked—and she hardly ever took a breath."

Welch nodded. He'd heard Diane talk.

Diane had apparently focused every ounce of her genius on tearing Lew away from his wife. Channeled, her energy was formidable.

She had her rose tattoo improved. It was now almost six inches long—a full-blown red rose atop a slender stem. She urged Lew to get an identical tattoo. He refused.

Lew told Alton and Welch that he had finally moved into an apartment of his own. "I didn't call Nora, but I went over there on occasion to mow the grass and take care of that for her."

He still seemed bemused by the hold Diane had over him. "I drank

with the woman. I slept with the woman. That was all. We didn't *talk* ...
she talked at me, nagging at me—promising all these things she was going to buy me—that she thought I wanted—the wonderful life we'd have
when I left Nora and came with her. I didn't want anything from her, and
she sure as hell never gave me anything she didn't have a reason for. She'd
buy me whiskey to soften me up."

Nora said that Diane had called her often, using her lover's wife as a
message center, especially when Diane and Lew weren't seeing each
other. "When he'd broken off with her, she'd call to tell me it didn't hurt
anymore and I could tell him for her that it was over, and then she'd hang
up on me."

Nora received two letters from Diane. "In November, 1982, she told me
how my husband had said he was going to move out and get a divorce ...
He left—but he came back. During that week, I just rode with the tide."

When Lew returned home a week later, Nora said Diane wrote another
letter, a rather odd letter from a mistress to a wife, "telling me how wonderful I was and that she respected me and she loved Lew no matter what,
and he was—he was *gold* in her mind and things like that. But then she'd
call me all the time ... two or three times a day continuously and hang up
on me."

Christie, Cheryl, and Danny stayed with Steve through Christmas,
1982, and Diane sent over presents for them. Diane even bought Nora
Lewiston a Christmas present.

"She got me these wind chimes, shaped like a frog. That was like her.
She wanted my husband, but it wouldn't occur to her that it might look
strange for her to buy *me* a present."

Steve Downs sold the Palomino Street house in January, 1983. Diane asked
the children to choose who they wanted to live with. They chose her.
Cheryl and Christie were afraid they'd hurt her feelings if they said they
wanted to stay with Steve.

Diane assured Lew that she would find a way to build the huge house
she had sketched out so many times. There would be a nanny to oversee
the children. She had no collateral, but she was considering borrowing a
hundred thousand dollars or more to pay for it all. Lew told her that she'd
be laughed out of the bank.

Apparently undaunted, Diane proceeded with bigger plans.

Nora Lewiston showed the Oregon detectives a sheaf of newspaper clippings. With the fire insurance money and what was left of the payment for her surrogate baby, Diane had opened her own surrogate baby clinic!

She rented office space at 1801 S. Jen Tilly Lane in Tempe, Arizona. She had kept her eyes and ears open in Louisville; she connected with an attorney and physicians. To them she seemed to be a woman who knew a great deal about surrogate parenting. "I understood it inside and out. I took a copy of their [the Louisville clinic's] contract, changed it to suit my needs."

She had thick vellum stationery embossed with her own letterhead: *Arizona Surrogate Parenting.* Wearing a tailored suit and plain white blouse, Diane gave an interview to Gail Tabor of the *Arizona Republic.* She told Tabor that she had five surrogate mothers waiting for childless couples. In actuality, there were only two—the Frederickson sisters: Diane and Kathy.

Diane stressed that desperate parents-to-be shouldn't be overcharged. Her baby, Jennifer, had cost the natural father and adoptive mother $40,000; Diane's business would charge only half that much: $20,000 to $22,000.

She said that the Kentucky program was "bleeding the poor parents." Diane's surrogate mothers would be paid $10,000—just as Diane had been paid—but her company would take only twenty-five percent of the fee, with the remainder going for medical and psychological testing and hospital care at the time of delivery. (Since Diane *was* both the company and a potential surrogate mother, she would receive more than seventy-five percent of the fee.)

Diane explained that money was very important in a surrogate baby program. "If a surrogate does it strictly for money, that's a guarantee she'll give [the child] up."

And what if a mother would not give her baby up?

"I would fight tooth and nail with every legal tactic—and appeal to her conscience."

Her new business had been started, Diane explained, solely to fill a need. "I hope to find surrogates for as many people who need them. If the response isn't good, I'll let it die because it isn't needed. But as long as there's a need, I'll continue to do it. I think it's fantastic!"

Fantastic it may have been, but there was some question of its legality in the state of Arizona. Statutes forbade the payment of compensation for "placing out of a child." Diane said that her lawyer assured her she was on firm legal turf. The surrogate mothers would not be paid for *babies;* they would be reimbursed only for their time, their loss of work, and their pain.

A sidebar interview with two prospective surrogate mothers, young women called Rusty and Cindy, accompanied the piece. Coincidentally, Rusty and Cindy were the same age, had the same number of same-age children and the same marital circumstances as Diane and her sister, Kathy.

Rusty (Kathy) explained that she was in the process of a divorce and had a sixteen-month-old son. Kathy did not have Diane's grasp of the English language. "At first I thought it was wrong. But then I had my own kid and thought, 'What a bummer that people can't have their own.' You're not doing anything wrong. It's not like you're sleeping with him."

Cindy (Diane) enthused about having given birth to her first surrogate baby the year before. "It formed a bond, and it didn't make me feel bad a bit. It wasn't my baby. I didn't even know who the father was. When the baby was born, it was her baby. I can't imagine giving up any of my own kids, but a surrogate mother doesn't fantasize. She doesn't sit around and pick out names or wonder who it will look like. She knows she's not bringing it home."

Cindy's own children had been delighted, she said, by her first surrogate pregnancy. "The children think it's neat that Mommy had a baby for a lady who couldn't have one because her body was messed up. My daughter told all the neighbors, and they looked at me funny. They knew I wasn't married—but after I told one of them the whole story, they understood, and it was fine. I loved being pregnant with her. There was no pressure. I was very secure. I could do other things to make $10,000. I just loved being pregnant."

She admitted her own parents had had reservations about surrogate parenting. "My mother said it was a noble thing to do, but why did it have to be me? My father is very conscious of his status, and he didn't like it."

If Diane's business should prosper, it was clear that Wes and Willadene would have more to be upset about. Not one but *both* of their daughters were preparing to carry surrogate babies.

Diane gave a second interview to the Tempe newspaper. Again, she appeared in the interview in two roles: she was Diane Downs, founder and director of Arizona Surrogate Parenting, and she was also Jenny, an experienced surrogate mother.

Diane told Elizabeth Neason, the Tempe staff writer, that she had been in business for several months, and inferred that there had already been contracts, babies conceived, and that deliveries were expected. None of this was remotely true.

And there were certain glaring flaws in this fledgling surrogate business. Since anonymity is essential in such agreements, and even Diane had stressed that the parents and surrogate must never know each other's names or addresses, how had she—as founder, director, *and* surrogate mother—expected to keep her identity secret from the natural father and adoptive mother? Wouldn't they have noticed that she, the administrator, was pregnant and then suddenly not pregnant just as their child was born? Wouldn't she know who they were?

Diane had no experience in running a business, precious little medical or legal knowledge, yet she had undertaken a business desperately dependent on the maintenance of a delicate balance between human behavior and contractual matters. Moreover, Diane was still under contract to the surrogate parenting clinic in Louisville. She'd been scheduled to fly there to be inseminated for the third try in the first week of February, 1983. She hadn't informed them of her new enterprise. She considered it prudent to keep all her bases covered. It seemed to be simply a matter of where she conceived first—her own clinic or theirs.

Would even Diane *know* whose baby she carried?

Nora Lewiston said she placed a phone call to the head of the Louisville clinic after she read the article. He was appalled when she read the articles to him and stunned to hear about Diane's bout with venereal disease. The perfect maternal specimen from Arizona was no longer welcome in Kentucky.

Diane spoke of the wives of the natural fathers as women whose bodies were "messed up," always stressing that surrogate mothers must be healthy—that "most people want [a surrogate mother] who is happy, out-going, level-headed, and straight." Diane Downs herself had a perfect body and a superior IQ, but there were increasing signs that her *head* had become more and more "messed up."

The question Fred Hugi had to wrestle with was just how messed up Diane was. Her behavior had been—and was—outrageous. But was she insane within the parameters of the law? Had she been aware of the nature and quality of the act of murder? Had she known the difference between right and wrong at the moment of the crime?

Hugi thought that she had. He also thought that it had not mattered to her.

Arizona Surrogate Parenting never got off the ground. The first prospective parents split up before they could sign a contract. Her surrogate business was to have been a way for Diane to have both Lew and her children. Her plans for a six-figure income died—in utero, as it were. She needed to find another way.

As Paul Alton and Doug Welch extended their stay in Chandler, Arizona, Fred Hugi pored over Diane's calendars, actually a form of diary. The woman loved diaries.

Despite setbacks, Diane's hold on Lew Lewiston seemed to have grown stronger. Diane's calendar-diary had a single entry in February, 1983.

"I could hardly believe my ears today. Lew said he would live in the same house with my kids and me (of course). Then he said he would have to 'marry my ass.' But I think I can talk him into *all* of me. I'm so happy. Just when I thought Lew would call off our relationship, he said that he would marry me and live with my kids. But before I get too excited, I'll wait awhile. He could take another look at the situation and change his mind. I hope he doesn't. I sure love him."

Doug Welch asked Lew about this. Lew nodded. They had been drinking, and he barely remembered the half proposal. But Diane remembered it. Ignoring all the times he'd said he didn't want to raise kids, she chose to remember this one time.

Lew had once given Diane four red plastic cups; she took the gift as an almost mystic sign that he had accepted her *and* her children. Four cups. One mom plus three children equals four.

"I had them in Texas," Lew recalls. "And they were just old beat-up red plastic drinking glasses that I got from a little store along my mail route in Texas. I didn't need them."

Lew's apartment on South Dakota was as barren as a monk's. Guilt would not allow him to live in any comfort at all; he had betrayed Nora—and he wasn't even sure why. When he left her, the only thing he took was his mother's sterling.

"I continued to go home to mow the lawn for Nora, to do chores around the house. Then I went back to my apartment."

Diane came *this close* to winning Lew. But she began to push. Welch could see Lewiston was a man who avoided argument. But this time, Lew had refused to decide one way or the other.

During the last half of February, 1983, Diane was at Lew's apartment so much that he felt stifled. One night, she pushed him to the wall.

"Diane asked me who I loved the most—her or Nora. I said I loved Nora. She blew up. She ranted and raved and screamed at me. I'd never seen *anyone* act that way before. She just lost it. I know it sounds silly, but the final straw was when she broke my hairbrush."

Lew walked out, and Diane raced to her car and maneuvered it to block him. Calmly he clambered over the hood of her Ford Fiesta and strode off down the street. He called Nora from a phone booth at the 7-Eleven. Nora picked him up, and Diane followed them home.

"She pounded on our door all night long," Nora recalled. "We wouldn't answer. Then she called on the phone."

Diane was back the next morning. In uniform. She delivered mail to the Lewiston's house, but she reversed her route so that, on that day, she started at their address. She knocked on the door and finally Nora answered.

"She began to tell me what I should do about my marriage, my relationship with Lew—everything—and I just lost my cool. She'd hurt him so much. I don't usually swear. But I told her 'Fuck off!' and I slammed the door in her face."

Lew had told Diane more than once that he might just pack everything in and go back to Texas. "We went to Texas—not for good, but for a two-week vacation. While we were sitting at dinner at friends' one night, the phone rang. It was Diane.

"I asked her where she got the phone number, and she told me she memorized it. Well, I asked her where she memorized it from, and she wouldn't tell me. Then I knew the only place she could have got it was to go through my wallet while I was sleeping one night."

Stunned to find that Lew had gone to Texas without telling her first, Diane assumed the worst—that Lew had left her for good. Diane then flipped the first domino in what would prove to be a chain reaction; she requested a transfer from the Chandler post office to the Eugene area. She could count on a job. Wes and Willadene wanted her and the kids up in Oregon, and Wes had assured her employment was no problem.

Chandler postal administrators had accepted her application for transfer with alacrity; she was a strange, disruptive woman. Her affairs and her often scanty attire were common knowledge, and yet she refused to deliver copies of *Playboy* or *Penthouse* to subscribers on her route. Her temper tantrums had become legend.

"They put her transfer through effective in April," Lew remembered. "She called me in Texas and told me I wouldn't have to transfer; she was going to go to Oregon. I think she meant to scare me, and she was sure I'd follow her."

Lew came home from his vacation in early March to find that Diane had begun yet another project. She was taking flying lessons from Bob Barton, a co-worker at the post office. Barton said she was good, completely unflappable in the air. Diane paid $28.00 an hour to rent the Cessna-152 and $18.00 an hour to Barton.

When Lew and Nora returned from Texas, Lew didn't go back to his apartment right away; he stayed at home with Nora. Diane was stunned. For a time, she saw him only at work. When he moved back into his apartment, she gave him her picture; he gave her some raingear to wear while she walked her route in Oregon.

The physical affair resumed as it always had.

Lew Lewiston had felt guilty, a little sorry for Diane. He grimaced as he recalled making a gesture that was the second domino. Diane had only two-and-a-half weeks left in Arizona. Lew asked her to move in with him, stay with him until it was time for her to go.

From what the detectives knew about Diane Downs by now, Lew's invitation must have been—for her—as good as forever.

Welch remembered that she had told him and Tracy about it two days after the shooting: "Once I was cooking supper and he started—big old tears got in his eyes, and I went over and I kneeled down and I said, 'What's the matter?' and he said, 'It just makes me so sad when I think of you leaving.' I mean there was a bunch of promises that were made, so many dreams that were planned, and he says, 'I want you to ask the postmaster to let you stay,' and I said, 'OK,' and he had his gold chain . . . He's the only person that's ever worn that chain . . . I wear two gold chains with diamonds on it—and he goes, 'Take that shit off your neck,' and I went 'What? My gold and diamonds?' and he says, 'Yeah, take if off,' and I took it off and I said, 'All right, why?' and he goes, ' 'Cause you're going to wear this; you're Lew's woman,' and I said, 'OK,' and he took his chain off and he put it around my neck, and if that isn't love—I mean the chain that's never been off his neck . . . God, there's so many promises and so many deep feelings. I know he really cares."

Diane asked Gami to tear up her transfer request. He refused. But Lew's gold chain around her neck meant that he was bound to her forever. The one thing she wanted now was for Lew to get a rose tattoo.

"She made an appointment with 'Swede' for me. I argued about it, and then I agreed to do it. We had a few drinks and I got the rose on my arm." Lew rolled up his left sleeve, and showed the detectives the tattoo. He had balked at having Diane's name beneath it.

"She wanted me to meet her parents. They drove down to Chandler to help Diane (and Kathy and Israel) move to Oregon. Christie, Cheryl, and Danny were going to ride to Oregon with her folks, and she was going to go on April second."

Wes had told Lew that he could have his choice of three jobs in the Eugene area if he wanted to move up there. Lew was uncomfortable as he sat at Sunday dinner with the Fredericksons. "I looked at him, and I remembered that Diane said he'd fooled with her when she was young."

Lew was on the fence. Diane was being so loving to him; she even picked all the lima beans out of a package of frozen mixed vegetables because she knew he didn't like them. The sex was as good—better—than ever. Everything was great until he went home to help Nora around the place, and until Diane started to nag at him.

He hadn't had a clue in hell what he was going to do.

"I kept saying to Diane, 'If it's meant to be, it will be.'"

In Diane's mind it was all set. Her kids were already up there, her belongings. Her job was over in Chandler. It was time to leave and wait for Lew. The drive to Oregon took Diane two days. She had a wonderful time. "I wondered what Oregon looked like; I wondered if it would be like the Oregon I remembered from seeing it in childhood. I remembered a fantasy land.

"I played tapes, and I got a suntan through the sunroof of my car. I thought I'd see Lew again."

Diane sang along with the New Wave tapes on her cassette deck. Duran Duran sang of love and desire, loneliness and passion. Their words told her she'd been right to believe in Lew. Damn Gami for telling her she would never get Lew. She *had* won! Couldn't she feel the warmth of Lew's gold chain around her neck, burning a hot circlet into her tanning skin?

Diane swore by omens and tokens of love. Roses first. Then gold. And finally unicorns.

"That chain meant that *I* was Lew's woman. He never sends his chain anywhere he isn't going to be shortly."

She went ahead only to prepare a place for him.

CHAPTER 16

Lew recalled to Doug Welch that his affair with Diane had continued right up to the day she left for Oregon in April 1983. And then it was over.

Even as Diane sang along with "Hungry Like the Wolf" as she headed north, she had lost her desperate gamble. But she didn't *know* that Lew had already made up his mind to try to salvage his marriage.

"Once the sound of her talking stopped—once my head cleared—I could *think* again. I didn't want to be with Diane; I wanted to be with Nora. But I still couldn't go home because I didn't want Nora to see that damn tattoo," Lew said softly. "I was just relieved—totally relieved."

Diane called him each morning from Oregon. She sent him a profusion of romantic cards. Alton asked, "We understand you started refusing her mail. Why?"

"I just realized that I did not love Diane enough to divorce my wife and give up my job at the post office and move to Oregon . . . I finally just told her over the telephone that it was over. I wasn't coming and that's all there was to it."

"What was her response to that?"

"She didn't believe me. Before she had gone to Oregon, she had given me five hundred dollars in case I needed some money because . . . I had bills to pay. I had the house payment to make for Nora . . . I had all the bills. I gave her my gold chain for security. Over the phone, she told me that when she received the five hundred dollars back, she would know that it was over. Well, I wrote a check out that morning—April twenty-first—and sent it to her. She got it and she cashed it."

When Diane continued to call him, Lew asked fellow workers to say he wasn't there. "She would ask for other people at the post office and talk to them."

"About you?"

Lew shrugged. "I don't know if it was about me because I made a firm habit of not asking anybody what she had to say. I was afraid if I asked anyone what Diane had to say, she would interpret that as me caring and me wanting to know what she was doing—and I didn't. I didn't *care* what she was doing."

"Then the last time you saw her was when she drove off to Oregon at Easter?" Alton asked, knowing that the answer should be No.

"No. I saw her once more. She came back to give me my gold chain."

Alton had listened to the tapes Welch and Tracy had—Diane's recounting of a last bittersweet meeting with Lew: "He did ask if I would send it [the gold chain] back, and I said, 'I can't. I can't take it off,' 'cause he told me 'Don't you ever take that off,' and I went back to Chandler this last time to see him."

Lew remembered the surprise visit well. April 28—exactly a week since he'd told her it was over. Diane had borrowed a truck from another of her ex-lovers and she'd pulled up behind him on his route about ten in the morning. He'd had no warning she was in town.

"I sat in the jeep," Lew said as he lit another cigarette and stared at the smoke curling in the air. "She had on jeans and a kind of string bikini top. She stood outside—and I remember she was barefooted—and she had this package—this package she'd sent Express Mail and that I'd refused before. She showed me the contents of the package. There were pictures—some of them were of her new friends in Oregon. There were these dried up flowers—roses, other flowers—stuff like that. She told me that she'd smoked marijuana and snorted coke with Steve the night before."

Diane had tried very hard to put on a cheerful face. She would bleed to death before she allowed him to see her wounds, and she would smile as the last drop left her veins.

Lew knew how she worked and he was wary.

"I did not kiss her. I did not hug her. I didn't tell her I loved her. I didn't say anything."

Diane's taped statements to Welch and Tracy had been much more detailed and dramatic: "I just walked up and I said, 'Hello, Lew, how are you doing?' and he said, 'Just fine. What are you doing here, Diane?' and I said . . . 'This chain is not my chain. I don't care if it's $500 worth of gold or what, it doesn't mean a damn thing except the love that you put around my neck, and it's not mine. It's not mine to keep and if you don't want me, if you don't want me to be Lew's woman anymore, then I shouldn't have it,' and I said, 'I want you to have it back,' and I couldn't—I tried to take it off and I still couldn't. I said, 'I just can't do it. Would you please unhook it?' So he undid the clasp and then I took it out of his hand and I said, 'I'm going to do the same thing to you that you did to me.' I took it out of his hand and I put it around his neck and I said, 'You wear this 'cause I love you.'"

Lew winced as Welch paraphrased that scene for him, but he nodded his head. The story sounded just like Diane, only it wasn't true.

"I only said about twenty words to her the whole time she was there. I told her I wasn't going to Oregon. I told her I just didn't want to be a daddy. She talked *at* me—like always."

Out there on Lew's mail route, the morning was only half-spent. The sky was still blinding blue, and a couple of birds sang cheerily as if Diane's plans for a passionate reunion hadn't crumbled.

After Diane stopped talking and after Lew said the few words he intended to signify the absolute end of their relationship, the two of them stood—frozen in time—staring at each other. And then Lew was gone, caught up in a spume of road dust, continuing on his route.

One can picture Diane gazing after him. How naked her neck must have felt, vulnerable now that the heavy gold chain was gone. She had come so far to see Lew, and it was all over in twenty minutes of strained conversation.

"You didn't see her again?" Welch asked.

"Nope. When I got back to the post office, I found a rose in my box. Gami said Diane had been in. He said she was smiling when she told him she'd talked to me and everything was great between us. He asked her to leave because she was practically nude on top. She left that day at one o'clock and flew back to Oregon."

"You never heard from her again?"

Lew's hands trembled slightly. "Not until last week—she called to tell me about . . . about what happened."

"As far as you know, did Diane have any guns?"

"I saw a .22 rifle on the closet shelf of her apartment on West Ray . . . June of '82 was the first time I saw a .22 target pistol as she described it—and she told me it was Steve's. I didn't actually see the pistol—but I saw the case, and its weight made a dent on the waterbed."

"Any other guns?"

"Just before she went to Oregon, she had a .38 pistol *and* the target pistol in the back of her car. I actually saw both of them there."

"How long before she left?"

"The night before . . ."

Alton's face didn't change as he probed to assure himself that Lew had, indeed, seen the .22 in Diane's car. Lew described the red Nissan; he knew that car well. The guns—the .38 and the .22—had been in plain sight in the carpeted area just behind the rear seat.

Diane had told detectives that she offered it first to Lew "because Steve was threatening him," but Lew didn't want it. "Then I put it behind the seat in Steve's truck the week after that, before I left for Oregon."

Diane's reasoning was convoluted, to say the least. She had offered the missing .22 pistol to Lew so that he could protect himself from jealous reprisal from Steve Downs. How counter to her original intent for her to give the gun to the very man she'd characterized as so dangerous: Steve.

Lew had never seen Diane fire her guns but she had once challenged him to go target shooting. "I made a comment that, you know, I'm sure I was better than she was, and she said something like, 'Well, now—I'll just have to show you,' . . . but we never went shooting at all. She went hunting one time with a couple of guys from the post office—Jack Lenta and Bob Barton. At that time, she had—ahhhh—a shotgun."

Doug Welch asked, "Are you familiar with weapons, Lew?"

"Ahhhh—I was more familiar with them when I was in Vietnam. Since I have come back from Vietnam—which was in '69—I don't fool with guns. I don't own one, I don't ever intend to own one. It doesn't bother me that other people have them; I just have no use for guns. They're only good for one thing, and I left that back in Vietnam."

In Eugene Fred Hugi waited for the latest report from Alton and Welch. Lewiston fascinated him; Diane's diary had been so obsessively involved with Lew. Even the poems retrieved from her apartment had been about Lew, many of them masturbatory fantasies. Hugi could almost believe now that the love affair had been powerful enough—perhaps on both sides—that they might conspire to eliminate her children.

At 3:15 Oregon time, Hugi grabbed the phone beside him before the first ring finished its bleat.

"Lew was here all the time," Alton began. "We've got witnesses who saw him and his wife down at a local cocktail lounge all evening. Lew and Nora are both good witnesses—but they're scared—"

"Scared?"

Alton repeated the last thing Lew told them: "I think Diane shot her children—because of me—and I'm frightened. Not so much for myself—but for my wife. I'm probably not as afraid of her as Nora is, just because I'm a man and a little bit larger. I figure I can probably take a bullet and get to her before she could kill me."

"Welch asked him if he really felt Diane was capable of coming down here and doing physical harm to them—" Alton continued.

"... and?"

"And he says, 'I think if she gets away with this, if she is found not guilty of shooting her children . . . that there's a good chance that she would come down here and try to arrange something to "happen" to Nora, and then, at that point if I still didn't go back with her, I'm sure she would arrange for something to happen to me.'"

"He sounded that definite?"

"You bet he did. They're practically hiding out down here."

The case was beginning to fit together. Hugi felt even better when he learned that Lew had seen the .22 target pistol in Diane's car the night before she left for Oregon.

Fred Hugi saw that the picture Diane originally painted for detectives must now be erased and redone in entirely different colors and shades. There *had* been an affair; Diane hadn't imagined that. There had been a sizzling passionate affair for several months but, according to Lew Lewiston, the affair had ended the day Diane had driven off to Oregon. Hugi realized Diane had wagered everything she had that Lewiston would leave his wife and follow her and the kids. But Lew didn't want to be a daddy.

There it was—the motive—as distasteful as it might be.

CHAPTER 17

Grow in love and wisdom. Remember, nothing worthwhile comes easy. Don't give yourself and your love to anyone unless they are worthy. Then love with all your heart. And when the heart-break comes, don't try to chase it away. It can't be done. Accept the pain and learn from it . . . If you remain good, pure & honest, the good will finally come to you . . .

—Diane Downs, unmailed letter in her diary, to her surrogate daughter on the occasion of her first birthday: Mother's Day, May 8, 1983

Fred Hugi could practically recite Diane's first Oregon diary by heart. It was designed, he was sure, to be an advertisement for herself, and yet she was transparent in ways she did not realize. Combining the diary's day-by-day recounting of the month leading up to the shootings with information from Doug Welch, Paul Alton, Kurt Wuest, and Roy Pond, Hugi drew an amazingly clear picture of the woman he dealt with.

She rented the brown duplex but never really furnished it. She put the kids in school, but Willadene took care of them before and afterward, and when Diane picked them up, they usually stayed for supper at her mother's table.

One of the first things Diane did was have their television sets hooked up to pay TV. For three years Diane reportedly watched Music Television (MTV), the cable network that features visual interpretations of popular songs, many of them violent and overtly sexual. She loved MTV—so many of the songs reminded her of making love to Lew.

If Diane had a favorite song, it was Duran Duran's "Hungry Like the Wolf." She'd bought the Duran Duran tape "Rio" in February when Lew left Nora; they played it all the time. "Hungry Like the Wolf" is a sensual song of frustrated passion. In the video, the lover stalks the object of his desire—a half-woman/half-animal creature—through the jungle. The video ends with animal cries of orgasm.

Diane would always insist it was Cheryl's favorite video, not her own. "Cheryl is [sic] a physical person and the video for that one is very physical what with people crawling around in the bushes."

It was probably only a coincidence, Hugi mused, that the Duran-Duran tape was in the tape deck of the Nissan the night it was processed.

Still, he bought the album and pored over the printed lyrics. He underlined phrases and came up with repetitive themes, finally jotting down five phrases in his notebook:

(1) Self-centered—I, me
(2) In love
(3) Lost, Lonely, Afraid, Desperate
(4) Internal quandry, conflict, confusion, compelling emotions
(5) Take a chance, Dare to Do Someting Bold—Radical Action/ Consequences-Violence, Make the Decision.

It fit the state of mind he believed Diane Downs had been in before the shooting, but then half the songs on MTV seemed to be slated for that kind of personality.

Reading her diary, Hugi perceived that Diane had been genuinely astounded that Lew didn't follow her to Oregon, when Lew decided—according to reports from the investigators in Chandler—to cut his losses and run like hell. Diane obviously equated sex with love. And Lewiston had apparently given Diane mixed signals, which would be a foreign language to her. "Maybe" was clearly the same as "Yes" to her. So when Lew had said, "Maybe I could give it a try," that would have meant to her that he was absolutely, definitely, positively, coming to Oregon to live with her and the children.

Hugi talked to psychologists and sought out experts on human behavior; he read books, trying to pin down Diane's personality. In the end, it was Hugi—a layman at psychology—who would understand Diane best simply because he had immersed himself in her life completely. He had to know his opponent. Even so, just as the psychologists in Kentucky had discovered, Diane would never be irrevocably caught in any psychological slot. She defied categorizing.

In many ways, Diane—who resented men so much—reacted as a male would. Hugi believed Lew when he said he feared Diane might try to kill him and his wife. That was a male's reaction to sexual frustration. Hugi wondered if Diane might be an erotomaniac.

Erotomania. The term was newly coined, but the obsession was age old. Some males would rather kill the woman they wanted than let another man have her. They stalked, they waited, they flooded the love object with flowers and letters and phone calls. In his research Hugi found that it was an almost exclusively male disorder. Women might sink into depression, or, in extremis, kill *themselves,* but he found only one case where a female resorted to murder because she could not have the man she wanted.

Or was it possible that Diane—who seemed to consider her children as "part of me"—intended to kill them as a kind of sacrifice upon the altar of Lew's love? A symbolic suicide, but one that would let her stay alive for her reunion with him? Hugi—so used to rational thinking, lists, organization, and the firm parameters of the law—became more and more adept in analyzing theories behind what had seemed a completely mad crime.

He always felt that the gun was the most important missing link in the case. He asked psychologist friends what a woman like Diane might do with a gun. Would she allow it to get out of her control so that she could not get it back? Or would she need to know that it was somewhere, safely hidden, waiting for her to retrieve it?

Nobody could say. Not even the experts had run across anyone like Diane Downs.

Hugi kept at the diary, looking for something he might have missed before, and he read each new background report the detectives brought him with interest.

Diane's trail in Oregon was easy enough to follow; she'd only been in the area for eight weeks. Heather Plourd recalled that when she trained with Diane at the Eugene post office Diane mainly talked about a boyfriend in Arizona who would be moving to Oregon soon.

Diane had never been close to women. But detectives checking leads in Oregon found that Diane had "come on" immediately to the males in her new post office. What did that do to the erotomania theory? Lew *was* number one, but Diane apparently couldn't resist testing her powers at conquest of the male.

Within a week of her arrival in Oregon, she propositioned Cord Samuelson, one of the carrier instructors at the Eugene post office. He was tall, bearded, handsome—and married. They dated for happy hours after work for about three weeks. Samuelson learned that Diane liked punk rock, bourbon and coke, and sex. Even to Cord, she'd raved about Lew from the first day. "She expected him to move to Eugene too. She was confident of that . . . at first. After a few weeks, it looked like he wasn't coming, and she became bummed out."

Diane talked on and on of her love for Lew—but that didn't keep her from sleeping with Samuelson. Why? For sex? For comfort? To prove she could seduce him? From simple boredom? Or to drive away the fear nibbling at the edges of her mind, the old fear that she wasn't really pretty, that she was still such an ugly little girl that Lew would desert her?

Even as she was intimate with Cord Samuelson, Diane was flooding

Lew with mail from Oregon, telling him that Oregon was *their* paradise. But Lew never came.

Diane bragged in her diary/letters how popular she was. Hugi wondered if she had really expected Lew to read it someday. He thought so; Diane rarely seemed to do anything without device. She wrote that the guys at her new post office called her "Lady Di" and "Arizona" and "Beautiful Lady." A flower vendor had bowed and handed her a yellow carnation, saying, "You have the most beautiful eyes and sweet smile." Another day, she wrote that a cab driver pulled up beside her mail jeep and yelled at her to open her window. She did, and he handed her a lavender carnation, saying, "Have a nice day, mail lady."

See, Lew—I am beautiful and everyone loves me.

Hugi sensed Diane's accelerating panic as the diary continued, and she began to suspect that Lew might *not* come to her at all.

Diane's days fell into a dull pattern: work, childcare, and cleaning house. Cord pulled away from her, and other prospects in the Eugene office turned down her blatant approach. She began to call women she knew in Chandler, asking questions about Lew. Karen Batten told detectives that Diane sounded distraught when she learned Lew had moved back in with his wife.

The diary made it clear that Diane blamed Nora because she could not accept that Lew had just stopped loving her. Yes, Hugi thought, Nora Lewiston might well be in danger.

> *. . . Nobody else can fill your empty place in my bed, or heart.*
> *I guess I really have been bewitched . . . I wish you'd come around.*
> *Just before I left, you said you were too smart to fall for any of*
> *Nora's tricks. What happened? Good night babe. Sweet dreams.*

Diane's writings were a complete denial of reality. She seemed to believe devoutly that it was *she* who made all the sacrifices, she who had rebuilt her whole damn life for Lew. She ignored what he had told her on the phone. She simply blotted all ugly rejection out of her consciousness.

Fred Hugi could see how difficult it became for even Diane to rationalize—especially when the flowers she sent Lew by Express Mail came back: "Refused LSL."

The roses she sent had suffocated and died, trapped inside the unopened box. If Diane saw the rampant symbolism in that, she did not write of it in her diary. But she *kept* that box of flowers, carrying them back to Arizona to show Lew, and then leaving them in the trunk of the red Nissan. They were still there when Pex and Peckels processed the blood-soaked car.

Hugi read on, marveling at Diane's blind spots.

> *Are you playing games?*
> *Are you just pretending to go along with Nora so that when you get a divorce, it will look like it's on the up and up? Do you ache for me the same way I ache for you? Does your heart hurt, knowing the pain I feel?*

Of course, Lew never received the letter. It was only one of a growing number of desperate messages in her diary. She'd promised not to call or write.

Cord Samuelson told detectives that depression had settled over Diane like a smothering cloud. He'd seen her letters refused, and the long box of desiccated flowers returned. Suddenly, he said, Diane would seem to bounce back. But when she laughed, it was a near-hysterical laugh wrought tinny and hollow by anxiety.

The little diary in the spiral notebook had grown thick. It was all Lew. Or how men reacted to Diane's attractiveness or how Diane felt. Fred Hugi noted that Christie, Cheryl, and Danny were hardly ever mentioned, except to remind Lew that they were pining for him too. One Sunday, Diane wrote of driving her children to see the Sea Lion Caves, where the giant creatures play in natural rock caverns carved away by centuries of pounding from the Pacific Ocean. "I bought Danny a stuffed seal, and he wanted to send it to you. They all really like you."

How could her kids have "really liked" Lew? According to Lew, they hadn't known him. Christie, at least, apparently knew that her mother's moods depended on Lew.

Hugi grimaced as he read where again Diane pledged fidelity—to a man who had no wish to see her . . . ever.

"Don't doubt me, Babe—there's no one but you. I'll never let anyone touch me but you. You are my mate."

Diane had already let Cord Samuelson touch her; she didn't write that to Lew—not even in the diary. She occasionally referred to Samuelson, but only as a good friend she could talk to.

The diary entries seem written by a woman on an emotional seesaw. One day, she sounded suicidal; the next, she was full of ebullient plans.

On April 27, Diane told Lew/her diary that she had a good chance at an upgrade in the post office. "I was interested . . . from the beginning—but I was saving it for you." She got the job, a promotion to a 204-B and a transfer from Eugene to Cottage Grove. Her diary entry was bubbly and optimistic.

It would have been the next day that she flew to Arizona to give Lew his gold chain back. She was gone only twenty-four hours, according to airline schedules. Hugi jotted down the timetable, amazed at how swiftly this woman whirled and turned, flew a thousand miles in a day only to return the next.

When Diane got home, she rearranged the facts of the trip for her diary. As always, she continued to write her "letters" to Lew.

Friday: 4–29–83

I'm home!

Boy, what an exhausting trip. Oh, Lew, I'm so glad I went. I learned so much. I'm happy again, and so content.

You love me Lew—and that's all I needed to know . . . I know you love me.

I'm a little sad that she [Nora] has convinced you that the kids would be a burden because I know it would not be true. They are terribly independent and require very little care . . .

Hugi shook his head. Once again, Diane hadn't listened to a word Lew said.

Finally then, Diane was all alone with her kids. She had told Lew often that the kids practically took care of themselves. Spending night after night with them, she must have been surprised just how much care they needed.

The diary changed dramatically on May 5, 1983. Diane wrote her daily "letter" to Lew.

> *I guess today was my first day of total realization that I really do want to be somebody. I want to be bigger than Gami or Bobb Dunn [the postmaster in Chandler]. I want to look down on them . . . My dad's name pulls power—I'm a personable and intelligent person—and I'm female. Not to mention that I'm getting to know the right people . . . In time, Lew, I'll be someone that people know by name and sight.*

Well, she had that right, Hugi thought.

Reading the diary for too long at a stretch made Fred Hugi dizzy; it was wearying to track Diane's mercurial emotional swings. After many entries declaring her love, she finally blamed *Lew's* inability to make a decision for all their trouble, accusing him of deceit.

But he had *made* his choice. She could not accept it.

Diane was lonesome and sexually frustrated and sad. As the diary moved closer to the last entry, she was beginning to be angry. Hugi's careful reading caught the veering off, the passive-aggression.

> *Oh Lew, it saddens me to say this but I guess it's time to speak out loud—rather than keep it inside . . . it's all so beautiful. And I think about what a fool you are.*

And then it was May and she was still alone.

Jennifer's birthday coincided with Mother's Day. For that one day, Diane wrote to her last-born child instead of Lew, a long letter full of Victorianic advice, ending, "Goodbye Jennifer. I love you. I hope all good things come to you. Be good and kind. Always be fair. Never lie or cheat. Maybe one day, I will get to meet you (although I doubt it), and when I do, I truly hope I find you to be happy, healthy and fair."

After reading the diary so many times, Hugi was positive that it was bifurcated, as if the writer had come to some kind of a decision. The change took place suddenly on Wednesday, May 11, 1983. Christie, Cheryl, and Danny had become the focal point of each day's entry, almost as if Diane had just discovered her three children.

> *Well, sweetie—I love talking to you, but I have my own life here. I have 3 beautiful children that I love more than anyone else. I think I even love them more than you now. They stand by me—no matter what. Danny says he's my best buddy, and I'm his best buddy. He's always giving me kisses and hugs. Every morning, when I go to work, he waves and says, "Bye, Mom. Pick me up after work. I love you." He's beautiful—and always so happy.*
>
> *Christie & Cheryl are fantastic in their own right also. Chris is so smart. She always gets A's and she is always willing to help . . . [she] drew a picture . . . You'll never believe what the picture was of. You! She drew you, with me in your thought bubble. Pretty smart huh? She's so very bright. I'll bet she really does become a lawyer when she grows up. She's been saying it for almost a year now.*
>
> *And Cheryl—so full of bubbly energy. She's so agile. Always doing flips and acrobatics. I've considered getting her into gymnastics . . . But, she's just as sweet and cuddly as Danny. When I get to my mom's house after work, she always wants to sit on my lap and be close. And, she's the one that always thinks of giving me flowers . . .*

Diane thought she might even love her children more than she loved Lew! It seemed an entirely new concept for her—a sudden lightning bolt—well worthy of notation. She loved her children more than her lost lover!

Hugi shifted at his desk. The lady was protesting too much.

Diane wrote about the outings they took: to Hendricks Park to see the flowers, to the river, and to the beach.

Well, I've decided where I'm going to take the kids—back to the beach. They really enjoyed it last time, and I told them we'd go back in a month. I know it's only been 3 weeks, but why wait?

Hugi read on, and he felt a chill at a single—seemingly innocuous—notation in the spiral book:

Oh, I found a beautiful brass Unicorn in a store window. I'm going to buy it for Christie & Cheryl & Danny. Then I'll have it engraved. I know they'll like it.

Diane picked up the unicorn on May twelfth, and took it to be engraved, saying she needed it by May thirteenth. Why? It wasn't anybody's birthday. No special anniversary that Hugi could discern.

Friday, the thirteenth.

On Friday, Diane delivered the cake she'd made to the Cottage Grove post office, even though it was her day off. Then she drove her children to the Pacific Ocean.

The whole day was spelled out in the diary: gray and cloudy all morning, the sun finally breaking through at noon. They flew a kite, Cheryl discoverd a crab claw, Christie found some seashells, and Danny was content just to dig holes and watch the sea creep into the hollows.

Hugi couldn't find anything sinister there.

Diane wrote that she couldn't find a place to build a campfire, and everybody was hungry. They drove home, stopping here and there while she looked for the perfect spot. It was a long drive, and the kids were tired. Still, Diane didn't go back to the townhouse on Q Street; she headed for the banks of the McKenzie River. They didn't stay long; Cheryl had pleaded that she had to go to the bathroom.

Diane picked up her nephew Israel—she had promised to babysit—and, inexplicably, Diane had taken her exhausted children back to Hendricks Park. The trees there cast thick shadows in the twilight. They then returned to the river's bank where Diane had to lead the kids along in the gray light. The park and the river were dark and spooky after sunset. Diane kept driving from place to place, taking the kids home only when it was so dark she couldn't see and they were whining and ready for bed.

Fred Hugi stared from the diary to the photograph Jon Peckels had snapped of the unicorn on top of Diane's television set. Why had it been so damned important to have it embossed with the date: May 13, 1983? Was something supposed to happen on that day that would make the date the ultimate symbol? God—it was so obvious. The unicorn was to be a memorial to her three children who were supposed to die on May thirteenth.

Nothing bad had happened. If there was a plan, it had been aborted. Or simply abandoned for the moment.

If Diane had been capable of subtlety, the diary might have been a masterpiece. Hugi saw it as an alibi before the fact: Diane had been so anxious for the cops to know about it—and it was, in its second half, a paean to motherhood. Anybody reading it would believe Diane would die for her kids.

But then he read over a statement Roy Pond had taken from a woman who lived next door to Wes and Willadene Frederickson. In spite of all the people the investigators had talked to, there were few with viable information. Nobody outside the family had actually seen much of Diane's children. But this statement came from Sada Long, who had talked to Cheryl Downs the day before she died.

She described to Pond a little girl with long, taffy-colored hair who had walked up beside her as she knelt to weed her flowerbed. Long said she'd looked up at her—a skinny little girl, with a slightly nervous smile, who blurted out a string of seemingly disconnected sentences.

"I'm Cheryl. My grandma lives over there. My father's in Arizona. My mom and dad are divorced . . . I'm scared of my mom . . . We went to the park last night, and my mom jumped out from behind a tree and she scared me."

Ms. Long had sat back on her heels and studied the child.

"Maybe your mom was just playing hide-and-seek with you?"

"When she jumped out at me?"

"Yes—maybe it was just a game?"

"Yeah . . . I guess so . . . I like that T-shirt—I'd like one of those," Cheryl said.

"Well, go ask your grandma what size you wear. Maybe I can get one." The little girl skipped off, but she didn't come back.

Sada Long had wondered if she should say something to someone— perhaps talk to the grandparents. She hated to think of a child being so frightened, even if it was over a game. But then, she decided that she was being ridiculous.

She was horrified when she heard on the news that Cheryl was dead, murdered. Long felt it might be important to tell the authorities about her brief encounter with Cheryl. It was. No one else came forward to speak of Cheryl Downs's terror.

According to Diane's diary, the last week before the shooting had been deceptively normal. It sounded almost boring, Hugi thought. Diane wrote about doing the kids' laundry and scrubbing the bathroom on Sunday, May 15. She had taken the kids to the river again that night.

Wes and Willadene went to Seattle for a convention early in the week. They came back in time to help Kathy pack to fly to Oklahoma to rejoin her estranged husband.

Two days before the shooting, Diane damned Lew in her diary, but in the next breath she adored him. She would wait forever—if she had to. "I miss you Lew, and I love you very much. Where are you? Why aren't you here? We were so happy"

Christie brought home that little bouquet of tissue-paper roses—all the colors she could find, even purple—with stems of pipe cleaners, a present for her mom.

They went to the river almost every night. Diane wrote that the kids just loved it.

On May 18, Diane drove Kathy and Israel to the airport for their flight to Oklahoma where Kathy's husband attended Oklahoma State Technical College in Okmulgee.

Hugi noted that Diane kept close tabs on her menstrual cycle; that figured—she would have needed to know to the day when she ovulated, so she could get pregnant when she wanted. Her calendar showed her last period had begun Friday, April 22. Hugi checked with women advisors.

They explained that would make Diane premenstrual during the week before the shooting, with her flow due to start by Thursday or Friday—the nineteenth or twentieth.

On that last Thursday night, May 19, Diane did the dishes after supper, and then called an acquaintance, Barb Ebeling, in Arizona. She confided that she missed Lew's lovemaking more than usual. "Horny" was the word she used. Diane cried a little bit and raved to Barb about Lew's sexual prowess. "That man can come three times in one night!" Barb was embarrassed; she didn't know Diane that well, and she didn't feel comfortable talking about such intimate things.

Diane chatted away for about an hour, according to Barb. Hugi looked at his time chart. It would have to have been right after that when she called the kids and told them to get in the car, they were going for a ride . . .

He looked at the diary. There was no real entry for May 19 in Diane's letter-diary.

All she'd written was: "Thursday: 5–19–83."

The rest of the page was blank. The diary had ended.

CHAPTER 18

Eight days after the shooting, Doug Welch and Paul Alton talked with Stan Post in Chandler, Arizona. The distaste Diane had often evinced toward Post, her ex-husband's sometime-employee, longtime-friend appeared to be mutual.

Diane had told the detectives that Stan Post was "crazy about guns." Welch and Alton figured then that if anyone had kept track of the perambulations of the missing .22 Ruger, it might be Post. They were right. Post remembered guns the way some men recall treasured hunting dogs. He told them that he and Steve Downs had shared a home three years earlier with a man named Billy Proctor. The semi-automatic .22 had been Proctor's; Post himself had fired between two and three thousand rounds from that very gun.

"Where's the gun now?" Welch asked.

Post flushed. "Steve took it from Proctor. As far as I know, Steve had it for some time, but then somebody swiped it from Steve. I don't know who has it."

Alton held out two colored photos of a Ruger with a six-inch barrel.

"That looks identical to Billy Proctor's gun," Post said. "It's possible though that Billy's gun may have had adjustable rear sights, and this one doesn't.

"Three years ago," Post continued, "me and Mike Hickle went on a hunting trip out at 96 and the Freeman Ranch. I shot a porcupine that must have weighed in at maybe thirty-five pounds . . . had to shoot him twenty times to get him out of the tree. I was using Billy Proctor's .22 Ruger."

The search for the moldering porcupine took Paul Alton and Doug Welch farther into the desert than they had any desire to go—way out to the 96 Ranch near Florence, Arizona. With Chandler officers they headed southeast in a four-wheel-drive rig. The roads grew narrower and more rutted, and finally, there was no road. They drove on for miles over the desert itself. The heat was relentless. The Chandler detectives were well dressed for desert prowling in tough boots and snake leggings. Alton and Welch wore jeans and light running shoes. They had sunglasses, but no hats. When they could drive no further, they got out and walked. Mike Hickle walked in front of the pick-up as a scout. Suddenly, he shouted, "Snake!"

It was a rattlesnake—close to six feet long. Welch, who is pathologically afraid of snakes, had just crawled down out of the rig. "I jumped straight up. They told me I didn't even bend my knees."

The Arizona cops guffawed. Stan Post pegged the rattler with the .45 he was carrying, and it flopped, decapitated, in the sand, its blood already turning dark in the heat.

They hiked past more snakes, scorpions, and tarantulas, through stinging cactus under unforgiving skies, until they could no longer see the truck. They found no porcupine.

On two trips to Arizona, Oregon detectives would scour the desert.

They never found the bullet-riddled porcupine, not even from the bird's-eye view of a helicopter. There was nothing but hardscrabble sand, rock, vegetation apparently growing without moisture, and lean herds of range cattle.

Stan Post said he'd shot the .22 in other areas around Chandler, in a gravel pit, at other unofficial shooting ranges, "and there might be some empty shell casings in my old pick-up truck. I fired the Ruger a lot while I was standing alongside it with the door open. That gun ejected to the right, and I'm positive I saw a bunch of casings in the truck before I sold it."

"You *sold* it?" Welch's voice reflected his disappointment. A bunch of casings as precious as diamonds to the investigation might still be nestling somewhere inside a truck that had been sold.

"Yeah. I sold it in October, 1981. A black Ford Ranger pick-up, three-quarter ton."

Computer checks showed that the vehicle had been purchased by a Mexican national who lived in Phoenix. He had sold it to a Jesse Pinon who resided on Phoenix's Gila Indian Reservation. Chandler detectives went up to Phoenix to see if they could trace the truck. But two years had passed. The truck had been sold, resold; the last owner of record had taken it with him to Mexico. Nobody knew for sure where he was.

That news wasn't nearly as disappointing to Fred Hugi as it might have been. Chuck Vaughn had just called him with astoundingly good news. Vaughn had discovered a most curious match during ballistics tests. Hugi excitedly marked his notes of the conversation with seven red stars and heavy underlining, ending "No doubt!"

Vaughn and Jim Pex had discovered that some of the cartridges Dick Tracy had removed from the .22 Glenfield rifle in Diane's bedroom closet had, at one time, been worked through the action of the very gun that fired the bullets into Christie, Cheryl, and Danny!

The tool marks left by the extractor were microscopically identical— the same marks on cartridges in Diane's possession as those on the casings found next to the river! The .22 rifle wasn't the death weapon, but the cartridges inside had once been in the clip of the missing Ruger!

Hugi was elated. This ballistics finding ruled out the possibility of a random shooting; it would take great suspension of disbelief to think a stranger could have gained access to *both* Diane's rifle and the Ruger pistol. What was she going to say? That somebody had sneaked into her apartment and put those cartridges in her rifle—cartridges that had been worked through the action of the death gun?

The .22 rounds fit both weapons. The tool marks showed that the cartridges had been mechanically manipulated through the receiver of the same weapon. Not fired—only loaded, unloaded. Had someone changed his—or her—mind and returned the cartridges to the chamber where they'd been originally? Or had it been an aimless thing? Someone sitting on a couch—indecisive maybe—or only bored—playing with a gun, unaware that minute tool marks were being stamped into the unfired cartridges?

Fred Hugi felt he had a breakthrough in physical evidence, enough to more than make up for the disappointing news from Arizona. But Vaughn cautioned the assistant DA that explaining the findings to a jury would be difficult because photographs wouldn't really show the three dimensional aspects of the marks left by the extractor and ejector of the Ruger. Pex and Vaughn and Hugi might see those marks as clear as neon, but would a lay jury? Even so, Hugi was still up. The case had begun, finally, to unfold in an orderly way.

As for locating an actual slug fired from the Downs .22 Ruger, the calls coming up nightly from Chandler weren't optimistic. There *was* one other chance to find a slug or casing from the elusive gun: the bullet Diane had fired through the bathroom floor of her trailer in her hysteria the previous September.

Alton called Hugi to report that all the trailer movers and crews had laid off for the long Memorial Day weekend. "The soonest they can move the trailer is Tuesday—and it's going to cost a thousand dollars . . . or we can have the trailer jacked up three feet off the sand by another company for four or five hundred dollars, but they won't work until Tuesday either. Either way, somebody has to crawl under it to disconnect plumbing and other pipes in thirty or forty spots, and that would disturb what might be under there."

Hugi assured him that DA Horton had OK'd the funds to move Diane's trailer. "He said, 'Go for it!'"

"We may just crawl under—if we can find somebody to spray bug killer under there," Alton said. "The bugs down here can kill you."

As it turned out, they crawled under without benefit of an insect spraying. Waiting until it was safe would have delayed them into the next week too; freshly sprayed, the stuff was potent enough to kill them as well as the bugs.

On May 28, Welch and Alton, accompanied by Chandler officers Bobby Harris, Ed Sweitzer, and Reed Honea, picked up Steve Downs and headed for Diane's deserted trailer. A few miles outside of town the grandly constructed gateway of the Sunshine Valley Mobile Home Park appeared. Beyond it, an oasis of fenced land with each space occupied.

18250 Arizona Avenue—Sunshine Valley—was meticulously maintained. The detectives drove along the promenade of towering palm trees, past the club house and pool. Park residents gazed curiously at the two-car convoy of police units.

Each handkerchief-sized yard was a segment of a giant mosaic; the grassless lawns with their raked rock chips—rose, purple, gray, magenta. Every yard had its own orange tree; bougainvillea spilled crimson over the fences. Terra cotta planters shaped like burros and wheelbarrows and Mexican sombreros abounded—enough to stock a roadside stand.

Diane's mobile home was in the very last row of the park: Space 363. Here the tiny yards were more utilitarian; children's trikes and wagons lay wherever they'd been dropped. The trailers were nice enough, but they hadn't been fancied up with awnings and patio furniture.

The mobile home no longer belonged to Diane; when she'd defaulted on the payments, the manufacturers had repossessed the unit, much the worse for fire damage and neglect. They had yet to repair it.

There was an eerie quiet inside. Walls and floors bore scars left by firefighters' axes, shards of melted insulation hung down from the gutted ceiling, the Naugahyde arms of the living-room furniture oozed charred stuffing. A thick layer of desert dust and ash clung to everything. The gutted back wall was protected by heavy plastic, which hung limply in the no-wind-at-all of a baking afternoon.

Doug Welch gazed along the blackened hallway, his imagination catching him unaware. Danny, who probably would never run again, had raced through this hall and bounced off the waterbed. This was the trailer where Diane said the Four Musketeers had enjoyed a fun-filled summer only last year. There was no sense of fun here now, only bleakness.

The temperature was well over a hundred degrees.

Welch glanced down at a book that lay where someone had dropped it, its pages sooty: *Understanding Emotions.*

Steve Downs led them to the bathroom and pointed out the single hole barely discernible in the patterned vinyl floor. Welch got down on his hands and knees to look for the slug's casing.

"Don't bother," Downs said. "That wall between the bathroom and master bedroom is new. The old one was torn out after the fire."

Welch felt his skin crawl. That meant they had to go for the bullet *underneath* the trailer, and it might not even be here at all. Being out in the desert in the sunshine had been bad enough, but at least he could *see* snakes and crawly things out there.

They pulled away the metal skirting beneath the mobile home, exposing the area beneath the flooring. Something alive scuttled away from the sudden blast of sunlight. Welch shrugged on coveralls before he crawled beneath the trailer, another layer to trap the heat—but hopefully block snakes. His face and hands were exposed as he slid, belly up, toward the spot beneath the bathroom floor.

Paul Alton poked a white wire coat hanger through the hole in the floor. Welch guided the metal probe through a layer of insulation until it touched the ground. With any kind of luck, that slug would still be in the sand where the coat hanger pointed.

Nothing.

There was a layer of debris under the trailer—nuts and bolts, nails, staples, charred wood, and insulation. The Chandler cops scraped it out tenderly; Welch sifted all of it through a screen on the chance a .22 slug might appear.

It did not.

Just before six, they gave up. Five hours of digging, sifting, probing, with no luck at all. Alton and Welch returned to the Holiday Inn. They ventured out to the pool to cool off and immediately felt curious stares. Their faces, necks and hands were sunburned—the rest of them was white as sowbelly. Welch's fair, freckled complexion had begun to blister. The next day was Memorial Day, but they had no plans for the holiday beyond digging in the dusky space beneath #363.

They began again at 7:00 A.M.

It was 115 degrees outside the trailer; beneath it, the heat telescoped in on itself and then expanded—five, ten, more degrees.

Perspiration made mud of the dust on their faces, and each breath was agonizing. Cobwebs drifted down and covered their noses, eyes, mouths. Something skittered across Welch's face, something with many feet. He shuddered, but stayed put.

"Sifting through the sand in the dark down there, I remembered the rattler in the desert. I had goosebumps underneath my sunburn blisters." Welch grins. "For some damned reason, I think of being under that trailer whenever I watch *Miami Vice*. The trouble with real police work is there's no music.

"I figured we'd try one more angle. I twisted the white coat hanger until it formed a perfectly straight probe, and I let it find its own direction through the floor—like a Ouija board—through that particle board until it touched the sand. It was only two inches away from where we'd been the day before. Paul held it there.

"We'd been taking turns outside where we could stand upright and pour water over our heads. The air tasted like hot straw."

Alton eased one more chunk of clay from the shadowed ground. It felt too heavy to be pure clay. Hell, it was probably some old trailer part they'd missed when they'd scraped. Sliding out on his stomach, Alton cradled the heavy chunk of dirt carefully against his chest.

They poured water from a thermos over the lump of soil. A glint of metal appeared. They passed a metal detector over it; it *was* metal.

Lead.

The .22 slug Diane had fired in a fit of hysterical rage eight months before lay in the palm of Paul Alton's hand. They jumped up and down like crazy desert prospectors, hooting and hollering. It was a copper-jacketed slug like some of the bullets in Oregon.

But this bullet had gone through the particle board trailer floor, impacting with the hard sand beneath. It was mashed and distorted. The pH factor of the desert—acid—had eroded the copper and eaten even into the signature lands and grooves, the striations that Jim Pex needed for a match.

Alton wrapped the .22 slug in blue tissue paper and carried it with him constantly. If enough markings remained on the bullet that had lain in the hot darkness under Diane's trailer, and if they should prove to be identical to those on the bullets removed from her children's bodies, it would be irrefutable proof that the same gun had fired all the slugs.

He called Hugi immediately. "We've got it! The slug under the trailer. I'm holding it in my hand right now!"

Alton explained it was still covered with about five layers of crystalline clay. He would leave it undisturbed, treat it like a precious gem until he could get it back to Oregon.

If it matched, Fred Hugi knew they would have their probable cause to arrest Diane. Alone, the extractor markings on the bullets from her closet might be iffy—too difficult to explain to a jury. But combine what they already knew with the right bullet from Chandler and they were home free!

Their mood was good, but to be safe, Welch and Alton kept searching for little .22 casings, and they found hundreds of various shooting ranges around Chandler. They bagged everything to carry back to the Oregon State Police Crime Lab. Literally clinking and clanking as they walked, they had to explain themselves to security guards at Sky Harbor Airport in Phoenix. They showed all of the voluminous metal would-be evidence to the security chief at Sky Harbor and were passed through.

Louis Hince met them at the Eugene airport. The slugs and casings were driven immediately to the Oregon State Police Crime Lab. The "trailer slug" was very damaged. The other slugs and casings were as valuable as a lottery stub. One in a million might pay off.

Fred Hugi waited to hear the lab results like an expectant father.

> *Exhibit #45*—One plastic vial enclosing one damaged copper-washed .22 caliber bullet wrapped in blue tissue paper. (The bullet found under Diane's trailer.) The total weight of this bullet is 36 grains. Microscopic examination reveals approximately one half of the lands and groove impressions are destroyed. Microscopic comparison of this bullet to bullets in Exhibits 1, 2, and 7 (the bullets retrieved from the victims) reveals the class characteristics are similar. Due to the type of bullet (copper-washed) and subsequent damage, the writer is

unable to effect a match. However, it is the writer's opinion that this bullet *cannot be excluded* from having been fired through the barrel of the same weapon as the bullets in Exhibits 1, 2, and 7.

Close but no cigar. Pex was saying that the battered bullet might well have been fired from the gun that shot Cheryl, Christie, and Danny, but that he could not say absolutely that it had.

None of the other possibles even came close.

"Some criminalists would say 'yes' to the .22 bullet from under the trailer. Others waffled on it. It wasn't safe to gamble. .22s are just plain hard to call," Alton explains, with passage of time dulling his disappointment.

On June 1, twelve days after the shooting, Fred Hugi remembered Diane saying to him, "I'm getting stronger and stronger and stronger."

She was, and she didn't even know it yet; they had just lost the best piece of evidence they had going.

"Let's put a chink in her armor," Paul Alton suggested at the next early morning meeting. "She doesn't know the bullet was in such bad shape. We tell her that it *did* match—she'll spill her guts."

They considered it, tossing it around. But that was what cops did in the old days—no more. They'd find another way. The case was still young.

Any day now, they could get lucky. They had no way of knowing then that luck would be elusive—if not nonexistent.

CHAPTER 19

By June 1, 1983, Kathy and her baby Israel had moved from Wes and Willadene's house, but Diane's youngest brother Paul had moved back home. He had been living with one of Wes's brothers who died suddenly, leaving Paul $25,000 so that he might go to college.

Diane was almost twenty-eight, but in her father's house she had to obey as if she were still a teenager. She couldn't drink; she couldn't date. She continued to tape her thoughts, backing up her cassettes with written comments in a ledger book. She was angry in both voice and script. She had cooperated with the detectives, she'd trusted Dick Tracy and Doug Welch—and now they didn't believe her. She suspected they were trying to lead her into some bizarre admission.

Diane balked now when the investigators asked for her help. She would not give her consent for minor surgery to remove bullet fragments from Christie's shoulder, nor would she allow the children's wounds to be photographed.

They did it anyway. Diane blew up at Dick Tracy. Wes Frederickson, however, assured Tracy that Diane was anxious to take a lie detector test. Diane was served with a grand jury subpoena one afternoon while she visited Danny and learned that her polygraph exam had been scheduled for the same day. They were really piling it on her, she thought bitterly.

The grand jury system dates back to twelfth-century English law, and it is the only legal process in America still held in secret. Often under fire as antiquated and unfair—a tool designed to favor the prosecutor—the grand jury system allows selected members of the lay public to meet and decide if a suspect should be indicted. The judge's role is minimal—he is there only to maintain order. No defense attorneys or reporters are present at the proceedings. (Witnesses may, however, request permission to leave the room to consult with attorneys.) Only the prosecuting attorney and the witnesses—all of whom are sworn to secrecy—are allowed in the room. There are twenty-three members in federal grand juries; in Oregon, there are seven.

The Lane County grand jury met first to discuss the Downs case in late May, 1983, and it would continue to meet—chaired by a Eugene homemaker, Claudia Langan—once or twice a month for a much longer time than anyone could ever have expected. Witnesses passed into the secret chamber, testified, and were dismissed. No one knew what they said there.

When Wes heard about Diane's subpoena to the grand jury, he felt it was high time she got herself an attorney. A minister recommended Jim Jagger, a man active in church activities. James Cloyd Jagger was thirty-eight and the father of two children close to the ages of Diane's children. A clever, competent attorney, he had practiced law years longer than Fred Hugi. He had been a deputy prosecutor in both Coos and Lane counties and in private practice since 1975.

Jim Jagger is either friendly and open by nature—totally approachable—or he chooses to appear that way. There is a puckish air about Jim Jagger, a mischievous quality as if he knows secrets no one else is privy to. His suits are off the rack, his brown hair is thick and constantly tousled. He smiles a great deal. He misses nothing. In the courtroom he is as enthusiastic as a television preacher. His acquittal record is good.

Diane did not appear immediately before the grand jury, nor would she for many months. For a victim to refuse to appear before the grand jury is almost unheard of. How can a prosecutor be expected to act on the victim's behalf if she will not testify to her loss in grand jury? DA Pat Horton asked Jim Jagger about Diane's refusal to appear and Jagger answered obliquely. "You know who shot the kids, and I know who shot the kids."

Jagger also decreed there would be no lie detector test at the county's pleasure. Instead, he arranged a private polygraph session. Diane flunked it. No one knew.

Jagger had immediately discerned a recklessness in his client, a seeming inability to shut her mouth—even when talking meant danger for her. He urged her to consult with him before she gave statements to detectives or to the media. She promised she would but she hated to take advice, particularly from a man.

Jagger wrote to McKenzie–Willamette Hospital: "This letter is to serve as a demand on behalf of Ms. Downs that law enforcement agencies and Children's Services Division . . . not have access to Ms. Downs, or her room, or the room(s) of her children, and that such parties, including hospital personnel, immediately cease and refrain from any interrogation or questioning of Ms. Downs' minor children, and/or Ms. Downs, as to any events leading to their injuries."

The gloves were off. Elizabeth Diane Downs, assisted by her attorney, was telling the cops to leave her children alone.

When the story hit the early edition of the *Register-Guard* on June 3, the public realized for the first time that Diane Downs—the mother herself—might be a suspect. Most were shocked; many were downright indignant—and vocal in their criticism of the authorities' insensitivity.

Diane visited Christie and Danny constantly, snuggling close to Christie, whispering. Deputy George Hurrey overheard snatches of conversation. Christie was beginning to speak—haltingly—but he could understand her. On June 10, he watched as Christie smiled cautiously at her mother and said, "Paula was here today but I didn't talk about nothing."

There was an ugly scene between Diane and George Hurrey; she'd been upset when Danny was moved, and more so when Christie was not allowed to phone him. Fred Hugi had ordered the phone removed; he didn't want to risk the chance that someone might threaten Christie over the phone.

When Hurrey told Diane that Christie could not make calls, Diane whirled toward Christie. "These heartless bastards won't let you talk to Danny . . . You're just a prisoner of war. I promise you, Christie. I'll get them. I'll get every one of them!"

Christie, mute again, stared back at her. Hurrey stepped between Diane and Christie; and Diane dared him to hit her.

There was the ever-present danger that Danny's and Christie's memories might be contaminated. Trauma and shock had done enough damage already. No one must be allowed to alter what they still remembered.

Diane's animosity toward Paula Krogdahl grew. The enmity was returned, although Paula kept her feelings hidden.

Christie Downs knew now that her sister was dead and that her brother was hurt—but she didn't talk about it. Sometimes she cried, but she couldn't explain her feelings. Her mother came to see her every day, but the guards were always there too and they wouldn't let her shut the door and talk to her alone.

One day her mother brought in the shiny unicorn—the one she'd brought home for them. When? It seemed like a long, long, time ago. Anyway, her mother put it on the bed with her and showed her where it said their names and "I love you, Mom" on it. Her mother told her that unicorns never died, and that the unicorn belonged to Cheryl now "so that means that Cheryl will never die."

It was awfully confusing for Christie. Cheryl wasn't a unicorn. Cheryl was dead. Didn't her mother remember that?

Mostly, Christie wanted to sleep. She didn't want to talk, and she didn't want to remember. She liked John Tracy, her speech therapist, but it felt safer somehow just to drift off. John kept waking her up.

In early June, Diane was readmitted to the McKenzie–Willamette Hospital for surgery on her injured arm. Jagger had stipulated there be no investigators present in her room and/or the operating room.

She was soon comatose under an anesthetic dose of sodium pentathol. She said nothing. Indeed, if she *had* said something during the operation on her arm, it would have presented her surgeon with a delicate ethical problem, another facet of privileged communication.

A single bullet had shattered her left radius. Dr. Carter removed a large blood clot and minute pieces of the slug. The bone fragments were drawn into place and held firm with a metal plate. Carter grafted a thin slice of bone he'd shaved from Diane's left hip to her arm where the bone had been blown completely away.

Diane remained in the hospital for four days, her injured arm encased in a heavy cast. She learned the day after surgery that Christie and Danny had been removed from her custody. At Hugi's request, Lane County judge Greg Foote signed an emergency protective order placing both Christie and Danny under the temporary care of the Oregon State Children's Services Division. Hugi had had no other choice; Diane had said she was going to take her children out of the hospital and nobody was going to stop her.

"Dr. Miller and Dr. Wilhite informed me. When I woke up in the recovery room, they told me they wanted me to know about it before I saw it on TV. They said, 'We just want you to know you can see Christie whenever you like,' as if they had the right to give me permission to see my own child! Jim [Jagger] explained that the DA said I was hindering the investigation."

One evening, Jim Jagger and his associate Lauren Holland came to McKenzie–Willamette to see Christie. When sheriff's deputies and nurses balked, there was a disturbance—almost a scuffle—and in the furor, Holland spent ten minutes alone with Christie before she was ushered out.

Diane told her tape recorder: "I dreamed about the shooting. I had the impression that he knew me."

"... *the impression that he knew me ...*"

Diane whispered to her tape recorder that she thought maybe the gunman had recognized her. She told no one else. Not even Jim Jagger.

As Diane underwent surgery in the McKenzie–Willamette Hospital, Kurt Wuest was at Sacred Heart Hospital talking to Danny Downs. Danny knew Kurt well, and he was used to seeing him around. Wuest had no kids of his own; Danny Downs got to him.

"He was so smart—so very, very extremely smart. He was a real heartbreaker for me. One time, he was sitting in his wheelchair and he looked at me, impatient and confused, and he said, 'How come I can't get up? I wanta get up.' And I didn't know what to tell him, so I didn't say anything."

They played games together, and one of the games made Wuest and everyone in the playroom turn pale. "Danny pointed his finger at me, as if it was a gun. Then he goes, 'Psshhow! You're a bad boy!' like he was firing at me."

Wuest talked to Danny in the third-floor playroom as Danny's nurse, Janet Jones, sat beside the little boy. Wuest spoke in a casual, soft voice—deliberately interspersing unrelated topics with the questions that were vitally important.

"Do you remember going to see some horses a little while ago?"

"Yeah."

"Did you go in the car?"

"Yeah."

"Where did you sit?"

"Back seat."

And then the harder questions, painfully, tediously asked.

"Danny, do you know how you got hurt?"

(No answer.)

"Did you see Christie get hurt?"

"Yeah ... next to her."

"Was it in the car?"

"Yeah."

"Did she cry?"

"No."

"How did she get hurt?"

(No answer.)

"Did your mom get hurt?"

"Yeah."

"How?"

"Cat did it."

"Were you in the back seat when you went out in the country?"

"Isn't any more country."

"Who was driving?"

"Aunt Kathy."

"Did you see how Christie got hurt?"

"Somebody poked her."

"Who?"

"I don't know."

"Was it somebody you know?"

(No answer.)

"Where did Christie get hurt?"

(No answer.)

"In the leg?"

"No."

"In the stomach?"

"No."

"In the arm?"

"In the arm."

And then Danny became very still, his face a blank mask as he looked into the distance.

"Are you afraid to talk about this, Danny?"

"Yes."

Wuest immediately stopped questioning Danny. The usually rambunctious little boy had grown so still, and his eyes were filled with tears. Janet Jones moved to take Danny back to his room and he said softly, "Not supposed to answer . . . not supposed to answer."

Danny Downs was three years old and someone had shot him in the back. It was doubtful that a toddler, not much more than a baby, would ever be accepted as a witness in a murder trial. But Kurt Wuest saw something haunted in Danny's eyes.

Later, Danny was sitting at the window staring down at a screeching ambulance below.

Suddenly he turned to his nurse and asked, "Who shot me?"

"I don't know, Danny. *Who?*"

"That man . . ."

"What man? Was it outside or in a car?"

"That man—Jack."

"Did you know him before?"

"That man was mean to me."

"What man?"

"That man Jack . . ."

"Who shot you, Danny?"

"Jack—like Jack in the Beanstalk . . ."

Did "Jack" mean something to Danny? Or was truth and fantasy as conjoined in his young mind as it is in most toddlers'?

"It's obvious to me they suspect my daughter," Wes Frederickson told the *Springfield News.* "Every time she moves and breathes, they move and breathe with her. I believe in my daughter's innocence. My daughter loves those children. I do not believe that she did—or that she could—kill those children."

Diane demanded, and got, a hearing on June 6 to question the State's right to remove her children from her custody. As in all legal maneuverings, there were pluses and minuses in Hugi's move to place Christie and Danny under protection of CSD. The juvenile court proceedings gave Diane a forum, and like all legal proceedings, the paperwork was the easy part. It would have to be backed up with hard evidence at a fact-finding hearing or a trial later. For the State, the advantage of juvenile court proceedings is that a judge alone presides and the standard of proof is a preponderance of evidence, not proof beyond a reasonable doubt. A judge would tend to err—if at all—on the side of the children.

The disadvantage of the juvenile court hearing for the State is that the defense is entitled to rights of discovery. They can legally seek any evidence that the State and sheriff's office might have. In a criminal case, such discovery would not be handed over until the suspect's arraignment on indictment.

Jim Jagger could now tailor Diane's defense to the evidence and exploit any holes in the State's case. And there were still plenty of holes. "Like all legal proceedings," Hugi comments. "It was easy to start—but like a tiger by the tail, impossible to turn loose of gracefully. This proceeding might be used to call us out before we were ready."

If Jagger chose, he could have *two* trials, call all the witnesses who might appear in a later murder trial to the juvenile hearing where all he had at stake was the custody of the children. Indeed, he could call Christie Downs to the stand.

Up until June 6, 1983, Diane Downs was an unknown quantity to the public. Willadene had given a brief press conference, Wes had been quoted often, but Diane had appeared only in old photographs reproduced on local front pages. In the television footage filmed that June day, Diane approaches the juvenile hearing clinging tightly to Willadene's arm. She limps slightly, and her left arm is encased in plaster and supported by a navy blue sling. Glancing sideways she realizes she is being filmed by the television cameras. In the space of a heartbeat, her limp becomes exaggerated. There was no reason for her to limp. There would have been miniscule, if any, pain from the hip shaved for the bone transplant, but on that day Diane limped. As the cameras commit her every move to film, Diane gulps noticeably, cuts her eyes again toward the lens, and then she smiles—as if she has just been given a wonderful surprise. Her limp becomes even more pronounced. The cameras follow a beautiful—almost fragile—woman in a modest blue ruffled dress until she disappears.

Whatever else might prove to be true or untrue about Diane's life, it is apparent that she has, in this very instant on videotape, discovered the dazzling power of the television camera. And the camera clearly loves Diane; it traces her every movement lovingly.

It is as if Diane had waited her whole life for this moment.

Diane lost at the custody hearing; she would hereafter have to "make appointments to see my own children." But she'd won the media. The cameras had warmed her, and she could hardly wait to get home and tell her diary about it.

Elizabeth Diane Downs had become the darling of the Northwest media; she loved them all back, and the honeymoon would last for a long, long, time. Only Eugene at first, but then Portland and Seattle, and Washington, D.C., and Los Angeles, and New York. All those cameras, and microphones, and notebooks. How she had longed for someone to listen to her views. At last, she had an audience.

Diane no longer shared information with the detectives. They hated her. Paula Krogdahl hated her. Susan Staffel, the kids' caseworker for the Children's Services Division, hated her.

"Stupid women. Stupid liars. I have met some of the lyingest people since I've come to this state, and they're sheriffs and legal people."

Henceforth, if Diane had something she wanted to say, she would tell it to the press.

To hell with the detectives.

Diane didn't even mention Fred Hugi in her sweeping denunciation of her tormentors. She had forgotten him—if he'd ever registered at all. She had no idea he stalked her more relentlessly than any of them.

CHAPTER 20

"Look," Fred Hugi reminded the disgruntled group of cops and investigators. "This isn't an organized army we're fighting; it's one young woman. Only one woman against all of us. She's bound to make some mistakes."

Inside, he was not nearly as sure, thinking, "How incongruous . . . What has happened to our legal system that would allow a mother to drive her kids out on a lonely road, shoot hell out of them, pitch the gun, drive them to the hospital—and get away with it. How can such a thing happen?"

The daily meetings had disintegrated after two weeks. The cops were angry because all Hugi had managed to do was get a juvenile court order. They were sure they had enough for a murder charge, and he was sick and tired of nagging them, nagging the crime lab, of barking out orders when he knew his list of supporters grew shorter by the day.

This huge joint meeting in Harris Hall, adjoining the courthouse, was on semi-neutral territory. For hours, they went over everything they'd come up with so far.

It was enough to arrest Diane, but in Fred Hugi's opinion it wasn't enough to *convict* her.

Although a lot of people in Lane County believed that a bushy-haired stranger had shot the Downs family, the deluge of tips coming into Sheriff Burks's department slowed to a trickle. Detective Roy Pond handled most of them. Pond canvassed each home in the Mohawk Road area with little success. He worked his eight-hour shift at the hospital guarding the victims and then he went out mornings, evenings, and nights—so that he wouldn't miss anyone. He had made at least one hundred fifty contacts, with only slight information coming out of them.

He had perhaps thirty to thirty-five written reports on possible clues or sightings from people who had theories on where the detectives should look for the death weapon. Some citizens called to suggest the shooting might have happened somewhere else—in the Marcola Valley, for instance. They told Pond to look in creeks, trees, culverts, wells. Searchers had already tried all those spots. Some were blunt: "You don't need to look any farther. Check on *her* and her boyfriend." Some tips came from psychics and proved to be about as valuable as a look in a cracked crystal ball.

Many of the tips had been generated by Wes Frederickson himself, who was vocal in his criticism of the Lane County Sheriff's Office. Frederickson's input was followed up along with the rest of the leads offered by citizens of Lane County.

Heather Plourd's best guess of Diane's departure time on May 19 was 9:45 P.M. Determination of the exact time the Downs family left the Plourds' was vital to the investigation. Detectives had to account for the location of the family from the moment they left Heather's trailer until

Diane called for help at the McKenzie–Willamette Hospital twelve and a half miles away just before 10:30 P.M.

Dolores Holland, who lived in the mobile home next door to the Plourds, gave a much more precise departure time: 9:40. Holland, a department manager at Albertson's supermarkets, had been reading a romance novel in her living room. She'd heard the car door slam outside, and the sound of tires backing out of the Plourds' driveway.

"I finished the last few pages of the book, and I looked at the clock to set the time on the coffeepot for morning. It was ten minutes to ten then. The clock's accurate—it's my husband's 'pet clock.'"

One of Wes Frederickson's best tips seemed to correlate with that time period. Basil Wilson's property abutted the Fredericksons' yard, although Wes and Wilson weren't very well acquainted. Wilson had seen something peculiar on the night of May 19. Basil Wilson was very active in the Springfield Country Club. The country club's buildings, grounds, and golf course lay between Marcola Road and Sunderman Road, with its entrance off Marcola. Diane would have passed the club's grounds three times on the night of May 19. First, she would have driven by its southern boundaries both going to and coming from Heather's trailer on Sunderman Road. Next, when she exited Sunderman Road after the visit, she turned away from Springfield and headed toward Marcola. She then would have passed the entrance to the country club. When Wes heard Basil Wilson's story, he was particularly impressed, given the proximity of the club to the shooting site.

On the night of May 19, there had been a board meeting at the country club from 7:00 to 9:30. Wilson remembered an odd duck who appeared at the club about nine. That Thursday was also "Calcutta Night" at the Springfield Country Club, but the man who bumbled in was certainly neither a member nor a guest.

Wilson had been sitting with the club's assistant golf pro when he looked up to see a shabbily dressed man enter the meeting room. The stranger, who had a green and blue crocheted bag slung over his shoulder, looked either bewildered or lost.

Wilson had nudged the assistant pro and kidded, "There's your relief—you can go home now."

After the man left, Wilson checked the men's room to see if the intruder had ducked in there. But he had left the club, and Wilson saw him just outside approaching a bicycle, apparently his own. Wilson himself left the club about 9:30, and he didn't see the stranger with the crocheted shoulder bag again.

Basil Wilson didn't go to the police immediately after the shooting. He went to see Wes and Wes bypassed the sheriff's office, going directly to the local TV reporter with the "flash" that the suspect had, indeed, been seen near Marcola Road. It made the five o'clock news.

Sometime later Wilson spied a young man who lived down the street from him, and he was struck by his resemblance to the man on the bicycle. The more he thought about it, the more it seemed that Tommy Lee Burns probably *was* the same man. Again Wilson contacted Wes and told him that this time, he could give a name to the suspect.

When detectives went to check on Burns, they found he wasn't in residence; he was in jail serving a short sentence for a nonviolent offense. Kurt Wuest and Doug Welch started to question him, but the instant Burns opened his mouth, he took himself off the list of suspects. Diane had been adamant that the stranger had had no unusual speech patterns and no accent.

Tommy Lee Burns sounded exactly like the cartoon character Elmer Fudd. Doug Welch and Kurt Wuest had never heard a more pronounced lisp. "I wasn't awound that wiver woad and I didn't shoot nobody with no Wuger," Burns said fervently.

They believed him.

John Hulce, seventy-two, had made a point of scrutinizing every yellow car he saw after he read the papers. Four days after the shooting and forty miles away, Hulce was driving on a forest service road east of Oak Ridge when he spotted a yellow car approaching. He looked at the driver as their vehicles drew abreast. The man was in his thirties, and his face was scrabbly with several days' worth of whiskers. John Hulce turned to his wife and said, "That fellow sure matches the description!"

All Hulce was able to tell detectives about the car was that it was an older yellow car with front end and left front damage—"minor wrinkling." It was a Chevrolet, dirty, early seventies model.

On June 13, Roy Pond contacted yet another informant, a citizen who had been driving north of Springfield on Thursday, May 19. He had left a message that he might have something to add to the investigation. Pond set out with little enthusiasm.

His attitude soon changed.

Joseph P. Inman, who worked for the Springfield Water Board and lived in Eugene, explained that he'd had relatives visiting from Southern California on May 19. He had taken them to his sister's home in Marcola earlier that evening. Inman and his wife and two children left Marcola at ten minutes after ten and headed toward Springfield.

"I had to go to see someone in Coburg to get papers notarized before 11:00 P.M., so I decided to go by Old Mohawk Road, Hill Road, and then over McKenzie View Road."

As Inman drove along Old Mohawk Road, he had to slow to a crawl because there was a red car with an Arizona license plate in front of him, traveling only five to seven miles an hour. Inman's own speedometer bounced near zero. The red car was new and foreign made—either a Nissan or a Toyota.

"We followed it for two or three minutes. I assumed the driver was lost or looking for an address. The car wasn't being driven erratically, and it was on the right side of the road. My son said something about cars from Arizona always being red, and cars from Texas always being white. [To match their license plates.]"

The Inmans didn't see passengers in the car, and it was too dark to see the driver. The two-car, accidental caravan inched along for a few minutes. The road was too curvy for Inman to risk passing the slow-moving red car. When they came to a straight stretch, he'd pulled ahead and left it behind.

There were no other cars driving or parked along Old Mohawk, and he'd seen no one walking along the road. But he was definite about the car, its color, the Arizona license plates, and his family could bear him out. Roy Pond was puzzled. The Inman family had seen a car exactly like the Downs car barely moving along the road—immediately *after* the shooting had occurred. But they hadn't noticed anything peculiar about it.

Pond took Joe Inman back out to Mohawk Road so that he could determine exactly where he had seen Diane's red Nissan.

The encounter had taken place eight-tenths of a mile west of the probable shooting site (where the casings were found) and Inman had followed the red car for about two minutes.

And yet, none of the Inmans had heard a cry for help, or a horn honking, or screams. Only the red Pulsar slowed to the pace of a turtle, inching toward Springfield.

Pond's statement from Joe Inman was the first eyewitness account Fred Hugi had heard. And it tainted Diane's version even more.

Diane had declared that she'd raced to the hospital with her bleeding babies, driving as fast as she dared to get them there alive. ". . . and I just kept going . . . kept going . . ."

Deputies painted two white lines across Old Mohawk: one still marks where Joe Inman first spotted the red car, the other where he pulled ahead and passed.

The darkened red car had been silent. For two full minutes, Inman was behind it—with his windows open. He would have heard a cry for help. No one called out. Not the driver. Certainly not the passengers.

Diane might not have known there was a car behind her—never noticed it as it passed. She was concentrating on sights and sounds *inside* her car.

CHAPTER 21

This whole thing was started because the detective pestered my children. I won't have them treated that way. Let her [Christie] heal! She may be the only person that's ever going to exonerate me . . . If I had shot my own children, I would have done a good

job of it. I would have waited 'til they died and then cried croco-
dile tears . . .

—Diane Downs, press conference, June, 1983

Diane was eminently accessible to the media. She held official press conferences often, castigating the DAs and the sheriff's offices. A month after the shooting the cops were coldly angry, some even suggesting that Fred Hugi be removed from the case.

No way. He wasn't ready to file charges yet, much as he wanted to. The probe was moving along, even if it sometimes seemed to be sliding backward. Beyond circumstantial evidence that pointed to Diane and virtually eliminated any other suspect, there was Joseph Inman's statement now, and there was *some* physical evidence: the tool marks on the cartridges and Jim Pex's discovery that high-velocity blood spray misted the exterior of the passenger door's rocker panel. But the physical evidence was so esoteric, perhaps more than a lay jury could fathom.

Small discrepancies continued to pop up. Diane told Doug Welch and Dick Tracy that Christie stared at her out the rear window of the Datsun, beseeching her mother with her eyes to save her. Paul Alton pointed out that it had been pitch dark outside the car, and the dome light was on inside the car. Christie could not have seen anything but blackness out the window. She could not have seen her mother—unless her mother was inside the car.

Fred Hugi believed that Diane *had* indeed seen that look on Christie's face, because Christie was terrified—horrified to see the gun in her mother's hand. The expression on Christie's features had not been "Mommy, why is *he* doing this to me?" The expression must have said, "Mommy, why are *you* doing this to me?"

He figured Diane couldn't erase the memory entirely, but she could incorporate it into her story of a helpless mother, impotent at the hands of a gun-wielding stranger.

The bloody beach towel meant something too, but so far, the criminalists and detectives weren't sure what. They folded it and refolded it, but they couldn't break the code that had to be there spelled out in blood.

Hugi kept thinking that today—or tomorrow—or the day after—the .22 semi-automatic Ruger would turn up.

It was common knowledge that Diane was the prime suspect. The media said it out loud, printed it on the front page. Rumor said she had done it for her lover. Some believed the rumors; more did not. The dichotomy of opinion would continue for a very long time.

The Eugene *Register-Guard* featured a huge color picture of Diane and her father in profile, the same intense expression on their faces as they sat together in Wes and Willadene's living room. Diane wore her usual modest blouse, white eyelet with a bertha collar and ruffles. So pale, without makeup, her left arm encased to the armpit in surgical dressing, she turned angrily toward both still and television cameras: "I will not confess to something I did not do. There's no evidence. I didn't do it and there can't be any evidence if you didn't do something."

Questions were called out from the press corps, and Diane fielded them confidently.

"Why did you go out so late? Why did you stop for a stranger?"

"We never went out 'til nine. We enjoy sightseeing and exploring, even at night. That's just us. They can't change us. I was raised not to fear people like that. If I didn't stop, I'd be responsible for someone on the side of the road dying, if there had been an accident. I had no idea he'd harm my children."

"Why were you only shot in the arm?"

"Thank God that's all. If he'd got me in the stomach, we all would have died."

A reporter asked a question about the "man" she had lost, the possibility that he might have been a motive in the shooting. Diane smiled with faint condescension. "That's like taking the first sentence in a book and saying that's the whole book. I know the man will never come back. He doesn't like trouble and death is the worst trouble there is."

In Arizona, Steve Downs answered reporter's questions carefully. "There's no need for me to put my judgment on her. If she's guilty, they're going to find out. There's no need for me to crucify anybody."

Christie Downs was still in the McKenzie–Willamette Hospital, visited every day still by her mother. But Christie had strong support from Paula Krogdahl.

The most important thing was to protect the surviving children—their minds as well as their bodies. Hugi would not consider questioning Christie until he was sure it wouldn't damage her. Was it too soon for Paula to ask her some careful questions? Danny, buffered by his youth, was more open—and he *always* related his injuries to his mother. His nurses were sure he knew the truth. But he confabulated: "I can't stand up—my mommy ran over me with the car."

They would have to question Christie.

On June 16, Paula, Bill Furtick (appointed by the court as Christie's attorney), Candi McKay (Christie's nurse), and Deputy Jack Gard gathered in Christie's room at 11:00 A.M.

How to start? Paula knew she couldn't just jump into the bitterest questions.

"Christie," she said. "I want to talk to you about—about a jigsaw puzzle. I know you were hurt, honey—but I need to know how you got hurt—if you can tell me."

Christie murmured, ". . . nothing." That was her way of saying that she couldn't remember.

"What color was your car, Christie?"

Christie pointed to Paula's skirt. Red.

That was hopeful. Christie remembered the red car, and the Nissan had been only a few months old when the shooting occurred. She hadn't blocked out all the memory for that period.

"Were you going to see someone that night?"

"Yes."

"Was it a man or a woman?"

Christie was silent.

And then, more slowly, Paula asked, "A man?"

"No."

"A woman?"

"Yes."

"Who?"

". . . hard . . ."

"OK. I'll say some names. You tell me if I say the right one. Sue . . . Mary . . . Linda . . . Laurie . . . Heather—"

"Yes."

"Did you ever go there before?"

Christie shook her head, No.

"Was it dark outside?"

"Yes."

"Was it past your bedtime?"

"Yes."

"Were you sleeping before you went to Heather's?"

"No."

"Did the ride to Heather's take very long?"

". . . long time."

Paula asked Christie to try to remember what happened on the visit to Heather Plourd's house. Christie indicated that they'd seen a horse. She remembered the horse. She didn't remember going into Heather's house.

"Did you see anyone there besides Heather?"

"No."

"What happened after you saw the horse?"

Christie's face changed. She was frightened.

Paula Krogdahl changed tack. She asked about the "hurts" to Christie's family.

"Were all the hurts the same?"

"No. Mom . . . different . . ."

"How?"

Christie shook her head in frustration; she couldn't find the words to explain how Diane's injuries were different.

"Remember when you lived in Arizona?"

"Yes."

"Were you ever afraid of anything when you lived there?"

"Yes."

"What?"

"Two . . . choked . . . in the hospital . . . choked."

Christie was remembering a time when she was two, when she had a sore throat—crouplike—and couldn't breathe.

Paula asked her if other things had frightened her.

Christie gestured that other things had scared her sometimes in Arizona.

"What, Christie?"

"I'm not telling . . ."

"Did Mom ever hit you, Christie?"

"Yes."

"Where?"

Christie raised her good arm and touched her face.

"Why?"

"It was me—my fault."

"Did Mom ever hit Danny?"

Christie showed Paula on a doll that Diane had spanked Danny.

"Did Mom ever hit Cheryl?"

Christie indicated that Cheryl had been slapped in the face.

"Did that happen that very often?"

"Lots."

But when Paula asked Christie if she liked to live with her mom, there was no answer. Paula sensed that Christie Downs harbored some terrible guilt that *she* was in some way responsible for the tragedy that had wrenched her family apart. Just as children often take personal responsibility for their parents' divorce, a catastrophe of this proportion almost certainly had left Christie wondering, "Was it my fault?"

"Do you think that bad things happened to you because you were bad?" Paula asked Christie softly.

The room was quiet. No one seemed to breathe. Finally, Christie nodded slowly.

"Christie, you're not bad. You're not bad at all. You're good," Paula soothed. "Sometimes bad things just happen and little kids can't help it."

Asked if she feared her mother, Christie said, "Sometimes," and then, quickly, "No."

Christie answered yes, her mother had guns—two of them. They didn't look the same. One was long (she extended her arm to show this) and one was short. Christie could talk so little that she needed her good left arm to communicate.

She tried to draw a picture of the shorter gun on art paper.

"Have you seen Mom carry the gun?"

"Yes."

"Where?"

Christie drew a picture of a car.

"Did Mom shoot the gun?"

"Lots."

"Where?"

Christie drew a picture of a target and indicated Arizona on the map.

"Was the gun kept inside of anything?"

Christie nodded. But she could not find the word. Paula asked her if it was closed by something you find on clothes. Christie nodded, and Paula pointed to a button, a snap, and finally a zipper. Christie nodded again. Now Christie drew a picture of a pouch for a gun with a zipper.

"Christie, did you see the gun in the red car in Oregon?"

"Yes."

"Did you see them the night you went to see Heather?"

"Yes."

"Which gun?"

"Both."

"Where?"

Christie indicated the trunk of the car.

"Who put them there?"

"Mom."

Paula hated asking these questions, but she had to go a little further. Painstakingly, because Christie was so hampered verbally, Paula phrased questions carefully to the child to answer. The guns were sometimes kept in the front seat area, but Mom had put them in the trunk that night.

Paula drew a picture of the red Nissan Pulsar. "Is this where the bad thing happened?"

"Yes."

Paula drew a line from the trunk area of the car to the front door areas. "Is this what happened?"

"I think—I think, Mom."

"Did anyone tell you not to tell, Christie?"

". . . Mom."

"Was there anyone there that night that you didn't know?"

"No."

"Was there a man there you didn't know?"

Christie shook her head.

"Was there a lady there you didn't know?"

Christie shook her head.

"Was it just your family there?"

Christie nodded.

"Is there anything missing from the picture?"

Christie shook her head.

"Was anyone crying in the car?"

"No."

"Was Mom crying?"

"No . . . yes."

"Were Danny and Cheryl crying?"

"No."

"Why wasn't Cheryl crying?"

". . . dead."

Paula Krogdahl didn't want to ask the next question. But she had to. "Do you know who was shooting, Christie?"

"I don't know . . . I think—"

Christie stopped talking.

"Who do you think, Christie?" Paula said softly.

"I think—" Christie's eyes filled with tears, and she stared off blankly into space.

Christie tried to draw a picture of the person with the gun. She labored over it. The person had come from the trunk of the car to the front door. But the person in Christie's picture had only a blank face. It could have been either a man or a woman.

"What do you think about the person that did the bad thing, Christie?" Paula asked gently.

"Yuk."

"Are you still afraid?"

"Yes . . . sometimes . . ."

It had been a scary thing for Christie just to tell Paula what she remembered. She wasn't anywhere near ready to testify in court.

Not yet.

Christie had said, "I think—I think, Mom."

A defense attorney would make mincemeat of her.

It was essential that Christie—and eventually Danny—be placed in a foster home where they would be nurtured and supported both emotionally and physically. Susan Staffel conferred with other CSD caseworkers and there was unanimous agreement; the *ideal* foster home would be with Ray and Evelyn Slaven. In a dozen years, the Slavens had given long-term foster care to a half-dozen youngsters, and they had also taken in *over two hundred* babies and children for shelter care. The shelter-care children were taken to the Slavens when police or social workers had to remove them from their homes *at once*! Two hundred babies thrust into Evelyn's arms wailing and bewildered.

"They came in the middle of the night, on holidays, any time," Ray Slaven, a big, comforting man with just a trace of Tennessee drawl, recalls. "Sometimes they didn't have any clothing; sometimes they had lice—or worse—but there are ways to take care of that. They just needed someplace safe to go to until a foster home was found for them."

Evelyn Slaven is as petite as Ray is large, a softly pretty woman with a melodious voice. She was born in Eugene; Ray on a farm sixty miles east of Knoxville. When farming got rough in Tennessee in the early fifties, Ray Slaven and his folks moved to Oregon. He was fourteen. When he met Evelyn, he was studying medical X ray at the Oregon Institute of Technology in Klamath Falls and working summers as a millwright for the Georgia-Pacific plywood mill. It occurred to him that his summer job paid more than he would make in the X-ray field after two more years of college. He went to work full-time for Georgia-Pacific in 1961. Two years later, he married Evelyn.

By 1971 they had three boys of their own and a big house with extra bedrooms. Evelyn spotted an ad seeking foster homes for young children. "I was just drawn to it," she remembers. "We talked it over, and Ray felt the same way. I come from a family of six, and there are seven kids in his family. It seemed right that we take in some foster kids."

For eleven years there were always kids at the Slavens' house. Their own three boys—who were seven, five, and three when it began—enjoyed the foster and shelter kids. "So much so," Ray laughs, "that they'd get bored when it was just them. They'd say, 'When are we going to get some *kids* around here?'"

"One Christmas, I counted sixteen kids," Ray remembers. "Our boys always voted on whether we should take more, and they always seemed to want more. They got really good with scared little kids; they'd play with them but never pressure them."

Brenda Slaven joined the family when she was adopted. In 1983 she was almost exactly the age of Christie Downs. The CSD wanted the Slaven home for Christie and Danny. But by 1983 Evelyn and Ray had been without foster kids for a year. Their own boys were almost grown up, and they'd decided to take at least a few years off.

"I don't know how many times they called Evelyn and asked her to consider taking Christie and Danny," Ray says. "We just kept saying no—because we knew how much would be involved. But then, finally, we just had to say yes."

The family had taken a vote—and Christie and Danny Downs won.

The Slavens were not naive; they knew that mistreated kids rarely responded to kindness with gratitude. These kids would have every reason to act out, to distrust them. They'd been through it before, but never with kids as damaged as Christie and Danny must be. Once they made up their minds, however, Ray and Evelyn vowed to do everything they could to bring the children through as whole and secure as it was possible for them to be.

"We started out by visiting the kids in the hospital," Ray says, "so they would get to know us. Christie came home first, of course—and we spent months visiting Danny. So when they came to our house, it was already like they were one of the gang."

On June 22, 1983, after five weeks of treatment, Christie was released from McKenzie–Willamette Hospital. She was very thin and wan, her right arm still paralyzed, but the fact that Christie was leaving the hospital *alive* was in itself a miracle.

Susan Staffel drove Christie to the Slavens. Their address was known to only a few trusted people.

"We don't know where she's at," Willadene told a *Register-Guard* reporter. "All they told us was something about her going to a foster home the first of this week."

Evelyn Slaven is even tempered and infinitely patient. She found Christie "very, very fragile—both physically and emotionally."

"Christie observed us for a long time. She needed to be sure that we were the same all the time—that we wouldn't be nice to her one day, and then angry the next. It took her quite a while to trust us."

The Slavens' adopted daughter Brenda and Christie clung together. "They went *everywhere* together," Evelyn laughs. "And I mean *everywhere*—even to the bathroom!"

Diane's visiting privileges with her children had been rescinded. Christie never mentioned her mother, never asked about where Diane was or why she didn't come to visit.

Christie still had great difficulty with speech, but she grew a little more verbal each week. She talked about Cheryl once she began to feel safer—but not in the context of the shooting. Instead, she remembered past times with her sister, good and bad. Cheryl had always been in trouble, Christie confided—for sucking her thumb, for wetting her bed.

Although Christie was only eight when she came to the Slavens, Evelyn was amazed to see that she was used to doing the laundry for a family. "She told me she always had trouble folding her father's pants—because she was too short."

Christie had been the mother in her family. Evelyn saw that Christie assumed that's the way it always was—that little girls cooked and did dishes and laundry and babysat.

On June 27, Susan Staffel referred Christie Downs to Dr. Carl Peterson, a child psychologist.

"Christie is currently living in a shelter home . . . visiting weekly with her brother," Staffel wrote. "She has been unable to totally recall the events on the night of the shooting, however, she has maintained that there was no one present 'when the bad things happened' other than her family. Christie has awakened regularly at night crying, and frequently becomes visibly upset when contemplating her scars. She has been unable, however to express her feelings."

Christie's nightmares where charted: 6-22, 6-23, 6-27, 6-30, 7-6, 7-19 . . . As she began to feel secure, the time between bad dreams lengthened.

Evelyn ran to Christie the moment she heard her cry out, so that she wouldn't wake up alone.

The Slavens walked a fine, fine line. They provided Christie with love and security, but on the advice of experts they could not validate what she said—one way or the other. They bent over backward not to show surprise or shock or confirmation at anything she said. "All we could say was 'Oh,'" Evelyn says. "We knew Christie needed some answers, but we knew the best way she could find them was with Dr. Peterson. Still, it was so hard for us—always having to let her wonder if what she'd said was right—or a dream—or whatever."

Something terrible obviously weighed on Christie's mind, and crept out in her dreams, but she would not share it.

CHAPTER 22

On June 28, the levy to fund the sheriff's and district attorney's offices failed.

Sheriff Dave Burks—frustrated and angered by his inability to protect the public—parked row after row of empty patrol cars in the lot across from the courthouse. Let the citizens of Lane County see them there and know that the failed levy had taken away funds needed to put officers into those units. A county bigger than either Rhode Island or Delaware was virtually without police patrols.

Paul Alton was laid off. Doug Welch and Kurt Wuest were given a reprieve—but only for a month. They had until August 1 to clear the Downs shooting. Thereafter, Dick Tracy would handle all major crimes in the county, a job even Superman couldn't have managed.

Fred Hugi still had his job, but he had no investigators. He agonized over his decision not to charge Diane. She didn't know where Christie was, but he feared she might find out. He watched Diane's televised press conferences and listened to her spin out her stories of bereft motherhood. It seemed as if every time he turned on his set, Diane was on the screen, mocking him. Diane and her father continued to snipe at the detectives, the DA, the sheriff. And Diane was free. She could drive wherever she wanted.

The decision to prosecute Diane Downs for murder and attempted murder had been made even before May eased into June—back at the mass meeting of all investigators, criminalists, and DA's men in Harris Hall. But the question of *when* the arrest would take place had sparked the corrosive arguments between Hugi and the sheriff's detectives. The onus of the decision to wait fell on Fred Hugi.

Now, the money was gone. The bottom had fallen out. Hugi lay awake nights, juggling the components of the case. Diane told her diary she was "beginning to feel like everyone is against me." Fred Hugi could empathize with her. In certain circles, he too was a pariah. The detectives all felt they had a "go." But Hugi refused to budge, urging them to get out there and dig for more. He had seen jurors disregard simpler and stronger evidence than they had so far and bring back not-guilty verdicts.

If they arrested Diane, Hugi had to be prepared to go to court within three months at the most. Oregon adheres rigidly to the right to a speedy trial. According to Peterson, there was no way Christie could be ready to testify in sixty days. She could barely speak, and she was too frightened to remember.

During the day at work Hugi had so many things to do, so many other cases that came and went, that he could often forget the Downs case for the moment. "But always, when the immediate tasks were over, my mind would return to it. It wasn't going to go away by itself. I was the only one who could make it happen."

Hugi wrote dialogues in his head, playing devil's advocate.

If they went ahead without Christie, the defense would cry, "Why hasn't the State waited so that the eyewitness—Christie—could testify and clear her mother?" Hugi could almost hear Jim Jagger as he said, "And how will you, as jurors, feel if you find Diane Downs guilty—only to have Christie remember later that the 'bushy-haired stranger' *was* the shooter?

All this could have been avoided if the State had simply waited. Why are they in such a hurry? The children are safe. Diane isn't going anywhere. What are they afraid of—the *truth*? That they have made a mistake by focusing on Diane and allowing the real killer to escape!"

It made a dandy defense, and if Hugi had thought of it, Jagger certainly would.

At night Fred Hugi tossed in bed, listening to some damned rooster crow far down the road—and pictured another scenario. OK. They would wait—they *were* waiting. That allowed a whole new set of problems to rear their ugly heads. Maybe Christie was *never* going to be able to talk. Or say she did regain her speech: Christie might try to protect her mother by going along with the bushy-haired stranger story. That was a paragraph right out of that essay Diane had written about child abuse. She knew that kids often stuck by their parents . . . no matter what. God only knew what Diane had said to Christie as she'd spent hours visiting her in the hospital before the court order stopped her.

If Christie was brainwashed, it wouldn't be a surprise to Hugi.

Would the long wait make the public—the potential jurors—lose confidence in the case? Jagger would go for that too: If the State had such damn good physical evidence, why did they need to wait for Christie?

Hugi gave up on sleep and went out on the deck to watch the sun rise. He tried to focus on the bright side. With the passage of time, Christie *might* talk; she might remember everything. He knew he could count on one thing. Diane would keep on talking, keep changing the composite drawings, and altering her versions of the shootings. She opened her mouth so often, she was bound to put her foot in it.

It wasn't that he didn't want to see Diane behind bars. It always came down to the kids. Remembering, even two years later, his face is agonized. "How could I ever face those kids if I lost? Especially if Christie remembered later that Diane *was* the shooter, and she *could say it*. Double jeopardy would attach, and we'd be helpless—a truly bungled prosecution."

They wouldn't be able to try Diane again if she was acquitted; she could pack up her two living kids and take them anywhere she wanted. Hugi shook with chills at the thought of it. The only time he knew where Diane was for sure was when he saw her on live television. Danny was safe; he was still under guard at Sacred Heart. But Christie was the biggest threat to Diane's story. What if Diane waited until she saw Christie in the street—and ran over her? If that happened, it would be his fault. Hugi believed that whatever happened to Christie and Danny from here on out was his responsibility.

A thousand times in the summer of 1983, Hugi went over his decision not to press charges until he was ready. A thousand times, he concluded that he had gone the only way he could.

They had to wait until Christie was ready.

Or until they found the gun.

The essence of Diane's press conferences seemed to be that she thought the murder probe was pretty much over; she was striving to get her children back.

Diane was shocked to learn from friends in Chandler that Doug Welch and Kurt Wuest were again in Arizona. The two young detectives had more people from Diane's past to interview, and they were making a final stab at locating cartridges or slugs from the missing .22 Ruger. Dick Tracy was in Oklahoma to interview Diane's sister, Kathy, and then would travel on to Louisville, Kentucky, armed with a search warrant for all of Diane's records from the surrogate parent clinic. An Oregon law allows an exception in the privileged communication statute between patient and doctor when the protection of children is concerned.

Diane called yet another news conference in late June. Around her neck, she wore Cheryl's gold chain with a tiny gold ingot added to it. Diane had had the gold bar engraved with the dates of Cheryl's birth and death. This was her new talisman, her new symbol.

She sat on a black leather couch in a room panelled with birch. A box overflowing with children's toys rested on the floor at the end of the couch. Wes Frederickson was nearby.

Eyes blazing, Diane turned toward the cameras.

"I ask any mother out there if someone came to her house and took her kids, wouldn't she act mad? Stamp her feet?"

Diane explained that Danny would recover completely. "Your mind controls your body, and if I can love Danny enough, I can make him walk."

No one in the watching public knew about the abuse her babies had endured, and it was easy for her to make Fred Hugi and the sheriff's detectives look like villains.

"I can't believe I've come to this. If the detectives had done their job—"

Diane had learned how to deal with detectives. She explained that it was now her duty to share her perceptions with the citizens of Lane County. Cognizant of the publicity on the lost levy, on the millions of dollars needed to run a sheriff's office, she advised the viewers that their tax dollars were going to pay inefficient, cruel, dishonest detectives. Her message was clear. What had befallen her could happen to anyone watching her.

"I gave them access to my house, access to my body. I let them do tests, gave them my personal letters. They know I didn't do it. Now they're too proud to back off. They sacrifice the mother of the children . . . I was never afraid of the dark, but now I am. I see it all over again. I have nightmares and I cry. I've always been able to help and I couldn't help my kids. We had a lot of memories and now we have to make new memories when Cheryl isn't there, so the hurt gets (will get) softer. I loved her and somebody took her—"

Diane began to cry and then pulled herself together. She explained that she had to be strong for Christie and Danny.

Fred Hugi strode to his set and started to snap it off, resisting the temptation to kick it. The woman was good; he had to give her that.

"What will you do 'after'?" a reporter asked.

"I don't know. Right now there is no future . . . They're [The police] supposed to be finding the man that hurt me and who could come back again and hurt me. They're *helping* him!"

Through it all, Diane's voice remained sweet and soft, the voice of a woman in so much pain that she couldn't possibly be shading the truth.

"Why did someone shoot us? I don't know. Why did someone shoot a 7-Eleven kid for $30? Why did someone kill five people down in Chino [California]? I don't know why people do things. Why does anybody kill anybody? It's insane."

The more astute viewer noticed that when one of Diane's arguments seemed to work, it would be repeated often. Even the inflection of her words remained the same, as if she had merely replayed a tape. She never stuttered or stumbled over a phrase.

Just keeping track of Diane's television appearances was a full-time job. Wes and Willadene kept three sets in their living room. One was tuned to KVAL, one to KMTR, and one to KEZI. Little notes listing the respective times of news broadcasts were taped to the sets.

Forbidden to see her children, Diane was still very busy. She had her diary, she had her tapes to dictate, she had the police to joust with, she had a media interview anytime she chose to ask for one. As the summer lengthened, she gave literally dozens of "exclusive" confidences to members of the press and TV, in addition to her large press conferences. And soon, she would have her postal job back.

Diane made a number of calls to Chandler. She called the Maricopa County Sheriff's Office to turn Steve Downs in for arson and insurance fraud, explaining that Steve had deliberately burned her trailer, and that he'd reported his sports car stolen—when it was really safely stored—so he could collect insurance. She was very angry with Steve for telling the police about the .22 Ruger.

Best of all: unbelievably, incredibly, Lew was back in her life.

Doug Welch and Kurt Wuest found Lew Lewiston still wary about what Diane might do. And he grieved for the kids—those somber little kids that he'd tried not to think about when he and Diane were together. He believed that if he hadn't started with Diane, she never would have shot the kids.

In an effort to get her to admit what she'd done, Lew decided to call Diane—and tape the calls for the police. If she ever admitted the truth to anyone, he thought it would be to him. She always told him he was the only one who really understood her.

It was legal. Both Oregon and Arizona statutes put forth guidelines for taping phone calls. Calls may be taped surreptitiously if "at least one of the parties taping is aware of it," preventing only a third party from taping callers unaware.

Lew was deceiving Diane. If not lying outright, he certainly left much unsaid. It didn't bother him. She was the champion of deception, of manipulation. She could lie and wheedle and cry and laugh and pout and charm at will. She always had, and he suspected she always would. Playing fair with her now seemed a negligible concern.

If she wasn't locked up, Lewiston fully expected to see Diane Downs again soon and, quite possibly, there would be a gun in her hand the next time he saw her. If a woman could shoot her own children to get a man, she would have no compunction at all about shooting his wife.

Whatever there had once been between them, any attraction, fascination, love, or desire that Lew had felt for Diane Downs was dead.

The smoky-whiskey autumn nights were gone, but there were ghosts. Sometimes, when Lew turned a corner, he could almost hear a phantom clink of empty glasses in the back ... and muted music, the strange, harsh music Diane had preferred to his country western. Times like that, it seemed as if her scarlet-talon nails were still clutching him and that she would never, ever, ever, let him go until she had destroyed all of them.

CHAPTER 23

In Chandler, Kurt Wuest, and Doug Welch obtained permission from the new owners of the house on Palomino Street to dig up their recently landscaped backyard; Steve Downs remembered that he'd once shot at some cats there with the elusive .22 Ruger.

"The new owners had built a patio—concrete slab—and beyond that, they'd put down river rock over black Visqueen," Welch remembers. "We ripped the whole thing out. When we were down to sand, we found some old guys—retired—who had metal detectors and they went over it ... We didn't find the casings. The county paid to have the backyard put back together again."

That left Mexico.

Jesse Pinon had sold Stan Post's old truck—which might still carry some of the .22's casings in it—to his brother: Raphael Pinon Acosta, who lived God-only-knew-where in Mexico. Welch and Wuest needed an interpreter and a guide.

Manuel Valenzuela was a retired Chandler police captain, a private investigator, and a polygraph expert. He had given the lie detector tests to the Chandler witnesses. Manny spoke such exquisite Spanish that no one would ever peg him as an American. He explained how to contact someone in Chihuahua: "You don't pick up the phone and call Raphael. You have to find someone in Mexico who might possibly have a phone. They get on a CB and contact somebody who lives closer to Raphael. Then, if they feel like it, they'll go hunt him up, Raphael will get on the CB and eventually his message will be transmitted to the guy with a phone."

It took Valenzuela three days to find Raphael Pinon Acosta. The most expedient way to get to him was to charter a plane. However, the area was rife with drug smuggling; low-flying planes were an endangered species.

Yes, Raphael still had the black truck, but he lived a hundred miles beyond Janos, the hamlet Valenzuela suggested for a meet. He doubted that his bald tires were up to the trip. Manny coaxed and cajoled. It was agreed. On July 5, the truck would be presented in Janos, Chihuahua, Mexico, for processing by two cops from Oregon.

An American police officer carries little authority south of the Mexican border. Indeed, carrying a badge is often dangerous. Valenzuela agreed to accompany Wuest and Welch. Hell, he said he'd *drive* them, which was just as well. The trip to Janos would take six and a half hours over highways that did little to merit the name.

Minus guns or police identification, they crossed the Mexican border at Douglas/Aqua Pieta. Guards, lounging in tilted-back chairs, stared blankly at the trio. Valenzuela spoke softly out of the corner of his mouth, telling the Oregon detectives to keep calm. They needed a visa; for that a driver's license would probably do. Kurt Wuest decided not to confuse the issue by saying he was born in Switzerland; he simplified his birthplace to "Chicago."

The Federales, their .45s dangling from their gunbelts, searched Valenzuela's car, grunted, and lazily waved them on.

They were in another world, mile after mile of bad roads with precipitous curves. Every so often, they came upon a checkpoint. Sometimes they were signaled to stop; sometimes not. Near most checkpoints there were burned-out car hulks, their windows shattered by bullets.

Laughing, Wuest asked, "What's that? Somebody who didn't stop for the checkpoint?"

Manny didn't smile. "You got it."

They arrived in Janos in the heat of noon. The Pinon pick-up was parked in front of the Cafe Harris ("Pollo Empanisado, Hamburguesas, Sandwiches, Tacos, and Burritos").

Manny took Raphael aside and explained something to him. Wuest and Welch could hear him say, "ninos children ... morte ... bang, bang ... Madre," and saw Pinon's eyes widen in horror. He nodded solemnly and gestured grandly toward his truck.

Welch had just begun to pull up the carpeting in the cab when the local policeman pulled up. His expression was not friendly.

Once again, Manny explained in Spanish, and once again they were waved on. Welch's fingers moved over the truck floor. And—almost miraculously—there were bullets there! Seven live rounds and a couple of casings!

The entire population of Janos had by this time gathered around the truck, staring. Welch contained his enthusiasm as he nodded triumphantly to Wuest and Valenzuela.

Doug Welch recalls his naiveté then; he was so caught up in cops-and-killers real live drama. "Here we were in an *international* investigation. We had to go to a foreign country to solve it, but we'd done it!"

He paid Rafael $50.00 for his time and trouble—and the temerity to drive 100 miles on tires with no tread at all. It was three weeks' wages. Rafael was elated. They were all elated.

But how were three "civilians" going to get bullets and casings across the border to Aqua Pieta? Welch solved that by tucking the seven live .22 rounds and the empty casings in the only hiding place the Federales might not search: his jockey shorts.

"I figured unless they actually 'honked' me at the border, I could get those rounds out of Mexico—and we wanted those rounds."

When they reached the border after midnight, the Federales didn't bother to search either Valenzuela's car or its passengers. Once they got far enough into Arizona, they stopped so Welch could fish the bullets out of his shorts, and he breathed—and sat—more easily.

It was now Doug Welch's thirty-second birthday. He felt he had much to celebrate. He'd bought a bottle of Tequila in Mexico. He discovered it had leaked all the way to Aqua Pieta. The leaky Tequila may have been an omen. Not one of the bullets, and none of the casings, matched those Jim Pex had.

The case was a nightmare, the kind of investigation that sands the promontories of illusion off an eager young detective in a hurry. Dick Tracy could have told them that. The ones that look as if they're going to work throw you the hardest.

At Oklahoma State Technical College in Okmulgee, Dick Tracy talked to Kathy Downing. Tracy could hear Israel in another room, screaming from the oppressive heat of the humid little apartment, or perhaps a nightmare.

Kathy Frederickson said she'd married Downing on March 16, 1980, in Flagstaff, but they'd only lived together a couple of months. Diane had driven Kathy to the Eugene airport the night before the shooting. Kathy explained that she wouldn't be staying with her husband long; she was going into military service in October.

Through mere coincidence Diane had married a Downs and Kathy a Downing, but Kathy had emulated Diane's behavior in many ways—first, as a potential surrogate mother, and now as a potential Army recruit.

Kathy said she'd seen guns in Diane's possession, but she didn't recognize the picture of a .22 Ruger semi-automatic and the bone-handled steel revolver Tracy showed her. She had helped Diane pack for several moves but didn't remember seeing any guns. Kathy did remember back to the time in September, 1982, after Steve had blacked Diane's eye; Diane had got the rifle out then and was loading it and threatening to shoot Steve if he came back. "But it worked out OK. Steve didn't come back, and Diane cooled down."

Diane often loaded and unloaded guns when she was mad at Steve. Her Aunt Irene recalled to Welch a time when Steve was late delivering Diane's new waterbed. Diane sat on the edge of the couch, loading and unloading, threatening to kill "the son of a bitch."

Seeing how troubled Kathy was now, Tracy asked her the obvious question: "Who do you think shot the children?"

Kathy admitted that her first reaction to the news of the shooting was, "Diane did it." She still believed that.

CHAPTER 24

...I'm glad you called. I need somebody to talk to. I was thinking about you real bad last night...

—Diane Downs, Lew's first call

Lew placed his first phone call to Diane on July 2, 1983. Diane *was* glad to hear from him, but wary. She still wanted him; she no longer trusted any man—even Lew.

In four days, it would be a year since they had first made love. *Only one year.*

Her surrogate baby Jennifer had been only two months old when she began with Lew. In the year since, Diane had sold the Palomino Street house to Steve, bought the mobile home, ended her affair with Jack Lenta, reconciled with Steve, engaged in a violent physical fight with Steve, attempted to commit suicide, returned to Louisville for insemination (twice), arranged to have her trailer burned, started college, learned to fly, begun her own surrogate business . . . and then moved to Oregon and to all that had taken place there.

The average woman would have long since crumbled, but by July, 1983, Diane Downs had completed an almost mystic process of renewal. She was as resilient as a robot whose damaged parts had been replaced. Diane was ready to go back to carrying the mail. She was in wonderful physical condition, despite the cast on her arm. Her voice on Lew's first tape is girlish and cheerful, as if she had spoken to her lost lover only a day before.

Lew pretended to be annoyed by the police. They were bothering him, asking him to take a lie detector test.

"Don't do it," Diane counseled.

"Well, I got nothing to hide."

No, she told him. It was a matter of principle. He must not fall for the cops' "bluff."

Lew's voice was laconic, lumbering, counterpointed by Diane's breathy, cheerleader's voice.

"How's everything?" she asked.

"Nothing's changed."

"That's good. Things have changed a lot for me."

"Yes, I can imagine so."

"I have a steel plate in my arm. The scar won't be very bad ... it's going away already. I get to go back to work next week."

Diane told Lew she was planning another trip to Arizona. That didn't surprise him. He expected to see her every time he turned a corner.

"You had a .22, Diane. I know that."

There. He'd tossed it out. He'd seen the .22 Ruger, and she knew it.

Her voice stayed cheerful, but it took on an edge, as if Lew was a very slow pupil who had to be drilled on his facts.

"Yes, I did—and Steve got it back."

"Steve got it back?"

"Yes, he does."

"OK" (doubtfully).

"When—*think*—I want you to think about this—because I know they are going to ask you," she prompted. "Do you remember *when* you saw that .22?"

"I saw that .22 at your trailer and I saw it before you left for Oregon."

"Two weeks before I left. Correct?"

"Oh, hell, Diane—you were packing the day before you left. You had it in the back of the car."

"No, Lew—think about it. I had a microwave and I had a TV and I had a whole bunch of stuff. The day that you say you saw the .22, I opened my trunk and my trunk was empty. Was it not?"

"Except for the .38 and the .22."

She would not budge; Lew's memory had to be flawed. Diane apologized to Lew for the inconvenience of having police on his doorstep.

"Well, it's just the breaks," Lew muttered.

"I know—but it's not fun—it's—I don't know—it's unusual. Everybody knows me—wherever I go—"

"Well, I imagine so. Keep your ass off TV."

"I *have* to go on TV. I have to tell them the truth because the cops won't listen."

Diane warned him once more about taking a polygraph: "Lew, would you listen to me and think rationally. If you were at work the day before and the day after this, there is no way in hell that you could have gotten up here and done that."

"OK. So there's no reason why I shouldn't take the lie detector test."

"... All right—I miss you."

"Thank you for returning the call."

"No problem."

"All right. Bye-bye."

"Take care of yourself—"

"Yup. Bye-bye."

"I love you . . ."

"Bye."

Lew removed the tape, labeled it, and slipped it into an envelope for the Lane County investigators. She was just the same as she'd always been. Words. Words and words. She'd hardly mentioned the kids. Only her arm and her money, and for him to keep his mouth shut. He wondered what she was afraid he might say.

He poured himself a shot of Jim Beam to get the bad taste out of his mouth. It was hard to remember now that he had ever loved her.

Diane felt secure with the support of the public. She couldn't even walk into a store without several people recognizing her, as if she were a movie star. Once when Diane collapsed in tears, a perfect stranger—a woman— came along the street and just held her hand and cried with her.

That seemed to Diane to be the difference between human beings and cops. She had a word for cops and social workers. *Evil.*

The more Lew called, the more Diane appeared to open up to him. Often Lew had to tell her to stop and take a breath.

"Say, you did it," Lew prodded. "You get rid of the kids, you get rid of Nora, and then you can have me. Right?"

"No. That wouldn't help. You know why?"

"Why?"

"Because you don't like trouble."

"Well, I certainly don't. That's the truth."

"You hate kinks and I know that, and this has got to be one of the kinkiest things that's ever happened. All I'm trying to do is protect you."

Theirs was, perhaps, the strangest dialogue between ex-lovers ever to buzz along telephone lines. Diane patiently explaining to Lew that she loved him, but not enough to kill for. Lew questioning her, picking apart her obscure explanations about suspects, intrigues, plots against her.

"Jesus," he breathed. "You have been watching too many cops and robbers movies."

"Oh, Lew," she cried. "I'm *in* a cops and robbers movie . . ."

"*I can't* be implicated, Diane," he reminded her.

"Oh, Lew, you can. I took a lie detector today."

"*You took it?*"

"Yes, I did. Don't tell anybody."

"What's the big deal?"

"Because the lie detector turned out the way *they* wanted it to. They didn't give me the test. It was a private test, taken on the side. Don't tell anybody. They asked me, 'Are you going to tell the truth?' I said, 'Yes.' It said I was telling the truth. They asked if a white male stranger was holding the gun that shot my kids, I said yes. It said I was telling the truth. They asked, 'Were you holding the gun that shot your kids?' I said no. It said I was lying. It can't go both ways. Either he's holding the gun or I'm holding the gun. See what I mean?"

Diane went to great pains to explain police strategy. They could not be trusted. "Why do you think the press is on my side? Because the judicial system here is rotten. It's fucked up. It's warped. They will sacrifice anybody to keep up appearances. They haven't lost a murder case here in ten years. Lew, they fucked up this one. They didn't look for the guy and he's probably fucking out of this state by now, and now they have to pin it on somebody or they've lost a murder case, a big one, a very well publicized one."

She was deluded about the media. The press simply knew a good story when they saw it, and Diane could always be counted on for an interesting quote.

His ear sweating against the phone, Lew watched the July sun lowering to the horizon, the barred windows throwing dark shadow-stripes across the yard of his newly rented house—a house Diane had never seen. That gave him a modicum of serenity; Diane didn't really know where he and Nora were. She didn't have his telephone number, except for the post office phone. But Diane had a way of finding things out. It was a fine line he was walking. Too fine.

He had to decide. If he was in it at all, he had to force her hand. He had to make himself available to Diane. So far, she'd only been playing games with him, giving him a spiel almost rehearsed. Lew dreaded giving her his phone number at home, but he sighed . . . and gave her the unlisted number.

"I don't want any hang-up phone calls, Diane."

"Lew—"

"Now just don't say anything. Don't call me late at night, and don't call me in the morning when I'm getting ready for work. If you want to talk to me, call me after work. All right?"

She asked him why he had changed his phone number.

"I've had my number changed four hundred times."

"But it used to be an 838 number."

"I don't live there. That house was sold."

She relaxed. "Oh—very good!" She assumed he had left Nora. But then he could hear the gears in her brain grinding.

"Can I ask you something?"

"Yeah."

"Are you and Nora together?"

"Yup."

A sharp intake of breath. A few beats of waiting, and then she spoke, with forced breeziness.

"OK. Just curious . . . Why would you allow me to call then?"

"I'm giving you a chance to act right. OK?"

"Yeah—you're crazy."

"Well, I probably always will be, so if you want to tell me something, you call me. All right?"

"All right. I love you, Lew."

"I know that, Diane."

He didn't doubt that she did, that she loved him in the way she always had. Lord, she'd told him that three dozen times a day. But she couldn't love him and let him be. With Diane, loving was the same as devouring.

He shivered.

CHAPTER 25

I don't care if you keep Diane a suspect forever. Just release the kids. My grandchildren are prisoners of war.

—Wes Frederickson, July, 1983

Christie and Danny were only in protective custody. Christie was seeing psychologist Carl Peterson. He was very gentle, very soft spoken. His emphasis was on *non* directive counseling; they would proceed at Christie's own pace. Although the aphasia left by her stroke compromised her speech, he could discern that she was very bright.

Christie's life had been turned upside down. She was not sure what she wanted to do. She liked Ray and Evelyn and trusted them enough now to relate memories of physical abuse that she and Danny and Cheryl had suffered, stories that made the Slavens ill. Sometimes Christie thought she might like to live with her father in Arizona, but only if Danny could go too. And Danny wouldn't be able to leave the hospital for months.

When Dr. Peterson asked, Christie drew pictures of Cheryl, Danny, and herself. Cheryl wore braids and jeans in the picture, but her eyes were closed, as if she was asleep. In the Christie picture and the Danny picture the figures smiled tentatively and their arms and hands were very large in proportion to the rest of their bodies as they reached out, almost in supplication.

Later, Christie drew the red Nissan for Peterson, and two guns: a long rifle and a short pistol. She drew a diagram of Heather Plourd's house, with children playing in a field with a horse.

Christie's memory—when she would let herself into it—was excellent.

But she needed a safe, therapeutic environment where she could work through her trauma, where she might one day feel safe enough to relate what had happened after they left Heather's house on May 19. Her terror had to be defused gradually.

Carl Peterson found Christie cautious and guarded. He didn't hurry her; he tried to find a mirror in her mind that would reflect what she was trying to keep hidden. Peterson never doubted that Christie *had* a memory. "The memory was put away—memories put into a vault until it was safe enough for them to come out. When they come out, it is like a flood, basically—a flood of memories."

Christie's emotional well-being was paramount. The best of all possible resolutions would be for Christie to remember that someone other than her mother had been the shooter. Peterson was not concerned with the prosecution's case nearly as much as he was dedicated to saving the child.

Christie loved her mother; that was evident. That didn't necessarily mean that her mother hadn't shot her. When Peterson asked Christie to write a list of the people she loved most, Diane's name topped the list. And yet, Christie could not talk to him aloud about her mother. There was a gap that shut Diane completely out of Christie's verbal communication to Peterson.

The green fairy hills in the Willamette Valley were gradually shading to umber. The summer of 1983 was much different from what Diane had expected. She shouldered her mailsack and walked her nine-mile route in Cottage Grove. The heat in Oregon was a pale imitation of what she was used to, but it reminded her of better days. And she felt healthier for the exercise. Back in Wes and Willadene's house, there was nothing for her to do but *think*. Her mother did all the cleaning, cooking, and laundry. Diane, as always, needed action.

The first day back after her long lay-off, Diane came home with blisters and aching muscles. She called Lew to tell him how bad she hurt. He'd never been sympathetic with her; he seemed even colder now.

At least work helped to keep her mind off waiting. If Diane had one fatal weakness, it was an inability to wait. No matter how many warnings she got from Jim Jagger, Diane could not wait for the detectives and the prosecutor's office to make the moves. If she didn't hear from them, she contacted them—with new clues about the stranger with the gun, with new memories that constantly superseded the old. Diane knew she was smarter than the cops, so she saw no danger in talking with them.

Not much was happening on the case by July. Dolores Holland, Heather Plourd's neighbor, finally remembered the name of a man she thought resembled the composite sketch of the shooter. She mentioned it to Heather, and was soon visited by Wes, Diane, and Diane's brother Paul. Mrs. Holland told them that the composite looked a little like her daughter's friend—a young man of Indian descent: Samasan Timchuck. She showed Wes and Paul an old snapshot of him.

The next day, Paul Frederickson drew a new sketch and took it—not to the detectives but to the Eugene *Register-Guard*. The *Register-Guard* published it: "Downs Revises Assailant Sketch." Diane suddenly remembered that the shaggy-haired stranger was thinner in the face and parted his hair differently than the subject in the first composite. In fact, the second sketch looked amazingly like the picture of Sam Timchuck.

Roy Pond and Kurt Wuest ran Sam Timchuck's name on the computers without success. They sent out teletypes requesting information on Timchuck and got no response. If Timchuck had been along the Little Mohawk that night, no one saw him. Indeed, no one had seen him for months.

Kurt Wuest shook his head when he saw the second sketch. The first composite showed a man with a couple of double chins—the kind of guy you would expect to have a beer belly. The new sketch portrayed a cadaverously thin man whose haunted eyes stared back from a gaunt face. Quite a difference.

"Do you think she could identify the guy if she saw him?" Wuest asked Diane's brother.

Paul shook his head. "The guy could walk right past her and she wouldn't know him. She just doesn't know if she can ID him or not."

"Why bother putting that second sketch together then?" Wuest asked.

"We were testing you," Paul Frederickson grinned slyly. "Just to see how long it would take you to contact us."

Wes Frederickson monitored Kurt Wuest and Doug Welch continually. It was Wes Frederickson's belief that Diane was being railroaded by the Lane County sheriff's office.

Frederickson reminded Wuest and Welch often that he was a very influential person with access to all types of information. He told them he knew Christie was at the Slavens' home. He had not told Diane where she was. When Fred Hugi heard this, he felt stark dread. If Wes knew where Christie was, it surely would be only a matter of time until Diane found out too. During the day Hugi knew Diane was in Cottage Grove delivering mail, and he relaxed a little. But not much. There was no way he could know where she was *all* the time or what she was doing—or what she might be planning to do. If the DA or the sheriff had had any manpower left, Hugi would have put a tail on Diane. But there was no one.

"That whole summer was cat and mouse," Hugi recalls. But it was sometimes a question of who was the cat—and who was the mouse. One afternoon, Hugi spotted Diane tearing out of the courthouse in a rage. Obviously, it wasn't one of her on-camera days. She was braless in a cut-off T-shirt; Hugi saw no trace of her pious television image. He was curious. Was there someone she would run to see when she was this angry? He stayed just far enough behind to keep out of sight as he followed her to her car, then he quickly slid behind the wheel of his.

"She didn't even know I was behind her," Hugi remembers. "She went up I-105 at seventy miles an hour, cutting in and out between cars. I kept up with her—long enough to see she wasn't going anyplace special—she just liked to go fast; there was a wild side to her."

Mad or not, Diane always drove that way. She was stopped twice in one day in Cottage Grove for speeding by a state trooper. When Hugi asked the state cop why he'd only given her one ticket, the cop shrugged and said, "It would look like we were really piling it on her."

Diane was back to driving her old Ford Fiesta; the red Nissan was still in the Lane County shops, held as evidence.

When Steve Downs flew to Eugene to visit Christie and Danny, their meetings were supervised and held at the Children's Services Division. This eased Fred Hugi's mind. Of all the people in Diane's life, Hugi considered Steve the most volatile. He had vacillated between love and hate for his ex-wife for over a decade; he was an unknown factor. Diane wanted

her children and Hugi feared Steve Downs might relent and help her get
them back.

Eight weeks after the shootings on Old Mohawk, Diane still walked free,
but the only person who seemed to believe totally in her innocence was
her brother Paul. Lew kept questioning her, and her dad wanted proof
that somebody else had fired the gun. Doug Welch and Kurt Wuest were
totally prejudiced. They wouldn't believe she was innocent if they'd been
there and seen the whole thing. Diane detested Welch and she was rapidly
growing disenchanted with Kurt Wuest.

On July 15 she called Sheriff Burks. She wanted to talk to *him*—not his
detectives. Burks agreed to see Diane late that same afternoon. Accompanied by her brother Paul, who carried a tape recorder, Diane arrived at
Burks's office at 4:45.

She had grievances. Dave Burks let her talk; her voice was almost a
monologue on the county's tapes. Every so often, the sheriff would throw
in a question, but it wasn't easy to find a break in her chain of sentences.
Diane explained to Burks that his investigators were looking in the wrong
direction. "I don't want to cause trouble for you guys. All I want is to get
some facts laid out. I'm afraid I have an advantage over you in that I *know*
I'm telling the truth . . . It looked like I did it, I'm sure, but I didn't do it."

Diane explained that the killer was still out there, and she was concerned that he might murder someone else. For three and a half hours,
Diane reprised the case for Burks, stressing that Christie was being brainwashed by detectives who cared nothing for her. Her own detective work
had revealed a subtle conspiracy—intended to sacrifice Diane Downs.

Naturally, there were some things she still didn't remember about May
19. Other things were clear.

"I knew that every second counted . . . The only thing that kept me going was Danny's crying. Danny just kept crying. He didn't stop once. Just
real soft and quiet. Just constant crying, and if it hadn't been for Danny, I
really think I'd of flipped out and run because of the sight of Christie in
the back seat. All the blood and the sounds and the smell . . . it's terri-
fying."

Burks had heard about Diane Downs's compulsion to talk, he'd read
transcripts of interviews, even heard tapes—but he wasn't prepared for

this "verbal vomit" as Doug Welch characterized it. The woman never seemed to breathe; she just kept talking, explaining, dismissing, criticizing, condemning, rationalizing. The day waned to dusk, past dusk, and then full dark outside before Diane had said all she had to say.

Diane suggested to Sheriff Burks that it was the Oregon State Children's Services Division that he should be investigating. She had evidence that CSD was deliberately brainwashing children, making them emotionally handicapped so that the state could bring in another $260.00 a month.

Did she *really* believe that? Burks stared at her dumbfounded.

Diane had intended that her marathon interview with Sheriff Burks would change the thrust of the investigation, but she had failed.

If there were such a thing as a rule book for murder suspects, the first chapter would strongly advise against dialogue with authorities. Even a neophyte defense attorney knows that. Diane was talking too much. To too many people. She had accused police of putting her under a microscope, of tunnel vision. And yet it was Diane who kept pulling attention back to herself. Diane Downs was figuratively jumping up and down, waving her arms, and crying, "Here I am! Look at me! *Look at me!*"

Diane complained about Burks to the papers.

Usually taciturn, Burks had had enough. "I'm not going to carry this media exhibition on with Mrs. Downs. If the press wants to write that and answer to every beck and call of Mrs. Downs, and go to her press conferences, then they can do that . . . I don't think it's appropriate to try a case in the media."

Diane rushed to the *Springfield News* and told them Burks had likened the press games to charades. This term initially infuriated Diane, but she grew to like the sound of it. "If they want to call what I'm doing a charade, well I'd call this *investigation* a charade," she cried.

Charades is a game played without speaking. In this of all games, Diane could never hope to excel.

CHAPTER 26

My God! My kids are the only people that loved me no matter what. I know you used to love me, but it's when it's convenient for you, and they always loved me—no matter what . . . God, I miss them. Why did all this have to happen? Who could hate me this much? . . . God, I just want somebody to hug me and tell me everything's going to be OK—even though it isn't . . .

—Diane Downs, phone call to Lew, July, 1983

Diane was in one of her spinning phases, hell-bent for destruction. Jim Jagger couldn't stop her from jousting with the police. She still talked to Lew on the phone frequently—long, long meandering conversations. He was definitely living with Nora. In fact, when Diane called Lew, Nora sometimes answered the phone. And she was just as sweet as pie, just took a message or handed the phone over to Lew.

Weird! Diane thought.

Diane told Lew exactly nothing that would help the State's case against her. She cried a good deal and begged for sympathy. Lew found it hard to respond.

"The whole world's gone crazy. I don't know what's going on," Diane said.

"Naw," Lew grunted. "The whole world ain't gone crazy. The whole world is just the same as it always was and always will be."

"*How come I'm so alone?*" she moaned. "All I want is my life to be normal. I don't want anybody to know me. I just want my kids. I want somebody to . . . say I love you."

There was such bleak irony in what Diane said. Her kids *had* loved her, and Christie and Danny probably still did.

With Carl Peterson, Christie was finally able to mention her mother aloud, although her speech impediment exacerbated noticeably when she did so. Carefully, he unfolded a newspaper, showing her the portrait of her family published back in May. Christie studied it silently.

She knew that Diane's birthday was coming up soon. She had always gotten a card for her mother and made a present. She worried about whether she should do that now. Christie was still unwilling or unable to remember the bad things, but she was not testing Evelyn Slaven as much to see if Evelyn would still be there in the middle of the night, or in the morning when she woke up.

Evelyn was always there.

If Diane could stay away from the detectives, she stood a good chance of avoiding indictment. If no charges were brought, sooner or later the children would be returned to her. The mixture as before. Cheryl was gone, of course, but Diane knew she could have other babies.

Although Fred Hugi was still figuratively walking just behind Diane—always—she never thought about him, much less counted him a danger. She saw Kurt Wuest and Doug Welch as her prime adversaries. But not for long; the extra month the county had given them on the case was almost gone. In less than two weeks, they had to file away their Downs follow-ups and go back into uniform.

It was galling. They would do what they could on their own time, but they knew it wouldn't be enough.

Diane continued to spend a great deal of her time on the telephone: calling Lew, calling the TV stations, calling the print media. And most unwise of all, she couldn't resist calling Kurt Wuest. Diane was ambivalent about Kurt. He'd always attracted her; he looked a good deal like Danny's father, Russ. Diane phoned Kurt almost every day. She complained about the sheriff, and Tracy, and Welch. She was flirtatious, suggesting that she had things to say to him—if he would come to see her alone. Diane dangled tantalizing carrots of information under Wuest's nose. Little teasers about the case.

On July 19, the two-month anniversary of the shooting, Diane asked Wuest to come over to her parents' home. "I would like for you to come over—and your buddy. You guys run around like Mormons—there's always two of you."

"What do you have planned?"

"I want to talk to you guys . . . I told you everything about the case—
except for one thing, and that was the true conversation that I had with
this joker . . . Please be very discreet or I will get killed and I'd just as soon
stay alive."

Wuest was ecstatic—until Diane called to cancel the meet. She was
frightened. She told Wuest that she had suddenly remembered that the
person with the gun had known her! Steve was "making waves." Her own
life didn't matter much to her, but she was afraid for Christie and Danny.
Diane thought perhaps she might come down to the sheriff's office the
next day. Wuest reminded her that he would have to read her the Miranda
rights again. She was still technically a suspect. That was OK with her.

But Diane didn't show up. She called to say she needed time to gather
her courage to share her new information.

"Besides," she added. "Is it *really* important that he knew me?"

"There's a big difference between a . . . person that has some association with you, or just some bum walking out of the woods," Wuest replied
through clenched teeth.

"Yes, I understand. I understand and I apologize—but like I told you
yesterday—if you were just a little girl with three kids—cut down to two
kids—I don't think that you'd be running to the cops and telling them
that—[not] if somebody said, 'Don't say anything 'cause you're going to be
killed!'"

She sounded like that little girl, her voice all crumpled in with fear. She
said Jim Jagger had suggested that a counselor or a hypnotist might help
her remember more. She told Kurt that maybe she was so scared she
didn't want to remember . . . to go back to the blood and the pain.

"Give me a few days . . . I swear to God I'll get back with you because if
I can tell you guys something that's going to help clean this up, I'm damn
sure going to do it—because I'm sick of this whole thing too, and as scary
as it is for me to have to relive this whole thing, I'm willing to do it just to
finish it."

Hell, they didn't *have* a few days, Wuest thought. He reminded Diane
of that.

Diane insisted she was petrified even to try to remember.

Christie, who had every reason to be even more afraid, was working
determinedly with Carl Peterson, and isolated images had begun to flash

across her mind more frequently. She'd known all along; it was just so hard to try to say it aloud.

Welch and Wuest conferred with Fred Hugi and DA Pat Horton.

"Diane's calling us, hinting that she wants to get everything straightened out—that she remembers the guy knew her. Should we go for it?" Wuest asked. "If we can get her in to our office, should we try for a heavy duty interrogation?

"Go for it," Hugi said. "It may be the last chance we're going to have. Get her talking . . . and see what comes out."

But Diane continued to back off every appointment she made with Wuest. He and Welch decided to give her another reason to come in. They had obtained a mug shot of Samasan Timchuck, the man Dolores Holland knew.

Wuest called Diane and asked her to come in and view a mug laydown of six possible suspects. Even though Jim Jagger advised against it, Diane told them she'd come in after work. "I pay Jagger—he works for me—and *I* decide what I want to do."

Welch and Wuest were elated; they were going to get one more chance! It wasn't difficult to decide which one would be the "bad guy," the irritant: Welch.

Diane arrived at the detectives' offices in the courthouse at a quarter to four, still wearing her postal uniform. They moved along the corridor to Welch's office, a twelve by fifteen room with two small windows looking out on a private courtyard. Diane sat across from Doug Welch's desk. She could see green leaves, birds, an occasional butterfly through the dusty little windows above his head. On the wall behind her, there was a huge print of some nameless lake, evergreens, snowy mountaintops. The walls of the room were once white, now faded blah beige.

It was like any detective's office; piles of teletypes rested on clipboards on a table nearby. But it was hardly the stereotypical interrogation room with a single light over the suspect's head.

Diane appeared relaxed.

She perused the photos Wuest showed her and commented that Timchuck's looked "real close"—but his cheeks were "too puffy."

Wuest and Welch held their breaths. Would she get up and leave now that she'd finished viewing the mug shots?

. . . no.

What eventually came to be known as the "hardball interview" began. Diane wanted to discuss the "good" suspects in the case.

"Steve Downs—my ex-husband. I divorced him two years ago, and he hated me for that."

"OK. Let's go on to Number Two," Welch suggested. They already knew that Steve had been in Arizona on the night of May 19.

"Stan Post is Steve's best friend . . . If one can commit a crime and get away with it, the other one will do it. They are like a stepladder and they keep pulling each other up, and Stan hated me while I was pregnant [with Danny]—"

Welch cut in, ending the flood of words. "OK. Let's talk about Nora."

"Her main motive is the fact that Lew loves me . . . We have been together for a year and it was an affair. I was his mistress and I'm not ashamed of that—it's just the way life is sometimes . . . He left Nora several times . . . I'm here, and therefore Lew would have to either move up here or bring me back there . . . but her *motive* . . . if she destroyed my kids, she would destroy Lew's desire for me because Lew is a person that doesn't like complications—he doesn't like hassles."

Diane's accusations were all a disappointing rehash of her earlier diatribes. Welch reminded her that she'd said she remembered now that the shooter had called her by name, and that he'd mentioned her tattoo.

Yes, she recalled that. He—they—had said they would come back and kill her if she told. She'd been afraid to tell.

"So this person knew you, referred to you by name, referred to your tattoo," Welch began. "Do you think it's logical to assume that this individual was sent up here from Arizona?"

"I would think so because there's nobody—only a couple of people up here—that know about my tattoo . . . I'd only been here for six weeks . . . I hadn't been here long enough to get any enemies . . . so if they referred to my tattoo, that means they must have come from Arizona—or were sent from Arizona."

"The kicker—the kicker," Welch mused.

"I know, I know," Diane cut in eagerly.

"How—"

"How would they know that I was going to be on that road? I don't know ... If I was set up, how would somebody know that I would be on that obsolete road? I don't have the foggiest ... Burks asked me the other day was I followed? I don't know—but who looks to see if they're followed?"

Kurt Wuest came up with another "kicker."

"Wait a second. If you *were* followed, how could they ... get somebody in front to wave you down?"

"I don't know ... I don't understand it in the least."

"The whole thing's bizarre," Wuest agreed.

"All I know is that I can tell you what he said ... anything that I can remember to tell you. OK? If it doesn't fit in, well—damn it—you syphon it out then."

"We'll work it out," Welch said.

Diane rushed on. The yellow car was important—but she didn't know why. "I could see the trees and I could see the bends in the road, and I see again my kids getting shot, and it was something that my mind would just fight with and the yellow car was there ... it's so weird. At the time that the person threatened me ... I wasn't supposed to say anything because I would be killed ... it didn't seem that it was somebody that knew me, and I don't know why because that's insane too ... You're concerned about your kids living or dying and one of them did die, and you've got so many things on your mind, your sense of hope, you're so flipped-out about everything that you've seen, everything that you've felt, and maybe your mind just doesn't let you feel that it's your fault—even though it was somebody that hated me that much that did that, and so you block out the fact that it was somebody that knew you."

Diane looked up and caught the detectives' expressions. "You're making faces, but it does make sense—"

"I don't understand," Kurt Wuest said. "You mentioned something about being your fault?"

"Somebody hated me enough that they would do this. So it *is* my fault."

Diane said she was terrified when the last thing the gunman said was—her name. She had just been shot, and she was still outside her car when he breathed her name and threatened to kill her if she told.

"But we had armed guards on you and the children when we interviewed you in the hospital." Wuest was puzzled.

"But I had to go *home* from the hospital."

"That was quite a few days later."

"I didn't know that. Can't you put yourself in my place and quit being a detective and just be a person?"

"I am a detective," Wuest said. "I am a person and—but . . . if you had fear for your safety and your children's safety, it would seem to me that would have been the best time—when you had all the policemen around, armed guards on both your kids . . . not now."

"Correct," Diane agreed. "But the person has no reason to come get me now, because you guys are chasing *me*. He couldn't be safer."

"They don't know that," Wuest countered. "We are still showing pictures in the paper."

"You guys are still calling me suspect . . . Who in the world would feel safer? The person that did this."

Diane was not as happy with the debate as she had been. She hinted that she would prefer another time. "I have very little patience with men."

"We're getting anxious," Wuest said frankly.

"It's kind of exciting, you know," Welch said.

"Yes, it is." Diane brightened. "It's scary—"

They checked the tape, whirring in the background. Welch took off his tie, undid his collar, and rolled up the sleeves of his white shirt. He was sweating.

Welch asked her why she had turned away from the route home after she'd left the road Heather Plourd lived on. It was late and very dark then.

She had only been looking for a scenic route—to sightsee. "For what reason did you stop and turn around again?" Welch pushed.

"Well, because I looked in the back seat and Christie was asleep. There was no sense in going sightseeing—I had already seen that route."

"Oh, kids had konked out?"

"Yes, Christie had. Cheryl was still awake."

"How about Danny?" Wuest asked.

"I don't know—he was quiet—I'm assuming he was asleep."

How fast had she been driving after she turned around and finally headed toward home, only to impulsively decide to turn off the main road again and drive along the little road that curved beside the river?

Forty miles an hour.

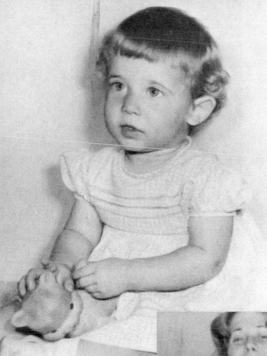

Elizabeth Diane Frederickson at 10 months.

An ebullient Diane, age 16, with Steve Downs at a Baptist Church New Year's Eve party.

Diane, an "A" student, graduated from Moon Valley High School in Phoenix in 1973.

Below: The Downs family in early 1980. Left to right: Cheryl Lynn, Steve, Diane, Steven Daniel, and Christie Ann.

The Downses' new house on Palomino Street in Chandler, Arizona.

When Diane left Steve, she bought this new mobile home, only to have it burn mysteriously a few months later.

Below: Christie, left, age 4, with Cheryl, age 3.

Above: Danny Downs learning to walk in 1980.

Diane's red Nissan in the emergency room entrance the night of May 19, 1983.

Christie's shoes and airway were left in the car as doctors and nurses fought to save the youngsters' lives.

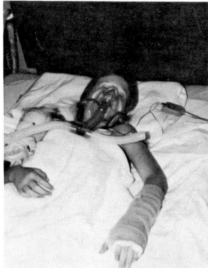

Christie Downs in the Intensive Care Unit after the shooting. Shot twice in the chest and hand, she survived profound blood loss, heart stoppage, and delicate surgery.

Below: Diane poses for a police photo to show where she suffered a gunshot wound to her left arm.

The scene of the crime: it was here, Diane claimed, that the "shaggy-haired stranger" flagged the car down.

An aerial view of the crime site and surrounding area. For days, divers scoured the "chute," searching for the murder weapon.

Detectives' original composite sketch of the "shaggy-haired stranger," left, and the revised version, right, that Diane had drawn later.

Lane County Detectives Dick Tracy, Kurt West, and Doug Welch investigated the Downs shooting for almost a year before an arrest was made.

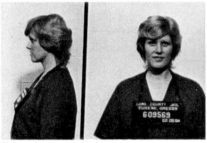

Diane's mug shots.

Willadene Frederickson, left, holds Diane's hand as Wes Frederickson accompanies them to a Juvenile Court hearing. (*Betty Udesen*)

A very obviously pregnant Diane, escorted by personal deputy Chris Rosage, leaves the courthouse. (*Betty Udesen*)

Below: Circuit Court Judge Gregory Foote presided over Diane Downs's long trial in the spring and summer of 1984.

Diane Downs, locked in the Oregon State Correctional Center for Women, continued to proclaim her innocence. *(Michael Jones)*

Diane Downs's escape from prison in July 1987 made her front-page news once again. Recaptured by Oregon State Police, she was later transferred to a maximum security prison in New Jersey. (*Gerry Lewin*)

After the shooting. How fast then?

Diane didn't know about Joe Inman's statements. She had no idea that someone had followed her down the black corridor of Old Mohawk, *after* the shooting.

"But after—after the shooting, you really scooted to the hospital?" Welch asked again.

"I don't know."

"You don't remember?"

"I have never been on the road, and it was dark. I was looking in the back seat most of the way, so I can't tell you that I was driving fast. I was driving slow enough that I didn't go off the road . . . I remember almost hitting the fence. I remember reaching over and rolling Cheryl's window down because I couldn't get my arm down to open my window."

"Where was your arm? Was it in your lap?"

"Yeah, I picked it up and put it in my lap."

"Was it bleeding pretty good then?"

Diane had calmed down; she was weighing each answer carefully, and she was doing well. She had her rhythm back. "I don't remember. I know that when I got to the stop sign, my arm was cold. I looked down to see if I was bleeding a lot, and there was a towel wrapped around it, and I don't remember putting the towel on there either."

"OK. So you don't know if you really raced to the hospital or if you just drove super slow?"

"Or if I stopped. I don't know—I have no idea at all."

Diane's recounting of events had changed subtly. She had been definite in her first taping in the hospital that she had "kept on driving, kept on driving" to the hospital.

Welch reminded her of that.

"I was very definite about everything that I told you—I was not definite about the things that I didn't know—"

"What do you remember telling us about your speed?"

"I don't remember what I told you, but I can tell you I remember I was going fast enough to get to the hospital on time, and slow enough to stay on the road and not wreck."

"*On time?*" Welch asked, puzzled.

"They were all alive . . . I had accomplished my goal, which was to save the kids. *They* killed Cheryl. I didn't. I wasn't the one that took too long driving to the hospital or whatever. My dad tries to say—maybe I blacked out."

"You think you did?"

"If I did, I don't want to think it."

"Whoever had the gun in their hands is the one who killed Cheryl," Wuest said quietly.

"I agree—but I'm the mother and I was there. Why didn't I do something? . . . I don't know why."

They talked about a time lapse, and why Diane had so much trouble remembering.

Wuest proceeded cautiously. "You're probably going to get mad at me."

"Go ahead," she said. "I've been mad at lots of people."

"Yeah, but you haven't been mad at me yet."

"Give me a chance."

"You've been under a lot of stress—you said something earlier—you were possibly blocking out this horrible thing that you saw."

"Yeah?"

"You may have forgotten a lot of these things when you blocked them out on purpose. Do you have any kind of idea at all what this horrible thing could have been?"

"No, I don't. So what are you saying?"

"What I'm trying to say is—"

"What you're trying *not* to say is—"

"You said it was more horrible than watching Christie get shot . . . and bleeding and everything else, and I can't think of anything more horrible than that."

"Neither can I."

"So what would you have to block out that would be more devastating than that?"

"I don't know. I told you that talking about it with you guys wasn't going to fix it."

Diane had come perilously close to the edge, and now she pulled all the way back.

"I gave it a shot," she said. "I really did; I tried."

The interview had come to an end—or at least to a turning place. Diane made no move to leave.

Would she consider seeing a psychiatrist, they asked.

She waffled. Maybe "I could open up without feeling pressed, without feeling that I'm in trouble if I say the wrong things—that maybe my mind really still believes that I'm going to get killed if I say it. And it doesn't feel safe because you guys are my enemy . . . as much as the person who shot me is my enemy."

"Have you been totally truthful and candid with us thus far?" Welch asked her bluntly.

"Yes . . . yes, yes."

"There's nothing you have knowingly omitted?"

"The only thing that I knowingly omitted from you was telling you that the man used my name."

It had come to her in a dream, she said, but by that time, the police had begun to persecute her, and so she had not told them.

"We're talking about a murder investigation, and we can't play little games like we've been playing," Wuest reminded her.

"This is a big game," Diane corrected. "It's not a little game. My daughter's dead—there's nothing more serious than that . . . You should have come to me straightaway," she lectured them, "and said, 'There's a discrepancy. We think you did it and this is why.' You shouldn't play games."

They waited.

"You don't lie to me—but *you don't lie to me for one thing.* Don't ever lie to me, 'cause I hate lying more than anything in the whole world."

Her voice was playful, but the veneer of hostility was there.

Kurt Wuest reminded her that she was free to leave anytime.

She nodded. "I know. As soon as this tape's over, I will be too . . . I'm sorry if I don't trust you. I think that if I did trust you, things would be a lot different."

"Do you think that you'd be able to come up with this *suppressed* information—if you trusted us?" Welch asked.

She didn't know. She laughed. "You are starting to look like a pouting child, Kurt. You're sitting there with a whole bunch of questions and you're just not going to play ball if I don't let you bat."

Diane's war with men had not slackened; she was good at male-female repartee, skilled at keeping men off balance by being alternately seductive and ingenuous, soft and caustically witty. On this July night as the interview strung itself out longer and longer, Diane clearly considered the detectives only men. She might have been rapping with the guys back at the post office. If she even remembered that Kurt and Doug were policemen, one cannot hear it on the tapes.

The interrogation turned a corner; Diane never realized it.

"You want to play hardball?" Welch asked flatly.

"Yeah—I want to find this guy . . . At first—like I said—it didn't matter whether you caught him or not. But now it seems that the only way for my life to get back to normal is to catch him."

"It's very important to us."

"I guess so," Diane agreed. "It's like the forbidden door . . . there's something behind that door that really happened that night—something bad."

"More horrible than watching Christie bleed?" Wuest asked softly. It was a point he would not let go. He had only been waiting.

"Watching Christie get—yeah . . . there was something there . . . I want to know—but at the same time, my mind knows better than my conscious mind. That it's bad and you're not supposed to look."

Wuest continued to question Diane quietly. "There's an emotion that— the only thing I can think of that—that's more horrible than watching a little girl get shot and bleed, and blank your mind out—is if *I* had some involvement doing it."

"I agree," Diane said pertly.

"That would be—"

"That would be horrible," she finished.

"That would probably be more horrible than watching the little girl—"

"You're right," she said. "That would be terrible." Diane caught herself up sharply. "I know for a fact that *I* didn't do it."

Doug Welch played the smart-ass, demanding more explanation, throwing out impertinent questions that annoyed Diane. But only a little. She could deal with him.

"Why?" he asked now. Why did she know she hadn't done it?

"Because—"

"You can't remember," Wuest said.

"I know that I didn't do it."

"You don't remember," Welch said. "You're telling us that you don't remember."

"I remember seeing Christie get shot. I remember the man reaching in the car and shooting her."

"Diane," Kurt Wuest said, "I'm being flat-out straight with you. You say there's a void there, that something's missing and—you're saying whatever it is, it's more horrible than seeing Christie bleed and I say that the only thing I can think of that would be more horrible is if I had the gun in my hand and I saw that."

Diane didn't flinch. "I agree with you. That would be devastating."

"Right, and that would create . . . a void."

"Or perhaps," she began slowly, "it's knowing that it's going to happen and that you could stop it somehow . . . I know what would be horrible, is—it's worse—" She looked up. "If the world was going to end tomorrow, would you want to know about it?"

"Yeah," Wuest answered laconically.

"Figures . . . Would you?" Diane turned to Welch.

"Yup."

"I wouldn't because . . . I would live the whole rest of this last day in agony, trying to do all the things I couldn't do—or trying to stop it—when you knew that it was futile, and just knowing that it was going to happen, what if the man taunted me with it? What if he was telling me how he was going to do it? I don't know."

The tape ran out.

They expected Diane to leave. But she gestured to them to put on another tape. It was twelve minutes to five in the afternoon, and now they could hear flies buzzing in the hot room. The leaves through the tiny windows were still. All the birds had left the courtyard.

"We just took a short break," Kurt told the tape recorder. "Diane, you indicated that you wanted to stop after the last tape?"

"Yeah—I was in the middle of a thought . . . We were talking about what could be more horrible than seeing my daughter get shot, and I was simply relating the fact that I can think of something more horrible, and that is knowing that it's going to happen and not being able to stop it."

But that thought, she was quick to point out, was only an assumption—not a true memory.

Doug Welch asked her if she was afraid at the present time.

"Of whom?" she asked.

"Us."

"No."

"Not at all?"

"No."

"Are you worried?"

"No."

"I think I started to say this earlier," Welch said. "I've been working this case since the beginning and involved very deeply in the investigation—and there are some things which just don't jibe."

"OK," she said.

Kurt Wuest stood up, and paced the small office. Diane casually propped her feet up on his vacant chair and waited to hear Welch's theory, a half-smile on her face.

"Is it possible—we know that you told us numerous times, you loved your kids deeply—they are basically your whole world—"

"Yeah."

"And you have also talked about fits of depression that you've had since; you said that Steve used to get you to a point where you contemplated suicide."

"Yeah . . . yeah."

"Is it possible that you were in one of these states of depression that night? And wanted to commit suicide, but couldn't stand the thought of your kids being without a mother, and decided to take them with you so they could be with you?"

"No. First of all, I don't have the right. Nobody has the right to judge whether another person lives or dies. If I chose that I should die, I would take pills—because it's painless."

"But who would take care of the kids?" Wuest asked.

"Whomever. My parents would, of course. If I were to kill myself, I would take pills, because I don't want to hurt. I don't like pain. I'm very bad with pain; I can't even stand a splinter. I would not take my children's

lives because God gave them life to do with as they saw fit. He simply
loaned those kids to me to raise in the best way possible. So that when
they became adults they would have a better start. It is not my decision
whether their lives should stop or not and so I wouldn't do that. So even
in a fit of depression, I wouldn't do that . . . God decides when you go—and
crazy men decide."

Kurt Wuest suddenly asked Diane about Lew. Yes, she was still in love
with him.

"Would you call it," Wuest began tentatively, ". . . an obsession?"

"No, an obsession is something that you can't let go of—there were
times in the past when I became obsessed with him."

"*Have* you let go of him?"

"Yes . . . I still love him . . . you don't hang on just because you still love."

They threw the tough question out harshly. Had Diane shot her children to get Lew back?

She shook her head impatiently. "He doesn't like trouble. If I had gone
to the extent of shooting my kids, that would never bring Lew back."

"Not if you weren't caught," Wuest put in.

"Oh that's insane. Even if I wasn't caught, Cheryl is still dead . . . It's
going to affect *me* emotionally—probably for the rest of my life . . . Lew
can't handle that. It's the stupidest motive in the world to kill—to kill the
kids for Lew's sake."

And yet. And still. It was the most cogent reason they had come up
with.

Diane turned suddenly to Doug Welch. "I'm learning to play the game.
This is very interesting. You can twist a word and make somebody look
guilty."

The tape rolled on. The little office was full to bursting with the sound
of Diane's voice.

"As the days progressed, I saw you guys were assholes. You couldn't be
trusted as far as I could throw you. And I may be strong, but some of you
weigh a lot."

She was growing angrier. Wuest reminded her that she could leave at
any time.

"I also know that I am not guilty; I have no reason to get up and leave until you become offensive—and you're working on it—you really are. You're getting close. Borderline." They were cops again. How could she have forgotten that?

"You have something to say?" Wuest asked.

"Oh my God," she cried. "You are so fucked up. I've told you everything I could!"

But she had lied to them, they pointed out. She had withheld the fact that the gunman knew her.

"You told us everything you could a month and a half ago, two months ago," Wuest said. "And now we get more stuff and who knows what the hell we will have next week?"

"Tell you what, guys—I'll make you a deal ... OK. Next time I remember something, fuck ya. You can find the guy yourself, 'cause I know I didn't do it. You can chase your little tails for the next twenty thousand years if that's what it takes. You don't like my help—you can fuck it."

They offered the door. She shook her head.

"I'm having too much fun."

But she wasn't. Somewhere along the way, Diane's control had wavered; she had lost the debate. These two young detectives had turned nasty on her.

She wasn't going to leave until she won.

Doug Welch was the worst, nipping at her with his questions. He had been polite, respectful, bitten his tongue for two solid months. Now, he could allow enmity to creep into his voice. He told her she hadn't had the guts to commit suicide.

"No guts? If I had the guts to shoot my own flesh and blood, why wouldn't I have the guts to end it all and not remember any of it?"

"Diane's a pretty important person, Diane's Number One; Diane always has been Number One," Welch hammered. "Steve wouldn't be a good father and you don't want him to have the kids."

"You're right. I agree with that."

"And you're very—you're possessive of those kids."

"I love my kids, yes."

"Well, it goes beyond love. It goes—there's a lot of possessiveness."

"It goes to being willing to die for them, yeah—" she said.

"Wait a second," Wuest said. "Would you give your own life for your children?"

"Yes."

"And you stood there and watched them get shot? And you didn't do a damn thing."

"I guess so. I don't know."

"Figure that one out," Welch said. Diane was as enraged as he had ever seen her. Would she get angry enough to tear the sarcastic, superior facade away—to "remember" what was in the void? "You stood by and watched your kids executed, lady."

"Yeah—I agree with you."

"And then you hung around long enough for the guy to talk to you."

"No."

"Yeah."

"He didn't say anything afterward, except 'Don't say anything.' That's not talking."

"But there was other conversation. You just don't happen to recall it."

"That's right."

"Or want to—"

"Right. Before the shooting, because I remember from the shooting on. Something was said before the shooting."

"What?"

"I don't know."

"Back to the void again."

"I forgot I wasn't going to try with you guys. You're assholes. You don't really want to know the truth. You just want to find a way to clean this up—"

"We want to know the truth—"

"No, you don't."

"From the beginning, you kept throwing us little bits and pieces . . ."

"I'm sorry if my mind—OK. I'll tell you what. I'll make a deal with you guys. You don't make deals—I forgot."

"We don't make deals," Wuest agreed.

"Well then, fuck you. I was going to say—give me two weeks and I'll give you the whole story in a pie pan. I can't guarantee that either, 'cause I don't know if I'll ever really remember."

"You can walk out, you can walk out anytime you want."

"I'm about ready to."

"How many mothers," Welch's voice cut through the tension, deliberately dripping venom. She half-smiled at him; they both knew he was playing a part. Still, his words shook her. "How many mothers who are good, wholesome, loving mothers—like you—are not going to protect their children in time of danger?"

"I have no idea."

"One was [killed], and Mom gets away with a little hole in the arm?"

"I don't know."

"Isn't that bizarre?"

"Yeah it is."

"Mom didn't do any fighting or anything. Isn't that strange?"

"And this guy is one hell of a shot," Wuest added.

"You were the biggest threat to this man," Welch continued. "He wanted your car. The kids weren't a threat as far as witnesses were concerned. You were. Why does he shoot the kids? And then lets you drive away, Diane?"

"Good question," she said. And then, in a rush, "I told you he didn't come to take the car."

"Not three little kids. He didn't—*what?*" Welch asked.

"He didn't come to take the car."

"That's what you've told us he asked for."

"Ummmm . . . you're right. I did."

"That's right."

"Oh crud," Diane sighed suddenly. "My arm hurts."

The corner was tightening around her, and her voice was softer and less sure. Suddenly, her wounded arm hurt.

"That guy's quite a shot," Welch droned. "He hit three little bodies in a dark car and hits them all dead center, and the big adult person—out in the open, standing right next to him. He hits you in the arm. Think about it, Diane."

"You're right. You're right. Hmmmmm. I've thought about it."

"Any response?"

"Yeah. I'm not going to tell you guys. God!"

"Scary, isn't it?"

"Yeah."

"Did you just remember something new?"

"Damned if I'm going to tell you guys."

"Why don't you get it off your chest?"

"Huh uh."

"You've been playing games since the beginning," Welch kept after her. "You thought you really pulled one over on us."

"I'm curious," Kurt Wuest said, "I'm curious about this incredible thought or remembrance—"

"No, you're not," she hissed. "No you're not. You're a lying asshole and if you say that, you're a double liar." Suddenly, Diane sat straight up, a look of dawning revelation on her face.

"I just remembered how—"

"But I'm not going to tell you guys," Wuest mimicked.

"You're right. I'm not—it's—"

"This man shoots three little bodies in a car—" Welch spat out. "Damn near dead center . . . and then a big adult gets winged in the arm—"

"The one that could have hit him on the head with a rock—or anything," Wuest said.

"The one that could have done something to prevent the kids from being shot to begin with—and who stands by and watches her kids be executed—" Welch echoed.

"All right," Diane breathed.

"And then doesn't tell the cops the whole story when she gets there, because she's afraid of this man who threatened her and who called her by name and referred to her tattoo. Come on, Diane. We are playing hardball here. Remember?"

Welch wondered if she was going to slap him.

"I know—Tell you guys what—"

"It's your turn at bat."

"OK! Since you guys seem to think I should have brought the guy in with me, I will get him myself and I'll bring him back. 'Cause I know who did it!"

"You do know who did it?"

"Yes, I do. I damn sure do!"

"You know this person," Welch said, surprised. "You know his name?"

"Yes I do. Yes, I do."
"You know him by name?"
"Yes."
"You saw him shoot your kids?" Wuest asked quietly.
"Yup."
"That's pretty important."

Diane was on her feet, poised for flight. "And I saw him grab my arm, and yank my arm out, and shoot my arm and say, 'Now try to get away with it, Bitch!' And I'm leaving 'cause I know who did it. Bye."

Doug Welch's office was open on one side; they could see Diane all the way down the hallway to the front door of the Criminal Investigation Division. She was running, jogging as fast as she could to get away from them. The door opened, slammed. She was gone.

Welch's voice follows a long silence. "The time is 17:46, and Diane has just departed the office. We are concluding the tape."

The two young detectives sat in Doug Welch's shadowy office. They had it all on tape—but they weren't sure what they had. They had pushed her into some manner of admission, but they'd lost her.

The phone rang, and they both jumped.

It was Diane.

They had badgered her into a "breakthrough." She remembered the whole night now, she knew who had done it—but that he "wasn't present." However, she herself would find a way to prove it.

"You're telling us that you know who shot your kids," Wuest echoed, while Doug Welch fumbled frantically with the tape recorder.

"I damn sure do. I remember the whole fucking night."

Diane would not tell them who the "shooter" was, but she assured them the killer was too scared to hurt anyone else.

"I'm not playing that game anymore, I'm not playing by your rules. I'm going to find the asshole myself."

It was uglier than she had realized, she told them. But she couldn't trust them. She didn't believe that the cops could bring the killer to justice.

"What was uglier than you thought?" Wuest asked her.

"The fact that somebody could hate me so much that they'd destroy my kids just to get even with me . . . If I don't say anything, maybe he'll never get another chance to shoot the kids—because the kids won't be a threat to him."

"What else do you have to tell us, Diane?"

"How the yellow car ties in. How many people were there. What they did to me. Why there's a time lapse and everything took so long.

"And just because I tell you exactly what happened that night, that doesn't mean you can prove he did it. It's a losing battle. I quit. I give up. If you guys want to throw me in jail, have at it. I—Steve wins this time. This is the ultimate. I quit. I'm not going to fight him anymore. He won. Goodbye."

The phone went dead.

Kurt Wuest and Doug Welch stared at each other. What the hell did they have now? Diane had changed her story again. And what had she meant that she'd "quit"?

She scarcely seemed to have quit at all. They had the feeling that she had only gone away for a while to gather strength.

Early the next morning, Doug Welch and Kurt Wuest were in Fred Hugi's office. They turned the tape recorder on and Hugi and DA Pat Horton listened along with them through the long, long tapes as Diane's voice rose and fell. She had told them everything; she had told them nothing.

And now, they were out of time. And the county was out of money. There was no arrest. To the outside observer, the Downs investigation appeared to be over.

It was not over; it had only gone underground. If Fred Hugi could have, he would have found a way to go back and save them all. Of course, he could not. But there was no way he was going to drop his mission to bring Diane into court. Without investigators, he was only slowed; he was not stopped.

Hugi lay awake long into the summer night, listening to owls and nighthawks in the forest outside. He went through game plans in his head but more often he worried about Christie and Danny. It had been easier, somehow, when he could sit outside the ICU and watch over them as they slept. They seemed more vulnerable to him now, as if they were still prey.

CHAPTER 27

In July of 1983, I changed the beneficiary on my $50,000 life insurance policy. It paid off whether death was natural, accidental, or suicide... I changed it so my children would benefit, and not the guardian [State of Oregon]. I also had a will drawn up. There was no reason for me to be here....

— Diane Downs, letter to the author, 1984

Diane believed she had thwarted Doug Welch and Kurt Wuest; it was an empty victory. As the summer of 1983 waned, she became steadily more depressed. She didn't have her kids back. Lew had turned out to be a total fink; it finally dawned on Diane that he was only calling her to ask questions for the cops. Her attorney confirmed her suspicions about Lew. Nobody gave a damn about her. She thought of suicide—just as she had when she'd slashed her wrist at thirteen; she even used the same phrase to explain her feelings: "No reason for me to be here."

Diane's pressures were all internal. The Lane County detective unit had virtually dissolved. The investigators weren't dogging her trail anymore.

Fred Hugi didn't feel much better. Jim Jagger had—through the defense's rights of discovery—laid his hands on every bit of information the prosecution had. Hugi wondered if he should just go ahead and argue his case in juvenile court. But if the State should lose in juvenile court, double jeopardy could attach and block any murder trial. There was a precedent case where exactly that had happened. Now that Jagger had discovery, he no longer pushed for the juvenile court custody hearing despite Diane's pressure. In the end, that long summer, Hugi and Jagger simply stood pat. Waiting.

On August 3, Diane had surgery to remove bone chips from her arm. It wasn't major surgery, but she dreaded a loss of will under general anesthetic, and the pills afterward to dull the pain. She needed a keen mind.

A second court hearing concerning her visitation rights to the kids was held on August 4. She didn't go; she didn't think she had a chance anyway to see Christie and Danny.

She was right. Diane was again denied visits with her children. Judge Gregory Foote explained that he would ask for psychological evaluations of both Diane and Christie before he considered further visitation requests. But he pointed out that if the police were unable to develop clear evidence against Diane, his only choice would eventually be to reunite Danny and Christie with their mother.

CSD worker Susan Staffel testified that the children seemed less afraid since their mother had been prevented from visiting them, and that doctors felt they might be able to unearth their repressed memories if and when they felt safe.

Diane was ordered to keep her health insurance, which covered her children, in force.

The next day, Jim Jagger got Diane to a psychologist.

Diane liked Polly Jamison, her therapist. Polly was a young woman too, new in practice, and Diane felt sympathy from her. Polly gave her an MMPI test. Just as they had when she was given the same test for the surrogate mother screening two years earlier, Diane's scores showed clumpings that indicated antisocial personality patterns. Diane explained that her answers would have been different before the shooting, and Jamison, finding that a cogent argument, gave her a repeat test where her answers came closer to a normal profile.

Diane's mood lifted appreciably when she received a birthday card from Christie on August 7. The picture on the card was a cluster of red roses. Christie had remembered! That proved to Diane that Christie still loved her, no matter what.

Christie had been ambivalent about Diane's birthday. Recognizing her painful indecision, Evelyn Slaven helped her pick out a card. Christie, the little mother still, felt responsible for Diane, and wondered who was looking out for her, now that she was all alone. No matter what was beginning to surface in Christie's memory, she seemed to view Diane not as her mother but as a lost little girl who had no friends. Christie's mind rested easier after she sent the card.

Steve Downs called Diane too. His love/hate feelings for her had apparently not changed, but he wished her happy birthday.

There was no card, no call—nothing at all—from Lew.

On August 13, Diane called Lew. She was ready to confront him.

"First of all," she demanded. "Are you still taping for the sheriff's department?"

He didn't flinch. "Are you?"

"Are *you*?"

"Uh huh."

"OK."

"And you're taping for you," he said placidly.

"You should know that I am not capable of doing something as horrible as that. It takes a person that's got a real problem to kill somebody, and to kill their own kids would be insane."

"*I* think so," Lew agreed softly.

Their voices on the tapes (his-and-hers tapes now) are flat and wrung dry of emotion. If they ever loved at all, one cannot detect it any longer. Diane sounds depressed; Lew has clearly grown tired of the games contrived to make her tell him the truth.

"I'm tired of fighting." Diane's voice is heavy. "I have very little energy left. They almost made [sic] me to the point that I was so depressed that I couldn't stand it anymore, and getting a card from Christie got me going again . . . I've got to help those other people and keep fighting, 'cause that's their biggest hang-up so far—is that nobody will speak out against the cops because they don't know what to say, but this case is so ripe, so fantastic . . . It's like the guy that rapes women over and over and over. If one woman will stand up and say he's the one that did it and this is what happened, it might start a trend and people will start speaking up and saying, 'Hey—yeah—he's the one that got me too.'"

She hinted that she wasn't alone in her quest. She told Lew that there was a "higher authority with much more power than the sheriff's department, and they're watching the sheriff's department, and they have been for quite some time, and they screwed up real bad."

But, in the next breath, Diane as much as spelled out to Lew that she was considering suicide. If he should ever receive a tape cassette from her, he must promise to listen to it. What would it be? Her confession, he suspected, rife with blame for him.

He mumbled something unintelligible. He had heard it all before. Threats and promises.

Accompanied by attorneys Jim Jagger and Lauren Holland, Diane flew to Chandler in the last week of August, 1983. They were looking for witnesses who could present a sympathetic picture of Diane. It might only be for a custody hearing; it might be for a murder trial. Until the other shoe dropped, no one could be sure.

Hearing of the trip, Hugi thought of another reason for it. If Diane should still have possession of the missing Ruger, she might arrange to plant it somewhere in Arizona. That would bolster her contention that the murder plot had originated in that state.

On her own, Diane had made up what she called a "vulnerability list" for Jagger. She listed the fears, secrets, and anxieties of people who had moved in her world. She had always ferreted out Achilles' heels. She wrote out the following guidelines for her attorney:

LEW: Threaten his job and/or himself.

KAREN BATTEN: [Diane's former co-worker who had let Diane live with her when her trailer burned.] Relieve her guilt. Tell her no one blames her for doubting me, and talking to the cops.

KATHY: "Guilt and God." [Diane's sister had called her after the visit in Oklahoma by Dick Tracy. Kathy had told Diane, "I know you're guilty ... but God forgives you."]

AUNT IRENE: "Appeal to her friendship."

ARLYS SIMMS: "Her husband hung himself." [Diane thought a reference to that tragedy would make an ex-neighbor vulnerable.]

GAMI: He owned some property, and Diane suggested that Jagger threaten him vaguely with the Internal Revenue Service—and accuse him of allowing someone to open mail addressed to her.

(Regarding several other postal co-workers in Chandler:)

BARB EBELING: "Hit her sense of fair play—I've always been good to her."

BARB B.: Diane knew a man who Barb was in love with. That would do to throw Barb B. off-balance.

LORA M.: "Prove how I'm innocent. Use guilt and pity."

RUSS PHILLIPS: [Danny's biological father.] "Use Danny. Say Danny will go to Steve if I'm found guilty."

It was an organized grocery list of emotional blackmail. Jagger didn't use it.

After five months in Oregon, Diane's second visit back to Chandler could hardly be called triumphant. Lew barely spoke to her when she confronted him as he came off his route. He said he'd consider talking with her and Jagger, but later he called and refused. Diane blamed Nora for that decision.

Diane was stunned by the cold shoulder she got from everyone. All of her old co-workers stonewalled Jim. She apparently had no friends in Chandler any longer. Diane spent her time sitting in a stifling hot car, waiting while Jagger and Lauren Holland worked their way through the people and places of her past. This was not how she'd visualized her return to Arizona. She and Lew were only a few miles apart, and yet he went about his life, making no effort to see her again.

Chandler was the same; but nothing else was.

Christie Downs was making tremendous progress living with the Slavens in her foster home. She still could not speak clearly, nor would she talk about the shooting. Her right arm still hung limp with paralysis. But she laughed now, and the nightmares were only sporadic. She was becoming very comfortable with Dr. Peterson.

Diane was permitted to buy clothes and shoes for her children, but she could not deliver them personally; they had to be left with Susan Staffel.

Christie started the third grade on September 6, 1983. Two days later, she was overjoyed; her little brother was finally released from the hospital after almost four months. Danny would be living with the Slavens too. Basically, Christie and Danny had only each other—the two of them who shared the same mother and the same memories, good and bad.

Danny was in a wheelchair; barring a medical breakthrough, he always would be. His physicians' worst possible scenario had come true; Danny had no feeling or control below chest level.

It had been love at first sight when the Slavens met Danny. They had spent hours and hours at the hospital with him. They were already Mom and Dad to him. As Diane had once said, he *did* have a wonderfully charismatic personality. But, in the aftermath of the shooting, Danny's moods swung wildly. "He was either way up or way down," Evelyn Slaven remembers. As soon as he adjusted to his new environment, Danny too would begin counseling with Carl Peterson.

The Downs shooting had dropped out of the headlines. Notoriety—like celebrity—is fleeting. There were articles once a month or so each time Diane was denied visitation rights.

Diane's life had become as aimless as foam on the ocean. Her emotional equilibrium—however tenuous—had always been rooted in the male in her life. The Number One male. She may have detested her father, and she might have hated Steve after their first few years of marriage, but they *had* been an integral part of her existence. She still hated men, and yet wanted them as much as she detested them. From the first time she'd had sex outside her marriage, through all the men she'd had affairs with, right up to Lew Lewiston, there had always been *somebody* close at hand. Some man to wind herself around so that the winds of change would not blow her away entirely.

Now, there was nobody.

Lew was no longer there for her on the phone. Cord Samuelson would listen to her, albeit nervously, but he wouldn't sleep with her. Kurt Wuest really appealed to her—but a cop who was trying to arrest her seemed a bit too much of a challenge.

Despite her constant theme that it was her children who had given her stability and happiness, reality shows that Christie, Cheryl, and Danny were in and out of Diane's life—sometimes there to hold and cuddle and play games with, but more often shunted to the side, or smacked, when they were in the way. But the *man*—whichever man it might be—was always there.

Diane felt relentlessly miserable as the fall of 1983 approached. She was drinking heavily that autumn, and thanks to her many press conferences, she was highly visible when she showed up stag at dance halls and taverns.

"We saw her at a dance at the Embers," a Springfield woman recalls. "She was alone and all fixed up. This man came in with some friends, and you could tell she hadn't known him before. She went over and started talking to him, and they danced, and then they were necking. And then she left with him. Just like that."

Feelings among the citizens of Lane County on the Downs case were shifting to more pronounced battle lines. Some considered Diane a beleaguered saint; others judged her far more harshly. No one seemed unaware of her, and no one seemed neutral.

"In September, I started drinking so I could be numb against the emptiness I felt . . . I stopped," she would explain in a letter to the author. "But I only stopped after I found a happy, healthy way to survive the waiting game. Even though I couldn't stop the grieving, I could love and be loved while the time passed waiting for Chris and Dan to be home."

The plan that Diane had formulated would become obvious—but not for some months.

Diane searched for *somebody*—some man to give her ballast in the storm. The dance-hall pick-ups didn't last. She always ended up back at Wes Frederickson's house, and in trouble to boot for coming in late, smelling of alcohol.

She was so damned depressed. She hadn't talked to Doug or Kurt—or anybody connected with the case—since the end of July. She couldn't fight shadows. She couldn't deal with the constant waiting, postponements of custody hearings, the nothingness that crept in when she was alone. One night, Diane suddenly remembered a special man she knew. It was quite possible that he could make her feel good again . . .

Diane had always dated attractive men, but this man was by far the handsomest. Better than Lew. Better looking, better educated than any man she'd ever known. He was perfect for the plan that had come to her. With his assistance, Diane could be a phoenix, rising from the ashes of her ruined life.

They had met first in late July in a park along her mailroute in Cottage Grove. He was a teacher on his lunchbreak; she was a mail carrier but she still planned to become a doctor—once she got her life and family back on track. The scene was tailormade for the first chapter of a Harlequin Romance novel—the beautiful tanned blonde woman in walking shorts, a cast on her arm, her huge greenish-yellow eyes meeting those of the wonderfully handsome bachelor.

He knew who she was; he would have had to have been in Siberia or illiterate not to know. He knew about the rumors, but he couldn't picture her as a murderess. She looked so wholesome, and so sad behind her obvious effort to be cheerful.

Matt Jensen was very tall with bright blue eyes, black hair, beard, and moustache—Diane's idea of a perfect male. He was younger than Diane by a year or so, even though the beard made him look older. He would be the first "civilian" (nonpostal) Diane had dated for a long, long, time.

Jensen remembers when he first heard about the shooting. "I'd been away for a week's vacation, and I got back to the Eugene area the Monday after the shooting. I'd left this quiet little area, and a lot of things happened that weekend: a bank robbery, a resignation of a police chief, and the Downs shooting.

"So—yeah—I remembered it."

Later, Matt spoke to Diane in the park. "I think most people had made up their minds that she was guilty—and I hadn't. I couldn't believe it—I wouldn't allow myself to think that anyone—not anyone I was sitting there talking with—could *do* that. We discussed children. I have a child by a former marriage—in the same age bracket. No, I couldn't believe she'd done it."

Matt withheld judgment. He felt sorry for Diane; he was nice to her. They talked once in the park and then, two weeks later, they met in the park again. Diane had had a dream; she said she needed to tell him about it. It had been a wonderful dream in a way—but not when she had to wake up.

The sunny park grew chill and even the bird songs seemed hushed as she spun out the dream for him.

"Christie came to me, and I asked her how she found me, and she said, 'Cheryl brought me'—and then Cheryl came walking out of the shadows and there was blood on her shirt and stuff. She had two little holes in her chest. I asked her, I said, 'Cheryl, I thought you were dead!' And she just goes, 'No, I was faking it. I knew they were going to take Christie away, and she wouldn't be able to get back to you.' So Cheryl brought Christie back, and then Cheryl showed us how to sneak Danny out of Sacred Heart and all that good stuff. It was just wonderful. Cheryl knew how to do everything. We were all together again."

Matt felt extremely sorry for Diane as he listened to her wish-fulfilling dream.

Later, Diane would relate the identical dream to KEZI reporter Anne Bradley. Diane's best dreams always involved Cheryl coming back to save all of them with her cleverness, there to lead them out of terrible traps.

Matt told Diane he lived in a little house not too far from the park. She smiled, and repeated his address to him. Of course she knew his address. She was his mail lady.

"I didn't want any involvement," he recalls. "But, somehow, she gave me her phone number—and I gave her mine."

Jensen, like most men, thought Diane's figure exceptional—slender and yet full breasted. He was a normal young male, and she was beautiful. Her story of being railroaded by the police fascinated him. But they had no common interests beyond that. She seemed to need a good listener, and that was fine with Matt.

He didn't expect to see her again. But, one night—a Friday in August—Diane called Matt Jensen, and asked him if she could come over, just to talk. He told her to come ahead and was somewhat surprised when she brought a bottle of whiskey. She had told him that she didn't drink.

"She lied a lot to me, but I didn't realize it until later."

They had a few drinks. Matt smiled at the way Diane downed her whiskey, holding her nose and grimacing. She hated the taste of it.

Jensen had no way of knowing that he'd won a lead role in a now familiar script. Diane could have walked through the part with her eyes closed; the dialogue was new to Matt. They sat on his living room rug and talked, but he made one proviso. "Look, I don't want to know about anything that happened that night. I don't want to know—I don't care to know."

Diane seemed to appreciate that; she'd talked about "that night" enough already. Despite his treachery, Diane talked about Lew; she always did, even with other men. "I have a reminder of him with me that will never go away," she confided.

"What do you mean?" Matt asked.

She looked at him with half-closed eyes, smiled slightly, and said, "I'll show you."

She stood up gracefully and removed her blouse, turning so Matt could see the red rose etched into the skin of her shoulder. She wore no bra, and she turned more, revealing her naked breasts. She didn't bother to put her blouse back on; she remained topless, sitting cross-legged on the floor in front of Matt Jensen's fireplace.

They were intimate that night. It was pleasant for him, but there was no commitment; they were both in their twenties, members of a generation with relaxed sexual mores.

"I didn't think much of it—but she seemed so desperate to have a friend, someone to talk to, to be with."

Matt Jensen was hesitant about seeing Diane again; Cottage Grove was a small community, and everyone knew Diane Downs. He didn't care to parade down Main Street with her. A double standard perhaps, but a familiar one. The woman *was* notorious, mostly through her own PR efforts; she was not the ideal companion for a young educator.

Diane had had plans for Matt Jensen almost from the first time she saw him—something beyond casual sex and light conversation. And yet they didn't have intercourse again during the rest of the summer. He had never intended to go that far in the first place and had been surprised; he was careful to forestall the opportunity for more physical intimacy. He was unaware that when Diane Downs wanted a man, it was virtually impossible to walk away from her. In the beginning, Matt was on hold, an alternate. When Diane realized that Lew was truly lost to her, she felt a tremendous vacuum.

She chose Matt to fill it.

It was September when Diane's pursuit of Matt Jensen began in earnest. Their dating lasted only three weeks, with Diane instigating their meetings. She called to ask Matt to go to a movie, or she brought Chinese food over to his little house, spreading out the little "goldfish" white buckets with great ceremony. Once they had breakfast together at a restaurant owned by the mayor of Cottage Grove. Matt squirmed some at that, but he didn't want to hurt her feelings.

They had so little to talk about. The subject of the shooting had been declared off-limits, and Diane's interests didn't coincide with Matt's. When they watched movies on TV, or listened to music, it was OK—but there was nothing more there. At least not for Jensen. Diane didn't read much. He was surprised to find that she often spoke in platitudes and homilies, sounding like a schoolgirl's C– theme. ("You can lead a horse to water, but you can't make him drink," "Everything always turns out for the best.") At first, he thought she was joking, and he laughed aloud. But she was serious. It was as if Diane didn't really understand the way humans were supposed to feel and used her trite quotations to guide herself.

She told Matt she found him an "escape from all the craziness." She clung to him more tightly.

During the single time they'd been intimate, Diane had been an eager sex partner, but something held Jensen back from further intercourse. In the end, in spite of her attempts at seduction, they would sleep together only three times.

Diane's views on sex matched the rest of her conversation—stilted and slightly unreal. Saccharine. "To me, sex is the ultimate way of showing a loved one that you love them," she wrote to him once. "I have tried to perfect the art of sex, to get as much pleasure out of it as possible, and to make my partner as happy as can be. Animals have sex outside of love. I feel that I am above animals. I have a heart and soul. I feel good and bad. Love is expressed through trust, hugs, remembering his favorite food, and patience. But sex is probably the most pleasant way of saying, 'I care.'"

More effective, perhaps, than sending a Hallmark card, Jensen thought wryly.

Diane had long since learned that men hated to be owned. She talked a carefree game, insisting to Matt that she wanted only friendship. She wrote him another transparent letter: "A woman is like a delicate butterfly sitting in the palm of your hand. If you try to close your fingers around her too tightly so she can't leave—she will be crushed and die. I prefer to think of the butterfly—not as a woman—but as love . . . Love cannot be suffocating or imprisoning. It must be free and giving."

Matt Jensen was beginning to feel like a cloistered butterfly, despite all Diane's platitudes on the benefits of freedom. His stomach churned at the sight of a red, white, and blue mail jeep. Diane knew where he worked, where he parked his car, his license plate number. She left notes for him under his windshield wipers. "She staked me out," he recalls ruefully. "She knew when I got home for lunch—or after work—and there she was at the door. She'd stop by my job."

Clearly, she considered him her candidate for a full-time lover. She told him that there were no other men in her life, but then she would slip and talk about going to bars, about all the men who were hitting on her. "There were so many different sides of her—even then. She was manipulating me.

"She played the vulnerable little girl with me—and told me how the police had mistreated her. I truly felt sorry for her—at first."

Diane told Matt that he was the only person she knew who could carry on an intelligent conversation. His brain was very important to her, she said. But all conversations with Diane were ultimately one-sided monologues, and as innately intelligent as she was—she was no intellectual.

When Jensen realized that she wasn't going to stop popping in to see him, he gave notice to his landlord and rented a place on the river twenty miles away. "I didn't tell her where it was."

CHAPTER 28

Christie was making good progress with Carl Peterson. He'd found her guarded and wary at first, but they'd come to the point where she almost felt safe enough with him to share secrets. Fred Hugi was so encouraged by Christie's progress that he had filed an affidavit with the juvenile court:

> I talked with Dr. Carl V. Peterson ... on Tuesday, September 27, 1983 and Wednesday, September 28, 1983. Dr. Peterson informed me that it is his professional opinion that Christie saw the person that shot her on May 19, 1983, and that Christie will be able to describe that person and events surrounding the shooting in the future. Dr. Peterson informed me he believes Christie should be able to do this within a period of four to six

months. Dr. Peterson is not in a position to know whether
Christie's recollection will corroborate or contradict Elizabeth Diane Downs' recollection of the event ...

Hugi asked for a continuance of the matter "due to its extreme gravity
and importance to all the parties. I believe that in fairness to all parties,
the case should not be litigated ... while there remains a reasonable prob-
ability that Christie Downs may be able to provide crucial eyewitness
testimony as to the identity of her assailant. In a case of this magnitude,
we should only proceed with the best evidence that can be reasonably
obtained."

The delay was granted.

Dr. Peterson sent a letter to Susan Staffel in late September. She had
asked him to evaluate the appropriateness of eventual visits between
Christie and Diane.

As you know, I have seen Christie on an approximate weekly
basis since therapy was initiated on 6-29-83. A letter to your
office on 9-14-83 outlined progress through that date. I have
since seen Christie three additional sessions ... I have helped
Christie to access some of the feelings she associates with her
sister's death. Throughout the duration of that work, I have
continued to be struck by the strength of Christie's resistance
or blockage to accessing feelings she undoubtedly associates
with the perpetrator of this crime. In part because of her
blocked feelings, I am of the opinion that Christie is currently
incapable of adequately protecting herself from the prospect
of further emotional damage. As if sensing her own emotional
vulnerability, Christie does not display the near universal
strong desire to be reunited with her mother that typically
follows a separation ...

Peterson said that any visits between mother and daughter would
have to be closely supervised. He hoped to meet with Diane before she
was reunited with Christie so that he could help her support Christie.

In the interim, Christie and Danny were doing better and better, living at the Slavens' house. For the first time in their lives, they lived in a child-centered home. Ray and Evelyn noticed though that Christie still tended to feel personally responsible for anything that went wrong. It was as if someone had said to her since birth, "It's all *your* fault, Christie."

Steve Downs made a trip to Eugene in late September to see Christie and Danny. He invited Diane's brother Paul to have dinner with them one evening. Paul reported to Diane that Christie looked fine and that Danny had laughed a lot and made cute remarks.

Fred Hugi knew Steve was in town, but he couldn't follow Downs twenty-four hours a day. Hugi did not know that the Children's Services Division now allowed Steve to take the children out with him all day, unsupervised. If it had even occurred to Hugi that such a thing might happen, there would have been fireworks. Nor did Hugi know that Steve Downs was talking and meeting with Paul Frederickson and other members of Diane's family.

Paul told Steve how lonely Diane was for Christie and Danny, what a rough time she was having. Time and distance had softened Steve's heart; he had forgiven Diane for turning him in to the police, and he'd changed his mind about thinking she could really hurt their children.

Steve called Diane on October 1 and asked her if she wanted to see the kids—not talk to them or anything, just have a look at them to be sure they were doing OK? *Of course!* Steve instructed Diane to be at a certain spot at a shopping mall and he would walk by with the kids. Diane agreed readily.

Steve called her the next morning and told her the mall was too public. Instead, he suggested that he bring the youngsters to Island Park under the bridge in Springfield at 10:00 A.M.

Steve felt sure he could control the situation.

Diane was at the park early. She saw Steve's car approach and watched as he led Christie to a bench over the rise of a little hill. He beckoned Diane to the car where Danny lay sleeping in the back seat. She peered in at her beautiful blond boy. He didn't look paralyzed to her; he looked as though he might wake up and run around the park the way he used to.

Diane had not seen Christie for almost three months. But she had fooled the cops, the DA, the damnable CSD—even Christie's counselor. And, especially, Steve. It didn't take her long to break down his arguments that she was just supposed to *look* at the kids. She wanted to hold Christie in her arms.

Diane would say later that Christie was thrilled and delighted to see her, that her daughter ran to her and smothered her with kisses and hugs. Diane remembers that even Steve cried. She took advantage of his emotional response to pry the name of his motel out of him. A meeting in the park wasn't enough; she wanted more time with her children—especially Christie. Steve agreed that she could come to his room at the Red Lion Inn at four that afternoon.

She was prompt. Diane peeked into Steve's car and saw a wheelchair. So Danny *was* still paralyzed. That, she knew, was the hospital's fault; all Danny needed was enough love.

Steve wanted Diane to sign custody papers giving him the children. Maybe he felt he had to offer her *something* as an inducement. He let Diane take Christie away with her—alone—for a ride.

They didn't come back when Diane said they would. Downs waited, frantic, pacing his motel room. He'd violated a court order to let Diane see the kids. Now she'd taken Christie away, and he couldn't even remember where she'd said they were going.

It was almost dark—and Diane still hadn't come back.

Steve was just about to call the sheriff—even though he knew he'd probably be arrested for allowing Diane to take Christie—when he saw a car turning into the motel's parking lot. He held his breath. It was the Ford Fiesta. Diane got out. And then he saw Christie, holding her dead arm in her good hand. Christie alive! All of his terrible imaginings vanished.

Diane laughed at Steve for being so upset. She and Christie had had a *wonderful* time.

"Christie and I went . . . to Hendricks Park for an hour and a half. It was so neat to hold hands and laugh. We talked about the old times, and a little about the good times in the future. We talked about Cheryl some and Danny's legs. We talked about school and reading."

Diane had pointed out that *she* was the one who sent Christie her clothes and shoes and candy. Diane insists that Christie asked to go home with her that night.

Christie had learned from Steve that Cheryl's body had been cremated, and that Cheryl's ashes were in Arizona. Christie had difficulty understanding this; she told Diane that she wanted to be in Arizona because that's where Cheryl was. Diane said Christie had asked about the shooting, but Diane insisted she had told her daughter she couldn't discuss it because she'd promised the police she wouldn't.

"We talked about the old days and Cheryl and doing cartwheels. She was angry that I wouldn't tell her [about the case]. I said, 'I'll tell you when it's over—I'm keeping a diary.'"

Christie asked about Lew. Diane answered, "He doesn't like me anymore."

"Why?"

"He believes everything people are saying."

And then Diane had had an inspiration. Why not take Christie to visit with Grandpa and Grandma Frederickson? "We walked around the side of the house to the backyard. Even my dad cried—and he *forbids* crying. He put her in front of the computer [to play]." Christie could use only one hand. Her reaction time was much slower, and her speech was garbled. But her brain was just as sharp as always.

Steve was so upset when Diane finally brought Christie back, that he wouldn't let her see Danny. She didn't get a chance to see if her theory that *she* could make him walk was valid.

Evelyn Slaven noticed something wasn't right when Steve returned the children that night. The kids had been so happy and relaxed lately, and suddenly they were like somber little mice.

"It wasn't something really obvious—but neither Christie nor Danny even said 'Goodbye' to their father. They just came in the house very, very quietly. I assumed maybe they'd had a bad day—I had no idea that Diane had gotten hold of Christie. Christie didn't say anything about it."

Carl Peterson found too that his optimistic "four to six months" until Christie could testify had lost validity. Since Christie's visit with her father, they were, mysteriously, almost back where they'd started. When he questioned Christie gently, she turned away. She had nothing to say.

Christie kept the secret well. No one knew that she had seen her mother—alone—for hours. Without preparation.

October 7 was Christie's ninth birthday. Diane and Paul took a cake and presents for her to the CSD offices, trailed by reporters and cameras.

Diane looked sensational in the pictures. Her hair was newly cut—as short as a boy's—in a shining blonde cap. She wore a long-sleeved sweater and tight jeans that showed off her perfect figure, and she smiled as she gazed down on a sheet cake that said "Happy Birthday, Christie: I Love You, Mom." The icing was white with—naturally—bright red roses in each corner. Behind Diane, Paul appears in the photographs, his arms heaped high with gaily wrapped presents.

They were not allowed to see Christie. Nobody knew that it was already far too late. Interviews had been set up with Carl Peterson for Diane on September 28 and October 14; she kept neither of them. There was no reason to see him. She and Christie understood each other.

Diane still smiled for the media cameras, but she wasn't really smiling much in private. Although she'd had her victories, they trailed far behind her losses. Anxiety and depression gripped her again.

On October 13, Diane scribbled in her diary, "I've been drinking a lot the past few days. I just wish I could be dead ... But I had a great idea. Tell ya later if it works! Gotta go—"

Matt Jensen remembers the night of October 13 well. It was a Thursday, and he was ready for bed when the phone rang, shortly after eleven. It was Diane Downs; he hadn't heard from her for a long time. Nor had he thought much about her.

"She wanted to come over," he remembers. "She went on and on about how lonely she was, and how she *needed* to come over. I wasn't interested. I kept saying 'No. No,' and she kept telling me she really *needed* to come over. I began to get annoyed, and I even hung up on her—but she called right back. Finally—I was kidding—I gave her this impossible situation— like if she could get an ounce of pot, and a six-pack of beer, and all this stuff—then she could come over. But it was late, it was Cottage Grove, Oregon, and there's no way she could have found all that stuff. So it was like I was saying no, but I was trying to kid her too so she wouldn't feel really rejected. I just wasn't interested.

"So she says she will, and I didn't think she would—but she came over. And she walks in with a six-pack, and the first thing she says is—'Guess what? I'm on birth control pills now,' and I said, 'Oh, really. I didn't think you were before,' and she says, 'No, I just started—I just got them.'

"So I asked her if she didn't have to take them for a certain amount of time before they were effective, and she said no. Just out of the blue, she was telling me 'It's safe. It's safe.'

"I guess I was a damn fool," Jensen says now. "Looking back I can see I was set up. It wasn't a seduction—it was a manipulation; she was using me."

Two days later, Jensen moved out of his house; Diane's late-night visit was almost forgotten.

Diane's diary entry for October 14 is gleeful: "It worked! Remember that guy I dated a couple of times? Well, I called him up and ended up going to see him. I talked him into doing you-know-what, because I knew it was my time of the month to get pregnant. I hope it worked. I just can't live without my kids."

Whether it had worked or not remained to be seen. Diane had been trying to become pregnant for a year; she had not conceived a second time even under the optimum conditions at the Louisville clinic. And now, she was under tremendous stress.

She continued to drink a great deal, but—even drunk—Diane could work out intricate plots. She did not want Steve to have custody of Christie and Danny, and she figured that the Children's Services Division would do exactly the *opposite* of what she wanted. If CSD learned that Steve had let her see her children, they wouldn't let him have the kids. Diane wanted CSD to know about her visit with Christie—but in a roundabout way.

On October 16, Diane wrote to Lew, telling him she'd seen her children, thanks to Steve. The letter is written in a drunken scrawl, addressed simply to "Lew, c/o Chandler P.O., Chandler, AZ, 85224."

Over the next few days, she called the post office and left messages for Lew: he *must not* open the letter she'd sent. He must send it back! If he opened it—and told anyone what was in it—she warned that his life wouldn't be worth anything. That would not only make him open it, but he'd get the information immediately to the Lane County Sheriff's Office, which was what she wanted all along.

It worked. It also scared Lew enough to file charges against Diane and request a restraining order.

Fred Hugi was appalled when he heard that Christie had been alone with Diane. It explained everything—why Christie had closed up with Peterson, why she was so afraid again. "I felt really incompetent," he remembers grimly. "I couldn't even protect one little girl. I wondered how many other times Diane had seen Christie. When you're dealing with crime, something that's admitted to *one* time usually means it happened a *lot* of times. Diane was getting more organized, stronger—just as she'd said . . . I didn't even have an investigator to check it out."

Those few investigators who were left in the DA's office were all busy on other cases. Crime had not stopped in Lane County in the six months since the shootings on Old Mohawk Road. Hugi had myriad cases to handle; so did everyone else. The Downs case was always with him, but he had to push it to the back of his mind in order to do the rest of his job.

Diane had managed to see Christie and foil Steve. She had seduced Matt. She was winning again. She kept her fingers crossed as the due date of her menstrual period approached. She would not allow herself to start bleeding. It was important to her survival that she be pregnant.

She was. Her sixth pregnancy had begun.

Later when her secret was out, Diane explained to television reporter Anne Bradley the symbolic meaning of this pregnancy, "I got pregnant because I miss Christie, and I miss Danny and I miss Cheryl so much. I'm never going to see Cheryl on earth again, I just— You can't replace children— but you can replace the *effect* that they give you. And they give me love, they give me satisfaction, they give me stability, they give me a reason to live and a reason to be happy, and that's gone. They took it from me."

And then Diane smiled faintly at Bradley, and remarked, "But children are so easy to conceive."

Matt Jensen—who had already made one grievous mistake—made another. He called Diane. A friend having dinner at Matt's new house commented he would like to meet the infamous Diane Downs, hinting that he didn't believe Matt knew her well enough to call her up. Loosened by a few beers, Matt called Diane. She was delighted and said she'd be right over.

Diane arrived wearing mini-shorts and high boots that clung to her calves. Jensen's friend eyed her appreciatively. There was no question that the woman was a knock-out.

"During the course of the evening," Jensen remembers ruefully, "she suddenly leaned over to me and whispered, 'I'm pregnant.' I was in shock. I didn't know what the repercussions would be. I was upset—I told her she'd set this up, that she'd used me—and I didn't want anything to do with her."

Diane had been amazed at his agitation. "Don't worry," she soothed. "I didn't mean to use you."

"I see what you were after," he countered. "I see what you did, and I don't want to see you anymore."

When Diane left, she was smiling. He would forgive her, she knew, when he began to understand. She would explain it all to him when he wasn't so bent out of shape.

Diane hadn't been to a doctor when she told Matt that she was pregnant. She didn't need to go; she was positive. But she went anyway on November 8, and she told her diary the great news had been verified: "Found out that I am positively pregnant! *YEAH!*"

She had done it. She was no longer despondent. "That is why on October 13, 1983," she wrote the author, "I chose to again get pregnant ... For nine months, I had love again. There was a child inside of me, kicking and nudging. Someone I could love who was with me. Each day, she reminded me that we had a future."

Diane wrote Matt Jensen letters, deluging him just as she'd inundated so many other men in her past. Diane, who seldom evinced guilt—about anything—was the consummate master of slathering it on others. To Matt: "I am writing this because I don't want to pop up on your doorstep and invade your territory. You seem to be a person who likes your privacy and invites friends over at your convenience. I respect that and hope you also respect me enough to take five minutes or so to read this ... Thanks."

Matt could see now Diane understood only facade; she did not grasp that deeds must follow words or words have no meaning.

"Anyway, Matt," she continued. "I am not that hard to figure out. Just look at me and listen. I am a romantic. I love the moon reflecting on the lake. I love to cuddle in front of the fireplace. And I will do just about anything to make a loved one happy. (Short of being a hooker, pusher, or murderer.)

"I am faithful to a fault. And I cannot cheat on a relationship . . . I always thought that everyone shared the same feelings I have, but I guess I was mistaken. I love you in that special way, but it is not meant to possess you. Just respect you.

"I have never thought of a baby as an obligation or problem. They are beautiful and full of love . . . A child will give more love and happiness than any other creature on earth . . . I thought you might feel that way—so I needed to tell you. That way, it was your decision to turn your back on the love of a child, or embrace it. Either way, you are not wrong . . . I just didn't think I had the right to decide for you, and never let you make the choice.

"I am not a siren," her words flowed in delusion after delusion. "I never intended, nor do I intend to trap you. I cherish your friendship . . . I'm still willing if you are . . . I never wanted to hurt you."

She signed it with a smiling face wearing a halo and then she added (in small printing) "P.S. I have been offered proposals of marriage by four different men in the past two years. None of which were bed partners, by the way. It should be obvious I am not husband seeking."

But there was something more. This letter was a code letter. A primitive code, certainly—because she had simply circled phrases to be sure that he understood *exactly* what she was saying.

> *My intention was never to "trap" you.*
> *I have read you wrong.*
> *Love is not possessing.*
> *Your decision to turn your back on love.*
> *I'll never tell who, I swear.*
> *Look bad for you.*
> *Nobody knows.*
> *My parents can't do anything—at all.*
> *You won't have to look for a new job or move or be embarrassed.*

He did not answer.

She sent him a Happy Thanksgiving card, addressed to "Hermit," with a note enclosed. She was quite restrained, wondering, "I don't know why you faded on me."

He didn't call her.

Matt Jensen avoided Diane, even though there were still occasional messages left on his car's window, even though it meant ducking into a storefront when the postal jeep approached. He had learned a bitter lesson in the temptations of the flesh.

His child was growing in the belly of a woman he suspected was a murderess. He remembered back to the clear-eyed, tanned woman in the park who'd seemed so unhappy. He knew now from painful experience that she took what she wanted.

CHAPTER 29

Despite Matt Jensen's rejection, Diane was calmer as October drifted into November. The new life in her womb gave her days purpose again. She met with Jim Jagger to work on her defense in a case that was—like the child inside—still embryonic. No charges had been brought, nothing was happening—but Diane sensed something or someone unseen moving behind her most of the time. When she turned around quickly, no one was there.

Doug Welch, back in uniform, and Fred Hugi had paced themselves for the long haul. The resolution would not come quickly, but it *would* come. Welch carried out the mundane duties handed to him. Hugi took a vacation, went fishing, worked around his property, and ran until the tension eased.

"It was all going to happen—sooner or later—and I knew it."

Diane was more impatient; she wanted a quick resolution to the investigation. Publicity was still important to her—the public must not forget who she *really* was, and what the evil cops were doing to her.

The media in Eugene were Diane's contemporaries—bright and imbued with the newshound fervor that demands a pace only the young can maintain. Their careers were just starting, and Eugene, Oregon, was proving to be a place where their baptisms by fire were assured.

Lars Larson of KVAL TV learned that Diane had filed tort claims against CSD, the Lane County district attorney's office, and the Lane County sheriff's office. He wanted the story behind her suits, and she was happy to oblige. Fred Hugi suspected that the *real* reason Jim Jagger had gone along with Diane's civil suits was to force the State's hand, to perhaps outrage the public so much that the State would have no option but to go to trial—*before* Christie could remember.

The tort claims were a replay of Diane's complaints about the sheriff's office and Paula Krogdahl: "Paula Krogdahl from the Lane County District Attorney's Office kept Mrs. Downs from having physical contact with her daughter, all without legal cause or justification. The same Paula Krogdahl removed Christie Downs from the hospital building, and took her outside into the night, in the evening, when it was cold, all contrary to health and well-being of Christie Downs..." (Paula had wheeled Christie just outside the door to the ICU on a warm June evening to show her that the world as Christie had known it still existed, that there *was* something beyond white sheets and disinfectant at McKenzie-Willamette Hospital.)

Fred Hugi too was singled out in the tort claim: "Finally, an assistant Lane County District Attorney knew of the aforementioned and did nothing to stop this illegal or tortious action and, in fact, harassed and intimidated Mrs. Downs—all without legal cause or justification. (The name of the assistant D.A. is Fred Hugi.)"

Diane's civil attorney had inserted Hugi's name; she herself was barely aware of his existence.

Diane's favorites among the media changed rapidly; if a reporter seemed sympathetic and appreciative, he or she moved toward the top of her list. Diane didn't care for hard, probing questions. Sometimes she liked Larson; more often she preferred Maureen Shine, the KMTR (NBC) anchorwoman. Because Shine was soft-spoken and seemingly compliant, Diane assumed she had control over Shine, that it was she who directed their interviews. Shine didn't argue with her—because Diane Downs, feeling confident, was a fascinating interview. If Diane Downs was a burr under the saddle of law enforcement, she was a newsman's plum.

Larson's KVAL story on November 17 led off: "Woman Threatens Suit for Shooting Probe: Eugene, Oregon— A lawyer for Elizabeth Diane Downs has threatened to sue three agencies for up to $700,000 because of their investigation of shootings last May that left one of her three children dead."

Diane invited Larson out to breakfast. On the way, she drove him by the Slavens' house to show him that she knew where her children lived. Over eggs and toast, she mentioned casually that she had once been a surrogate mother. It took everything Larson had to keep from jumping up and rushing out with this information. He forced himself to chew slowly.

Then afraid she'd favored KVAL (CBS) unduly, Diane suggested that Maureen Shine come by the house. She gave Shine an interview about Christie—stressing that Christie was OK, and that even the district attorney's office didn't mind that she had *actually visited* with Christie. "People do think of her and Dan a lot." Diane told every reporter who would listen—print and visual media—about her wonderful reunion in Hendricks Park with Christie, about how happy Christie had been to see her mother, about all the hugs and kisses.

It was too much for Fred Hugi, "She was so blithe. It only made me more determined than ever. The question was, 'Will she destroy our case—and Christie—quicker than we can put it together?'"

Diane's stolen visit had set Christie back weeks—if not months—in her therapy. How could a child of that age juggle her just-surfacing memories of horror with the smiling face of the mother who hugged her in the park and told her she must not tell secrets? Christie was wrenched by conflicting emotions: fear, grief, love, longing. She had just begun to adjust to her new world, and now her psychic scars had been ripped open again.

"We were on a collision course," Hugi remembers. "There was going to be a trial someday. There was the remote possibility that the gun would surface. Or that Diane would tell someone the truth—someone she'd soon alienate—or that Christie would be able to talk. If we don't use Christie, the defense has a big plus. They know I've committed myself. At some point, I'll have to go ahead with or without her."

Both Diane and Steve Downs were charged with contempt of court for flouting Judge Foote's order that Diane must not visit the children.

A "show-cause" hearing was set for December 9. Steve and Diane Downs would be called upon to show—if they could—that they hadn't violated Foote's order.

The specter of a court appearance didn't appear to make Diane apprehensive. With each interview now, she revealed more; she was a woman whose life was honeycombed with secrets, and she exposed them at her own pace, opening them for the media like so many Christmas packages.

Every time Fred Hugi turned on the television set, he saw Diane Downs criticizing the investigation, emphasizing her favorite line: "If I'm guilty, why don't they arrest me?"

Diane's television appearances in November and December were so frequent that it seemed only a matter of time until she had her own show.

Hugi felt like the loneliest man in the world. His case had sunk to its lowest ebb. He sat alone late at night with no one to talk to. Oh, he could have awakened Joanne, and she would have listened. But what the hell was the use? He thought about Diane all the time, out there in her beloved television land, laughing, maybe figuring out the next way she'd get her hands on Christie.

It had been more than five months since the shooting, and where were they? She was running them around like Keystone Kops.

Hugi got to his office after a sleepless night just in time to pick up the phone; Jim Jagger had news.

"Diane's pregnant."

Great. She was growing another baby for herself. His first thought was, "Are we going to have to wait *another nine months* to get this trial?" Now the public that hated Fred Hugi for relentlessly pursuing a young mother, could hate Fred Hugi for relentlessly pursuing a *pregnant* young mother.

Didn't anybody care about this case? Was he crazy for hanging on and hanging on? Sometimes he thought he was.

The public, always ambivalent about Diane Downs, had begun to believe that if the woman was guilty of anything, she would have been arrested months ago. Letters reflecting a certain outrage at her treatment reached the media and Hugi.

> Sir:
> There is something basically wrong with our governmental process when the judicial system can unilaterally confiscate property (or children) without ever filing charges of a crime committed! To be innocent until proven guilty is the basis of our judicial system!
> The case of Elizabeth Downs exemplifies this fault. Were you or your wife to be murdered, do you believe that the survivor should have your children removed without even visitation rights? GOOD LORD, I hope not!
> ... Yet the UNACCUSED defendant has been deprived of HER rights as a natural mother. There is only one solution, and her attorney should pursue it. Ask government to PUT UP OR SHUT UP! Another way to state it is "Ante up or surrender the pot!"
> ... Is justice only available to the rich? This situation could happen to YOU and that should scare YOU, just as it does me!!

DA Pat Horton had been quoted as saying that the Downs investigation was complete. So had Dave Burks. What did that mean? The rumor mills were alive with frenzied activity. A certain proportion of the population of Lane County believed there was a man with a gun out there, walking free. They figured they had good reason to be afraid. Subtle pressure was put on the DA and the sheriff's office. Pressure to *do* something.

As 1983 wound down, it looked doubtful that anyone would be arrested soon. The public, of course, could not understand the untenable situation Fred Hugi found himself in. Take a chance, and maybe lose in court—and the killer goes free, forever. Wait—and the good, but misinformed, citizens screamed for justice.

Hugi filed away the letters and fielded the phone calls. He knew the public was getting restless, just as he knew that some members of the sheriff's team were angry. He remembers November, 1983, as the worst

possible period in the progress of the Downs investigation. Progress—
hell, they were going backward by November.

DECEMBER 9, 1983

Diane appeared at the show-cause hearing dressed demurely. She wore a
pink overblouse, and a pink cardigan sweater was draped loosely over her
shoulders. Profile shots taken that day show a serene, pensive Diane—a
dead ringer for Princess Diana. She carried herself differently; the practiced eyes of the television cameramen told them she might be pregnant,
even though she was only two months into gestation.

This was a new Diane, far different from the bereaved victim, the enraged mother, or the brazen hussy. Very soft, moving more slowly, even
speaking slowly. On this day, she gained a nickname: "Lady Di," to most,
and "Lady Die" to doubters.

She appeared tired, and she cried often during her testimony, particularly when Fred Hugi asked her to read aloud the letter she'd written to
Lew—drunkenly but deliberately—to be sure the authorities knew she'd
seen Christie.

Diane testified that Steve had told her to lie about the visit, that she
was to say he had taken the children to the park, expecting only to meet
their Uncle Paul, that it was she who had surprised them by showing up
instead.

"He said I'd better stick to his version or he's going to 'take me out,' and
if you know Steve, you know that means he's going to kill me. What he
said really was, 'If they [the police] don't put you away, *I'm* going to take
you out.'"

Diane was unharried by Fred Hugi's questioning. She recognized
Doug Welch as an enemy, but she still hadn't spotted Hugi as anything
more than a tall, quiet man who worked for the prosecutor.

Hugi did nothing to apprise her otherwise.

Diane testified she had told Christie that the authorities said Christie
knew who hurt her, but Christie had insisted she could only remember
seeing the horses.

Bill Furtick, the children's attorney, cross-examined Diane next. He
was curious about why Diane hadn't simply notified CSD that she'd been
with Christie.

"Let me back up just a bit," she answered. "Steve said that if I cooperated with him, I could see the kids whenever he said . . . Steve was basically supposed to be set up as the *foster home* . . . I could abide with that, but that wasn't Steve's opinion. His opinion was that he would be the *custodial* parent. If you understand Steve like I do, that means he can use the kids to buy affection from me, to buy time with me. Steve is a possessive person, and it was his way of getting to me. If he got angry with me . . . I would not be allowed to see the kids . . . On Friday, I talked to Steve on the phone. He said, 'It's all set. Sign over the paper on the kids, and it will be done.' He made them sound like used cars. Those were my *babies* he was talking about."

Furtick's voice was incredulous. "Let me interrupt you. The man who you say threatened to kill you is trying to buy your affection—buy your . . . love?"

"Yes."

Diane testified that her only reason for telling Christie to keep their visit a secret was to avoid hurting the feelings of Christie's foster family.

Furtick got Diane to agree that Christie now knew that her mother was a suspect.

"If you'd like to know what I said to Christie—Christie said, 'Mommy, why can't you come to see me anymore?' And I said, 'I thought they told you that I'm a suspect.' She said, 'So what?' I said, 'They think that I'm the one that hurt you.'

"And she said, 'That's stupid. How could they say that?'"

What Christie had really said would remain a gray area; Christie would not appear at this court proceeding.

Carl Peterson testified that Diane's visit with Christie had caused a pronounced setback in Christie's progress. Peterson said that Christie was at present "obliquely aware of who shot her." Eventually, he hoped that she would remember the details.

"There certainly are elements of that evening that have been suppressed—because they have slowly begun to come out."

Susan Staffel told the court that Christie had to be continually reassured that it was all right for her to reveal she had been with her mother. Christie finally said Diane had "told me not to tell" about the visit.

Christie Downs was a pawn in a human chess game she could not begin to understand. If there was a way to bring murder charges against her mother without placing Christie on the witness stand, Fred Hugi would have leapt at the chance. But until the murder gun was found, there was no way.

Christie was it. And, despite the setback, Christie had not given up trying to remember. There was a resolutely gallant quality about that little girl; Hugi wondered if *he* would have had the guts at nine that she had. At nine? Even at thirty-nine, would he want to remember what Christie had seen? No way.

He contended in his closing argument that Diane had visited with Christie solely to protect herself against the possibility that Christie had incriminating memories of the shootings.

Diane faced jail for violating the order to stay away from her children. It seemed a definite possibility—until Jim Jagger rose to impart information that would make jail inadvisable for his client.

"My client is two- to three-months pregnant," he announced for the record. The courtroom buzzed.

"Everyone was shocked," Diane told her diary. "I blushed."

Not everyone was shocked. Hugi and the investigators already knew, of course. The press, however, was caught off guard. Lars Larson had just broken the news in an AP wire story that Diane had been a surrogate mother. The immediate assumption was that Diane was pregnant with another surrogate baby.

No, she smiled gently and shook her head at that suggestion when besieged with reporters later. But, yes, she was pregnant, and she was very happy about it, although the father's identity was not for public knowledge. He was, she said, a "very private person."

Rather than sentence her to jail for defying court rulings, Judge Foote gave Diane a one-year suspended sentence.

Diane admired Foote at this stage of the game. Gregory Foote is six feet four—a muscular blond man in his thirties, built like an athlete, which he is. He became a judge at twenty-nine—one of the youngest judges in Oregon history, and his consuming concern is the rights of children. He coaches a soccer team and spends untold hours counseling troubled teenagers. If Diane should go to trial for murder, it would be Foote's first homicide trial.

———

Despite all the roadblocks in his path, Fred Hugi felt that they were moving steadily now toward an arrest. Timing and Christie's memory were of paramount importance.

Carl Peterson reported—to his great relief and surprise—that a rebound effect had ensued after Christie's initial reaction to the surreptitious visit. For every backward step, Christie now leapt forward two or three. They worked with play therapy, with pillows and chairs. Peterson obtained a copy of the Duran Duran tape "Rio"—the one that had been in the Nissan's tape deck on the night of the shooting—and played that during their sessions. Sounds—like smells—can often bring back total recall.

They had reached a new plateau. Peterson gave Christie slips of paper and told her that if she wanted to, she could write the name of the person who shot her and Cheryl and Danny on the paper, put it in an envelope, and seal it. If she didn't want anyone to read what she wrote, she could burn the envelopes in his fireplace before she left his office.

Gravely, carefully, Christie wrote something on the paper slips and placed them in the envelopes. But she kept the envelopes with the names inside until the end of each session. And always, before she left Dr. Peterson's office, she flung them into the flames and watched until the paper curled and scorched and finally turned to unreadable ash.

CHAPTER 30

Of all the television reporters covering the Downs case, only Anne Bradley of KEZI (ABC) had never approached Diane about doing an interview, and this annoyed Diane.

Anne Bradley, the daughter of newspaper editors, had graduated from the University of Oregon at twenty, interned at KEZI, and was now an anchor-person. Pertly pretty and blonde, Bradley was a consummate media professional, although she had difficulty hiding her empathy for another's tragedy. Bradley was highly visible in Eugene's media corps, and her failure to appear at Diane's news conference left a noticeable gap. Bradley had stayed away deliberately, suspecting that might make Diane jump at a KEZI interview.

On the afternoon after the show-cause hearing, the time seemed right. Bradley didn't want to be premature; Diane Downs hadn't been charged with anything yet except disobeying a visitation order. But there was a feeling in the air, the heaviness of a major move soon. Bradley suspected that it was only a matter of time before Diane would be arrested for murder. Once that happened, there would be no more interviews.

Anne Bradley chose not to speak to Diane on the phone; that would water down a face-to-face taping. She asked her news director to call Diane. Diane was delighted to cooperate. The next day, a Saturday, she arrived at KEZI, accompanied not by her attorney but by her brother Paul.

In three hours on tape, Diane would give Bradley one of the most revealing views of her personality yet seen. The tape that resulted contained astounding footage. For Bradley, it would mean a tremendous struggle between conscience and ambition. Diane Downs and Anne Bradley sat side by side in the conference room of KEZI and talked for hours on camera. Diane recalled her thought processes on that ugly night in May.

"I have been through that night so many times; I have been through it with my psychologist. It's very hard, it's very tearful—there are a lot of memories that—I don't know. A lot of people if something traumatic happens to them, they suppress it immediately. *I* kept those memories because I knew that I was the only person that could be able to tell them what happened when we went to the hospital. And when I got there, the first thing I said was 'Call the doctor!' Second thing the blood type, and the third thing was 'Call the cops!' . . . And so, I had to remember as much as I could remember. When this man shot my daughter, my first reaction was to snap back to my childhood, to the pain that had happened to me back then, my marriage, my entrapment by society. This man was bigger than me; he was stronger than me; he had more power because he had a gun. He was in control and I was not. And I had—there was nothing I could do and I stood there, and I looked at Christie reaching and the blood that just kept gushing out of her mouth, and— *What do you do?* You just stand there trapped, and then—and then, the gun kept firing and firing and firing and it made it—it was monotonous . . .

"I pushed him. I ran. And when he swung around he was pointing—when he swung around . . . the gun hit the tips of my fingers and that snapped me, and I went *Wait a minute!* I'm not trapped by society. I don't care if he *is* bigger. If I stand here, and I say, 'Yeah, here—take the keys; there is nothing I can do—you win because you have the gun,' my kids are going to die. I'm not going to let my kids die. And so . . . I feigned throwing the keys. He did not take time to point the gun and shoot me, obviously, because he would have shot me the same way he shot the kids. When he was swinging in the direction of the keys, firing the gun, he hit my arm. Everybody says, 'You sure are lucky!' Well, I don't feel very lucky. I couldn't tie my damned shoes for about *two* months! It is very painful, it is still painful, I have a steel plate in my arm—I will for a year and a half. The scar is going to be there forever. I'm going to remember that night for the rest of my life whether I want to or not. I don't think I was very lucky. I think my kids were lucky. If I had been shot the way they were, we all would have died—except maybe for Danny."

Diane talked freely of her past, of her marriage, of her abortion, and of her search for a "good specimen" to father the baby that became Danny. But always she came back to her valiant fight to save her children.

Bradley noted that Diane lingered obsessively over the feel, sight, smell of blood. Again and again, she described how she could see "the blood coming out of Christie's mouth." "Driving to the hospital, I can smell blood."

"The DA has come up with this idea that someone was shot on the outside of the car—on the passenger side of the car . . . And that's why it was so—I'm going—'It *was* planted!' and . . . it just seemed, I mean it can't be real. Because they talk about blood spatter and when they say 'spatter,' I think of something being shot out. Like the blood spatter in the car—you know, it was so uniform. It was so regular. Same size droplets spread evenly in a pattern. And when they say spatter, that's what I thought of. And we saw pictures of this *so-called* spatter—It's *drops.* When they took Chris and Cher out of the driver side of the car, and it's blood droplets. It's when they picked the kids up and carried them over the threshold, there is blood dripping down the side of the car."

Bradley suddenly felt faint, her senses saturated with the continual talk of the children's suffering, their life fluid pouring out endlessly as their mother's car moved toward the McKenzie–Willamette Hospital. She touched Diane's arm.

"I have to stop," Bradley murmured. "I'm getting sick—"

Diane half-turned toward Bradley, and the cameras caught Diane's expression. It was a smile—but such a strange smile—her eyes narrowed, her lips in a smirk. *Freeze frame.*

Bradley noticed that when she threw unexpected questions, Diane's body language telegraphed subtle signals that she was disturbed, even though her voice stayed calm. Diane flushed visibly when she was caught off guard.

Bradley had discovered elements of the case that Diane had thought were privileged information, known only to the police, herself, and her attorney. The fact that she'd said at one point that *two men* attacked her, and the information that Cheryl's type O blood had been found on the exterior of the car had hit Diane with particular force.

"When I asked her about those things," Bradley recalls, "she was shocked... Her neck blushed scarlet, and she kind of pulled her head back and stared fixedly at me. And then I could see her composing herself... I perceived that inwardly she was frightened, but outwardly she could control it.

"When I asked her about the 'two men story,' Diane gasped so quickly that her breasts heaved as if she was trying to catch her breath—but she never flinched. If she didn't want to answer me, she had a coughing attack, or she asked for a drink of water. She needed to buy time to formulate the right answer."

It was the interview of a lifetime, and Anne Bradley was twenty-five years old. Conscience forbade her showing it to the public immediately. If she did, they'd never get an unbiased jury in Lane County. And her station's attorneys forbade her from showing it to law enforcement.

In the end, Bradley played fair with both the State and her station, and lost the sharpest edge of her scoop. She rewound her videotape, and placed it far back on a shelf—saving it for "someday."*

---

* Sections of the transcript of the Bradley tape appear in earlier chapters and are so credited.

Diane knew that the police had read much into the diary she'd sent them to retrieve the night of the shooting. Her second diary seems even more designed—contrived—to be read.

"Went Christmas shopping this evening. There was a little boy there, crying. His hands were so cold and red," she wrote in December. "I wanted to reach out and put his hands in my warm coat—but I didn't. Before all this happened, I would always comfort children in stores. It keeps them from getting hit by up-tight parents. People . . . said I had a special way with kids. Now, I don't try. I'm afraid they'll think I'm going to do something wrong . . ."

She gave Anne Bradley another interview. This time, Diane sat next to her parents' Christmas tree. She looked ill; she had purple circles beneath her eyes, and her complexion was pale green and blotched. The room, empty of children, spoke volumes.

Diane spoke of her desire to cooperate completely with the investigation—to do anything that would help Christie's memory return, although she herself didn't think it would be good for Christie to be forced to remember.

CHAPTER 31

Fred Hugi's New Year began not in January but in December. He had been so disheartened when he learned that Diane had seen Christie. However, by December the county had squeezed funds for the Downs investigation from their frugal budget—not much, but enough for a couple of detectives.

"Then it went from the worst possible in November—to the best in December," Hugi recalls. "We never had a point where we could say 'Aha! This is it'—it wasn't that kind of a case. All we ever got were little gains here and there, but they added up. In December, we started to get our investigators back—Paul Alton and Doug Welch came back. You could just feel it—all of a sudden we were starting to get stronger . . . And then, of course, we had Pierce—and that really helped."

Pierce.

Pierce Brooks lived just down the road a piece on the McKenzie river bank, a country-mile neighbor to Fred Hugi. Brooks's proximity for advice on a murder case is akin to Michael DeBakey's being on hand to assist a young surgeon in a heart bypass.

Pierce Brooks is a policeman's policeman; his name sparks instant familiarity in law enforcement circles. A cop for almost forty years, Brooks has led a life that sounds like fiction, but isn't. He signed on with the Los Angeles Police Department in 1948 when he was in his early twenties. A decade later Brooks was a homicide detective on his way to becoming a legend.

Brooks was the detective sergeant assigned to investigate the murder of a kidnapped Los Angeles patrolman in a desolate onion field north of Bakersfield. A bitter, tragic case for any cop—yet the lessons Brooks learned in this investigation (later the subject of Joseph Wambaugh's *The Onion Field*) made him an expert in the successful prosecution of the most difficult homicides.

Pierce Brooks spent ten years as an LAPD homicide captain. He was technical advisor to Jack Webb for both "Dragnet" and "Adam 12." His office and den walls are papered with commendations—and a movie still of a younger Brooks and a younger Jane Russell as he pilots a blimp high over California.

When Pierce Brooks retired from the Los Angeles Police Department in 1969, he was a long way from being retired from police work itself. He became first the police chief of Springfield, Oregon, and then chief of the Lakewood Police Department in Colorado. He returned to Oregon to take over the job as chief of the Eugene Police Department.

Lane County, Oregon, is where he prefers to stay—and few would blame him—after so many years of scrutinizing the gritty, murderous failings of his fellow humans. Brooks can well afford to retire. But staying home wars with his other interest, his avocation, his obsession. He is one of the definitive experts in America on homicide, particularly serial murder.

By 1980 Pierce Brooks was being called in as an investigative consultant on so many major homicide probes that he had to choose between consulting and being the Eugene police chief. He chose the former and went to Atlanta to work on the child murder cases there, and then to Chicago to assist in the Tylenol poisonings probe. In 1983 Brooks was nearing his goal of establishing a nationwide computer network to catch serial killers, but he was seeing little of the McKenzie River, and more and more of the inside of airplanes winging across America.

Brooks, who has a special investigator's badge presented by Sheriff Dave Burks, was talking with Pat Horton one winter day when Horton mentioned the Downs case. On the road so much in 1983, Brooks hadn't followed the case closely.

"I hear she might not be guilty after all," Brooks said.

"What do you think?" Horton tossed back, his face void of expression.

"I'd have to know more about it to give an opinion."

"Want to take a look at it?"

Brooks was hooked as cleanly as a trout skimming along the McKenzie. Fred Hugi drove him out to the scene, out to the bend in the road that came closest to the Mohawk River. It was cold and the maples were bare once more. The fields of wild phlox had been plowed under, the mountains' outlines muted by lowering rain clouds. The smell of blood had blown away long ago.

Brooks did a lot of listening in the next few days. He talked with Hugi, Jim Pex, and with Ed Wilson, the pathologist who had done the post-mortem on Cheryl. He watched a televised re-enactment of the shooting and noted that Diane laughed gaily as she demonstrated to Dick Tracy and Doug Welch how she had escaped the gunman.

Pierce Brooks and Fred Hugi spent a lot of time together. Brooks could feel Hugi's determination to someday, someway, gather the ammunition he needed to try Diane Downs for murder.

Brooks drove the Marcola-Sunderman-Mohawk routes with Doug Welch and Kurt Wuest. He was impressed that the young detectives were confident but not too cocky to ask questions of an old pro. He looked at the murder car, the shiny red Datsun still soaked with long-dried blood. Basically, Brooks played devil's advocate, throwing "What ifs?" and "Buts" at the detectives and at Fred Hugi.

Brooks listened to one of the last Lew tapes—the one that contained Diane's latest version of what had happened. Brooks's face was unreadable as Diane's breathy sobs filled Hugi's office:

"... God, I can't believe it and it is ugly—it's—it's as ugly as when I was a kid. Really bad. And I can't tell them now because I don't think that they would believe me. And it's just, it isn't important to prove it to them. Steve won. That's it. I quit—they can throw me in jail and I don't care, because I can't prove that Steve did it ... Uhhhh," she sighed, "I promised you that nobody would ever touch me until you and I got back together."

"Ummhumm."

"But I got touched—and I got threatened."

"Are you saying now that you got raped, and then he shot the kids?"

"It wasn't a he. It was a *they,* and no, I didn't get raped—I didn't. It was just the things they said, and the things they did, and only one of them talked. The other one didn't say a damn word. He just held me. And he had his hand over my mouth ... I *did* kick. That's why I got shot, by the way. He said, 'You have kids in the car; you don't want me to hurt your kids, do you?' So you try to be a good girl. Do what you're told, you don't argue, you don't tell anybody—because everybody will hate you and think that it's your fault. The same shit from when I was a kid."

"So they just—the two of them just held you there and talked to you and then they shot the kids and left?" Lew's voice rumbled.

"No, then they said—I don't remember the whole conversation—My God, it's been two months ... But there was ugly stuff, and then they mentioned Steve—"

"What do you mean ugly stuff? Verbal—or are you talking about—"

"Verbal and emotional—and physical. I don't like to be touched. I don't like guys—like I said, you're the only one that I really ever truly respected, and the touch wasn't bad—and I don't say that to impress you, damn it. You're the one that wants the answers. And so when somebody forces themselves on you, forces me to accept something and is gloating over it, I hate it. It's just—that is the ugliest thing that could happen to me in the whole world—having to relive what I lived when I was twelve years old ... and I couldn't stop it any more now than I could back then. It was awful and it's just one of these things where you just—you just space out, and go someplace else. It isn't real. It's not happening to me. It's just different, you know. It's somebody else—it's a movie or something. It's just not real. And then all of a sudden it dawns on you that they aren't there just to do that. That's just fun and games for them—because they know who you are. They use your name, they used *Steve's* name, they talk about 'plucking your rose,' and taking it with them, and I only know of one rose and that's on my back. And that scared me real good because as crazy as they were acting, for all I knew I was going to lose my shoulder. And then, they said, their motive basically was to get me off somebody's back, to get me out of somebody's life. That's why—I told the cops that it was Steve—but I don't know that it was Steve. Stan used to do crazy things—"

But Diane had fought, she told Lew through sobs. "We were going to get out of Steve's life, and he wouldn't have to worry about the kids any-more, if they were being taken care of or not being taken care of, and that Lew wouldn't get to raise his kids, and stuff like that. They said all those things. Then they shot the kids and I watched—Yeah, I watched. That's right, I watched, 'cause that son of a bitch shot me and I couldn't do any-thing. I hate—and then they turned around and he put the gun up to my head and I kicked him in the balls, and he says, 'Oh, you think you're real smart. Huh, bitch? And he grabbed my arm and he shot me, and I yanked, and he missed—so then he shot it again. And then they just stood there and said, 'Now, let's see you get out of this.' And left."

"Well, then you saw what they looked like, right?"

"Only one."

"So it's nobody you know—or is it somebody you know?"

"No—it's nobody I know. I only saw him because of one reason. They had ski masks on. When I hit the gun and kicked the guy, I grabbed his mask and pulled it off. The one behind me didn't say anything. I have no idea what he looks like. I can tell you that if—he was tall enough that his hot breath was in the back of my head."

Something rang up hinky in Pierce Brooks's mind. There were too many versions. He shook his head slightly. The two-man theory bothered Brooks. (It must have made Jim Jagger feel uneasy too; he called Fred Hugi and said, "Disregard that two-man story. Diane was only relating a dream.")

After reviewing the entire case, Pierce Brooks strongly agreed with Fred Hugi and the sheriff's detectives that Diane Downs had guilty knowledge in the shooting of her three children. He also told them that the long wait for arrest seemed unavoidable. Hugi's mind lightened when the old pro agreed with him.

Convincing an old homicide man and convincing a jury were two different things. In preparation for the "Onion Field" trial, Brooks had had to show the jurors the precise route of the police partners' abduction, exactly what it was like out there in the onion field in the dead of night—in effect, to re-create the actual murder. He had arranged for maps, aerial photography, mannequins to represent the victims. The crime scene had figuratively moved into the courtroom in a visual, palpable sense.

And it had worked. The onion field jury had been able to visualize the case as clearly as any detective working it.

"*You* have a very complex case here," Brooks said to Fred Hugi. "You have casings found lying out there on a rural road. You have tool marks on those casings that look like so many hen scratches to the layman. You have bullet angles, and you have blood spatter. What you're going to have to do is *graphically* display what happened. Look, if I have to draw myself pictures after thirty-five years in this business, you're going to have to *show* a jury."

Hugi agreed. The car could be reconstructed in styrofoam or plywood and brought into the courtroom; the children could be brought in to the courtroom too—as life-size dolls.

Pierce Brooks said he would be around for a while. When the time came to talk about arrest, he'd share his experience on that too.

Christmas, 1983, neared. Last year, Steve had had the kids, but Diane had taken them tons of presents. And last year there had been Lew. Lew was gone for sure, and Diane had none of her children with her—save for the fetus growing within her womb. It helped a little to listen to its heartbeat through the doctor's stethoscope. Diane hoped to have Christie and Danny back by January, if she could just light a fire under Jim Jagger.

Diane wasn't aware that Doug Welch was back in the detective unit. And she'd never even heard of Pierce Brooks.

It snowed five days before Christmas. Diane spotted Matt Jensen on the street; she'd been waiting in the snowstorm, watching his car, *needing* to see him. Jensen saw her and turned the other way. She couldn't understand why he was so mean and antsy when he saw her.

Everything was getting worse.

Diane carried the mail, trudging through the snow to deliver brightly wrapped packages, her stomach queasy in early pregnancy, fatigue heavier on her shoulders than her mailbag.

On Christmas Day Willadene did her best to make it seem like a regular holiday. It was a travesty. Of her five children, only Diane and her brothers Paul and James were home. John and Kathy didn't make it. Willadene had only three living grandchildren now, and none of them played under the tree. She cooked a huge meal, but it didn't help the pall over the house. Even Willadene was depressed; she, of all people, usually managed to keep a cheerful face. This year, she just couldn't. Israel was in Oklahoma, Christie and Danny were in their foster home. Cheryl's ashes were in Arizona.

Diane passed out the presents, and later somebody suggested they play dominoes and cards. They did. Wes lost—and he got mad.

"I guess I just figured it would be different when we got older," Diane wrote in her diary. "It wasn't. He still hates to lose, and I'm still affected."

Wes, Willadene, Paul, and James left for California the next day. Alone, Diane had too much time to think, and it grated on her. She filled pages in her diary. Lew came back to her in memory, as strong as if he were there in the room with her. Funny—when Lew's world was all desert and heat, and the snow kept piling up outside her parents' white ranch house, she still found it difficult to accept that Lew would let the police blackmail him, turn him against her.

In her isolation, Diane got sick. Her arm hurt, and her head ached and she had a fever and her vision blurred. She was sick to her stomach. She had only her diary to complain to.

December 29, 1983, was Danny Downs's fourth birthday. Diane bought him a Smurf Cake and a remote control race car that he could manipulate along its tracks from his wheelchair. She arranged for KMTR to be present when she picked up the cake, and then she took KVAL with her to the CSD offices.

On December 30, Diane was still sick, but she went to work. The doctor had said the pain in her arm might mean a crack in the mend, but it wouldn't help much to rebreak it and try again. She just couldn't stand pain.

On December 31, she wrote, "Well this is the last day of 1983. Big deal. I'm not much on sentimental New Year's. I may hope that 1984 is better. I want my kids home and start a new life."

The Eugene *Register-Guard* listed the ten top stories of the year. The Downs shooting ranked first. The failure of the levy to finance the sheriff's department and the district attorney's office was third.

Diane started the New Year by returning to church. She was accepted graciously at the Bethany Baptist Church in Springfield. Reverend Craig Brooks refused to judge Diane.

She was self-conscious now; people seemed to know her wherever she went, and it no longer warmed her. She felt comfortable only at church. She went often—not just on Sunday mornings. And she joined some of the church women's groups.

Diane said she didn't really care who the killer was anymore; she just wanted to get on with her life; 1983 had been a "bummer" for her, but she was ready to start fresh.

Christie was coming along so well after her setback that Dr. Peterson felt she would be able to testify in a grand jury hearing within weeks.

Cheryl would have been eight years old January 10, 1984. Doug Welch was glancing through the classifieds of the *Springfield News* when he spotted a notice in the "Personals" that made gooseflesh prickle along his arms. The first and only time he'd seen Cheryl Downs flashed across his memory; he was instantly back in the ER, viewing the dead little girl in the green shorts.

HAPPY BIRTHDAY
CHERYL LYNN DOWNS
Jan. 10th, 1976—May 19, 1983
We loved you very much
Jesus loved you too

He took you to heaven
When you were only seven
We miss you. Mom
Grandma & Grandpa

Welch recognized Diane in that poem. Her birthday wish for her dead child—it was the sort of symbolic gesture Diane liked. Names engraved on a unicorn. Names printed in a paper. Neat. Happy Birthday to Cheryl.

As if they truly were pitted against an army and not a lone woman, the prosecution team was quietly beefing up its troops. Paul Alton and Welch had been back a month in January. The Lane County DA's office had also scraped up the funds to rehire a six-year veteran who would be of immeasurable assistance in a case that looked as if it might finally be headed for trial: Ray Broderick.

Broderick, a one-time Chicago street cop and detective, is a dark-haired, lanky Irishman. Married young, the father of four, Broderick wrested a college education in night school from Loyola *after* he became a cop. Working the bad streets of Chicago, one memorable bloody shoot-out turned his thoughts to Oregon and a better place to raise his kids. Quickly hired by the Eugene Police Department, he stayed only two years. Broderick is, at heart and by natural propensity, an investigator, and it could have taken him too long to work up through the Eugene hierarchy to detective status. He talked it over with Pierce Brooks, and Brooks empathized. Investigators are a different breed of cat from a street cop. Some men excel in one area; some in another. Brooks, then Broderick's chief, agreed that he should resign and find a spot where he *could* be a detective again.

And so Broderick had moved over to the district attorney's office as an investigator. Ray Broderick's area of expertise is far afield of, say, Paul Alton's brilliance in firearms identification. Ray Broderick literally reads *people*—what they say, of course, but more than that—the *way* they speak. Body signals. Eyes shifting to the right or to the left, or turning up until the whites show. He is fascinated with the intricacies of conversation, the patterns that can be woven with words. His innate perception allows him to elicit a great deal from what is both said—and unsaid . . . a long silence, a quickening of breath, or a cessation of breathing for a beat or two. Ray Broderick is not a man with whom the guilty would choose to speak. He is personable and gregarious, a man of considerable wit—although given to atrocious puns. And yet he is always listening and evaluating on multiple levels.

Broderick had listened to the voluminous Diane Downs tapes and he had seen her countless times on television. He found her mistress of the pat answer, with the same words weighted *exactly* as they had been in other interviews. This habit of repeating verbatim answers was, he knew, a typical defensive pattern.

Broderick explains that when people who are able to feel emotion are bereft, their heads drop, their eyes lower, and their voices soften. In the individual who feels nothing, there is a flatness, a stilted quality, as he attempts to feign sorrow.

And, Broderick noted, Diane's "grief" seemed plastic.

"I am continually amazed," Broderick says, "at how many people will *believe* something merely because it is said aloud. It may be a patent lie, but it has been *spoken*—and therefore it must be true."

Broderick can spot a lie, but he can also recognize the truth—and that was what he heard on the afternoon of January 9, 1984.

To help Christie and Danny remember (and eventually to use them in trial), Fred Hugi had gone to a group that makes anatomically correct dolls used all across America in counseling victims of child abuse. Ginger Friedeman, Marcia Morgan, and Mike Whitney made three dolls the same size as Christie, Cheryl, and Danny Downs. Dr. Peterson had suggested that Christie and Danny take the dolls home to the Slavens' house so they could get used to them. Ray wanted to meet the children; picking the dolls up was his excuse.

Brenda Slaven and Danny Downs warmed to Broderick immediately.

"But Christie stayed away. I could see her watching me, judging me."

Broderick is a talented cartoonist, and he drew cartoons for the three children. They liked that, and he could sense Christie was edging closer to the group. "I felt an immediate affinity for Christie, and it seemed to be mutual."

But she was like a little rabbit at the border of a clearing. She was so bright, and she'd been so hurt. Christie was poised for flight during the first half hour or so the DA's investigator drew his funny pictures for them, making Danny and Brenda laugh out loud.

Ray reminded the kids he'd come to pick up the big dolls, and the three youngsters rushed to carry them back, playing with them for a while on the way. The dolls were deliberately dressed in the Downs children's old clothes. It was apparent to Broderick that the "Cheryl-doll" was, for Christie, an extension of her dead sister.

Casually, he asked where the dolls would have been sitting when they rode in their red car. Christie looked up at him, and he could see this new game was something she wanted very much to participate in.

"There was only one couch in the living room, and Christie said we needed two couches because the car had two seats. The Slavens said, 'Well, let's go downstairs; there are two couches down there.'"

"You put the dolls where they're supposed to be," Ray said to Christie when they were in the rec room. "I was amazed. She immediately placed the three dolls exactly where we'd all figured the kids must have been that night."

It was a tense moment, but he played it very quietly. Christie was anxious to tell him something.

"Do you want to tell me what happened?" Broderick asked softly.

Christie started to explain something to him, but he couldn't understand her. "Honey, that doesn't make much sense to me. You be your mommy. You play her part."

Christie hesitated for a moment. Then she moved over to the car that was made from two couches. No one in the room said anything.

"Kinesthetically, it was all right," Broderick recalls. "Christie walked to the 'front door' from the rear of the 'car.' She hunched over and she pointed her finger at 'Cheryl,' 'herself,' and 'Danny.' Of course there was no roof on the couch-car, but Christie's body bent over as if it *were* there."

Pow. Pow. Pow. Christie pointed her finger at the dolls.

"Emotion took over. She broke up and started crying. She said she could tell me more, but she was sobbing. I told her that it was OK—that we didn't have to."

Ray Broderick gathered up the dolls and went to meet Fred Hugi. "I was overwhelmed by the flow and the honesty of Christie's actions," he told Hugi. "As a technician, I was struck by how totally correct every move was—she hunched over because the car 'roof' was there."

Broderick sighed. "As a human being, I feel awful. But Christie's over the hump. Christie will make you a great witness."

CHAPTER 32

The list of people Christie trusted grew longer. She had confided in Carl Peterson, and she felt safe with the Slavens, with Danny, with Paula Krogdahl, and now with Ray Broderick.

She needed to trust Fred Hugi, perhaps most of all.

"We were rapidly getting to the end of our rope," Hugi remembers. "Something had to happen. We were running out of postponements with juvenile court. We had to appear there and be sure Diane didn't get the kids back. We always wanted to find the gun first, and then have Christie remember and tell us what she remembered."

There was no gun. And Christie was remembering, yes, but she could balk at any point.

It was essential that Christie and Fred Hugi become friends. There was little doubt in Broderick's mind that Fred already loved Christie—but in a removed, protective stance. He had been there in the hospital when Christie was critical, but that was a long time back and they hadn't talked. Hugi had watched over her, silently. He wasn't comfortable with children; he didn't even talk that much with adults.

The truth was that Hugi was scared to death of confronting Christie. He didn't want to do her any harm, and yet he needed to ask her questions. He had to become so familiar to her that he was like an old shoe. He prevailed upon Ray Broderick to sit in on their first few meetings—for Christie's sake, and for his too.

After Christie and Susan Staffel had visited Fred Hugi's office—with Broderick acting as buffer—several times, the little girl and the quiet prosecutor began to feel comfortable enough to talk cautiously together. Twice a week now Christie spent time with Hugi and Staffel. Hugi knew she didn't want to be there. The meetings usually started at 3:30 and ended at 4:15—but the forty-five minutes seemed hours long as Christie sat obediently across from his desk, and he searched for the right words. Again and again, Hugi found himself backing off, talking only about safe subjects. He couldn't bring himself to talk about things that would make Christie unhappy. After each failed meeting, he would blurt to Broderick, "I didn't get anywhere today, damn it!"

But they had. Christie had a child's clear perception of who really cared about her—and she sensed that Mr. Hugi did. Even on the days when they ended up talking about cats or fishing or just went out with Susan to buy an ice cream cone, they made progress. It wasn't something that could be rushed.

Christie knew Mr. Hugi was one of the good guys; she could not know how much her pain hurt him too.

Neither of them were huggers. It might have been easier for the little girl and the intense lawyer if they had been able to end their meetings with a hug, but they weren't touchers and that was that. Nevertheless, Christie understood that Mr. Hugi would protect her if the day should come when she must get up in a courtroom.

If they ever got to trial, Hugi would have to ask Christie devastating questions in court, and he hated the thought of that. But he had to prepare her. He explained to her everything about a trial; nothing would come as a surprise. He let her play witness and judge. She sat, such a small figure, in the judge's chair, gazing down on the empty benches of the gallery. And always, Hugi promised Christie that he would be there *for* her. Whatever happened, he would be her friend, instead of a threatening presence.

But in the long run—if they went to trial—he knew it would be hell for Christie. Could she actually point an accusing finger at her own mother and meet those strange greenish-yellow eyes without flinching?

Diane didn't talk much about the case in her diary anymore. She was fighting for her parental rights. She wanted to attend parent-teacher conferences; she wanted the children taken out of Dr. Peterson's care and assigned to another psychologist. She was still convinced, she wrote, that Danny would walk again, if only he could have proper rehabilitative care. She wanted him moved to the Philadelphia Spinal Cord Institute at the Shriners Hospital there.

Wes Frederickson did not help her with her bills now. Although she was still living and eating at home and had a good job, Diane had to take out a loan for her expenses.

The situation in Wes and Willadene's house was disintegrating. Diane's mother was beginning to pick up on veiled references to the secret Diane shared with her father—the stuff that had happened so long ago. Willadene resented it when Diane wouldn't tell her what was going on.

A fact-finding hearing to see if the children might be able to come home was postponed for sixty days. Sixty days! That was a lifetime for Diane. Jim Jagger warned her that at first she would probably only have visitation rights, then overnight visits, and then *maybe* one day the kids could actually live with her.

She had nightmares. She dreamed the kids were home, but Danny didn't remember her. He wouldn't give her kisses.

She felt sicker and sicker, and she began to vomit blood. The doctor diagnosed ulcers and told her not to worry so much.

Her written memories of the days with the children were perfect in retrospect. It had been heaven. Nothing marred her life then but the presence of Steve Downs.

"I had accomplished my goal. We were a happy family. Chris and Cher were almost inseparable and they never fought. And both of them catered to Danny, without thinking of themselves first. And when one of the girls got hurt, Dan would cuddle them and coo. There was love. Lots of love! We were also able to communicate. If they thought I was wrong, they spoke up without fear of punishment. And if I thought they were at fault somehow, I could say so without fear of them withdrawing in fear. We were happy. We were a success. We were a family!"

Diane's memory was selective; she had let everything negative slip away into oblivion as if it had never happened.

Wes was playing cat-and-mouse with her. He declared that he had no secrets from Willadene, and Diane was tempted to fling accusations at him—to remind him of the torture of anxiety and disgust she'd suffered fifteen years before. She said nothing; he still controlled her.

Eight months now. Eight months back in her father's house. She wanted to leave—but Diane had finally begun to worry that they might be up to something over there in the courthouse.

Things were too quiet.

She went to church and felt better. She didn't know that her new interest in religion was being monitored—along with almost all of her other activities away from home—by Doug Welch.

Attached beneath the frame of her white Ford Fiesta, there was a tiny radio signal that Welch could monitor from his car. Welch slipped the "bird-dog" under Diane's car on January 23, and it stayed there for a week and a half.

At first, Fred Hugi merely asked Doug to chart Diane's movements in the early morning hours. Welch parked his car around the corner from the Frederickson home, waiting in the cold from 5:00 A.M. until 7:30 for Diane's car to go by.

Hugi feared that Diane might learn how close they were to arresting her. "She might panic and do something rash. If she snatched Christie and took off for Mexico, she wouldn't be any worse off if she was unsuccessful. At this point, she'd be definitely better off if Christie disappeared. It was imperative that she not know that Christie was able to relate what happened."

Welch watched to be sure Diane didn't drive to the Slavens' house—perhaps to waylay Christie and Danny on their way to school.

There was also the possibility that she might move the gun—if she still had it—or even use it again to further her defense. It had been Diane's pattern in the past to stop at a lover's home on the way to work. If the father of the baby she carried had been part of a murder plot, and if Diane was as antsy as she was reported to be, she might drive to the father's house for comfort. Welch spent hours following Diane, listening for the telltale beep the bird-dog put out. The stakeout was tedious—and unrewarding.

His family never saw him. At length, Tamara Welch packed a picnic lunch, grabbed their two young sons, and announced that they would do a "family" stakeout for the weekend. And they did.

"When the kids and Mama saw how much fun it was to drive around aimlessly all day, and wait behind bushes, they decided I wasn't leaving them behind while I had a high old time playing James Bond. They also decided they'd just as soon stay home the next time," Welch laughs.

Diane was leading a circumspect life. Welch never saw her with a boyfriend. Work. Church. Home. She appeared to have no friends, male or female. If she wasn't with her brother Paul, she was alone. Diane never knew that Welch had been tracking her. On Wednesday, February 1, the bird-dog device was removed from her car.

Rumors were rampant now that an indictment was coming down, but the media could find no source who would verify it. Diane called Jim Jagger often to see if he'd heard anything, and he was usually able to calm her by saying some reporter had started it.

Even as her already tenuous world was beginning to crumble, Diane felt temporarily victorious because she had been allowed to talk to Danny's teacher and the report was good. He sounded like the old Danny—so intelligent and full of mischief—even if he couldn't walk. Diane had once told Lew in those phone calls that he'd taped, "of course Danny's paralyzed, but it really doesn't bother him."

Diane's cheerfulness was bravado. She grew more and more anxious. The entity she'd felt behind her was getting closer, and she glanced back more often.

She knew it wasn't her creepy phone caller. Some man had been calling her continually, pressing to meet her. He finally told her what he really wanted was to star her in porno movies—and she laughed. Eight thousand dollars for taking her clothes off! Jim Jagger laughed too when she told him. The weirdos were coming out of the woodwork.

The secret grand jury, after almost nine months of meetings, continued to weigh testimony to determine if Elizabeth Diane Downs should be charged with murder and a number of lesser offenses.

Lew and Nora flew into Eugene on January 26. Lew testified on the twenty-seventh, and they left for Arizona early in the morning the next day. Diane didn't even know he was in town. When she found out on February 9, she was shocked. "I don't know what came of that. But that's not unusual. They don't tell me anything."

Everyone was talking about her behind her back. Even her parents were holding secret conversations. She saw them sitting outside in their car, talking for a long time.

So what was new? It was the story of her life. What do we do with Diane? Send her here. Send her there. Put her on a bus and wave goodbye. Get rid of her. Badger her. Ignore her.

It was wearing her down. "I get so very tired of the fight. It is strange how you lose your self esteem," she told her journal. "The DA & Sheriff and Dept of CSD talk and act as if I am guilty. Everything reflects their convictions . . . I know that I am innocent."

And now, after she had spoken enough words to cover the highways from Eugene, Oregon, to Chandler, Arizona, and back, Diane began to wonder if it might not be a good idea to speak out less. She wasn't sure if it would help but "I'll say one thing for sure—it can't hurt to keep my mouth shut."

It could not hurt, indeed. But it was a little late in the game.

Perhaps she did talk less for a while. Her diary—her journal—became thicker. Each day's entry was now pages long, rather than the few sentences per day she had begun with.

She knew. Somewhere in her gut, Diane knew what lay ahead. It was coming down.

"Boy, my skin crawls when I hear those words. [Murder Trial.] There is so much violence and ugliness attached to those two words. They seem so foreign to me, and yet it is something the DA has made part of my life. All my old friends and the media are waiting for that trial. It is so sad."

On February 17, Diane went to a woman's seminar in Portland with ladies from her church. Three hundred women attended, and she was amused to see that the topic under discussion was how to be a submissive wife. Well, she could have given lessons on that one—but she was surprised when someone got up and said you could be a Christian and still not have to kneel at your husband's feet. The Baptist Church was making progress.

The trip to Portland helped take the strain off for a few days. The atmosphere in her father's house was oppressive. One by one, the whole family was being called to testify before the grand jury, and there was rampant suspicion about who would tell what. Willadene was sure Diane was hiding something; Wes was wanting to know what Diane was going to say.

Her parents were even abrasive with each other—a most unusual situation.

A whirlwind had come into their home, churning dark hidden sides up—into the light where they shouldn't be. Fifteen years since the Arizona state policeman had stopped them in the desert. But Diane remembered, and she knew her father did too. They circled each other like wary tigers—waiting to see who would strike out first.

But it was Wes Frederickson's house. Diane was only there under sufferance. She could tell her welcome was wearing thin.

On February 24, Ray Broderick met Diane for the first time when he served subpoenas requiring Diane and Paul to appear at the grand jury hearing. They would be next: Diane the suspect; Paul the relative in whom she apparently confided. Broderick had deliberately waited until he could meet with Diane in her parents' home—alone. He had noted that Diane seemed to choreograph her meetings with authorities; this time, and perhaps this time only, she was caught unawares. They talked for four or five hours. Diane explained to Ray Broderick fervently that "no one ever *listens* to me; they talk to me—but they won't listen to me."

Broderick had been trained to do exactly that. Listen.

He phrased his comments carefully. Diane talked about the night of the shooting, the "stranger" who had shot them. Broderick suggested that "All of us have a stranger within us—a stranger who might do things that we ordinarily wouldn't do."

She did not demur.

"She didn't resent my suggestion that she might be capable of shooting her children—an innocent woman's response would almost certainly have been one of hostility, protesting."

It was a subtle balancing of wit and mind. He could see that the woman was very, very intelligent—but she talked so much, she failed to listen. Diane would write in her diary that she had explained to Broderick "what love really is." She apparently had no idea that she had just jousted with a master interrogator; she felt positive about the whole conversation— that she had gotten her points across well.

Diane extrapolated what she wanted from Ray Broderick's conversation. As he left, he had looked directly into her eyes and said, "I do believe you. I think we both know who did this."

"It isn't that Diane doesn't *know* the truth, that she buries it in her subconscious somewhere," Broderick muses. "I think it's more that she picks what she chooses to discuss . . . deliberately. That seems to be her strength, judiciously emphasizing only self-serving statements."

For Broderick it was a fascinating exercise in human communication, both spoken and silent. "She was a woman with tremendous strength who was basically giving us the finger. Beneath it all she was saying, 'Prove it!' The chase was on, but as strong as our case was beginning to look, it could all collapse. We had over two hundred pieces of physical evidence to help us—but, even so, it was flimsy evidence. The mathematical combinations of what could go wrong were endless."

On Sunday, February 26, Diane had a doozy of a fight with her father. "Just when I think that things are as bad as they can get, somehow—it gets worse," she told her journal.

She had been on her way to church, but the argument ruined that. She went driving, "talking to God," and then bought herself a new outfit to wear to grand jury. After that, she sought out a movie, a comedy where she could laugh. But it started again at supper. A discussion that grew in intensity and pitch, until they were shouting at each other. It ended with Wes telling Diane that she had to move out because he couldn't stand to live with her anger and hate toward him.

At the height of the battle, Diane turned to Willadene and blurted out accusations against Wes. She told her mother, finally, that she had been molested by her own father. Willadene shook her head in disbelief. She would not believe that—ever. Diane had fantasized it.

It was possibly the worst scene ever in the Frederickson household. If she had to go to trial, Diane had decided to use what had happened to her when she was a child—and to find every medical record or police file she could from fifteen years ago to prove it—if she had to. If it came down to him or her, she wasn't going to spare her father. She was ready to tell the whole world that her father had molested her when she was too young, and too frightened, to fight back or tell anyone.

Willadene simply shut her mind to Diane's accusations. She'd been married to Wes for almost thirty years. She'd lost her grandchildren, her daughter might be arrested for murder, and now she was supposed to believe that her own husband had done sexual things to their own daughter? It wasn't so.

On February 27, the family went to testify before the grand jury. What was said there was secret, but some of it would leak out, hints and impressions. Wes reportedly acted shocked when he was asked if *anyone* had ever molested Diane.

That night, Wes ordered Diane out of the house.

"Obviously I have no place to go, because I used all my money to pay my bills. But I was [am] getting all my stuff together, hoping to find room with someone, somewhere."

She had no one. She had no friends. Willadene came and talked with her while Diane ironed a dress, and they made up. Willadene fixed supper early so that Diane wouldn't run into her father, and when Wes got home, Diane left.

Diane went to see Matt Jensen; he was, after all, the father of the baby she carried. She thought perhaps he would let her stay the night with him.

He wasn't home.

That left no one at all. Diane drove to Foo's, a singles bar on Centennial Boulevard in the shadow of the University of Oregon's stadium. It was a meat market, where both men and women prowled and preened, looking for instant love. She sat at a corner table, writing in her journal, sipping bourbon and water.

During the hardball interview, Diane had asked Kurt Wuest and Doug Welch if they would want to know the day the world would end. They said they would; she said she would not. Even as she sat alone amid the laughing dancers at Foo's, Diane was living through the last twenty-four hours of the world as she had known it. Her world was about to come to an end.

And she got her wish. She didn't know it was the end.

One by one, those connected to the Downs shooting had been called into the secret chambers of the grand jury—some from far away, some from the Eugene area. They had told their stories, and it was done.

A secret indictment, Number 10-84-01377, had been handed down. The State of Oregon vs. Elizabeth Diane Downs.

The charges listed were:

MURDER
ATTEMPTED MURDER
ATTEMPTED MURDER
ASSAULT IN THE FIRST DEGREE
ASSAULT IN THE FIRST DEGREE

The counts were listed individually, worded in the oddly archaic language of the law: "The defendant on or about the 19th day of May, 1983, in the county aforesaid, did unlawfully and intentionally cause the death of Cheryl Lynn Downs, a human being, by shooting her with a firearm; contrary to statute and against the peace and dignity of the State of Oregon."

Murder in Oregon is an unclassified felony; there are no degrees of murder in that state, and the death penalty was not extant on May 19, 1983. (Within the year, it would be.)

The attempted murder and assault with a deadly weapon charges are Class A felonies in Oregon.

Fred Hugi had called before the grand jury:

Christie Ann Downs
Elizabeth Diane Downs
Steve Downs
Paul Frederickson
Wesley Frederickson
Willadene Frederickson
Joseph Inman
Paula J. Krogdahl
Lewis Lewiston
James O. Pex
Heather Kathleen Plourd
Mark Christopher Plourd
Cord Samuelson
Richard B. Tracy

The secret indictment was signed by Frederick A. Hugi and by Claudia M. Langan, the grand jury foreman.

Diane's sixth sense had been right on. Everyone *had* been keeping secrets from her. She hadn't known Welch was following her, and she hadn't known that Lew had come to town, but she'd seen the emotional chaos of her parents' home, seen even her mother reduced to suspicion and hostility.

Fred Hugi and Pierce Brooks had discussed the best way to carry out the actual arrest of Diane Downs.

"I went in and we went through the tactics of the arrest," Brooks remembers. "Was the gun still hidden somewhere—in her room maybe, someplace in the parents' home, maybe a locker at the post office? I felt it essential that when she was arrested, there be at least one officer that she knew, and one policewoman—and that there be no handcuffs used."

The time had come.

After Christie's grand jury testimony, DA Pat Horton had turned to Fred Hugi and asked, "Any reason not to arrest her now?"

Hugi shook his head. There were no more reasons. The final decision to move on an arrest was his, and he had held back so long. Now, it was time.

Ray Broderick prepared the affidavits for search warrants for the Fredericksons' home and garage, for Diane Downs's Ford Fiesta, for her post office locker, and for the Rent-A-Garage on Franklin Boulevard where many of her possessions and household items had been stored.

Affidavits must show probable cause—demonstrate the pressing reasons why a judge would grant officers permission to invade the privacy of citizens. And they must list the items sought in some detail. The documents were seven pages long, a summary of one of the longest investigations in Lane County history. Succinct and convincing.

Diane knew nothing of the indictment, the search warrants. She was, quite literally, on the street. She had no money and no home. She had her Ford Fiesta, and she had her journals—the two blue ledgers that said "Record" on their covers. She carried them with her wherever she went.

It grew late in Foo's. It was still February 27—the longest day of her life. She had to be at work at seven the next day, but she had no place to sleep. She sat in the corner, and she wrote steadily. A lovely blonde woman, her voluptuous breasts swollen with pregnancy. She was into her fifth month but it wasn't apparent when she was sitting down and men approached her often, asking her to dance. She smiled and shook her head, noting each invitation in her journal.

With no one left to talk to, she was talking to herself.

"If a nice guy comes to talk to me, I crawl away inside myself. I'm afraid they'll figure out who I am, and then they'll run away from me. I know it sounds kind of kooky but I have seen the DA take my very best friends and close their hearts. They were lovers and friends and now they are adversaries. I guess I'm just afraid that the DA will find out if I have any new friends and do the same thing to them. That's why I stay away from 'Papa.' I've never even told him that I love him, because I'm afraid that someone will find out, and they'll drive him away. But, it's kind of ironic because I deny caring about him, and that has driven him away too. I guess I can't win. Perhaps when this ordeal is over and my children come home and our new baby is born, then things will settle down. Maybe then, I will be able to be open and affectionate with people again. Maybe I'll even find the courage to tell 'Papa' I love him. And if it isn't too late, then he will be able to share his child with me.

"Time will tell."

Diane would write seventeen pages in three hours that evening. Pure unadulterated fantasy. "Papa"—Matt Jensen—bolted at the very sight of her.

The music was loud—a lot of Michael Jackson: "Beat It" and "Billie Jean," which was a sad song for Diane because it was about a man denying paternity. "The child is not my son . . ."

She sensed her baby was a girl, but the lyrics stung anyway.

The club's air blued with smoke, and the music blared louder. The bass tones vibrated in time to the colored lights flashing on-off-on-off, and the child within her stirred and kicked too—light little taps to let her know she wasn't alone.

And still Diane wrote, aimless anecdotes, filling page after page. "I guess alot of things have happened in my life that are out of the ordinary for some people. But I take it all in stride."

Foo's would close at 2:00 A.M. Outside the rain was coming down steadily, making the rivers rise.

"Ya know, there are so many things I want to teach my children," she wrote. "I have taught them so much already, but there is so much left. They know how to love now, and trust. But they need to know that a life without love can be so bleak. I need to take them to see kids that don't have the love they have. Perhaps if they don't see the pain that can be caused by lack of love, they'll take it for granted and not love their kids. Na. That could never happen. If you love someone long enough and strong enough, they can't help but give it away."

More fantasy.

"I was just sitting here in my corner watching the people on the dance floor. I often wonder what possesses people to dance the way they do . . . I remember when Lew and I used to dance. I was dancing for him. I was seductive and erotic. I liked to make him smile and raise an eyebrow . . . I have to feel what I do, or it is all fake. And I'm not a fake person.

"Well, I just had the third guy ask me to dance, so obviously writing isn't working. I think I'll try to sneak into my parents' house and get about six hours sleep . . . That won't be enough but it's all I'll get.

"I can't keep this up every night. I'll be exhausted."

And so the second journal-diary ended, although Diane couldn't have known that this was her final entry.

God, she was tired. She crept into the house and nobody tried to kick her out. Willadene heard her, but Willadene would never have thrown her daughter out. Diane slept until it was time to get up at 5:30 and go to work.

CHAPTER 33

FEBRUARY 28, 1984

They gathered in Pat Horton's office at 5:30 A.M.—long before the courthouse was officially opened—almost all of the investigators who had worked on the Downs shooting for these nine months: Paul Alton and Ray

Broderick, Doug Welch, Pat Horton, and Fred Hugi. Chris Rosage, a female deputy, joined them. They would need a woman along when they arrested Diane.

Ironically, it had taken nine months and one week for the investigation to come to the point of arrest. A gestation of sorts. The State's "baby" had yet to be delivered. It could still turn out to be an uncontrollable monster.

The search warrants had to be served concurrently; the arrest had to go like clockwork. If they stood any chance at all of finding the gun, they would lose their advantage if there was a warning. They knew that Diane was getting antsy. But they were pretty sure she didn't know exactly when the arrest was coming down.

They would work in teams: Louis Hince and Paul Alton to the Frederickson home in Springfield, and Welch, Broderick, and Rosage to the post office in Cottage Grove, with Bill Kennedy and Carl Lindquist following just behind to search Diane's car after the arrest was made.

Diane was due into work at 7:00 A.M.; she had proved in the past to be unfailingly punctual. None of the arrest team knew that Diane had been kicked out of her father's house the night before. Ray Broderick would always wish they *had* known, wondering if Diane might have opened up more if she'd been alone and virtually homeless for a few more days.

But they could never know now.

The Cottage Grove team parked their vehicles at the side of the post office at 140 South Fifth. They peered through the thin gray wash of dawn light for the sight of Diane's Ford.

Headlights pierced the gloom from time to time. Some passed on by. Some turned in and parked, and other letter carriers walked toward the Cottage Grove post office.

They waited.

At exactly two minutes to seven, a white car came into view and pulled into the employees' parking lot behind the building. It was a Ford Fiesta, license number DQX 055.

Immediately, the police units turned the corner and came nose-to-nose with Diane Downs's car. Everyone got out. For just a beat, they stared at each other: Ray Broderick, Doug Welch, Chris Rosage, and the wan woman in the maternity postal uniform.

Diane was smiling at them, a tentative try at nonchalance—but her smile was a little crooked and her eyes were frightened. Her throat flushed scarlet.

Doug Welch spoke first. "Today's the day, Diane."

"Oh . . . OK." It was her little girl's voice, compliant, vulnerable.

Chris Rosage moved toward Diane. These two women who would spend so much time together were introduced for the first time. They were about the same height, but Chris was a few years older. Her hair was dark and luxuriant, twisted and coiled atop her head, her dark eyes fringed with thick lashes. Even in her man-tailored sheriff's uniform, she was clearly a well-built woman. Whether Rosage liked it or not, she too was about to become a media celebrity; Diane would be photographed thousands of times, and Chris would be, of necessity, there beside her, caught in the strobe lights.

"Diane," Rosage said quietly as she patted her prisoner down for weapons, "I'm probably going to spend more time with you from now on than anybody."

Diane Downs still smiled faintly, as her rights under Miranda were read to her, along with the five charges that the grand jury had returned. As they walked to the sheriff's car, Broderick asked her if they'd left anything important in her car.

Yes! Her diaries.

"She mentioned her diaries to me three or four times. She wanted to be absolutely sure that we knew about those diaries," he recalls. "It was reminiscent of Brer Rabbit insisting 'Whatever you do, *please* don't throw me in the Briar Patch.' Diane wanted us to have those diaries. I assured her that they would not be overlooked."

Diane, not handcuffed, sat in the back seat with Ray Broderick. Chris drove, and Doug Welch sat beside her. They took the old highway, 99, through Creswell and then into Eugene, driving through the melancholy rain. Once—it seemed so long ago—Diane had described the natural beauties of this very road to Lew in her first diary, as she pleaded with him to join her in Oregon.

Only the firs and pines were green now, and that was a dulled green of a gray day.

Exactly a year ago Diane had written on her calendar: "I'm so happy.

Just when I thought Lew would call off our relationship, he said he would marry me and live with my kids. But before I get too excited, I'll wait awhile. He could take another look at the situation and change his mind. I hope he doesn't. I sure love him."

No more.

Diane chattered on the way to jail—not about the case but about the trouble at home. She told them her dad had thrown her out of the house because he was afraid she'd tell about how he'd molested her when she was twelve. She told them she'd finally told her mother about the abuse but that Willadene hadn't believed her.

"It's strange," Broderick remembers. "I almost think she was relieved when we arrested her. She knew it was coming, and she had no place to go."

Behind them, Bill Kennedy and Carl Lindquist searched Diane's car in the Cottage Grove post office lot. There was not a great deal to be gleaned from the Ford. Certainly, there was no gun in plain sight—or hidden.

What were to become Exhibit #81 were the two blue notebooks labeled "Record": "Reported to be the diary of Elizabeth Diane Downs. Also included are two ballpoint pens. One is labeled 'Skilcraft–U.S. Government,' and the other is labeled 'Papermate.'" As she had planned, Diane's journal-diaries were in the hands of the police. All of her blistering attacks on the cops, her longing for her children, her memories of perfect motherhood, her feelings of loss, her protestations of innocence—now part of the police record.

What would become Exhibit #82 were: "Two sealed brown paper bags one inside the other, enclosing one 750 Ml bottle labeled 'Jim Beam Kentucky Straight Bourbon Whiskey.' This bottle is approximately ¹/₂ full of a light brown liquid. The odor is consistent with an alcoholic beverage. Examination of the area under the cap reveals a semi-solid material containing several epithelial cells."

Cells and crusted mucoid material from a woman's vagina, caught in the neck ridges of a bottle of bourbon . . . Lew's favorite bourbon.

Louis Hince and Paul Alton served the search warrant upon the Frederickson residence at 7:15—even as Diane was being transported to Eugene for booking.

Willadene was alone when she answered the door; Paul was still asleep and Wes had left for work. She was very upset. Wes Frederickson always spoke for the family and made the decisions. She looked at the search warrant and the affidavit attached and asked if she could call her husband. Alton assured her that she could.

She handed the phone to Alton, who was not surprised to find the postmaster of Springfield incensed at the thought of police pawing through his home. However, Frederickson understood the power of a search warrant. He said he would be right home.

Wes had paid the rent on the "store-and-lock" facility in the Glenwood district of Eugene where Diane's things were. He gave deputies his permission to search it.

They searched the rented garage, they searched Diane's room in the Frederickson residence, and they searched her car. The elder Fredericksons were cooperative in allowing the investigators to look wherever they asked for the missing .22 caliber Ruger.

They didn't find it. The gun, any ammunition, its pouch-type carrying case, all gone.

For the first time, Diane Downs was led through the "sally-port" into the Lane County Jail booking area. She was given a pair of green one-size-fits-all jail pajamas, fingerprinted and posed before the mug-camera. She stood against a light wall of concrete blocks, a chained sign around her neck:

LANE COUNTY JAIL
EUGENE, OREGON
609569
02 28 84

There are circles under Diane's eyes in this picture, and yet she smiles. She truly does—a faint, bitter little smile.

In her profile mug shot she appears quite pregnant, but she had a long way to go. There would be someone there for her, inside, for at least four months.

Diane was housed all alone in an intake cell. Bail was set at $15,000 on each of the five charges. If she were to be freed pending trial, someone would have to come up with $75,000.

No one would.

Did Diane sleep there in her jail cell? Only she knows that; she had been so tired, and she had been spinning down and down and down for so long.

As she always said, "Just when you think things get as bad as they can get, something worse happens."

And it had.

The headlines on February 28 and 29, 1984, were banners six columns wide and titillating enough to make the most devoted soap opera fan switch to real life for the duration. The AP wires picked up an URGENT flash—tipped by Lars Larson—that the arrest had been made at 6:55 A.M., February 28, 1984. He was off only by eight minutes.

POLICE SAY DOWNS SHOT CHILDREN FOR BOYFRIEND
POLICE ALLEGE ATTACK MOTIVATED BY LOVE FOR
A FORMER BOYFRIEND

When DA Pat Horton and Sheriff Dave Burks held their news conference that first morning, they stressed how difficult it had been for the agencies to wait so long to make a move. "The one thing that has underscored this investigation is patience," Horton remarked. "The real battle ... is in the courtroom."

Patience was a euphemism. Tempers had frayed and unraveled completely. The rifts healed tentatively as the sheriff's men realized that an arrest *was* actually going to take place. Ray Broderick had stepped into the role as buffer. With Hugi's full knowledge and consent—Ray would agree often that "Yeah, Fred's an asshole—but let's do it anyway. Let's go along with preparing for this trial."

Hugi nods, remembering, a rare smile breaking across his face. "If it was a choice between being Mr. Nice-Guy Fred and we lose the case, I'd rather be Fred-the——ing asshole—and win the case. I know I can be abrasive, but I also know what it takes to put a case together properly. I was not going into this trial half-assed prepared and try to wing it. Exhibits needed to be made; witnesses needed to be talked to and prepared to testify. There are a couple of days of behind-the-scenes preparation for every smooth day in court."

Hugi felt no elation when he heard that Diane's arrest had been accomplished. "That only meant that there was no going back for me. We lose control—as soon as an arrest takes place. The courts decide when and where. An indictment doesn't mean anything. *Conviction* is what counts."

It all hinged on Christie—on one frightened nine-year-old.

No one beyond the authorities knew that Diane had been evicted from her parents' home only hours before her arrest. Wes Frederickson gave no hint of the family schism when he spoke to the *Register-Guard.* "It's good to get it out . . . We've had nine months of hell already, and I'm not looking forward to nine more months of hell, or three months, or one month—or however long it takes . . . I don't know if my daughter did it, and I don't know that she didn't do it, because I wasn't there." And then he added a bit less charitably, "If my daughter did it, then I believe, in fact, she should pay. But nothing can take away the love a father has for his kids."

A picture of Diane and Chris Rosage walking through the jail's sallyport appeared on the front page of most Northwest papers. Diane's hands were cuffed, her arms gently folded around her pregnant belly. It was the sort of picture that Pierce Brooks had feared: the expectant mother in bondage. Diane's supporters in the public—and she still had many—were horrified.

The next day, she pleaded Not Guilty to all charges before Circuit Court Judge Edwin Allen.

Allen revoked her bail.

Her trial date was set for May 8; Diane expected to be free within three months—well before her due date of July 7.

She confided to Lars Larson, "He [DA Horton] finally screwed up . . . he can't back up those charges in court and everyone is going to see that." She didn't plan to give birth in jail but even if that should happen, no one was going to take her baby away from her. She was sure it would be a girl; she would name her Charity Lynn. Diane wasn't worried about obtaining a fair trial, she told Larson; Lane County would give her as fair a trial as anywhere else.

Almost immediately, the Downs case began to make national headlines again. Elizabeth Beaumiller was going to fly in for the trial—at least for a time—to cover it for the *Washington Post*. The *Seattle Times* devoted two full pages to Diane Downs. Wes Frederickson announced that San Francisco attorney Melvin Belli had tentatively agreed to defend Diane.

Belli—seventy-six years old and going strong, flamboyant and brilliant—had defended Jack Ruby after Ruby shot Lee Harvey Oswald. Belli had also offered his services—gratis—to Sirhan Sirhan after Robert Kennedy was killed. Belli was the grand old man of the celebrity lawyers: F. Lee Bailey, "Racehorse" Haynes, Marvin Mitchelson, and Gerry Spence.

The combination of Melvin Belli and Diane Downs was a parlay that any reporter might devoutly wish for. Guaranteed fireworks. The attorneys presently of record were not as entranced with the possibility. Jim Jagger had represented Diane for months, often for extended periods without payment. When he'd done all the scut work, why would he relish handing over the case to one of the big boys from out of town?

Fred Hugi wasn't enthusiastic about facing Belli in court either. Hugi would not suffer histrionics and antics kindly. He would not see Christie sacrificed for headlines.

On March 22, Diane filed an affidavit seeking to suppress evidence taken from her home and vehicle (the red Nissan) on the night of May 19, 1983. She claimed that she had been "extremely upset" and "sometimes disoriented" at McKenzie–Willamette Hospital and that she had not understood the forms she signed giving permission to search. Judge Foote denied the motion to suppress.

On April 7, Melvin Belli sent word that he would personally be working on the case. Since Wes Frederickson would have to liquidate some prime property set away for his retirement to pay Belli, he would settle for no underling.

Jim Jagger was anxious to go to trial on May 8. There is a softness, a vulnerability, in a woman heavy with child. How could any jury send his hugely pregnant client to prison? May 8 conflicted with Melvin Belli's plans to depart for Rome for the annual meeting of the Belli Society, an international group he had founded so three hundred lawyers could meet once a year to discuss legal and social issues. Immediately after what media wags termed "International Melvin Belli Week," the San Francisco attorney had another trial commitment. He could not come to Eugene until the fourth or fifth of June—only a month before Diane's baby was due.

That was cutting it mighty close. The Downs trial was expected to take two months. There had been so much pretrial publicity (before Judge Foote issued a gag order that quieted things down considerably) that simply picking a jury might take two or three weeks. And the list of potential witnesses was a mile long. Unless Diane could manage to stay pregnant for over ten months, there would have to be a recess in midtrial for the defendant to give birth, recuperate, and return to court.

A well-planned trial gathers momentum as it goes along; interruptions can dilute both the prosecution and the defense's case.

Fred Hugi argued that the trial should not be delayed by Belli's social calendar, and he wondered how soon Diane would be ready to stand trial after she gave birth. Jagger pointed out that Diane had a history of returning to work the day after delivery. She sounded as hardy as a peasant woman who squats to give birth in the fields and then slings the infant on her back, continuing to chop sugarcane or pick rice.

Foote's decision was swift. There would be no delay.

Belli was appalled. He took a verbal swipe at the young judge who was sitting on his first murder trial. "I very much wanted to represent this young girl. She's obviously in a lot of trouble and needs a lot of help. But the judge wouldn't give us the time of day . . . In my fifty years as an attorney, I have never heard of a judge doing this in such an important case . . . It's utterly outrageous, but I guess his majesty reigns up there. Thank God he's not in San Francisco!"

Foote was scarcely chastened. He remarked that Belli shouldn't have taken the case in the first place if he knew he was obligated to be in Rome. Christie and Danny needed to have the case resolved as soon as possible.

Belli left for Rome, and Jim Jagger continued to prepare the defense for Diane.

Fred Hugi had twenty-four volumes of evidence, statements, follow-ups, transcriptions of tapes—a mountain of possibilities to be winnowed down, and shaped, and molded for his case. He would work eighteen- to twenty-hour days. And so would the rest of his team.

"It's unusual," Broderick says, "for a prosecution team—to end up willing to share decisions. Of course—in the end—only one person goes into court with it."

Ray Broderick held a "witness school." The cops viewed it with a somewhat jaundiced eye—hell, they'd testified just fine for years. But most went along with it. Hugi told Broderick exactly which areas he planned to cover with which witnesses. Ray then played Fred's part or Jim Jagger's, playing from a script full of the worst possible eventualities. Broderick worked particularly hard with the staff from the ER at McKenzie–Willamette Hospital. They were used to privileged communication between doctor and patient, and it was difficult for them to discuss what had happened. Moreover, many of them were nervous about getting up "on stage" in a courtroom. Shelby Day and Judy Patterson grew dry-mouthed at the thought of it.

Everything was choreographed. "We had to plan the order of our witnesses, when the breaks would come—and we couldn't over-emphasize small pieces of evidence," Broderick explains. "Each witness had to get on the stand, throw a punch, and get off."

As Pierce Brooks had stressed, the State was ready to re-create the scene. A prototype of Diane's red Nissan had been constructed in two days by Ben Bartlett, a Eugene cabinetmaker. It was built to scale of heavy Styrofoam reinforced with plywood.

"In the end, it was 1/16th of an inch off in length—and that's pretty damned close."

There were the Christie, Cheryl and Danny dolls. Aerial photos had been taken in sequence so that the jury would be able to see Diane's alleged route from the shooting site to McKenzie–Willamette Hospital. And huge blow ups of the shell casings were developed.

They had never found the gun. And they still could not figure out what the bloodstain pattern on the beach towel meant.

Right up to trial, Paul Alton fiddled with it, folding, refolding, and . . . finally he hit the combination.

Bingo. Bingo. Bingo!

The prosecution team was elated, but they kept what they had found to themselves. The time would come.

Jim Jagger had his own problems preparing for trial. Diane did not understand that the face she presented to the world would not do. She smiled when she should be looking sad. She laughed when it would have been appropriate to sob. And there was a certain expression Diane so often wore—her imperious look—as if she *were* Princess Di, and the rest of the world only rabble.

When Jagger asked Diane if she thought she might modify her facial expressions a bit for the jury ahead, she looked at him, bemused. She hadn't the vaguest idea what he was talking about.

CHAPTER 34

I live in a locked room by myself. I am allowed out of this room two hours a day. During this time, I shower, make phone calls, read the paper and watch TV. I am also allowed out of my room to visit people from the outside . . . My pastor comes to see me once a week, and my attorney comes when the need arises. I do receive some mail, and always send replies . . .
— Diane Downs, letter to Matt Jensen, April, 1984

Diane's brother Paul never missed a visit, and she called her parents every other day. She had no visits from friends, although reporters still sought her out. Her Cottage Grove co-workers, once so supportive, had dropped away.

Diane's written correspondence became more important than ever to her. Even in jail and six-months pregnant, she needed some special connection with a male more than she ever had. She found someone—of necessity via the mails—or rather, he found her. Randall Brent Woodfield, thirty-four, was the handsome scion of a respected family on the Oregon coast—a sports prodigy, a former president of the Christian Athletes at Portland State University, a one-time draft choice of the Green Bay Packers . . . *and* a convicted voyeur, exposer, rapist, and killer of women.

Randy Woodfield's exploits up and down the freeway between Seattle and northern California had earned him notoriety as "The I-5 Killer."

His convictions for the execution-style rape-murder of a nineteen-year-old Salem girl, for the attempted murder and rape of her best friend (who had survived three bullets to the skull), and—in subsequent trials—for sexually attacking other females ranging in age from eight to forty, had put him into the Oregon State Penitentiary for life, plus one hundred fifty-five years. He remained the prime suspect in several sexually motivated murders up and down the West Coast.

Randy Woodfield wrote to Diane, using the pseudonym "Squirrely." He soon became Diane's "dear friend," even though she had not the slightest idea who he was. All she knew was that he was writing from prison. Woodfield had seen Diane in the papers and on television. He wrote to his "Blondie," going into explicit sexual detail about how exciting her pregnant state was to him. Since he too had been arrested in Lane County three years earlier, he felt a kinship with Diane.

Diane received a number of letters from "the guys" in the penitentiary; it helped her immeasurably to remain cheerful. Diane, the chameleon, slipped into the world of the con easily. She picked up prison slang as if she had always used it.

She found Squirrely's letters particularly charming, supportive, and stimulating. If they began on a friend-to-friend-in-the-same-boat tone, they invariably steamed up. Squirrely was not averse to describing his physical attributes, particularly the massive dimensions of his erections. These letters came to Diane in jail from a stranger. And to a perfect stranger, she wrote back—in the same vein.

Woodfield enthused, "I bet our kid would be a beautiful baby!"

Perhaps it would. They were both endowed with exceptional physical beauty, both of them strong and athletic. Diane Downs and Randy Woodfield were two sides of a coin: Narcissa on one and Narcissus on the other. If one should stare into a mirror, the other might gaze back through the glass. She was fair and he was dark. She could spot him twenty-five points on the IQ scale, even though he was the one who had almost four years of college.

They were two dark stars whirling in the same orbit. Each had always felt the world was unfair, that fate and luck and karma had failed them. Each seemed to exist for sexual pleasure, and excitement, and naughty games against the establishment—and, always, for a place where the sunlight of publicity shone upon them.

Squirrely wrote to Diane often as she waited for her trial. His letters sounded like the tomes sent to the Forum section of "Penthouse" by college boys. They exchanged photos. He politely asked if he might masturbate on hers, but promised to cover it with plastic first. When Diane wrote to him, she invariably enclosed religious tracts, and occasionally she sent him pictures of her children.

Censors at the Lane County Jail recognized Randy's picture. He'd been *arrested* in Eugene and spent time in that facility. Diane was not in the least disturbed to learn that she was corresponding with a convicted rapist and murderer. He seemed like a nice guy to her, and he was handsome with the full dark beard she had always preferred in men. Their letters flew back and forth, growing more erotic and intimate with each mailing.

It helped to fill her days.

Diane missed sunshine. Her skin was as green-white in the jail lights as the other prisoners'. The jail smelled like every jail: sawdust, Pine-sol, cigarette smoke, sweat, boredom, and tears. She never knew what the weather was like outside.

The ride to the courthouse would be only a few blocks long with little chance for her to feel the air or smell good smells. Anyway, it would probably be raining.

She was eager to get the trial over with. And then, Diane didn't care if she *never* saw the state of Oregon again.

TRIAL

CHAPTER 35

To attempt to accommodate the crowds, the trial has been moved from Courtroom #8 to #3—the largest in the Lane County Courthouse. It isn't even close to being big enough to hold everyone trying to get in.

Number Three has yellow-brick walls and, toward the back of the room, walnut-stained two-by-twos lined up vertically over acoustical tile. There are no windows, only recessed lighting above the dropped ceiling panels. Judge Gregory Foote, looking austere in his black robe, sits between the American flag on his right and the state flag of Oregon on his left. His court reporter, Kay Cates, and his clerk, Sharon Roe, are in front of him.

We of the press are only slightly more blasé than the anxious spectators; we have been assured of a seat—*if* we can fit all of us into the first row. As the trial progresses and the front row grows more crowded, we will learn to stagger our note-taking by sitting right-handed/left-handed/courtroom artist/right-handed

No cameras are allowed in the courtroom. A number of courtroom artists—some superb, some pedestrian—sketch furiously to catch a face, a mood, a certain shading of pain or fury before the witness steps down.

Ray Broderick occupies the end seat of the second row on the left side of the courtroom. The opening performance of his "play" is about to begin. (After he testifies, Doug Welch will sit in the end seat, second row, on the right side of the courtroom.)

This is a "young" trial. The judge is thirty-six, the prosecutor thirty-nine, the defense attorney thirty-eight, and the defendant twenty-eight. The press corps, for the most part, matches.

The jury's median age is older.

Women's voices—faceless—murmur behind the press row.

"I'm supposed to pick the kids up from school today—I hate to leave, but I'm in a pool."

"I plan to be here every Thursday," another voice whispers. "That's *my* day off when I try to do something nice for myself. Usually, I go bowling..."

And a deeper woman's voice, graveled with whiskey and cigarettes, "I'm with *her*. CSD took my daughter away, and they never even told me she hadn't been going to school. They're just out to break up decent families."

"Do you think she did it?" someone else asks sotto voce. "I can't imagine a mother doing that."

"Well, she slept around—with *anybody*. What do *you* think?"

"That doesn't mean she'd kill her child."

The gallery draws a collective breath when *she* walks in, for the first time, accompanied by her personal deputy Chris Rosage. Chris wears her deputy's uniform; Diane had chosen a blue maternity dress with a little white collar. She is very pregnant, but she carries herself gracefully. Her shoes—high wedgie sandals with thin straps around her slender ankles—are so new that the soles have no marks.

In person, Diane is a surprisingly small woman, her bones delicate, her skin translucent. She doesn't look like a killer. She smiles faintly as she walks through the judge's chamber door and bows her head in a slight beneficent nod to the masses who await her appearance.

Diane requested beauty aids—bleach for her hair, makeup—but prisoners are not allowed to bleach their hair or to have curling irons or scissors. Refused, she has chosen to forego makeup entirely, and her complexion is sallow. Diane's blonde hair is growing dark at the roots, and it is a bit long in the back. One lock falls often over her eyes, and she tosses her head to lift it—a gesture that will become familiar.

Diane's pregnancy was only one of the hundred variables the prosecution team has considered. In the end, Hugi has decided simply to ignore it. Her condition has nothing to do with this trial or with the events of May 19, 1983. But what will the jury make of it? It is hard to overlook her great belly.

Hugi has filed a pretrial "motion in limine"—a request to limit the defense's reference to the sightings of people who resembled the "bushy-haired stranger." Hugi submits that the fact there *was* a man in the general vicinity of the crime who resembled one of several descriptions Diane had given has only marginal relevance to the case. Ironically, among the cases Hugi cites to show that the inclusion of the BHS would serve to unduly distract the jury was "State v. Woodfield." Randy Woodfield too had blamed a stranger for his crimes. To bolster his argument, Hugi cites the many versions of the crime and the suspect Diane has given.

"The defendant has produced two different composites (5-20-83 and 7-12-83) of the suspect. The defendant has stated, 'I don't know who shot me and the kids. I haven't the vaguest idea in the world' (8-5-83). The defendant has stated, 'I know the person used my name and made a reference about my tattoo. That means the asshole knew me' (7-18-83). The defendant stated, 'I know who did it.' When asked, 'You know this person, you know him by name?' the defendant responded, 'Yes, yes I do . . . I know who did it! Bye' (7-22-83). The defendant stated, 'No, it's nobody I know. I only saw him because of one reason. They had ski masks on. When I hit the gun and kicked the guy, I grabbed his mask and pulled it off; the one behind me didn't say anything. I have no idea what he looks like' (7-24-83)."

Jim Jagger wants to use information on possible bushy-haired-stranger suspects. Jagger himself takes the stand. Then he calls Fred Hugi as a witness. When will the real *trial* start? The lawyers are playing musical chairs.

"Of course, there were sightings," Hugi agrees with Jagger placidly. "We received calls from all over the U.S. and Canada and even the eastern seaboard about sightings of people who looked like the composite." But are they relevant to the case? Is the State withholding anything from the defense? The likely leads were followed up and dismissed; those that were patently ridiculous were culled out. Foote ultimately rules that the defense can receive only two of the reports on bushy-haired strangers.

By Thursday, May 10, the jury files in: Daniel Bendt, foreman—a tall, bearded young man, an electrical engineer; nine women—a few young but mostly middle-aged and elderly; two more men—middle-aged—a truck driver and a pipefitter.

Three alternate jurors. Oregon law stipulates only one or two, but one of the empaneled jurors has already suffered a migraine headache. Most of the jurors are married and parents. Several of them live in the country, and at least eight keep pistols, rifles, or shotguns in their homes for protection.

They will not be sequestered; Lane County cannot afford to put a jury up in a hotel and furnish all meals for two months. They are instructed to avoid newspapers, television, and radio.

Now it begins—this ceremony of testimony and judgment.

Fred Hugi and Jim Jagger are as close to being opposites as men might be. Hugi does not smile and appears tense. He *seems* unaware of the gallery. He moves around the courtroom like a pool player sighting along his cue for the perfect shot; one gets the feeling that he will miss nothing.

Jim Jagger seems relaxed. His hair is as tousled as always and he wears an ill-fitting suit—the sleeves too short over his shirt cuffs, pants "high-water" above his unshined shoes, the coat's shoulders hunching up in an inverted V as he leans forward at the defense table. His clothes say, "Hey, you guys in the jury—I'm just like you. It's you and me against the rich guys." Jim Jagger's image is "folksy."

This seems to be a folksy jury. The women wear polyester leisure suits or summer cotton dresses, the men mostly western shirts—the kind with a center placket buttoned with mother-of-pearl studs. Jim Jagger isn't trying to convince a New York jury that his client is the victim of a monstrous mistake; he is talking to good, solid wives, mothers, grandmothers, most of whom look as if they would be more comfortable canning or serving Sunday dinner, to men who drive semis and work for Weyerhaeuser.

The State has begun. Fred Hugi has spent more time organizing his opening statement than anything else. He wants to put the entire case in perspective so that the jury will know what to expect and if the proof substantiates his opening statement, they will have no option but to come back with "Guilty."

Hugi is a model of organization, a teacher patiently outlining an entirely foreign curriculum. He never says, "Ahhh"; his sentences do not run on. Each point follows the next, from some outline perhaps in his own mind. He begins with the crime itself, and he tells the jury what happened next . . . and next . . . and next. He repeats Diane's remarks to police and medical personnel. He points out the discrepancies, as her recall changed. He tells the jury that Diane acted, initially, as a cooperative victim of a crime; later, she did not cooperate.

In an hour or so, he must encapsulate her astounding background and explain why and how she committed the crimes she sits accused of.

He unfolds his case. The motive: lust for a married man who did not want children. The method: the .22 Ruger that the killer had brought with her from Arizona. The opportunity: so easy—children safe and drowsy in their own mother's car, believing they were heading home to bed.

Diane Downs, Fred Hugi explains, wanted to marry Lew Lewiston, and the only obstacle she saw to his getting a divorce was her children. "The plan that emerges is probably one that seemed reasonable at the time. An *outside* force would remove the children."

In his soft, matter-of-fact voice, Hugi reads Diane's letters to Lew aloud. They are sexually graphic; they are masterpieces of manipulation. And they also show the fine crafty intelligence of the woman who wrote them.

And her consuming obsession: ". . . I want so badly to wrap myself around you and hold you so close and tight that you'll never go away again."

Hugi reads aloud what will be referred to as "The Masturbation Poem."

> *I lay here quietly,*
> *in the dark*
> *Deep inside me*
> *there glows a spark.*
>
> *The air breathes cool*
> *across my skin*
> *But desire burns fiercely*
> *from within.*
>
> *Thoughts of you,*
> *play on my mind*
> *Lying here alone*
> *seems so unkind.*
>
> *My temperature rises,*
> *I'm getting hot*

You should be with me,
    and yet you're not.

My fingers touch lightly
    the place of desire
Still I've not quenched
    that burning fire.

I need your presence
    towering over me
I need that passion
    I can see.

So, reaching deep,
    inside my heart,
I pull a memory
    that will not part.

This touch can conquer
    every fiber and bone
But look at me—
    I'm all alone.

My passion is finally
    laid to rest,
Yet none can say
    "This is best."

Tenderly, I think of
    your gentle embrace,
The way you gently
    caress my face.

Come to me now—
    lay by my side

How much more time
  must I bide?

I need you more than
  this rhyme can say
I need you every
  hour of the day.

I love you more
  than could your wife
Yet it's brought sorrow
  to my life.

I just keep hoping
  and hanging on
How much longer
  can I be strong?

I stand alone,
  just waiting to hear.
The day has come
  when you'll be near.

I long to hold you
  to my breast.
Then I will find
  great peace and rest.

The sorrow builds
  then ebbs away.
When I dream about
  that beautiful day.

Masturbation is not a topic generally discussed among middle-aged and elderly women in Lane County, Oregon. The courtroom hushes as Hugi reads. Diane bows her head and cries softly into her handkerchief.

He reads from Diane's first Oregon diary—the diary filled with letters to Lew, letters damning his wife, begging him to join Diane. All those letters never sent.

He has selected only a small percentage of Diane's writings; already the courtroom is saturated with her words.

Succinctly, dispassionately, Hugi has told the jury what he needs to prove to them in the weeks ahead. His words, transcribed, fill eighty pages. He has fifty witnesses on tap to back him up.

Jim Jagger stands up at three minutes to two, smooth and cheerful. He explains that there are only three key portions to this case: Christie Downs; ballistics testimony and crime lab evidence; and Diane Downs herself.

Yes. Yes and yes, Jagger admits. Of course, there have been lovers. No one is denying that; names will be named.

The ladies of the gallery react by shaking their heads in shock, covering their foreheads with their hands. One murmurs, "My God!" Their own horror delights them; the long wait in line was worth it.

Yes, Jagger allows, there has been an obsession with a male—but never to the exclusion of Diane's children, or her career. Jim Jagger agrees that Diane is promiscuous. He has no other choice—just as he must now explain the face that Diane Downs presents to the world. He cannot alter the protective smiling mask she wears. Nor is there any way he can keep her off the witness stand. Jagger tells the jury that Diane learned to hide her real emotions because she was molested by her father. They must not judge her by the way she reacts in court.

"She cannot react to pain by crying. She laughs, she jokes; everything is going to be OK—this is her habitual reaction."

There will be tapes. "When we listen to the tapes . . . you'll see she talks without thinking."

Both sides have their own reasons for revealing as much about Diane as possible. Jagger wants to evoke sympathy for a girl who has endured such a hard life that her quirks are not only understandable but forgivable.

"From my side," Hugi recalls, "I saw her as a classic case of child abuse—perpetuating that abuse. Each side felt that the more the jury knew about Diane, the better his case would be—that was why there were so few objections during the trial."

As Jim Jagger fights to save her, Diane's blonde head bends over her yellow legal pad. She is drawing something—what? It is a desperate face marked with shadows and heavy lines.

Indeed, there *was* a man—a stranger, Jagger assures the jury. He doesn't know who he was or why he shot Diane's children. "Whether crazy, drugged or whatever—he just shot. Christie Downs has—she has in fact identified the perpetrator as best she could."

Diane nods yes, but she does not lift her head from her drawing.

Jagger speaks of the trouble Diane has had with dreams after her desperate race to the hospital to save her children—a mother, hopelessly, helplessly, trying to save those she loved more than anyone in the world, confused later by her own nightmares.

Diane asks for a Kleenex, yet her eyes seem dry.

"I suggest to you that she [Christie] has identified who did it—in a special way. And we'll get to that in the trial."

Both sides agree. It will fall upon the fragile shoulders of Christie Ann Downs.

On Monday morning, May 14, Judge Foote, the jury, and Diane board a yellow school bus. They are driven to Old Mohawk Road; the jurors pile out and look at the river, the trees, the narrow roadway that looks so normal now. This is the precise week when it all happened—only a year later. The maple leaves are not the same maple leaves, but they look the same.

Diane remains in the bus, her face an inscrutable mask as she gazes out the window.

At the Lane County Public Works shop, the jurors look at the shiny red Nissan Pulsar where it has been parked for a year. The car has been washed in the interim, and the outside rocker panel on the passenger side removed for Jim Pex's analysis of the blood spatters found there.

———

Back again in the courtroom: Heather Plourd is the first witness. "It was about dark. I saw somebody driving up in the driveway ... She [Diane] said she was out sightseeing."

The next morning when Heather visited Diane in the hospital, Diane had voiced a fear. "She told me, 'I'm afraid Christie might blame me for what happened ... When Christie raised up, I'm the first person she saw.'"

Dolores Holland, Heather's neighbor, remembers firmly when she heard the car door slam and the sound of tires leaving the Plourds' driveway.

"Twenty minutes to ten."

This early testimony is important in matters of establishing time, but not sensational. Jurors #6 and #12 take notes, while the other ten pairs of eyes move from Jim Jagger to the witness.

Joseph Inman is next. He has a full reddish-brown beard, wire-rim glasses, and he speaks with a slight Texas drawl not unlike Lew Lewiston's. He wears western boots and a cowboy beltbuckle. He is a good witness. He describes coming up behind the red car with the red Arizona plates that was merely creeping along Old Mohawk. Inman identifies photos of the Downs car as the car he saw.

Deputies carry in a huge map eight feet long and three feet wide, an overview of the vital areas in this case: Diane Downs's duplex on Q Street, Heather Plourd's mobile home on Sunderman Road, the spot where the .22 casings were found on Old Mohawk Road, the point at which Joe Inman observed Diane's red car inching along the road, and the hospital.

The times the victims had been at each point are noted on the chart so that the jury can see for themselves.

The shooting had to have occurred at five minutes to ten. It was 10:15 when Joe Inman first observed Diane's car; he followed her for two-tenths of a mile for two minutes at a speed of six miles an hour. At 10:17 P.M., he reached a straight spot in the road and passed her.

Diane was only four and a half miles from the hospital at that point— and yet it took her almost twenty-two minutes more to reach the Emergency entrance.

Jim Jagger attempts to sway Joe Inman on his recall of time and speed. He cannot. Inman will not equivocate.

Judy Patterson leads off the McKenzie–Willamette ER witnesses. She is nervous, but she remembers it all—the Code 4, the page for all available personnel, her conversations with Diane.

"She told me the kids were laughing and talking, laughing at something Danny had said—and talking to Christie. That it was an awful thing to be laughing one minute, and the next . . ."

Patterson recalls the two versions of the shooting Diane gave. Only after she steps down does she realize she forgot one exchange. "Diane looked up at me, that first night, and asked flatly, 'Are they dead yet?' No emotion. Just, 'Are they dead yet?'"

One after another, all of them who were in the ER a year ago take the stand. Shelby Day is next. She had dreaded testifying, but she does well as she recalls that Cheryl was dead on arrival, with blood already clotted in her throat, a straight line on the heart monitor.

Rosie Martin tells the jury about her first sight of Diane standing by the driver's side of her car. "I asked her what was going on, and she said, 'Somebody just shot my three kids—'"

Rosie had suctioned Christie Downs's occluded airway. And then she had spent most of her time with Dr. Foster as he worked over Danny.

What does she remember about Diane Downs's wound, Hugi asks.

"I just remember an entrance and an exit—somewhere on the forearm . . . She asked how the children were, and I told her the doctors were in there working on them. And then she—the mother—laughed, and she said, 'Only the best for *my* kids!' and she laughed again and said, 'Well, I have good insurance.' I thought it was peculiar—but I was thinking about the kids."

The mother's demeanor?

"She seemed very composed."

As the hospital personnel continue their testimony about the night of May 19, 1983—particularly about the bizarre comments of the defendant—the jurors become more and more subdued.

At afternoon break, no one in the gallery leaves.

Diane doesn't wear handcuffs into the courtroom, but there is always a faint rattle of chains just before she enters the room after recesses. Every time she walks in, she smiles.

Dr. John Mackey is to be the next scheduled witness. But his beeper sounds and he rushes from the corridor on an emergency. Court recesses early. The gallery disperses reluctantly. There is the danger that they will not be able to get into the courtroom tomorrow.

TUESDAY, MAY 15

The lines are longer this morning, a huge crowd on Day Six, pushing against the rope barrier an hour before the courtroom doors will open.

Mrs. Mackey hopes to get in to hear her husband testify. A chatty woman who lives three houses down from the shooting site half-apologizes for the neighborhood. "It's real quiet—and nothing ever happens out there. This was so unusual."

The crowd is jittery; they rush through the doors. A man who was far back in line stomps out when he finds the courtroom filled. "I couldn't find a seat," he announces loudly to no one in particular. "There are three fat ladies taking up a whole row!" The three fat ladies stay put, but look annoyed.

Dr. John Mackey is a most articulate witness. He looks directly at the jury: "I found a small child gasping for air, crying weakly . . . and then I saw what I assumed to be a child—crumpled on the floor. I thought to myself, 'Oh my God, there's a third one. What will we do?'"

"What *did* you do?" Fred Hugi asks softly.

"Can I refer to the children by name—it would be a lot easier."

"Of course."

"Cheryl appeared to be dead."

Diane is immobile, her pale right hand—with long, carefully filed nails—droops languidly on her chair's arm.

"Cheryl—had dilated pupils, no respiration. We hooked her up to a heart monitor."

Mackey's voice is emotional and husky. For twelve minutes, he describes the measures they had tried. "I knew that Danny had been shot in the chest, I knew that Christie had been shot in the chest, and Cheryl also had been shot in the chest. Christie had actually begun the process of dying . . . the oxygen level in her bloodstream was incompatible with life . . . One of the most serious injuries you can have is a gunshot wound to the chest . . . we were just doing everything we could to bring those kids back."

One of Mackey's other jobs had been to report to the mother what was happening with her children. Dr. Mackey's encounters with Diane Downs had left him astounded. He told her all three children were critically injured, and that one of them had died—one of the girls. He started to describe the dead child—but stopped, realizing how similar the girls were in appearance.

"She said, 'Oh. She was to be my athlete' . . . She was extremely composed. She was *unbelievably* composed. I couldn't disbelieve she was a family member. There were no tears . . . no disbelief . . . no, 'Why did this happen to me?'"

Slowly, Dr. Mackey shifts slightly on the stand and turns to look at Diane as he speaks. "I told her that she would have to stay at the hospital," and she said, 'Well, will I be able to work tomorrow? I must work the day after at least.' I thought that was a truly inappropriate response."

"Objection, your honor," Jagger booms.

"Sustained."

"I felt—"

"Objection!"

"Sustained."

Hugi rephrases a question to elicit Dr. Mackey's observation.

"Objection."

"Overruled."

Mackey says that he observed a lack of concern by a mother for her children. "I felt that something was very wrong at that point—"

"Objection!"

They tussle with their legal points, and finally John Mackey is allowed to say a complete sentence or two about the woman he saw on the night of May 19.

"A woman very calm, very self-assured, excited—not tearful—but angry. Occasionally smiling, occasionally chuckling. I saw a woman who appeared to be in very good control of herself. That's surprising."

Fred Hugi asks if the police put undue pressure on Diane. No. "I felt they acted in a very professional manner . . . they were very cautious."

Asked about the normal reactions to grief—and he had seen many—
Mackey says people tend to react in a similar fashion with crying and
disbelief although men are less overtly tearful than women.

On cross-examination, Jim Jagger attempts to modify the picture
Mackey has painted. "All you're saying is that during the five minutes she
spent with you, she wasn't reacting? Isn't that true?"

"Yes."

"Would it be fair to say this was one of the most serious and emotional
situations you have been in in your years in the ER?"

"Yes."

Mackey offers that he had already formed an emotional attachment
to the Downs children when they were in the ER. "I'm that kind of
person . . . We were very proud of the fact that we were able to save a
couple of the children."

Jagger is careful; Mackey has clearly won over the jury. An overt attack
on the doctor could be disastrous.

On redirect, Fred Hugi asks Mackey if he was surprised when he heard
that Diane was suing the hospital.

"Well, yeah—we saved two kids . . . I felt we had been more or less
heroic."

Dr. David Miller is next. He worked with Dr. Mackey over Danny and
Christie when it seemed that they too were going to die.

"Christie was as near to death as anyone I've ever seen and come back."

Miller relates to the jury Diane's reaction when he told her that the
bullet had missed Danny's heart.

"She said, 'Far out!'"

And what was his observation of Ms. Downs's behavior?

"It was very consistent and remarkably unusual. She showed none of
the cultural concepts of grief."

Miller's animosity toward Jim Jagger is unmistakable, but controlled.
He explains that Diane made an attempt to remove Christie from the
hospital and to bar access to the children by law enforcement agencies
and CSD.

"It became clear that Christie's ongoing medical care might be compromised by attempts to remove her."

Christie's custody had been given over to the witness and Dr. Steven Wilhite.

Wilhite, the surgeon who operated on Christie Downs, takes the stand. He is a man with a presence. After racing to the hospital, he found Christie with no blood pressure, no pulse, dilated pupils, her skin blanched white.

"Essentially, she looked dead," he testifies quietly. He describes the emergency thoracotomy he performed to stop Christie's bleeding. As Wilhite speaks, his voice takes on a richer timbre; he describes what is—for him at least—the typical reaction of a mother who learns that her child has died. "Their souls are just wrenched from them." Diane's response was "what shall I say—a bit bizarre." Wilhite's voice grows heavy with remembered emotion. He offers Fred Hugi three examples that gave him pause as he confronted Diane Downs.

"I think one example was her concern for her car—and then that her vacation was 'spoiled.'"

But the third point—the incident that had troubled him the most—was when Diane entered the room where he was treating Christie. She had turned to Wilhite and said, "I know that Christie has sustained brain damage, and I don't want you to sustain her life."

"That was very unusual! And *inappropriate!*" Tests had yet to show any brain damage.

Each of the three physicians has demonstrated that doctors do not become inured to tragedy. Wilhite bristles as Jagger questions him about why no one signed permission slips before the children were treated.

"We're dealing in seconds here—*seconds* not minutes—finding someone who will sign a permit is ludicrous." Wilhite's voice rises, and he cuts off Jagger's next question. "I didn't *meet* Mrs. Downs until after surgery. When I'm in surgery, there isn't time for chit-chat."

Jagger and Wilhite are wrangling in earnest.

"What did you do after the conversation with Ms. Downs?" Jagger asks.

Wilhite smiles thinly. "I continued to prolong life."

"Isn't it possible that she said—*if* she has brain damage, is it realistic to continue to prolong life?"

"No."

"But isn't it possible—"

"No. I said what she said," Wilhite thunders.

"No further questions."

Carleen Elbridge, the X-ray technician, recalls her meeting with the defendant the first night. Diane Downs had worried about having her picture taken without makeup as her injured arm was X-rayed. Yes, even as her children were dead and dying.

Dr. Bruce Becker takes the stand. Becker cared for both Danny and Christie in the intensive care unit. He explains what Danny's wound means. There is no motor function or feeling in Danny's legs. He has lost organ function; he cannot voluntarily control his bowels or bladder. The chance that he will be able to use his legs again is "very slim." Christie has survived two chest wounds, a bullet through her hand, and a stroke affecting the left side of her brain. A middle cerebral artery clogged, and with that, Christie has lost the easy use of speech. Her right arm and hand are still paralyzed to a degree.

Becker explains how Christie's speech problems manifest themselves. He uses an angiogram (where air and dye are pumped into the brain to show areas of damage) and a chart of the left side of the brain to give the jury a crash course in speech pathology after a stroke.

"She searches for words. She may, for instance, find a symbolic value—she may call a pencil a pen. But her 'feedback loop' is intact. She will know whether she is right or wrong—but her signal process is delayed . . . Her comprehension is the same as it was."

Fred Hugi asks a very important question. "Do you have any evidence at all that she's experienced a memory loss?"

"To the best of our knowledge, it has not been damaged."

Dr. Becker explains memory, stressing that it is not easy to tamper with human memory. Stroke patients—patients with injuries to speech centers—may not be able to *say* what it is that they remember, but that does not mean they do not remember.

Christie Downs's speech difficulties would be exacerbated under stress, Becker explains. She might well make mistakes, but she will know instantly that she has done so. "Even when I first saw Christie, I was aware that she knew of errors and that she tried to correct them."

At the defense table, Diane flips her hair from her forehead, toys with a pencil. She is either truly serene, or she possesses an almost superhuman ability to appear so. She looks very pretty in a light blue, long-sleeved taffeta blouse, topped by a maternity vest.

She has heard medical testimony all morning—testimony that went into agonizing detail on how her children had suffered and how one had died. And she heard doctors and nurses say that she scarcely seemed to demonstrate grief.

And now. She must have known what was coming.

Christie.

Christie Ann Downs—the baby who was the first creature in the world to truly love her—her favorite child. Christie will walk into this courtroom, climb up on the stand—and what in the world will she say?

Diane has not seen her child for seven months—two weeks before she conceived "Charity Lynn," who kicks now in her belly.

After the lunch break, a shining gold unicorn statuette rests on the bailiff's bench rail. Few in the courtroom understand its significance, but it is certainly an item of curiosity.

Diane, of course, knows what it symbolizes to her. That gleaming unicorn is Cheryl—it means that Cheryl will never die.

All along Diane has told the television cameras and the newspapers about the love she and Christie share, about Christie's extraordinary intelligence: "She may be the only one to get me out of this . . ."

CHAPTER 36

They had planned this so carefully, cushioning Christie between two doctors—Dr. Becker first, and then Carl Peterson, each to explain why Christie expresses herself the way she does. Fred Hugi did not promise the jury *what* Christie would say. He did not know what—or how much—she would be *able* to say in this frightening courtroom environment.

"If there was ever a time that Christie might lie, this would be it," Hugi remembers. "She could say she didn't remember, to remove herself from the case—and who would blame her? She might be thinking that 'My mom's more powerful than the State—she got me back once [with that October sneak visit], and I'd better side with her—because she's the winner and she'll probably get me back again. Mom's all powerful. Mom blasted me—but I probably deserved it.' There were so many reasons for Christie to suppress her memory—and even to lie."

They have tried to make it as easy as possible for Christie. "We couldn't ask too many questions, but we set the groundwork . . . to show if she doesn't answer, that it isn't that she doesn't remember . . . We know she remembers—we can't be sure that she will be able to find the words," Broderick explains.

They don't know if Christie can do it—with her mother staring at her. Christie's entire foster family is in court to bolster her.

Hugi suspects that Jim Jagger is deliberately dragging out his questioning of Becker so that Christie's testimony will be spread over two days. Uncharacteristically, he mutters an epithet at Jagger.

Exactly three hundred sixty-one days after she clinically died, Christie Downs is scheduled to testify. It will take the rawest kind of courage for this little girl to do that. To get up there in front of a judge, fifteen jurors, eighty spectators.

And most of all . . . her own mother.

All morning there has been a conspicuously empty space in the left side of the second row. Just after lunch, Ray Broderick leads a child to that seat—a very pretty little girl with light brown hair cut in a pageboy with bangs. She looks to be about nine. She wears a navy blue suit-dress, trimmed with white lace at the collar and cuffs. The little girl sits down next to a teenage boy, also a new face in the gallery. He holds her hand protectively.

The room quiets, and then hums with expectancy. Is this the child who will tell what really happened that night?

Odd. Diane scarcely glances at the little girl. Her expression is bleak this afternoon, and she covers her cheeks with her hands—so that it is impossible to read her feelings. But Diane isn't crying.

She knows this isn't Christie.

The little girl is Brenda—Christie's foster sister and best friend.

Suddenly, a door beside Foote's bench opens and another child walks into the room. Her outfit and hairdo are identical to Brenda's. Christie looks first at the floor, and then, very slowly, she lifts her gaze. Her eyes meet Diane's. Mother and daughter stare straight at each other for a beat, and both begin to cry.

Diane looks away first, and Christie dabs at her face with a large lacy pink handkerchief, holding her left hand to the side of her face.

Her right arm hangs limp, useless.

This is the most difficult moment of the trial for Fred Hugi. "I'm thinking about what she was like when I first saw her and, before that, when the blood was gurgling out of her—and about when Diane had her for hours in October. And yet, Christie's still HERE. She's only talked about the shooting with me twice before the trial—and all those people are out there gawking."

Christie takes the stand, lifting her dead arm with her left hand and laying it carefully in her lap. Her face is full of fear and pain and a kind of hopelessness. The stroke has left her with slight facial paralysis; one corner of her mouth droops, making her words blur. She can say "yeah" more easily than she can say "yes." Mr. Hugi has told her that would be all right.

Christie occasionally glances down at the defense table where her mother sits.

No matter how much preparation has been done, no matter how many sessions with Dr. Peterson, no matter the presence of her dearest friend out there in the gallery. No matter that Diane sits smiling fixedly at her twenty feet away. Christie Downs is all alone. She cannot stop crying, but she will not run.

Diane leans forward at the defense table and smiles harder at Christie.

Fred Hugi walks close to Christie. She knows him; this is her friend, the same friend she's visited for weeks, who has helped her get ready for today. Now, she looks into his eyes and takes a deep breath.

He doesn't know if she can do it or not. He doesn't want to qualify her as a witness yet; first he has to be sure she can speak in the courtroom.

He will have to demonstrate to the court soon that she is competent—but first, he must cut the rest of the courtroom away from him and Christie, tune the gawkers out so she can say what she must.

Hugi's voice is very soft as he begins.

VERBATIM:

"Christie, do you feel okay?"

(Witness nods head.)

"You're going to have to talk to all these people here. Can you tell me your name?"

"Christie Ann Downs."

"How old are you?"

"Nine."

"What grade are you in?"

"Fourth."

"Do you know your teacher's name?"

"Yes."

"Can you tell us her name?"

"Miss Bottoroff."

"Did you go to school today?"

"No."

(Christie's voice is tremulous, almost a falsetto. She is trying so hard.)

"You had to come to the courthouse?"

"Yes."

(Christie's face is very red.)

"We've talked about this day before, haven't we?—That this day would happen? Have we talked about it?"

"Yeah."

Hugi holds his breath. He has to ease Christie into this. At grand jury, Christie burst into tears when he asked her only to say her name.

"OK. Christie, do you remember back to the day when you got shot? Can you remember?"

"Yes."

"Do you remember if you went to school that day or not?"

"Yes, I did."

"Do you remember where you went when you came home from school?"

"Yeah."

(Judge Foote interrupts Hugi's questioning here to remind him to inquire as to Christie's competency.)

"Yes," Hugi said. "I haven't lost sight of that."

"Very well."

"The judge wants me to ask you some questions about if you understand the difference between the truth and a lie. Do you understand the difference?"

"Yeah."

"If I said this piece of paper was black, would that be the truth or a lie?"

"A lie."

"And you know that when you come in the courtroom like this, that you have to tell the truth. You understand that?"

"Yeah."

"Do you promise to do that?"

"Uh-huhh."

(Diane has not changed expression. She flips her hair from her eyes several times, watching Christie intently.)

"Do you promise to do that?"

"Yeah."

"So everything we talk about in here now has to be the truth as best you can remember. Do you understand that?"

"Yeah."

The courtroom is so very still. But now, the doors to the corridor creak open, and a young woman tiptoes in, looking for a seat.

"I lost it," Ray Broderick recalls ruefully. "It was some reporter from one of the smaller papers. I told her to either find a seat or get out, and she said, 'But I'm with the *press*.' And she just stood there in the aisle. If she stayed there, she'd detract from Christie's testimony, from everything we'd done to assure she would have the right setting up there. I still can't believe I said it, but I turned to that girl and whispered, 'Get the fuck out of here. *Now!*' She left."

"On the day this happened, you went to school and you came home from school. Do you recall that?" Hugi asks, his eyes never leaving Christie.

"Yeah."

"Whose house did you go to?"

"My grandparents."

"Did you eat there?"

"Yeah."

"And after you ate, where did you go then?"

"To my mom's house."

"Back to her apartment where you were living?"

(Witness nods head.)

"Did you go out that night?"

"Yeah."

"Did you go for a ride?"

"Yeah."

"Who went with you?"

"My mom, Cheryl, and Danny went."

"And do you remember the car?"

"Yeah."

"What color was the car?"

"Black and red."

"Can you tell us where you went? Do you remember where you went to?"

"Yeah."

"Where?"

"My mom's friend's house."

"And was that in the city or was it in the country—were there buildings—tall buildings—or was there a lot of grass?"

"A lot of grass."

"Do you remember what you did when you got there?"

"Yeah."

"What did you do?"

"We went out and petted the horse."

"Did you give the horse food?"

"Yeah."

"What was your mom doing when you were petting the horse and giving it food?"

"She was talking to her friend."

"Do you remember her friend's name?"

"Yeah—Heather."

"When you left Heather's, do you remember if it was light out or dark?"

"It was dark."

"Who was in the car when you left Heather's house?"

"My mom, Cheryl, and Danny, and me too."

"Do you remember if there was any music playing in the car?"

"Yeah."

"Was that from the radio or was it from the tape?"

"Tape."

"And do you remember there was a time when the car stopped?"

"...yeah."

(Christie begins to cry again, Hugi pauses, and Christie takes a deep breath.)

"When the car stopped, did you see any other people around?"

"No."

"Did you see any person standing in the road?"

"No."

"When the car stopped, what did your mom do?"

(There is no sound at all in the packed courtroom, nothing beyond Fred Hugi's soft questions, and the witness's tear-choked answers. No breathing, seemingly no heartbeats from the jury or the gallery.)

"She got out and she pulled the lever that went to the trunk."

"I'm going to show you a picture here. It's called State's #335. Is that the lever you're talking about?"

"Yes."

"After your mom pushed the lever that went out to the trunk, were you able to see her do anything after that?"

"I didn't look at the back."

"O.K. Did you see her come back into the car?"

"Yeah."

The next question was one Hugi had asked Christie only twice before.

"It was going to scare her again. Here I was putting her through the meatgrinder again—knowing what she was going through. Her courage was amazing. Now she was going to avenge Cheryl's death, and put the killer away. The drama was more than *I* was up to."

But he asked the question, for the third—and hopefully last—time.

"What did you see then?"

"She kneeled down and—"

(Christie begins to sob, burying her face in her hands. And her sobs are echoed in the courtroom as spectators break into tears too. Diane turns her head away from Christie.)

"Would you like a recess?" Fred Hugi asks his witness.

(No response.)

"What did you see? You told us she leaned across the seat?"

"Yeah."

"What happened then?"

(Diane is crying. Christie puts her hand to her face as if to block out the memory.)

"She shot Cheryl."

"And you *saw* that happen?"

"Yeah."

"Was the music still playing?"

"Yeah."

"Can you tell us what that was?"

(No response.)

(Christie's face is scarlet with the effort not to cry, to keep going. But she cannot say the title of the song that was playing on the car's tape.)

"Maybe I'll come back to that," Hugi says. "Do you remember what happened after you saw Cheryl get shot?"

"Yeah."

"What happened then?"

"She leaned over to the back seat and she shot Danny."

"What happened then? What happened after Danny got shot?"

"She standed up and went to the back of the seat on the—"

(Christie can no longer hold back tears. In the gallery seats, Brenda lets out a wail of anguish and Evelyn Slaven cuddles her tightly, rocking her. Brenda cannot handle Christie's testimony. The Slavens' son carries her out of the courtroom.)

(Christie is not alone. She has Mr. Hugi. And Mr. Hugi is trying to help her finish what she must say.)

"Do you remember when you got shot?"

"Yeah."

(Her voice is thick, clotted with tears, and she holds her pink handkerchief to her face.)

"Who shot you?"

"My mom."

"Do you remember the music that was playing?"

(No response.)

"Can you just not think of it right now?"

"I can't think of it."

"Do you remember what happened after you got shot?"

"No."

"I'm going to put before you State's #334. Have you seen that before?"

(Hugi picks up the golden statue from the bailiff's bench and holds it out toward Christie.)

"Yeah."

"What is that?"

"It's a unicorn."

"Where did that come from?"

"My mom bought it for us."

"That was before you got shot?"

"Yeah."

"If I said the name of that song that was playing, do you think you'd remember it?"

"Yeah."

"Is it 'Hungry Like the Wolf'?"

"Yeah."

"No doubt about that?"

"No."

"Christie, has anyone ever told you to lie about this?"

"No."

"What you've said here is the truth?"

"Yeah."

"Christie, do you still love your mom?"

"Yeah."

(Almost everyone in the courtroom is crying—from the burly deputy beside Chris Rosage to the reporters in the front row and the jurors.)

"I'm going to offer the two exhibits that were identified by the witness at this time," Hugi says quietly.

The Court: "Show them to counsel, please."

Jim Jagger has no objection to the admission of the unicorn and the picture of the car's trunk-release lever. He now has to cross-examine a little girl whose face is streaked with tears.

VERBATIM:

(He begins)

"Do you know who I am?"

"No."

"Do you recognize me?"

"No."

"I'm an attorney just like Mr. Hugi, and I'll be asking some questions for your mom. OK?"

"OK."

"You know Mr. Hugi, don't you?"

"Yeah."

"And you think he's nice, don't you?"

"Yeah."

"Do you know when the last time was that you talked with him?"

"Today."

"About testifying here today?"

"Yeah."

"You believe very much that what you've said today is the truth, don't you?"

"Yeah."

"And that hurts and makes you feel really kind of bad, doesn't it?"

"Yeah."

"Do you know when you first started to think that this is what happened back then? Do you remember at all?"

"Yeah."

"When was that?"

"In the hospital I remembered."

"Do you remember if you told anybody—"

"Yeah."

"—about it? Who did you tell?"

"My caseworker."

"And you remembered back then who shot you and Danny and Cheryl?"

"Yeah."

"Do you remember her name?"

"Yeah."

"What was her name?"

(No response.)

"Would it be like a Paula or Susan?"

"Yeah, I telled Paula and Susan first."

"And you remember telling both of them about who shot your brother and sister and you?"

(Witness nods head.)

"When the car pulled over to stop, do you remember if you were—do you remember if you were lying down or standing up or sitting up?"

"I was sitting up."

"And what was Danny doing?"

"He was sleeping and his head was on the—"

"Was he in the—were you in the front seat or the back seat?"

"I was in the back seat."

"And was Danny in the back seat or the front seat?"

"Back seat."

"Was his head closer to you, or away from you?"

"Away from me."

"The back seat—the back has a part that you can put your back against?"

"Yeah."

"Was his back—was Danny's back to the back seat or on the bottom of the seat or towards the front of the car, or was he lying on his stomach?"

(Judge Foote leans toward Christie, his body language protective. The gallery is impatient with Jagger. He is trying to confuse the child. Christie is hanging in there, fielding questions.)

"He was lying on his side."

"Do you remember where Cheryl was?"

"Yeah."

"Where was she?"

"She was sitting up."

"She was sitting up?"

"Uh-huh."

"And where was she sitting up?"

"In the front seat."

"She wasn't asleep?"

"No."

"Do you remember what she was wearing?"

"No."

"And you remember that—do you remember if Cheryl was awake or asleep?"

"She was awake."

"Can you tell me which way she was facing—front or side or back?"

"Front."

(Jagger confers with Diane, and they nod their heads. He walks back to Christie. Clearly, Diane has suggested that Christie is confusing the fatal night with the other car trip—the trip they'd taken to the beach a week earlier.)

"Do you remember going to the beach with your mother and Danny and Cheryl?"

"Yeah."

"Do you remember the drive to the beach being a long ways or a short ways?"

"It was long."

"Do you remember Danny sleeping—Well—forget that question. I'll ask you again. Do you remember where Cheryl was sitting on the ride to the beach?"

(No response.)

"Do you remember if she would have been sitting in the front seat or the back seat?"

"She was in the back seat."

"Do you remember about coming home if he [Danny] was in the back seat?"

(No response.)

"We can go back to that in a minute. Do you remember Danny sleeping on that trip to and back from the beach while in the car driving?"

(No response.)

(Jagger's questions jump around. He starts one, drops the core of it, and asks something else. Christie begins simply not to answer.)

"We can come back to that—or do you want to think about it more—or do you want me to ask you another question?"

"All right."

"I'm sorry?"

"It's all right. You can ask me another question."

"Do you remember helping your mother at all—taking things from the trunk of the car or putting anything into the trunk of the car?"

"No—only our clothes."

(The defense attorney shows pictures to Christie—the composites of the bushy-haired man. She has never seen him.)

"Have you talked with Mr. Hugi about testifying here? Can you tell me about how many times you've talked to Mr. Hugi about what you would say here in court or about testifying here?"

(No response.)

"Have you been talking to him each week, or do you remember?"

(No response.)

"Do you want me to ask another question?"

(Brenda returns to the courtroom, her face puffed from crying.)

"It's all right," Christie tells Jim Jagger. "If you want to."

(Diane smiles faintly.)

". . . Have you practiced being a witness in a courtroom before?"

"Yeah."

". . . Did you practice being a judge? Do you remember that at all? Did you do that too?"

(Witness nods head.)

(Christie laughs, her eyes turn down shyly—then she glances up at Judge Foote. He smiles at her. The gallery is getting restless and antsy. A woman in the second row mutters under her breath, "Come on! That's enough.")

"OK. Did you practice sitting where the attorneys sit?"

"No."

"Have you had some—when you were driving to your mom's friend that night, were you and Danny and Cheryl—what were you doing on the drive out to her place?"

"Listening to the music."

"What music was playing?"

"The tape of Duran Duran."

(Diane is staring intensely at Christie. Her face contorts—as if she is trying to convey something to her daughter.)

"Were you all laughing or talking?"

"Not talking or laughing."

"Just listening to the music?"

"Maybe we were talking sometimes."

"Do you remember if on the way out there, you got lost at all?"

"Nope."

"Do you remember seeing in the hospital some things on the television about your mother and you and Danny and Cheryl?"

"Yeah."

"What do you remember?"

(No response.)

"Do you remember if you saw any TV programs about it?"

(No response.)

"Do you feel like you know what the answer is to my question but you just can't say it, or maybe you don't know if you saw TV or not?"

(No response.)

"Are you feeling a little tired?"

"No."

"I wouldn't mind if we had even a break at this time. I'll be asking a series of more questions, taking more time," Jagger offers to Judge Foote. "This might be an appropriate place to break. Fresh in the morning might be better."

This was what Hugi had feared. Christie had dreaded the witness stand. He didn't want her to have to go through another night of anxiety. Foote agrees. He orders only a ten-minute recess.

Jagger is going on too long with the child. He asks the same questions several times—obviously trying to show that Christie has confused the trip to the beach with the trip to Heather Plourd's. He hints that Christie has been coached until she is brainwashed by Susan Staffel, Paula Krogdahl, and Fred Hugi. But it isn't working.

Christie knows what she knows.

It is 5:05 in the afternoon. Jagger begins again.

VERBATIM:

"Do you remember some time ago you being told by anyone—erase that—Do you know what a suspect—do you know what the word 'suspect' means?"

"No."

"That's the reason I want to stop for a second. Do you remember ever being told by someone that some people thought your mother was the one who shot Danny and Cheryl and you? Do you ever remember that?"

"No."

"Do you remember Susan Staffel ever saying that to you?"

"No."

"Or Paula Krogdahl?"

"No."

"Or your mother?"

"No."

"Do you remember some time after you got out of the hospital and before now, do you remember ever wondering if your mother had done the shooting—kind of wondering 'Maybe she did—or maybe she didn't, I wonder?'"

"Yeah."

"Isn't the reason that you were wondering that—because you heard from someplace that some people thought she had?"

"I didn't hear."

"I couldn't hear you."

"I didn't hear."

"OK. You never remember ever thinking that—something like this—that my mother must have done it because of what other people are saying? Do you remember ever saying anything like that?"

"Nope."

"Do you remember when Paula Krogdahl would talk to you, if she ever brought you any nice presents or anything to play with?"

"No."

"What is your name at school?"

"Christie Ann Slaven."

"It's not Downs?"

"Nope."

"How long has that been?"

(No response.)

"Do you think it's been as long as you've been in school—erase that. Has it been as long as—that you've been living with the Slavens?"

"Yeah."

"The Slavens have a nice house, don't they?"

"Yeah."

"They have a TV?"

"Yeah."

"And some things to play with?"

"Yeah."

"And there are some children there your age?"

"Yeah."

"You've talked to the children there about what happened when you were shot, haven't you?"

"Yeah."

"And they—your friends have talked back to you about it, haven't they?"

"Yeah."

"Danny has talked about it too, hasn't he?"

"Yeah."

"Danny has said that his mother did it, hasn't he?"

"Yeah."

"But you know that couldn't be true because Danny was asleep, right?"

"Yeah."

"In fact, *you* told him that, didn't you—when he said that?"

"Whenever he's—I talked to other people about that, he listens too."

"Have you talked to a lot of people about that?"

"No."

"Do you remember Danny saying that a monster with long ears did it?"

"No."

"Do you remember if Danny has said that anyone else did the shooting?"

"No."

". . . Do you remember your mom—before you got shot, some days before—looking for a larger house to live in?"

"Yeah—but not a couple days."

"Do you remember if Cheryl—when the shots were being fired—did Cheryl ever get out of the car?"

"No."

"Do you remember if the person who shot Cheryl and Danny and you, if that person got in through the driver's—the side where the steering wheel is—or the other side?"

"The driver's seat."

"And which side were you sitting on—the driver's seat or the other seat?"

"Behind the driver's seat."

"You remember seeing your mom through the back window of the car, don't you?"

"I didn't look at the back of the window."

"Do you remember seeing—the back window of the car—do you know what I mean by 'the back window'?"

"Yeah."

"One you'd look at as you drive straight ahead, and the other one is the back window. Do you remember before the shooting took place—do you remember seeing your mother through that back window?"

"No."

"Isn't that because you were lying down?"

"No."

"Were you sitting up or standing up?"

"I was sitting down, but I didn't look at the back window."

(Jagger asks the bailiff to show her pictures of guns—pictures Christie has seen before in Dr. Peterson's office. They look to her like guns Diane had.)

"You've seen her with those two before?"

(Witness nods head.)

"See, there's a long one and a shorter one, right?"

"Yeah."

"Do you remember seeing the shorter one in the trunk of your car when you were going to the beach or coming back from the beach?"

(No response.)

"We'll make it two questions. OK? The first one is this: Do you remember before you went to the beach if you saw that short gun in the trunk of the car?"

"Yeah."

"Was that while you were getting some clothes and things in the trunk of the car?"

(No response.)

"Is it hard to remember back then?"

"It was in the trunk of the car."

"Do you remember seeing it there when you got back from the beach?"

"Yeah."

"... There was just one in the trunk of the car that size, wasn't there—the smaller one?"

"Yeah."

"Do you remember talking to Dr. Peterson about whether or not you could be safe with your mom?"

(No response.)

"Is it that you don't remember talking about being safe with Dr. Peterson?"

"With my mom? I was safe with my mom?"

"Yes."

(No response.)

"I'll ask you again later, or were you going to—"

(Witness shakes head. Jim Jagger's questions are impossible to follow, and Christie is tired.)

"...Did you go ahead and draw a picture of who shot Danny and Cheryl and you?"

"I was trying to draw."

"And do you remember if you actually did draw it or not?"

"I was not finished."

(The bailiff starts to hand Exhibit G—her unfinished drawing of the "Killer"—to Christie.)

"I'll ask you—before you do it—when I—when I have a picture shown to you, I'll ask you if that's the picture you drew of who hurt you. OK?"

(Witness nods head.)

"That's the one that you drew of who hurt you, isn't it?"

"Yeah."

"...and that was the—even though maybe it wasn't finished, it was the best job you could do on drawing that, right?"

"Uh-huh."

"...Do you remember anything on the drive to the hospital?"

"No."

"Things happened very fast, didn't they?"

"Yeah."

"Has anybody ever told you that your mom saw a person there who shot Danny and Cheryl and you?"

"No."

"Has anybody ever told you that somebody out there within—a little while before this happened—saw someone who looked like the person your mom said did the bad things to you? Has anybody ever told you that?"

"No."

"When Mr. Hugi asked you if the person who hurt you was kneeling and leaning across, I think he motioned across the seat to the shelf, and that's what you remember?"

"Yeah."

"Now the car seat in the front seat of the car—is that a seat that goes all the way across from one side of the car to the other, or is there a hole in the middle?"

"It was a hole in the middle."

"Was the person—" (Jim Jagger seems suddenly to realize that he has alienated the jury.) "... are you getting tired?"

"Yeah."

"Do you still wonder sometimes if your mother did it or not?"

"No."

"Have you thought about it so much now you think she did?"

"Yeah."

"It would be nice to know—it would be nice to know that she didn't, wouldn't it? That would make you feel better if she didn't do it, huh?"

(Witness nods head.)

"Do you know what made you change from wondering to then thinking she did? Do you really know?"

(No response.)

"Has talking to Dr. Peterson helped you? Is that what you think?"

(No response.)

"You don't really know what has made you change from wondering to now thinking that's what happened. Right? Is that right?"

"Yeah."

"Have you had dreams about this?"

"No."

"You don't remember—strike that—another erase, OK? I don't have any more questions for you."

Christie is limp with exhaustion.

Fred Hugi approaches Christie on redirect. He wants to let her go with no more questions. But he cannot. She has been on the stand for such a long time, and it's almost 6:00 P.M.

VERBATIM:

"Do you know who shot Cheryl?" (He asks gently.)

"Yeah."

"Who was that?"

"My mom."

"How do you know that?"

"I watched."

"Were there any strangers there, anybody that you didn't know?"

"No."

"How about with Danny—was there any stranger there when Danny was shot?"

"No."

"Who shot him?"

"My mom."

"How about you—when you got shot—were there any strangers there?"

"No."

"Who shot you?"

"My mom."

"Do you know that because you saw her do it?"

"Yeah."

"Was she close to you when that happened?"

"Not close."

"In the same car—was she in the same car or standing outside?"

(No response.)

"Do you remember when the shooting happened, do you remember when Cheryl got shot?"

"Yeah."

"Was your mom inside the car then?"

(No response.)

"Was part of her outside the car and part inside the car?"

(No response.)

"Are you pretty tired now?"

(No response.)

"I don't have any other questions."

Nor does Jim Jagger. Judge Foote leans over and says, "Thank you, Christie, you can go now."

Hugi watches Christie step down.

She has done it. By God, she has done it.

CHAPTER 37

"Hey, those people took cuts—hey! Get those people—they're shoving and pushing."

"How unfair. That little boy could sit on your lap and we could get one more in there."

After Christie's testimony, the crowds are even bigger. The State has leapt far ahead, and the followers in Diane's camp are fewer. The bailiff opens the door at ten on May 16, and a hundred people surge in and somehow squeeze into eighty seats.

Dr. Carl Peterson is the first witness of the day.

"I never really doubted that she had a memory."

Peterson explains that when Christie heard the tape of "Hungry Like the Wolf," memories flooded back. But she was afraid to tell him what they were.

"I told Christie that it was OK to feel happiness, sadness, anger, fear."

Christie had drawn a number of pictures—of Cheryl and Danny, of their car, of the pistol and the rifle. She had drawn the Plourd trailer. And she had drawn a picture of the shooter.

Drawn March 4, 1984, it is not a picture of a male. It is a female with short hair and bangs, whose eyes have pupils afloat in white, whose mouth is turned down angrily. The gun is an excellent rendering of a .22 Ruger. The shooter holds the gun in her left hand—not her right, as Diane would have, but then Christie herself is left-handed. It is not a major discrepancy. The picture is incomplete; it shows the figure from the waist up only—the part of the body Christie would have seen from her position in the back seat.

Peterson recalls some of the things Christie said—testing the waters. "If my mom shot me, Cheryl, and Danny, I'd want to go back with her—'cause she was probably really, really angry and it wouldn't happen again."

Jagger accuses Peterson of planting a conditioned response in Christie's mind to implicate Diane.

No. Christie tested *him,* Peterson explains, to see if it was safe for her to remember. "She said, 'Now my mom can't be with her boyfriend because he thinks she done it—It almost *seems* like she done it.'"

Dr. Peterson hadn't commented. But on December 19, he'd asked her once again if she wanted to write the name of the person who had shot them on the slips of paper and put them in the envelopes.

Yes.

And this time, she had not burned the envelopes; she had told him he could save them—if he promised not to open them until she said so.

After a counseling session on January 16, Carl Peterson asked Christie if she feared she might be shot again. Christie thought about it for a long time. "Maybe—if I lived with her again—but maybe she wouldn't."

Christie had finally confided that she no longer wanted to live with her mother.

"Maybe she didn't really love the family," Christie wondered. "She just loved Lew."

Christie wrote down two lists of people in her life. One list was a "safe" list; one was the "unsafe" list.

SAFE	NOT SAFE
Myself (Christie)	Mom
Daniel	Maybe my dad
Cheryl	
Dr. Peterson	
Evelyn and Ray Slaven	
Susan Staffel	
Ray Broderick	
Fred Hugi	

The safe people were all new in her life—all but her brother and sister. Christie Downs had had no "safeness" in the first eight years of her life.

On redirect, Fred Hugi hands the still-sealed envelopes to Peterson. Christie has given permission now to open them.

"Would you open the envelope dated January 2, and read what it says?"

Peterson's voice cracks as he reads the question: "Who shot Cheryl? The answer written here is 'Mom.'"

"Would you open the envelope dated December 19?"

Peterson read the contents: "Who shot Christie?" "The answer is the same. 'Mom.'"

"In the course of your entire association with Christie, has she ever indicated that anyone other than her mom shot her?"

"No."

"Has she ever given any other version of the story?"

"No."

"Are you aware of anyone influencing Christie not to talk with you?"

"Yes."

"Who was that?"

"Mrs. Downs."

"Has Christie expressed an apprehension and fear of her mother as well as love for her mother?"

"Yes."

"Did she indicate to you the order the children were shot in the car?"

Peterson nods. Cheryl was first, Danny was second, and Christie thought she herself might have been shot twice.

Carl Peterson testifies that Christie said she enjoyed living with the Slavens because "they don't yell or spank."

He has heard Danny say to Christie, "We might get shot again."

"Christie said, 'Sorry, Charlie.'

(This is a slang expression from a tuna fish commercial that means "It will never happen.")

"I asked her how she knew that, and she said, ' 'Cause *she* doesn't know the address of the Slavens.'"

Dr. Edward Wilson, who performed the autopsy on Cheryl, is next. As he speaks, the jurors pale noticeably. Diane is absolutely immobile, her hands quiet on the arms of her chair.

Wilson's photographs are accepted into evidence. "The cause of death was two gunshot wounds through the upper body, through the aorta. She bled to death."

Juror #12 looks nauseated as Wilson continues in his description of the last moments of Cheryl Downs.

None of the jurors—save #8—will look at the defendant.

The parade of policemen begins. Policemen say "Sir" when they testify. They do not volunteer information; they answer questions.

One by one, they tell of their contacts with Diane Downs, of what they remember of May 19, 1983. Most of them refer to notes as they speak. But only for specific details. The woman herself—who sits before them—they remember perfectly without prompting.

Rob Rutherford reads from his notes. Just before he left the hospital with Diane on May 19 to go back to Old Mohawk Road, Diane had laughed as she said, "I hope *you* have good insurance. If I die out there, I'm going to sue you! And I'll come back to haunt you."

Rob Rutherford is still on the stand the next morning. Jagger infers that he did not look hard enough for the gunman and the yellow car the night of the shootings. Rutherford will not be shaken. There was no sign that any vehicle had been recently parked along the road: the sheriff's sergeant had just completed a tracking course.

Tracy is next—the gallery tittering at "Dick Tracy."

Tracy verifies how incongruous the defendant's behavior was, recalling her continual babble about a boyfriend in Arizona instead of concern for her injured children. Diane told them where the rifle was, read the consent to search aloud, and then signed it. And Tracy had taken it to Sergeant Jon Peckels.

The best piece of physical evidence the State has is the microscopically identical match between the extractor marks on the casings from the death bullets and those of the two bullets in the .22 rifle home in Diane's closet.

Jagger suggests to the jury that the chain of evidence has been broken, the bullets mixed up. He asks for a play-by-play account of Tracy's day. He is looking for a slip somewhere. Most defense attorneys don't have the temerity of nitpick with civilian witnesses; cops are fair game.

Diane seems either exhausted or bored. Her eyes are puffy with fatigue, and her arms rest heavily on her chair.

"You didn't make any notes about the order of how the bullets came out of the rifle, did you?" Jagger asks Tracy.

"I did not."

"Detective Tracy, you've been investigating homicides where you know who did it—and couldn't prove it. Isn't that true?"

"Yes . . ."

"Isn't it true that you got a bullet from the scene, from another officer present—and put it in the rifle?"

Tracy's face turns a shade of magenta. You do not ask an honest cop a question like that.

"That is a lie," he says evenly. "That is not true."

"Do you deny then that you could have placed two bullets within the rifle, or you could have placed two bullets in an envelope—bullets that didn't come from the gun? You deny that, don't you?"

Tracy just may go for Jagger's throat. "You bet I deny that!"

Dick Tracy had solved every murder case he ever investigated; in his last year on the department, he was not about to start faking the evidence.

Judge Foote pounds his gavel—for a judicious break.

Jon Peckels is next. He has twenty-one years with the Lane County Sheriff's Office, assigned currently to the Identification section, and in charge of preserving the physical evidence in the shootings. At fifteen minutes to midnight on May 19, Shelby Day gave him one bullet, a bullet that had fallen from Cheryl's clothing as she was placed on the treatment table. Dr. Wilhite gave him another bullet.

Ever since that night, Peckels has watched over the chain of evidence. If even one link is broken, the evidence is flawed. He has guarded the children's clothing and the bright colored beach towel. He has the gun residue kit and the trace metal tests made at the hospital at eighteen minutes after midnight.

Roy Pond slowly opens the brown bags containing the small garments. A miasma, real or imagined, seems to rise from clothing sodden with long-dried blood. Pond pulls out a green shirt with a yellow collar with a dark red blotch in the center. He I.D.s Danny's OshKosh B'Gosh jeans, Christie's maroon pants.

Diane turns her head away and stares down at her hands. She begins to doodle again on the yellow pad in front of her.

Tears run down Roy Pond's face as he holds up Cheryl's gore-marked purple and white T-shirt, cut at the seams by someone in the ER a year before, and then the postal sweater—Diane's—that Cheryl had around her shoulders when Shelby Day carried her in.

"These are the shorts from little Danny Downs." Pond's voice cracks. They are such improbably tiny white jockey shorts.

Diane has not looked up since Pond began.

Diane's ex-husband takes the stand.

Steve Downs is still a handsome man, compactly built. He wears gray slacks and a navy blue jacket; he speaks quietly. Steve goes through his twelve-year history with Diane. Her expression indicates that his testimony is a joke.

Occasionally, Steve Downs *is* laughable, and Judge Foote must admonish those in the back not to react with chuckles at his testimony.

The marriage was good, and then "iffy," and then bearable, and then bad. He was aware of his wife's lovers. He had thought her a little crazy, sometimes suicidal; she tried twice to shoot *him* in a three-month period in 1982.

"Have you beat her?" Hugi asks Downs. "If you have, tell the jury about it."

Downs nods. "The first time—when I found her with Russ Phillips in bed."

Diane gazes down at the defense table.

Another beating: "She picked up the girls when they were living with me and left me a note 'You are a%%%####&& father.' I was gone—the kids were next door with a neighbor. I went over to her house—her mobile home. Cheryl and Christie were playing outside. I was pretty pissed-off about that . . . She was on the phone—ignoring me. I took the phone away from her and put my hand on her throat. Then we just really got into it. I pounded her—pounded her hard. There was blood. Cheryl saw me hitting her mother."

Hugi asks Steve if he has been convicted of crimes. He will beat Jagger to it.

"Yes, I have—grand theft—auto. I reported my car stolen to the insurance company. It wasn't stolen. I was convicted last summer, in July, after the shooting happened here. Diane saw that I wasn't in her camp with the whole story. She called down to the Chandler Police Department. I owned up to it."

"The mobile home fire—" Hugi begins. "Tell us about that."

"Diane and I planned it. She talked about pouring gas on it. I told her it needed to be done with some discretion. It was started by me—in the bedroom . . . The insurance paid."

Diane shakes her head in disgust.

"Did you ever show Diane Downs how to operate that weapon [the missing .22 Ruger]?"

"Yes sir. I gave it to her when she was living at the mobile home by herself . . . I got it back . . . I assumed it was on a shelf in the closet where I left it. She wanted the guns. I didn't see any need for her to have them."

On cross, Jim Jagger asks Steve to discuss the sexual relationship between him and Diane after the divorce.

"It happened one time—it was very cold and callous. I absolutely could not bat against the guy [Lew]."

For once, Diane agrees with Steve. She nods vigorously. And then she grins and passes a note to her attorney.

Steve Downs admits to stealing guns from Billy Proctor. "Technically yes."

"Isn't it true that you were having affairs?"

"No. Diane said that to justify her own affairs."

"You two have some pretty hard feelings, don't you?"

"Yes. They've [the DA's office] showed me what they have and I'm satisfied with it."

"Did you look for that gun?"

"Once the kids were shot, I looked for the gun."

"In a phone call a week after, she told you about what vehicle the gun was placed in?"

"Yeah—it was her idea, and a wild one in my eyes. That gun was not in my house or storage place . . . I never looked for it until after the shooting and when I did look for it, it wasn't around."

"You wouldn't have been inclined to give that gun to the police in any event—"

"Yeah. I would have immediately given it to the police 'cause they could have matched the bullets to the gun . . . I knew then that she had absolutely nothing, no caring at all for the kids."

The weekend comes and with it, real spring—sunny, warm, and full of promise: May 19 again.

CHAPTER 38

Diane's due date is supposed to be in July, but rumor says June. Female spectators watch Diane with the eyes of experience to see if she has "dropped." She *looks* close to term. The emotional strain alone would be enough to send an average woman into premature labor. But then Diane has never been average.

She sweeps in dramatically Monday morning, May 21, dressed in a royal blue maternity dress patterned with flying gulls. She smiles at the relieved sighs in the gallery. She looks very well.

It is the prosecutor who seems to be wasting away day by day. Fred Hugi has lost so much weight that he has to cinch his belt several holes tighter. He cannot hold down solid food, and he exists on milkshakes and yogurt. If he could spare the time to run, he might work through some of the tension—but there is no time.

He is scarcely eating, and he is not sleeping. Every night, like clockwork, he awakens at three with a throbbing pain in his jaw that brings him right up out of bed. He went to his dentist on May 18 but X rays revealed no overt problem. His dentist, aware of the trial stress, diagnosed, "It's all in your head. Ha. Ha."

During the day, Hugi is so wrapped up in the trial he can ignore the pain. But it comes back every night. He is aware that tension can trigger psychosomatic pain, but this is beyond anything he ever imagined. (After the trial, when the pain continued, he insisted upon another X ray, and his dentist found the problem. Hugi had clenched his teeth so hard that he had split a tooth vertically, such a clean crack into the nerve that it looked normal in the first X ray. An oral surgeon attempted a root canal filling, but the tooth fell apart. When it was pulled, the pain "in his head" vanished.)

On May 21, the courtroom has been transformed. The mock-up of Diane's car is in place, filling much of the space between Judge Foote's bench and the defense/prosecution tables. The roof is off and set to one side. This car is not red, it is pale blue—so that the outlines of blood pools will show. The names of those who bled there are written in. Just like the real Nissan Pulsar's, the front seats are buckets with head rests, the back a bench seat.

The dolls are in the courtroom this morning. They aren't as realistic as the car is—only large white rag dolls that will bend into different positions. Their eyes are black felt, mouths rosebud pouts. The Christie-doll has hair of reddish brown yarn, and the Cheryl-doll's hair is made of lighter brown yarn. The Danny-doll's hair is bright yellow. They are exactly the size the Downs children were on May 19, 1983.

"Cheryl" and "Christie" wear blue jeans, and "Danny" wears tiny shorts and small running shoes. A single lock of yarn has worked loose of its stitching and hangs over "Cheryl's" eyes. Unconsciously, Fred Hugi bends over and brushes the lock of "hair" away from her eyes. Hugi invariably cradles the "children" in his arms as he talks about them. Jim Jagger, on the other hand, tends to toss them on the floor when he finishes with them—as if to underscore the fact that they *are* only rag dolls.

This is a mistake. It jars the heart each time one of the dolls crumples to the floor.

Jim Pex will attempt now to give the jury a crash course in forensic science. Pex and Chuck Vaughn have inserted a wooden dowel into a cutaway of a .22 Ruger semi-automatic pistol, and then held the gun close to the dolls' "wounds" to determine angle. A rigid white probe ran from the gun's barrel through the wounds to show the bullets' paths. Pex demonstrates on the rag dolls.

It is a standard procedure in autopsy to help forensic pathologists ascertain the height of the shooter, his position, and the position of the victim. It is horrifying for the layman to watch. This morning, the jurors and the gallery can see the children as they were when they were shot.

Jim Pex uses an overhead projector to demonstrate how close the shooter was to the victims. With a .22 caliber gun, the maximum distance barrel-debris (particles) will travel is two to three feet. All of the children had heavy stippling around their wounds.

Pex used a number of tests to verify his findings: the Sodium Rhodizonate test (which turns purple in the presence of lead); the Greiss test (for sodium nitrates); a soft tissue X ray; the appearance of the skin itself; the swollen fibers of clothing where the bullet penetrated.

The gun barrel had been between six and nine inches from the wound in Diane's forearm.

The gun had been nine inches or less from Danny's spine.

The gun had been nine to twelve inches away from the two wounds in Christie's chest (wounds so close together that they could be covered with a half-dollar piece), but only one or two inches away from the hand she held up in a vain attempt to block the second bullet.

The gun had been six to nine inches away from Cheryl's right shoulder—the first shot—but it had been right next to the skin—a near-contact wound—at Cheryl's left shoulder.

Pex places the doll children in the car mock-up. Danny is on his stomach on the left side of the back seat. "He would have been paralyzed immediately upon being shot." With the gun-on-a-stick, Pex becomes the shooter. He shows how "he" would have had to lean into the car to shoot Danny.

At Judge Foote's invitation, the jurors stand to get a better look at the demonstration.

Diane looks away.

Pex shows that Christie would have had to be sitting up on the rightrear seat. The first shot would have knocked her into a half-reclining position. The second bullet had gone through the back of her hand into her chest.

Cheryl's first wound occurred, Pex deduces, as she lay on the floor of the front passenger seat. In an almost reflex action, Cheryl had apparently reached for the door handle and tumbled out on the road. Cheryl had suffered a fatal wound to her upper right shoulder, but she was still moving. Her killer had either reached across the front seat—or run around the outside of the car—and placed the .22 Ruger against her left side and fired once more.

Pex takes the probe and shoves it through the Cheryl-doll's left side. The courtroom is as still as death itself.

Because that wound was contact, or near-contact, there was "back spatter"—high-velocity blood that flew back from the wound to the rocker panel of the Pulsar, leaving a characteristic scarlet spray along the aluminum ridges.

Either bullet would have killed her. The second shot may well prove her killer a liar. Christie cannot remember seeing Cheryl shot a second time.

But Christie has retained one remarkably clear memory. She is positive that a tape was still playing, even as the shots were fired. "Hungry Like the Wolf" wailed inside the car, keening lyrics of thwarted lust. When Christie heard it in Dr. Peterson's office, her expression had reflected a dawning memory of terror.

Diane had always said it was Cheryl's favorite song. Or was it Diane's own theme song? Passion and longing and the mouth full of juices, the huntress on the prowl, the she-wolf warning her lover that she would never, ever, ever, give up until she stalks him to the wall, and leaps upon him by moonlight? Fred Hugi felt that "Hungry Like the Wolf" had given Diane the courage to do whatever she had to do to get Lew back.

It would have been the last thing Cheryl heard.

Jim Pex found something interesting when he checked the condition of the tape deck at the Lane County shops. The tape deck would not play unless the keys were in the ignition! Diane had stressed continually that she put the keyring around her finger as she got out of the car to talk to the stranger on the road. She has related a dozen times or more how she pretended to throw the keys after the man shot her children.

If the keys were in her mother's hand—outside the car—how *could* Christie have heard "Hungry Like the Wolf"? Why did Duran Duran continue to sing as the bullets fired monotonously?

Pex's findings suggest that Diane Downs lied about throwing the keys.

It makes her whole story of fighting the gunman suspect. Can the jury pick up on the significance of this?

Jim Pex's next chore is to explain what the identical tool marks on the bullet casings mean. It helps to have gun owners in the jury.

The Crime Laboratory Information System lists 12,000 different weapons and all of their characteristics; 3,468 of them are pistols. The best fit for the death weapon used on Old Mohawk Road is a Ruger semi-automatic pistol.

Several witnesses have said that Diane was the last person in possession of the .22 caliber Ruger semi-automatic that Steve Downs stole from Billy Proctor. The casings on the road fit that gun. When an extractor pulls a cartridge from the chamber, unique scratch marks are left on the cartridge. When an ejector flips the casing to the right or left, it too leaves distinctive marks.

Pex moves to the huge display board where blow-ups of the parts of a pistol, magnified many times, are mounted.

"Nine cartridges were found at 1352 Q Street—in the Glenfield rifle," Pex explains. "Two of the cartridges found in that rifle had been mechanically manipulated through the weapon that was used to shoot the children."

Despite the huge blow-up showing the matches in tool marks on cartridges from the rifle in Diane's closet and on the casings of the death bullets, Chuck Vaughn was right when he warned Hugi that photographs would scarcely show a lay jury that *those* two cartridges had once been in the missing .22 Ruger. Cartridges were not as convincing as bullets.

Pex admits that the bullet Paul Alton and Doug Welch found under Diane Downs's trailer in Chandler, Arizona, was too badly damaged to say it had *identical* characteristics to those fired on the night of May 19. In forensic science, a very strong possible doesn't count.

Pex had purchased a Styrofoam-lined zippered case for a Ruger, placed a gun similiar to the missing weapon inside, and put it into water to see if it would float.

"It did—without even getting the zipper wet."

If the shooter had thrown the gun—in its case—into the Mohawk River, it might well have floated until it reached the McKenzie or the Willamette, moving gently north on the current that links rivers and reservoirs in a seemingly endless chain to the mighty Columbia.

Possibly never to be found.

Diane supports her belly with her hands often now—as if it is very heavy. She has moved to Jim Jagger's chair so that she can watch Pex's tool mark demonstration. His explanations tear jagged edges along her own script of what happened that night.

Jim Jagger is on his feet, moving around the mock-up, the display board, taking notes.

Pex describes spraying Luminol in the death car and along the roadway. It showed blood inside the car, and on the rocker panel, but, oddly, none on the road itself. Pex deduces that immediately after Cheryl was shot for the second time as she lay on the ground, the shooter threw her back into the car—before any blood had seeped from the wound. The initial bleeding was internal; the pool of blood on the floor of the front seat had come from Cheryl's mouth.

Cross-examination of Jim Pex is spirited. Jagger needs to shatter the theory that Cheryl was shot outside the car. He asks if the door angle might not have been different than assumed, if certain blood spatters might not have come from another source, at a different time.

"That's affirmative," Pex says calmly, "*if* you have an alternative."

Jagger bears down on Pex. Jagger, the master of the scattergun, convoluted question, is at his best in this kind of courtroom warfare. Blood spatter, gun residue, ejector marks, extractor marks—all of it is confusing anyway to anybody outside a forensic lab. He obviously wants to cloud the issue, to ask Pex the same question so many different ways that the jurors will run out of endurance or interest to keep up.

Finally irritated, Pex responds to one of Jagger's long, long questions, "Well, we're not talking about a basketball here—we're talking about a *liquid*."

"Well, you recognize that some experts in the field would differ with you on that," Jagger counters.

"No, I don't recognize that—" Pex's voice rises a shade.

Fred Hugi makes no move to object. Pex is quite capable of taking care of himself.

Jim Pex stares without expression at Jagger, who continues to question him about blood spatter, and says finally, "Perhaps you could draw this— you've got *me* confused."

Jagger wants to get to the top of the mock-up so that Pex can explain where the blood spatter was. Fred Hugi bends to lift the heavy top portion, turning to Jagger to ask tersely, "Want to help?"

Judge Foote steps down from the bench to help lift the top of the "car."

Pex explains that the blood spatter on the roof of the car had been "medium velocity"—traveling at five to twenty-five feet per second. This was consistent with blood from Christie's injured hand flinging back—the drops much larger than high-velocity blood spatter.

It has been an endless blue Monday. Diane seems glum and dispirited. She has been kept busy turning her eyes away from displays. They are all over the courtroom. Dolls with probes through them, a car like hers, the terrible glossy pictures of Cheryl—dead.

Diane wears a different outfit each day. On Tuesday, it is a gray and red diagonally striped maternity top. She always wears the red identification wrist band of a high-risk prisoner—but she makes it seem a part of her outfit.

For the most part Diane appears relaxed, her right arm draped always over the chair. It stays there sometimes for an hour or more, her limp white hand motionless. Her nails are long and unpolished, and her hair is lank, the dark roots showing more; her skin is flawed and muddy.

The testimony is still about blood. Who would have thought that blood could be seen so many ways? To maintain a modicum of serenity, it is important to forget where all of this blood under discussion came from and to concentrate only on the scientific aspects of Jim Pex's prolonged cross-examination.

Yes, there was a blood-spatter pattern on the exterior of the car. Yes, Pex believed that aerosol-like spray on the rocker panel had come from Cheryl. Bullets free *high-velocity* blood, blood that travels at more than twenty-five feet per second. "It doesn't change much when the subject is moving slowly."

Laconically, Pex is saying that the victim can be almost dead, but his blood will still travel at high speed if he is shot.

Pex patiently explains that he has tested all manner of objects for blood patterns: hand-whipped blood, a bloody sponge smashed with a hammer, with a sledge hammer. Pex tacked butcher paper up lab walls, over lab ceilings to catch blood as it was flung from a variety of sources. Humans do much damage to one another with any number of weapons, and there are distinct differences in the way blood leaves their veins and arteries.

Jim Jagger suggests that the blood on the *outside* of the car didn't come from Cheryl's being shot outside, but was only deposited there when Shelby Day lifted Cheryl out. The sleeve of the postal sweater must have dipped in the pool of blood on the floor and left those drops on the panel.

No. That would be "cast-off blood" Pex explains. Cast-off blood is not like back spatter. Cast-off blood comes from a whipping hand or a dripping sleeve. Pex cannot be shaken. "I made my opinion on the source of that blood the day we wheeled the car outside."

The postal sweater, its lower left sleeve saturated with blood, is admitted: "Exhibit #53."

Jim Jagger picks the Cheryl-doll up from the front of the red car, wraps her in the gray sweater, and demonstrates how the sweater's arms would have trailed through the blood, and then dripped on the rocker panel. Jagger must go through a most complex series of dips and whirls to make his point. Pex shakes his head slightly.

Finished with the doll, Jagger drops her into a sitting position at the rear of the plywood car. The loose strand of yarn falls back over her face. The black felt eyes stare straight at Diane.

Diane runs her long sharp fingernails over her pregnant belly again and again, as if she is stroking and comforting Charity Lynn. She does this often now—caressing her own abdomen, and then raking it with her fingernails. It is somehow embarrassing—disturbing—to watch her.

Danny's blood was on the back seat, although very little of it. "The bullet clipped his lung—he may have lost blood through his nose or mouth."

Wait—if Diane was the shooter, why hadn't there been more blood on the sleeve of her plaid shirt? Jagger is curious about this.

"I made a paper apron, I held the gun twenty-two inches from the paper—the blow-back spatters occurred. [Closer up] I held the gun in my right hand—and I only got a few droplets on my sleeve. Most of the blood went up."

Pex was, of course, not shooting at a human body—only at a blood-soaked sponge wrapped with plastic to simulate skin. More enthusiastic—and less sensitive—criminalists and pathologists have testified to the same experiments with cadavers and animals, a practice that instantly alienates a jury.

To refute further the theory that the blood on the outside of the car had come when the ER crew removed the children, Pex had tried another experiment: "I went to McKenzie-Willamette Hospital, and I poured a cup of blood on the asphalt surface. We stomped in that blood, and we attained some blood spatters on paperbags. We got spatters only two and a half inches up. We did not produce *any* spatters more than two and a half inches from the ground—eleven inches away."

Whoever the shooter was, Pex is absolutely convinced that he/she fired from the driver's side, reaching around the driver's seat or between the bucket seats.

John E. Murdock, director of the Contra Costa County Crime Laboratory in Martinez, California—and one of the country's leading experts in firearms and tool mark metals examination—verifies what Jim Pex has said: Tool marks are almost as good as fingerprints.

The extractor removes the casing from the gun after the gun is fired. Then the extractor is forced back to the ejector and out the ejector port, where the cartridge is removed. Murdock had examined the suspect cartridges— both from the Glenfield rifle and the death car—under a stereo-binocular microscope for extractor marks on the rims.

"The extractor marks were close enough so that I concluded all of them had been fired from a gun with an identical extractor. I'm quite comfortable that the same extractor made the marks. When the claw-shaped metal moves over the softer rim, it marks it. If you unload a gun by hand—very, very gently—you may not leave a mark; but if you do it forcibly, you leave a nice mark. Every expert I consulted on these extractor comparisons agreed that it was a classic example."

Diane sits placidly with her hands folded over her stomach as the California criminalist testifies. She seems unaware that on the display board behind her the blow-up of a black Ruger semi-automatic is directly above her head.

She is anxious for her moment on the witness stand. She can explain all of this away. She is confident that the jury will believe her.

CHAPTER 39

Dick Tracy testifies again about helping Diane draw a composite picture of the suspect with an Ident-a-Kit on May 20. "We began with the hair, and she picked a shaggy head of hair, and then she wanted more hair added. She wanted 'meaner-looking eyes.'" They had worked over the first sketch for a long time, and finally, after changing the chin line again and again, Diane had said, "That's close enough . . . that's close enough."

Tracy was present at the day-long search of Diane's duplex unit. All of the minutiae of her life, the stuff from the back of closets, papers jammed in drawers, now become Exhibits #220 to #333: letters, romantic cards, poems written for Lew, essays, calendars, half-filled-out bankruptcy forms, polaroid pictures. Tracy's voice drones as he reads off the list of items retrieved.

A television set and VCR are wheeled into the courtroom. Diane re-enacted the crime for Jon Peckel's television camera four days after it happened. Dick Tracy portrays the suspect. Diane portrays Diane. It is a bizarre videotape. The slender blonde woman on the screen wears a sling-supported cast on her left arm. She is laughing as she tells Tracy how to approach her, changes her mind, and repositions him.

"I'm throwing the keys, OK?" She laughs again.

And then Diane jumps into the driver's side of the car. She yelps and giggles. "This is worse than—"

Her sentence stops in midair. She has hurt her arm on the doorjamb as she made her "getaway" and it seems that she was about to say, "This is worse than—the real thing."

"Cheryl Lynn was on the floorboard in front . . . with a sweater over her. She was asleep at the time. Danny was sleeping in the back."

Again Diane laughs on camera. Nervous laughter?

The television screen goes dark. Diane is smiling a little—here, now, in "real life." She trails her talon nails up and down her belly.

The court clerk carries in a portable stereo.

"Hungry Like the Wolf" blasts through the small courtroom. The first sound on the tape is—eerily—a woman's trilling, heedless laugh. "I'm on the hunt—I'm after you . . . I'm hungry like the wolf—"

The act of murder is caught somewhere in that music, assaulting the ear unaware.

Covertly, listeners glance at the defense table. Diane is smiling broadly. It is enough to raise the hairs on the back of the neck. She whispers something to Jim Jagger, giggling.

Why doesn't the sound of this tape make Diane cry—or vomit—or *something*?

She jiggles her foot in time with the music, snapping her fingers. When the title phrase comes around, she mouths the words: "Hungry Like the Wolf" in time with the tape.

The song lasts forever, bouncing off the acoustical ceiling and walls of the courtroom. The arrangement features extraneous noises in the background of the tape. Sharp reports—like gunfire. A snare drum, maybe. And screams. On the MTV video, the piercing cries are the sound of the tiger-woman in orgasm. In the courtroom in Eugene, Oregon, for those ignorant of the visual script, the sounds are gunshots and children screaming in terror and agony.

Fred Hugi—who has barely glanced at Diane during the first weeks of the trial—turns in his chair and stares fixedly at her, his great dark eyes unblinking. She does not look at him.

The sounds like pistol shots come again, and then the breathy words and the chilling, high-pitched screams. Finally, the tape sighs to its end.

Diane still grins, her foot still moves rhythmically. The courtroom is as silent as if it were empty. The jurors' faces are gray.

Diane looks terrible the next morning, her skin green beneath the pallor, mauve tracing the circles under her eyes.

Cops continue to take the stand. Jerry Smith, the detective sergeant from the Springfield Police Department who carried Diane's first diary to her—the diary full of unsent letters to Lew—begins the day's testimony, recalling impressions of the night a year ago.

Paul Alton testifies only to those things that he has been able to prove; the jury will never hear about his frustration in digging in the heat beneath Diane's trailer, of all the avenues followed to a blank wall. Alton's presence on the stand is professional, dispassionate. He recalls learning from Steve Downs a few days after the shooting that Downs had owned a .22 Ruger semi-automatic pistol, which Steve had last seen in Diane's possession.

Alton identifies the Montgomery Ward sales slip for a brass unicorn.

Lt. Bobby J. Harris of the Chandler Police Department has accompanied Steve Downs up to Eugene. The Arizona detective holds in his hand a theft report filed by Billy Proctor on January 6, 1982, on a .22 Ruger. The serial number of the gun was #14-76187, Model RST6—according to the Chandler Gun Shop. Proctor bought it on January 30, 1978.

Harris verifies that he arrested Steve Downs for car theft on June 7, 1983, as a result of a tip from Diane Downs on the car theft insurance scam.

Paul Frederickson is a hostile witness for the State. Paul—who much prefers to wear his hair and clothes "punk"—looks presently as "All American Boy" as possible. Short and slight, he wears gray corduroy trousers and brand-new black shoes. His brown hair is as straight and short as Beaver Cleaver's.

Hugi elicits that Diane has confided a great deal in Paul. She told him she was going to change her story from one man with a shag haircut to two men in ski masks. Frederickson testifies that he advised her, "If it's not true, don't do it—but, if it is, do it."

And Diane had assured him, "It's true."

Diane had "morning dreams," her brother tells the jury. "The kids were all alive. Danny was walking. Cheryl had blood on her shirt—but she was OK. They were all running from someone—and it was always Cheryl who knew which way to turn to avoid danger."

As far as Frederickson can recall, the dreams dissipated after Diane began therapy sessions with Polly Jamison.

"Did she display emotion—when she was in her room?" Jagger asks Paul Frederickson on cross-examination.

"Yes—she was crying—it was muffled. To her, it was something personal."

"Muffled—" Jagger prompts. "How—"

"It was muffled with a pillow—or something."

Ahh. Good. Jagger wants to show that his client *is* capable of tears.

"When it was just me and her, she showed emotion—but not with my parents . . . In our family—my dad's quite the tough-type person . . . with a strong, bold front. He feels you should be able to contain your feelings and remain professional. Sadness and that stuff should remain private."

Cord Samuelson's fleeting affair with Diane has come back to haunt him. It is excruciatingly embarrassing for him to take the witness stand. Fortunately, Samuelson has already confessed his indiscretion to his wife.

"It was the day before the grand jury hearing," Samuelson recalls. "Diane came out on my route, and she asked me, 'Do you want to know what really happened?'

"I told her I thought I already knew. And then she said, 'It wasn't a shaggy-haired stranger—there were two men with ski masks. They called me by name, and they referred to my tattoo. They said, "If Steve can't have the kids, neither can you," and they began to shoot. They said, "Watch this, bitch," and they started shooting the children.'

"I asked her, 'Why don't you tell the police?'

"And she said, 'As crazy as it may seem, I want to protect Steve—because of the trouble he's already in—because of the arson charges.'

"I advised her to tell the cops the truth, and she said that her lawyer said it doesn't look good to change your story in the middle of a murder case. She told me not to tell anyone what she'd told me. She was convinced the cops didn't have the murder weapon. She asked me, 'How can they prove it without a murder weapon?'"

"You were quite familiar with Diane Downs prior to the shooting?" Fred Hugi asked.

"Yes."

Tactfully, Hugi left it at that.

"Call Lewis Lewiston."

The gallery gasps. No, it is more a wave of sighs. *He* is actually here—the male lead of Eugene's "General Hospital."

Just as unabashedly curious, the entire press bench turns to gaze toward the double doors at the back of the room. Judge Foote raps his gavel for order. Diane has not moved, or turned her head even slightly.

Lew strides in from the corridor, and despite Foote's warning, the sighs reach a crescendo. He looks the part—every inch the southwestern hero, tall and tanned, his beard and moustache trimmed neatly. If he is nervous, he doesn't betray it as he moves forward to be sworn.

"I can't believe it's really him," a woman breathes. "Right here in Eugene."

Somehow, sometime—during the weeks of being cloistered in the windowless courtroom—reality has drifted away for many of the spectators. They are totally caught up with the leading characters. The trial has become fiction, an exciting diversion from their own lives.

Hugi steps almost immediately into Lew's intimate life. They must sting, these questions about the affair that began when he broke his elbow in 1982.

When Lew speaks, his voice is a rumbling drawl.

"My wife became aware of it on my birthday—September 12. I told my wife I has having an affair because Diane accused me of giving her gonorrhea. I said no . . . [but] I had to tell my wife because I'd probably given it to her. On September 13, I tried to break it off. A gun discharged in Diane's trailer that day."

There is no need for Lew to give the details of that gunfire—Steve had already testified to Diane's hysterical despair when Lew left her for the first time.

But the affair had continued; it accelerated, Lewiston says. Diane pushed him to leave his wife, to file for divorce. Sometimes he said he would—but he changed his mind. Back and forth, he'd wavered, with Diane pulling at him.

The children?

"I didn't see very much of the kids."

"From Christmas on," Hugi asks, "how were the ... two relationships?"

Lew makes a Freudian slip as he tries to frame his answer: "Worse with my life—er—my *wife* because I continued to lie to her. Diane wanted me to divorce my wife and live with her and the three children. I told her I just didn't want to be a daddy to her kids. I never wanted kids—or to be a father."

A crimson flush creeps up Diane's neck; otherwise, she shows no reaction. The man on the witness stand might be just another detective.

Still, if one looks closely, there is a tenseness in her body; every muscle under the seemingly blasé exterior is taut. She leans over to Jim Jagger often, whispering and laughing derisively. She *has* to act as if none of Lew's testimony matters—who could possibly believe that she ever cared enough about this man to hurt her children? But, even as she works to show disinterest and scorn, Diane's eyes fall on the new wide gold wedding band on Lew's finger.

She has not seen Lew for eight months—Lew, her golden man she once could not live through a night without. When he leaves the witness stand, it is unlikely that she will ever see him again.

Answering Fred Hugi's questions, Lew moves verbally through the seventeen months he'd known Diane before she left for Oregon. By that time, her conversation had become "an every-day push for me to get a divorce, sell my house, and get up to Oregon with her. She wanted me to do it quick enough to come with her. I always said, 'If it's meant to be, it will be.' I just hadn't made up my mind."

And the gun? What about the .22 Ruger?

"The few days before she left—four or five days before—she offered the use of her .22 pistol to me. Her ex-husband, Steve, was not my best friend to say the least ... Steve threatened to beat me up."

Lew testifies that he turned down the pistol offer after considering the gift for a few minutes. "I saw it in the trunk of her Datsun the night before she left—the .22 Ruger."

"What day did she leave?"

"April 2, 1983."

Once Diane was in Oregon, Lew recalls, "It was basically a relief that she was gone, and I started to patch things up with my wife. Diane usually called me every day in the morning or evening. She sent letters every day. I began to refuse both the calls and return the letters. I was back with my wife in two weeks."

As Lew explains that her absence was "basically a relief," Diane's armor cracks visibly for the first time since he began to testify. She stares at him with an expression of ineffable sadness. He had not missed her; he'd only been *relieved*.

Diane came back once, Lew continues, to give him his gold chain. "After she left on the twenty-eighth, I assumed it was over. She gave back the chain; I didn't want to come to Oregon, and I was back with my wife."

Lew recalls the morning he learned of the shooting. "Diane sounded the same. She asked me, 'How are things? How is Chandler?' and she said, 'See, I've been leaving you alone. No letters. No calls.' And I said, *'Why* did you call?' and that's when she told me about the shooting."

"Did she sound upset?" Hugi asks.

"Not at all."

There is a whhsshing sound in the courtroom. Not a sigh—more a massive intake of breath.

Hugi questions Lew about the rose tattoo on his shoulder, and Lew nods. Diane got her tattoo first and had his name written beneath it. For months, she had begged him to get one too. After a few drinks one night, he'd agreed to go with her to get the rose tattoo. But he had refused to have her name written under it as she wanted.

"Is there a name under your tattoo now?"

"Yes."

Diane freezes, listening.

"What is it?"

Lew stares down at Diane and says deliberately, *"Sweet Nora."*

Her chin snaps up—takes the blow. Instantly, she recovers, nodding with bitter weariness, as if to say, "I knew it all the time—I knew he'd buckle under to her."

Lew lifts the lid from the box of dried roses and nods. This is the box Diane brought to show him when she flew down to return his chain. He identifies the uncirculated 1949 silver half dollar found in the glove box of her car. "I gave it to her—that's the year I was born."

And then a virtual torrent of letters from Diane to Lew. Some of them mailed; some handed to him. Many were letters she'd written before she left and hidden in his drawers, in his bathroom, all over his apartment—for him to find and read after she was gone, a web of words left behind.

The longer Lew talks—hours now on the witness stand—the deeper his voice grows with strain and fatigue, total Texas drawl.

Jim Jagger suggests to Lew that Diane was not nearly as obsessed with him as the prosecution would have the jury believe. Diane whispers and prompts during this period of cross-examination.

"You spent only an hour or two with her?" Jagger asks referring to their usual daily meetings.

"No sir."

"How late?"

"In my apartment, she would spend the night."

"When you were living with your wife, how late did you get home?"

"At that time, it [the assignations] would be after work. When I was with my wife, Diane and I were together eight hours a day at work and two more after—on the average."

Jagger stresses that this is a married man, who lied to his good and faithful wife all the while he seduced Jagger's vulnerable client.

The defense attorney elicits answers that show Lew actually likes children, inferring that the State's purported motive—that Diane shot her children so that Lew would come back to her—is patently ridiculous. Lew counters that he never wanted to have his *own* children. Diane had always said she didn't need him to be the father of her family. Yes, once he'd said: "Maybe I could give it a try—"

"You see her as being just incredibly in love with you?" Jagger asks, sarcasm heavy in his voice.

"Yes sir."

"She told you she loved you at least twenty times a day?"

"Yes sir."

Just before Diane left for Oregon, Lew testifies he told her that Nora simply wouldn't give him a divorce—not until "she was good and ready."

"What was Diane's reason for leaving Arizona and going to Oregon?"

"So that I could make some decision about leaving my wife and going to Oregon."

Jagger hammers at Lew. Wasn't Diane's moving away without any fuss at all the ultimate fair play—strange behavior for a woman who told Lew she loved him twenty times a day, for a woman Lew characterized as so incredibly in love with him?

"Yes sir."

"Were you aware of any other intimate relationships Diane Downs had while she was involved with you?"

"No sir."

(And, indeed, Lew was not aware of her later affairs. He did not know how quickly Diane had bedded down with Cord Samuelson.)

Lew Lewiston is on the witness stand most of Wednesday. The tangled debris that he and Diane had made of their affair, his marriage, her children's lives, was laid out for the jury—and the gallery—in meticulously painful detail. Lewiston, a man who hates dissension, had found that once he began with Diane, there was nothing *but* dissension in his life.

He admits that he worried after the shooting that Diane or the police might implicate him as a suspect, adding that later his biggest fear was that Diane might come gunning for him or, worse, for Nora. "I was afraid that if Diane could shoot these children, the only other obstacle in her way would be my wife—that's why I made the tapes."

Sitting there in his gray-blue suit, his pale blue shirt, navy tie, and beige boots, this bearded witness resembles more a wealthy rancher than a mailman, the ex-lover of an accused murderess. Lewiston has made no effort to paint himself any more honorable than he is. He will not forgive himself. He will never believe that he is not in some way responsible for what has happened. Perhaps allowing himself to be so mercilessly exposed in this courtroom is an unconscious penance. There is a gritty honesty in the man's description of a time in his life that was less than honest.

It is finally over, and Lewiston steps gratefully down from the stand. As he heads for the doors, he is—for the time it takes to draw a quick breath—within two feet of Diane.

Surely, she must turn and watch him walk away.

She does not turn around at all. And still, when the doors shut behind him, she flinches almost imperceptibly. So many, many, times Diane feared that Lew had left her. This time, he was gone.

Really gone.

"When I finished testifying," Lew remembers, "and I was walking down the street, these two women drove by. Now, I was thinking I was invisible. I didn't know anyone in Eugene—except the detectives and the DA, and . . . Diane. We just wanted to get on a plane and go home. I didn't realize I was public property. People recognized me.

"These women yelled out the window, 'Way to go, Lew! Way to go!' It was so strange—just cheering for me, like that. Like it didn't matter about the kids . . . It made us want to get out of there and go home even more."

CHAPTER 40

The court clerk begins to play the tapes on Thursday morning. There are twenty-five tapes, some of them over two hours long. The proliferation of tapes is in direct proportion to the loquaciousness of the defendant. It is a kind of black farce. The detectives taped their interviews with Diane. She recorded her own tapes to double-check their tapes. Lew taped her phone calls to give to the police. Diane taped Lew because she didn't really trust him. And, in between, she carried on a running taped diary.

As the jurors are each handed a hugely thick black binder full of tape transcripts—so that they may follow the printed word as they listen to the spoken voices—it looks as though the trial will last the whole summer through.

Reporters pull out fresh yellow legal pads, scribbling frantically; the gallery settles back to listen.

Diane has heard all of the tapes. She was a participant in them to begin with, and through the defense's rights of discovery, she has listened to copies of the tapes. Even so, how humiliating to have to sit still and listen to your own voice, unguarded, unaware—sometimes manipulative and wheedling, sometimes sobbing, sometimes angry, sometimes throaty with unspent passion—played back in a courtroom.

Diane doesn't like her voice. It is a pretty, feminine voice, although she talks so fast that she often sounds like a 33⅓ LP record played at 78 speed. It is impossible to picture her as the shy child she describes.

On the Lew-tapes, he is unresponsive to Diane's constant calls, to her breathy declarations of love. Can't she hear that? Why did she bat herself against such an inhospitable source of warmth—like a moth with one wing paralyzed by the glow? Did she truly not recognize the goodbye in his voice?

Days later, we are almost finished. It is the last of the last—the hardball interview—which requires hours to hear. No one wiggles. No one coughs.

"You know this person?" Welch's voice asks finally.

"Yes I do . . . and I'm leaving because I do. Goodbye!"

The jury looks puzzled. Why would Diane keep that information to herself?

The State has called thirty-three witnesses; four hundred twenty-eight items of evidence have been logged. On the last day of May, 1984, Fred Hugi steps aside. The prosecution rests.

"Diane Downs!"

He's going to let her on the stand. The moment she gets on the witness stand, the door is opened to questions from Fred Hugi. Diane doesn't care. She *has* to explain.

She makes her way to the witness stand, a bit more ponderous than on the first day of the trial, her slender ankles seem too delicate to support her gravid belly. Diane wears a navy blue print tent dress, with a ruffled white bodice. She looks very young and very sweet.

She gives her age, twenty-eight, her birthdate, August 7, 1955.

"How do you feel?" Jagger begins.

"Scared . . ." she answers in a high, light voice.

"Anything else?"

"Glad to finally be here—it's been a long wait. Scared—and anxious to finally have a chance to say what really happened."

"What does 'control' mean to you—the word 'control'?" Jagger asks suddenly.

"Control is just you don't show emotion. You don't show you're hurting or people may hurt you more."

"You really believe that?"

"Yes."

"Are you a trusting person?"

"No . . . it depends on the person, I think."

"Do you like that part of you?"

"No, you don't find many friends . . . You go out of your way to trust certain people and you get hurt worse . . . You don't like people telling you what to do—anyway I don't."

Diane's favorite poem is the one about how easy she is to read—the one ending, "Speak of me as *you* find." But all through the prosecution's case, she has smiled and laughed at inappropriate moments. If the jury goes with her poem's sentiment, Diane doesn't have a prayer. Jagger attempts now to draw out a frightened little girl from behind the insolent mask.

Is she aware, he asks, that—even as he questions her—she is smiling?

"No. It's not supposed to be there." But now Diane laughs aloud.

"Why?" Jagger asks. Why is she laughing?

She blames her father. "You had to sit or stand and listen. Don't smile. Don't cry. You end up mirroring what's on his face. You learn not to have any face at all."

"You realize this is real serious," Jagger reminds her.

"Yes *Yes.*" She is impatient.

"But you say that with a *laugh.*"

"They're two emotions that are closely related. I've really never been allowed to cry—so I laugh. I know it's serious."

And, again, she laughs.

Perhaps she *cannot* help it. Perhaps she really doesn't know about the face the world sees.

Diane tells the jury about her early life—her bullying father, her mother who dared not defy him. She has always considered her father an intruder into her life. Her parents, potential witnesses, are, of course, not in the courtroom as she discusses them. They are barred until after they testify.

No, she never confided to her mother about the incest, the fumblings and fondlings in the night when she was twelve.

"I didn't tell anyone until I was sixteen."

Her enmity toward Wes Frederickson laces everything Diane says. "Because of my dad, I can't stand to be touched by dominating men."

Jagger asks her to discuss control.

"I didn't like it, and I've always been controlled by somebody else until I got my divorce. I vowed I'd never be controlled again!"

"Do you like to control others?"

"No. It can't be done. Or I'd be dehumanizing them. Just to gain control over yourself is enough. People say I like to control and manipulate—but I don't . . . I thought my dad was a terror—but he was Santa Claus compared to Steve."

"At the time they [the incest incidents] were occurring, how would you cope?"

"Blank out. It just didn't exist. I didn't exist. It's like a nightmare. Not real."

She explains she never cried or fought back. Her father was the authority figure. She could not resist him. And she could not tell.

"And so Steve dominated you later—did you remain quiet?"

"No. We'd fight. I'd end up getting hurt worse. I would almost fight until he choked me, and if I blanked out, and lay there, he said I was crazy."

"In response to your father, did you feel you had the opportunity to run away?"

"Yes and no. I packed my bags five times . . ."

"Immediately after the shooting," Jagger continued, "you indicated on the tape that . . . was one of the most rational times of your life. Is that true?"

"No. It's easier to look back and see things as they really were."

"Why do that?" [Why tell the detectives she was rational?]

"I'm a Twinkie inside. I'm soft. I try not to let others see. I don't like people to think I'm soft or weak."

Jagger asks her about the incident in September of 1982 when she scratched at her face and shot through the floor of her trailer.

"I turned my anger inside—because you can't strike out at other people—so you hurt yourself."

"You never struck out at your father?"

Diane seems appalled at the thought. "N-o-o-oo."

"When people batter you with questions, what do you do?"

"You go inside yourself. That's the same as blanking out. You're screaming—shut up inside. At some point, you can't contain it, and it comes out."

"Did your father show softness, tenderness, or caring?"

"No."

"Mother?"

"When I was little."

"Steve?"

"When we were dating. Miraculously, it stopped on our wedding day."

"Your children?"

Diane's face glows. "Kids are different from other people. From the time they're born, they cry for you; they need you. They don't ask for anything in return."

Jagger asks her who had the children during those bad times their ex-neighbor, Dan Sullivan, had testified about—when the kids were barefoot in the cold, and hungry.

"Steve did. I'm glad that came out. Steve would leave them alone for two hours!"

"Who were you living with then?"

"Myself."

Steve had the children from September, 1982, until the middle of January, 1983. But, Diane insists, when she had the youngsters, they were always properly clothed, and in bed by eight.

"I was pregnant. We all went to bed by eight."

"What kind of a parent were you?"

"The first year, I was learning—the next few years, I was a bad parent. Steve and I would fight, and Steve would walk out the door. Then Christie would come sit by me and I'd yell at her. Cheryl was into everything, and I was always screaming at her."

"What did you do about being a bad parent?"

"Stopped it."

"Did you realize that things Steve and your father did might have affected you?"

"Yes."

They talk about Diane's essay on child abuse. She wrote it in July of 1982 because, "It was important. People don't have a right to do things to other people—especially children." Diane lowers her eyes modestly. "—I'm not a public speaker . . ."

She felt better after writing the paper—it had helped her. "Even though I wasn't the kind of mother who beat her kids with a two by four—but I wanted to say it."

Jagger has done well—showing a woman from a loveless home, sexually molested by her own father, terrorized by her own husband, pushed around and abused until she'd freaked out and struck out at her babies. But *she* had caught herself in time. She even tried to stop other parents' abuse with her essay. This is a good person, but a woman whose emotions have long ago frozen inside—somewhere back behind her derisive little laugh, her irritating smirk.

"I can only see me from the inside," Diane tells the jury. "I don't know how other people see me. I only know how *I* feel."

Now, after all Diane has already endured, the State has taken her surviving children away and is trying to send *her* to prison for something a maniacal stranger did to them all.

Diane admits she doesn't remember everything about that night, about going to the hospital, but she remembers there was no one to help her. Her memory of May 19 is spotty; some things are crystalline—others obscured.

She remembers filling out the insurance forms—but she can't recall telling Judy Patterson that the gunman had shot through the window. She hadn't wanted to leave her wounded children and go back out to the scene—but "a nurse knelt and put her hand on my knee and said, 'One might not make it,' and I thought I might as well go . . . everyone was telling me to go—so that insurance statement was blurted out."

"Wasn't that stupid to say?" Jagger asks.

"I say lots of stupid things. I'm practiced."

Of course she had cried at the hospital. She'd begun to cry when her mom showed up in the little lounge next to the trauma room. She remembers coming back from the scene to have her arm treated. Dick Tracy and

Doug Welch were there. When she first got back, someone told her one little girl was in surgery, but that Danny would be OK.

"They didn't mention the other little girl. Doug said, 'Did you know Christie died?' I screamed at Doug—I was angry—sad because Christie wasn't the one who was doing badly . . . I was afraid that if Christie was dead, then Cheryl would die too, and I'd lose both of them.'"

There is a definite pattern in Jagger's direct examination of Diane Downs. He does not stay with a particular line of questioning for long. Whenever Diane begins to smile, he quickly switches to questions about her childhood, or introduces pictures of her children. Jagger is using Pavlovian signals. He has to remind Diane not to laugh. He cannot tie a string to her ankle and tug on it—he uses pictures and questions to pull her back. She has taken scores of pictures of her children. Christie at eight months with the cat, Christie at three months, laughing. Fred Hugi quickly picks up on the reason for the photographs. The wash of sadness that sweeps across Diane's face is instantaneous whenever Jagger hands her a new picture to identify, like turning on a switch.

"I felt like standing up and saying, 'The State will stipulate that every time Diane is handed a photo, she will look deeply moved and concerned. Now, let's get on with the trial,'" Hugi says.

Jagger asks a question that would seem a given: "Did you develop a real deep love for those children?"

"Yeah."

"Did you ever develop a love for any man —like Lew—to pick him over the children?"

"That's ridiculous."

More pictures are introduced: Christie trying to eat right-handed; Danny and his sisters; Christie, two years old on a farm.

"Do you miss the children now?"

"Yes—very much."

Diane details the outrages perpetrated on her injured family.

Jagger tenses; if he doesn't leap in at the right moment, Diane slides away on a tangent, just as she always has with detectives.

She explains that she yelled at the deputies in the ICU because of her concern for Christie's elbow. Christie had two bullet holes in her chest, a stroke in the left brain, a hole through her left hand—yet her mother's main concern is for her elbow.

"Her right elbow was really bad. She wasn't scheduled for physical therapy. When she was shot the first time, she raised up. When she was shot the second time, she fell. I was concerned that she'd snapped a tendon."

Diane goes back to the moment in the hospital when she'd had the worst news of all. But even in an hour's testimony, her story has changed. She no longer blames Doug Welch for breaking the news.

"They told me Christie had died. I flipped out. I sat there mourning for Christie and for Cheryl too. Then they said Cheryl had died. I said, 'Both?' And they said, 'No, Christie is alive.' I felt like a traitor because I'd been mourning for Christie and when they said it was Cheryl who was dead, I felt like Cheryl was standing there in the room, saying, 'Didn't you love me, Mom?'"

Diane suddenly begins to cry. For the first time in the long trial, she appears to be mortified. She apologizes for her tears and pulls herself back together with a smile almost at once.

There are more pictures of the kids in the afternoon session: the girls together; Christie with hair in her face; Cheryl grinning at the camera. So many pictures of the children that the A through Z designations are used up, and now the photos are lettered Exhibits AA through ZZ.

Diane smiles happily as she thumbs through and identifies photos.

"You're smiling," Jagger reminds her.

"It makes me feel good to look at them. Those were the good days."

"Your children are handicapped?" Jagger asks later in the day.

"Yes. But I want them back. That doesn't change their hearts—that doesn't change their minds."

Jim Jagger jumps into the center of the State's motive theory. Had she loved Lew that much—

"Yes, I loved Lew—even after the shooting," she answers, cutting her lawyer off in midsentence.

"Assume you believed the children were standing between you and Mr. Lewiston . . ."

Diane shakes her head vehemently. Lew was the original man who didn't like trouble, kinks. "I loved Lew," she sighs. "But he was a lot of work—a lot of trouble . . . I loved him, but talk about a headache . . ."

She had left Arizona for Oregon simply to get away from her old life. Not to force Lew into making a decision—only to begin again.

Why does she say that?

She has to remember that her first diary is in evidence, all of her plaintive letters, her aching loneliness and growing sexual need for Lew documented in her own handwriting. At this point in the trial—over the long Memorial Day weekend—the jurors have already *read* them. She cannot obliterate them with words.

And still Diane describes Lew as a headache—too much work to bother with.

Fred Hugi had had a good reason to read so many of Diane's own writings in his opening statement, his dispassionate voice adding a touch of irony to the letters.

To Lew—this man she now denies so forcefully and had written from Oregon in the weeks before Cheryl died:

> *You and I make each other very happy. We fit together so well. Yet you say you are willing to discard all that happiness because of my children. That is foolish. You've said all your life that you can't live with kids. But how do you know if you can do it or not? You've never done it.*
>
> *Even you admit that I have good kids. They are obedient and well-behaved. I know that you are concerned about living in a little two bedroom apartment with three kids, but I've told you that by the end of August I would have a huge house to get lost in.*
>
> *The Nanny will take the responsibility for most of the kids' spare time, and I'm sure you wouldn't go stark raving mad spending a couple of hours a night with them.*
>
> *If it ever got to be too much, you could go upstairs and watch TV or we could. But I just find it so hard to accept that you would throw away our good feelings because of a fear that has never been proved...*
>
> *I'll always be waiting for you. I'll always say yes.*

Too much work to bother with?

Do you remember how we used to snuggle up in your easy
chair? I miss that so bad. It was so nice to watch TV at night and
get all lazy before bed. Then you would tuck me in and give me
such a warm, loving kiss.

I love you, Lew, and you truly loved me. I miss waking up in
the morning and making love before breakfast. We were so
happy . . . Why?

She denies him now, as if she had never written that agonized, plaintive "*Why?*" All she's ever wanted was her kids. She sounds very convincing. Her words are right, but expressions flicker unwarranted across her
features. Sometimes she wears one face, and sometimes another. And
often, as she herself has described it, Diane seems "to wear no face at all."
The courtroom artists, working briskly with their clutch of colored pencils, find no expression to capture. Their renderings emerge curiously
empty of any sense of feeling—as if they had tried to draw a ghost.

Diane will spend an unprecedented four and a half days on the witness
stand. She explains her entire life. She corrects, modifies, sets straight,
and smooths over things done (or not done) for the jury.

Diane tells *everything.*

With Jagger's indulgence, she recalls how much fun they had on the
beach trip a week before Cheryl died. She explains that is why Christie
was confused about *when* she'd heard "Hungry Like the Wolf."

"There were only six thousand miles on the car before the murder. We
had four tapes: 'The Beat,' 'Saga,' 'Men at Work,' and the one with 'Hungry
Like the Wolf.' We played the tapes constantly. We must have played Duran Duran's tape for about four thousand miles."

"Did you have any guns—"

"I brought two guns to Oregon—the .22 rifle and the .38 revolver. The
.38 had cream color with brown carving on the handle . . . We took Danny's
kite to the beach . . . the .38 was in the trunk in clear view. They [the chil-
dren] were in and out of the trunk all day. The .22 rifle was in the bedroom
closet. It probably had no bullets in it."

Diane agrees absolutely with Jim Pex that a tape will not play with the
keys out. Christie must have only *thought* she heard "Hungry Like the

Wolf" during the shooting. "It's impossible. When the keys are out of the ignition, the tape player's off."

Jagger asks Diane if she is aware that she "unnerved" some of the spectators in the courtroom by her reaction to the song.

She smiles. "That tape has no bad connotations. That tape was Cheryl's favorite tape. It can't make me feel bad—I'm sorry." Of course she realizes that she grinned and tapped her foot and sang along. "I was just being me."

But when she speaks of telling Christie that Cheryl was dead, Diane begins to cry again. She blushes. Talking about illicit sex does not faze her; expressions of grief do. She hurries along with her story: "That's when we decided the unicorn was Cheryl. Unicorns are magic. They never go away . . . The unicorn says 'Christie, Cheryl, Danny, I love you, Mom' . . . That was for the kids. They had a new free lease on life in Oregon. It was a new beginning."

Why—on the night of May 19—had she voiced her regret about buying the unicorn to Deputy Rutherford?

"I said, 'I shouldn't have bought the unicorn, and maybe none of this would have happened. I meant that all the freedom, the unity— Maybe I was getting too arrogant, and God was slapping me in the face. The names engraved for all eternity was too arrogant—for the Baptists, *God's* first. I put my children first."

She has touched on the essence of this endless trial. If Diane truly put her children above all other considerations, then she had had no reason to shoot them. If, as her letters and tapes suggested, her obsession with Lew was paramount, the State's case looked good.

It would take a modern day Medea—a monstrous excuse for a mother—not only to shoot the three children of her own womb but to continue to play the martyred mother, to portray herself as a long-suffering victim and not a killer.

Or it would take someone who had learned to blank out the ugly segments of her past, and believe that they had never happened.

CHAPTER 41

Another weekend interrupts the flow of the trial. Will Diane be back? Or has she been spirited away to give birth?

She is not here. The bailiff looks solemn. That must be it; the strain of testifying has brought labor on early. The gallery is restive, disappointed.

"I didn't wait in that line to see nothing!" someone complains bitterly.

Suddenly Diane appears, rubbing her wrists as if her handcuffs were too tight. She is still with us, but she looks ghastly. Very tired. Very sad. Always before, she has walked into the courtroom confidently. She only shrugs now as the bailiff instructs her to go directly to the witness stand.

The vibrant hue of her cherry-red dress accentuates her pallor. Diane has learned that the child in utero is not hers, but the State's. "The Lane County juvenile court judge has ordered them to take my baby—the one who's not even born yet. I won't even get to see it. I'm angry and depressed—but I'm gonna fight."

From now on, Diane will cradle her belly more often. They cannot rip it from her womb. It is as if she has vowed to stay pregnant. If she does not deliver the baby, they cannot take it away.

Jim Jagger moves to begin again with questions. Diane sighs and picks up her life at age twenty-two: the abortion of Steve's baby, his vasectomy, her realization at the Right-to-Life booth, her rape by her boss, her seduction of Danny's father, her triumphant pregnancy with the baby that became Danny, her surrogate pregnancy...

From time to time, a juror blinks and shakes her head.

Jagger returns to the aftermath of the shooting. Yes, Diane may have asked about going to work the day after the shooting. She *always* showed up for work.

"I don't know ... it was a crazy night."

"That's a light phrase," Jagger reminds her. "Some people might not understand . . ."

"No . . ." she rephrases rapidly. "It was a *nightmare*. I'm in a dream I can't wake up from."

Jagger asks her about her feelings that night—in the hospital.

"Scared—stripped of all my power. I've always been able to control things—so my kids were happy, healthy, well-fed. They weren't listening to me. They [sic] threw Danny over [his] shoulder. I felt invisible. They kept throwing me out of the room . . . all the cops, asking questions . . .

"They kept asking me how tall he was, and what he looked like. If they'd just gone out there with a tape measure and caught him, then they would've known how tall he was."

Diane accuses the hospital of crippling Danny. A nurse deliberately picked him up, causing the paralysis. "This might not be the time for revenge—but I hope she burns.

"I believe in God," Diane explains somberly. "And He'll give you anything you ask him. Danny will walk. I know he will."

Diane's recall of the night in the ER room is completely at odds with the memories of the medical staff.

"They kept comin' up with real whoppers. They threw me out six times. I got up off the table and they pushed me down. I never saw Cheryl until she was in her coffin. I still haven't really accepted it—like they're all in foster homes, or maybe they're all dead."

She didn't have the .22 pistol—she'd given it back to Steve. She wasn't even sure how to load or unload that anyway. "If I never hear about another .22 handgun again as long as I live, I'll be in heaven!"

"How do you feel about talking about it today?" Jagger asks quickly.

"Oh . . . I want to talk about it. I want to get it cleared up."

All she remembers of the shooter and the gun he held is an impression that the man was a "leftie" and that the gun was shiny.

"How do you feel about talking about the attack?"

"Sadness predominates. But I've told the story so many times now, much of the pain is gone."

Diane talks—on and on and on—inserting a stone in the mosaic of her life—and the crime—here, and a bit of colored glass there, identifying more pictures of her children.

The courtroom is filled with women. Most of the jurors are female. Diane tells her story to other women who have given birth and made do with too little money while wrestling with diapers, colic, chicken pox, and cleaning up vomit. Most have had less-than-perfect husbands. Most have suffered disappointments in love and in life. You can read it on their faces, a silent judgment. *If that had been me . . .*

The women of the jury seldom take their eyes off Diane.

Finally, Diane and her attorney have come to the summer of 1982. Diane talks about Lew, and her confidences are so intimate that she might well be talking to a girlfriend.

Harm her children for love of Lew? It made Diane feel like laughing. "The two have nothing to do with each other."

What about the nanny? The big house? Jagger presses.

"Maybe 'governess' is a better word. I don't know—*Hazel,*" Diane giggles. "The vision of the house got bigger the worse Steve got. I guess it was an escape."

Jim Jagger puts the finishing touches on the portrait of the little family who had had it all. Who hadn't needed a father to make them happy.

In Oregon, Diane and the kids loved to explore. "It's fun to drive through all those streets on the hill above the park, and get lost trying to find your way out. The kids liked that. They thought they were lost—which we *were*—but I never told them that."

Yes, Diane had gone back once to Chandler—but only to return Lew's gold chain personally. "He told me not to take it off for anything—'You're my woman' and all that mushy stuff. I gave him my word. And we all know what my word means, I think—"

In Chandler, Diane had called Steve.

"I had a couple of drinks so I could tolerate Steve. I spent the night at his place. Steve and his friends were doing coke."

After a few more drinks, she had fallen asleep.

Jagger urges her to expand on the events of that night at Steve's. Diane looks down, hesitant.

"Were you intimate with Steve that evening?" Jagger pushes.

"Do I have to answer that under oath?"

Jagger nods.

"I woke up cold, naked, and in pain. My mouth tasted horrible. I had a fuzzy head. I ran a cold bath. I can only remember coming out of a deep, deep darkness and I was crying. I heard Jeff yelling, 'Steve, leave her alone; she doesn't even know what's happening!' Jeff didn't help me, and I passed out again. When Steve took me to the airport the next day, he asked me, 'Do you remember making love last night?' I said, 'No.' And he said, 'Too bad because we had fun.'"

Why hadn't she taken a cab to a motel? Why had she called Steve Downs to pick her up at the airport in the first place? Past experience had taught her there might be trouble.

Fred Hugi notes the incongruity; he scrawls something on the legal pad in front of him.

The time has come to go over the night of May 19 in detail. Diane sounds tired as she recites the story again. The trip to Heather's, driving under the dark trees to the mobile home.

"I feel that I'm relating something over and over and over—

"The kids were in the car and we talked through the window [after they'd petted the horse]. She asked me if Lew was coming and I said, No, he wasn't."

They left Heather's at ten minutes to ten.

She has shaved ten minutes off Heather's estimate. How can she explain the entire twenty-five missing minutes between leaving Heather's and arriving at McKenzie–Willamette Hospital?

She went back the way she'd come, south along Sunderman. But she'd turned away from town at the intersection with Marcola Road, thinking she would find the pass where Deerhorn Road went past a waterfall. But then, though Cheryl was still "babbling away," she realized that Christie and Danny had probably fallen asleep.

"I pulled off to debate where I'd go."

Diane remembers talking to Cheryl: "We talked about school, about her bloody noses. I said the next day she had off, we'd go to an ear-nose-and-throat specialist. She wanted to go for a ride still. But she was pretty easy. She was going to take the unicorn to school the next day.

"We stayed parked there for a while, and then Cher curled up on the front floorboard. I pulled the seat back for her—and she covered herself with my postal sweater. She was on her left side, in a fetal position. I was looking in my checkbook 'cause I had to buy school lunch tickets that next week."

Diane has just about filled in the missing time. But is it believable? Why would she stop along a lonely road—in the dark after 10:00 P.M.—to balance a checkbook when they were only fifteen or twenty minutes from home? This testimony is the first time she has ever mentioned the checkbook.

Jagger asks her when she remembered it.

"I *always* remembered—but the detectives didn't ask specific questions."

After she put her checkbook away, she headed the red car back down Marcola toward Springfield. She turned off onto Old Mohawk, a soft right turn. There was a house on the right.

"I saw a man in the middle of my lane, flagging me down with his left hand . . . my thought was 'He's a leftie—and he's in trouble . . . No—he's got too much energy to be in trouble.' I stopped rather quickly. None of the kids woke up. I looked to see. I took the keys with me—a standard safety precaution."

"How did you feel about the police who doubted you?"

"It made me angry. It made me feel a disbelief in myself. Do I remember what I think I remember?"

But Polly Jamison has helped her to feel secure with her own memory.

"I felt like I was going crazy back then. I really didn't know what was real and what wasn't real."

Diane began revising her original story because of the dreams she was having. It was easier for her to believe that there had been two men—rather than just one—because it helped her convince herself that there had been nothing at all she could have done to save her children.

"How do you feel about going through the facts now?"

"I feel emotion—but not as strong. I'm scared. It was an ugly night—a crazy night. I still can't remember everything."

Jim Jagger stops his client repeatedly when she becomes defensive; he gives her a chance to expound on her feelings and memories, allows her to let logic dictate some of the sequences of that "crazy night."

"My own memory messed me up good," she says feelingly.

Diane takes a deep breath and continues more calmly. "I stopped the car. I looked around to see if the children were still asleep or awake. I opened the door, got out. He was standing at the point of the car door. He made a comment about wanting my car.

"I said, 'You've gotta be kidding.'"

Jagger cautions her, "Don't fill in, Diane."

"He shoved me back toward the back of the car—a few feet. I didn't fall. I had to catch myself. He moved toward the car. I looked in the window—and Christie was shot. It was almost simultaneous."

"You're not crying," Jagger offers quietly.

"No."

"Why?"

"There's nothing I can do about it now."

Diane's attorney comes finally to the end of his direct examination. Jim Jagger asks Diane, "You didn't shoot your kids, and you didn't cause anyone else to shoot your kids, did you?"

"No, I did not."

Fred Hugi rises slowly and walks toward Diane. It is one year and twelve days since their brief meeting in the corridor outside the intensive care unit of McKenzie-Willamette, that moment when she assured him that no one would beat her.

The time has come for cross-examination.

Hugi is ready. He has thought about this confrontation a thousand times, ten thousand times—at night, driving, during the lunch breaks while he sat alone in the little park across from the courthouse sipping a milkshake.

Adrenaline heightens Hugi's senses and blocks out the pain in his tooth. At last, Diane sits there on the witness stand. It is his turn.

He expects no major revelation. "We knew Diane was not going to confess on the stand. The goal of cross-examination was to try to let the jury see her under some stress—to see her convoluted reasoning, inconsistencies, the improbability of her story . . . to show the development of her antisocial personality."

It is going to require infinite patience, and Hugi knows he risks alienating the jury. Jagger did that when he pushed too far with Christie. Christie is handicapped by her age and disability, but Diane is pregnant. She looks fragile—not at all like the suntanned hardy woman she was last year.

Only her eyes are the same.

Fred Hugi has a narrow path to walk.

At all cost, he has vowed to appear courteous and reasonable. He will not respond with hostility unless Diane deliberately provokes him. His goals are modest. He wants only to expose what lies beneath Diane's facade; he is quite willing to settle for a "few small victories and not get carried away with myself. After all, this isn't a high-school debate."

Diane waits for him now on the stand, full-blown with child, faint pastel circles beneath her huge eyes. It is apparent that she holds Fred Hugi in low esteem.

Occasionally, as Hugi questions Diane, he glances toward the gallery, but his eyes never really focus on anyone. All his energy is directed toward Diane. He respects the mind behind the mask. In no way does he underestimate her.

Fred Hugi too begins far back in Diane's life. The mosaic is about to be rearranged once more, flooded with a different light. He speaks to her as gently as if she is a child, his voice kind and interested.

And still Jagger objects; he wants Hugi to sit down while he questions Diane.

Fortunately, Foote overrules him. Hugi has stood to question witnesses the entire trial; he is more comfortable thinking on his feet.

"Let's go back to your childhood. Was it happy? Was it sad?"

"Sad . . . lonely."

"Why was that?"

"Because my father was quite strict—intimidating—and my mother remained in the background."

"You tried to interact?"

"No."

"You tried to please?"

"Of course."

"How?"

"I was obedient."

"You were a good student?"

"I got good grades . . . I hated lecturing by my father."

"You were frustrated at home?"

"Yes."

"Angry?"

"No." There. She has stopped him. She smiles. She wasn't angry, and he couldn't make her say it.

Unfazed, Hugi asks about the incestuous incidents between Diane and her father. "Could you be specific?"

"I'd prefer not to . . . it continued for approximately a year."

He asks her to explain.

She sighs. "Specifically?"

"Yes."

"Talking, touching, being told not to tell anyone—at my father's hand, in my house, in different rooms. The others were sleeping. My mother was working. In the car . . . there was fondling, touching of my chest—I had no breasts then—and other parts of my body where little kids aren't to be touched. I blanked it out . . ."

Her life is so sad, her problems as a child seemingly so overwhelming— and Hugi's voice so soft—that it is easy to forget that *this* is the prosecutor, not the defense attorney.

Yet, if one listens very carefully, certain words and attitudes are being elicited from the defendant. She talks often of being trapped, of being depressed, suicidal, reclusive, rejected. Fred Hugi is showing the jury a woman who has spent years absorbing the motivation to murder—a sponge storing up rage.

Diane is obviously intelligent, but she has blind sides. She cannot see where Hugi is going.

Her married life certainly *sounds* like hell. "I couldn't make it on my own, and I wanted children. It was a case of either staying with my parents and scratching my face or going off with 'Evil Steve.'"

"Your whole life has been stressful?" Hugi asks quietly.

"Not all," she blurts cheerfully. "We haven't even gotten to the good part yet!"

Hugi reads from the *Washington Post* and from her essay on surrogate parenting.

Suddenly, Fred Hugi has led Diane into more dangerous waters, and she has not seen it coming. She was too busy talking.

How was it that she found a suitable sperm donor for Danny? She explains that she really "liked" Russ.

"But I set it up so he wouldn't know about the pregnancy. I got pregnant for me—and my kids. I didn't have many feelings about how a prospective father would feel."

Hugi's tone has the thinnest veneer of sarcasm: "Your whole goal then was to 'interact' with these children?"

"I still wish that I could someday get married and have a husband who would interact with his child."

"Were you getting what you needed from your children?" Hugi asks rhetorically.

Apparently not. There were men in her life. She is quite willing to talk about past lovers. She divorced Steve, worked full-time at the Chandler post office, and met Mack Richmond.

"You flirted with him?"

"I flirt with everybody."

"Were there temper tantrums?" [On Diane's part.]

"Very much so!"

"What brought that on?"

"Mack and his wife. I couldn't stand the way they treated their kids."

Suddenly, Diane lifts her head. She has picked up on a change in the wind, aware at long last that Fred Hugi is not as innocuous as she thought—but she relaxes again. She finds him hostile, but a bumbler who misses the points she is trying to make. Diane is condescending with Fred Hugi. If he wants to talk about her lovers, it's fine with her. She has definite opinions on sex—about the fine points that differentiate dating, friendship, and sex. She "loved them all" though.

To expedite matters, she offers to list all of her lovers, the circumstances of their meeting, the details of the affairs. The press row waits—pencils poised—

Hugi demurs.

Diane still manages to slip most of the names in as her testimony flows. The press row keeps count; the roster grows longer.

"It ended up with Lew Lewiston?" Hugi presses on.

"No, I can't say that it did."

"Any others as intense?"

"How? You mean the cards and letters?"

"No—the intensity of the *emotion*."

She laughs harshly. "Lew was the only one dumb enough to tell his wife we were having an affair!"

Diane flushes frequently, the now-familiar wave of red suffusing her throat, but she never stops talking, detailing her affair with Lew, and her struggle to wrest him free of his uncooperative wife.

Even after Diane has denied that Lew means very much to her, she defines "heart love" as the only love that really matters. Heart Love carries with it no sexual connotations at all.

That was what she had found only with Lew, she tells Hugi.

Diane is amused remembering aloud how she was kicked out of Bible school for promiscuity. She is sad because she has always been lonely. The heller-vixen and the lonely child fight each other for a spot in the witness chair.

Guns and houses and men and relationships and even children have changed hands so often in Diane's life. She has not been able to hold on to anything.

Jim Jagger appears serene at the defense table. He cannot shut his client up; there seems no point in objecting. Diane is doing damage to herself, as Hugi hoped she would. He has opened the floodgates. He has only to stand aside and let her talk. Jagger will have another chance on redirect. Possibly he can patch the worst damage then.

During recesses, Ray Broderick sits on one of the long benches outside the courtroom, doodling his endless cartoons on the small pad he always carries. His humor is sometimes macabre, usually pun-oriented. Today, he draws an awestruck crowd gazing up as a woman floats down in billowing greatcoat and bonnet, clinging to her umbrella. And the crowd shouts in horror, "Wait—it's not Mary Poppins! It's Diane Downs!"

Cartoons—only some of them from Broderick's hand—have surfaced from time to time. At the CSD office, someone has tacked up a mimeographed copy of a cartoon drawn by an anonymous artist. It portrays a very pregnant Diane Downs attempting to escape from jail. She holds a pistol to her belly, warning, "Stop or I'll shoot!"

But, still, Diane has her champions. There are regulars in the gallery who cannot make up their minds and who may well reflect the jurors' feelings. A sweet-faced woman with tears in her eyes talks to a reporter: "It's confusing. Sometimes I think she's guilty, and sometimes I just feel like going up and giving her a hug."

There is a tall, quiet man who says nothing more than that he believes Diane's testimony.

Wednesday morning. Hotter today. Really spring. Diane is wearing the royal blue dress with the pattern of gulls flying. It is her prettiest maternity outfit and looks expensive. She finally is forced to repeat some of her outfits; the trial is going on so long.

Diane has had all night to mull over her response to Fred Hugi's cross-examination. Jagger has pointed out to her that Hugi deliberately let her rattle on. She is not such an unknowing adversary this morning. She watches Hugi warily as he approaches the witness stand.

Hugi begins not with the night of the shooting but back with the incident in the Arizona desert—as if he is reading a book, has put it down for a spell, and must reread a few chapters to remind himself of the story. The jury has heard so much in the past three days; they need this catch-up.

Diane acknowledges her terror as she drove with her father into the desert. That was the very last time Wes touched her. She recalls that she screamed, "You're killing me!"

Diane explains to Fred Hugi that even when she's "crazy," she's "rational"—that she promotes herself as more rational than she is so that she will appear strong.

"That's not telling the truth then?" Hugi prods.

"OK."

"Were you angry at your mother?"

"No."

". . . for not protecting you?"

"Not really. She was just as trapped as I was. She wouldn't have believed me. I was just a little kid and he was a grown-up man."

"You believe people should believe a grown-up over a child?"

"Not necessarily."

Damn! He has zapped her again.

Hugi holds Diane's essay on child abuse in his hand. As he begins to question her about it, she offers to read it aloud. She is very proud of it, totally unaware of the damage it can do here. Hugi hands it to her. Diane has just offered the prosecution a coup.

She reads well, her voice strong as she cautions parents and grandparents that if they abuse their helpless children, the vicious circle will continue endlessly, twisting in upon itself and harming children yet unborn.

As Diane finishes, the courtroom is hushed.

". . . Remember the cycle—generation unto generation."

She turns to Hugi, a genius deigning to engage in conversation with a dolt.

"Do you understand it, Mr. Hugi? If you can stop the cycle—*I* stopped."

"Is that how you stopped the abuse—by *eliminating* an entire generation?" Hugi asks bluntly.

"No, Mr. Hugi, I did not . . . I have never sexually abused my children. If you stop the cycle, you stop the abuse." She snaps at him, annoyed. "Mr. Hugi, you irritate me! You're not listening. You're not listening—"

But of course, he is. Fred Hugi is listening to every word the witness says, to every inflection. He cares not the least how Diane lectures him.

Diane has also written papers on peer pressure and drugs, smoking, alcohol. "I felt I was lucky—that it was beneficial that I had no friends—no bad habits."

So soon, she has forgotten the warnings to beware of the prosecutor. Diane talks almost as freely with Fred Hugi as she has with Jim Jagger. At times, when she chides him, they seem to be the only two people in the room. From her mythical "seventh level" of intelligence she sees him far below.

She is woefully mistaken.

Hugi asks about her sexual problems with her husband. Had they been her father's fault too?

"No. Because it was fine before marriage. After, he'd come home at 3:00 A.M. from being out with friends and expected me to please him."

And now, they speak of the unicorn:

"I saw it in the window for a week in Cottage Grove and I thought that Cheryl would really like it—but no favorites. I thought 'Hey, this is our new start on life—something eternal.' It *was* wild and free—a unicorn is a type of horse and a horse is wild and free—"

"Have you ever studied what a unicorn means?"

"No," Diane answers. "I heard from a detective that it was 'magical.'"

"Things *did* change drastically in Oregon?" Hugi asks.

"Yes."

"He [Lew] wouldn't accept letters, cards—?

"... after a point."

"How long?"

"One and a half to two weeks after I got here . . . I was hurt . . . I wasn't devastated, 'cause I already had a male companion. Mr. Samuelson was a better substitute than Lew. Mr. Samuelson paid his own way!"

Substitute for what?

No, Diane replies, she did not confide to friends that Mr. Samuelson was not as good in bed as Lew. Yes, she had lied to Lew about not having other men, " 'cause men don't want to believe you're fooling around."

She will not admit that she longed desperately for Lew Lewiston. "He told me to write him every day. I really expected him . . . I took a lot of time to make him feel loved and secure. He was *never* the only one. To an extent—I made a commitment to Lew—but he wasn't my whole life. I even dated people *you* aren't aware of . . ."

What is Diane trying to do? It makes sense for her to make Lew Lewiston sound negligible, and hardly all-consuming. But why is she so eager to present herself as a trollop, greedy for sex—with lovers yet untold? Only yesterday, Diane was too shy to tell the jury that her ex-husband had done something sexually disgusting to her while she lay unconscious from alcohol and, perhaps, drugs.

Is it "power" again? Is it because Steve forced himself on her—and sex is only permissible when *she* is the one who chooses? Or is she still only trying to convince herself—and everyone listening—that she is no longer the ugly duckling, that she is pretty enough for men to want her?

Fred Hugi asks Diane about the letter diary. Why had she written all those longing letters—but not sent them?

"If I kept these letters of undying love, I could show them to Lew when he showed up here. I knew he would show up here one day, and I'd show him the letters."

It would be Diane's way to show Lew how much she'd missed him.

"They were lies then?" Hugi's questions are short—quick jabs to the gut, and as effective.

"They were 'untruths.' 'Lie' is a strong word—like 'hate.' Like saying 'hate' for 'dislike.' The fact is I do love him and I was also relaying my love for him. I simply overdramatized what was the truth."

"You've done that before," Hugi says quickly. "You've never been told you were a histrionic personality?"

"What?"

He has her. She doesn't know the meaning of this word. "You never heard the results of your psychological tests?"

"I've never heard that word."

Diane hastens to explain her diary. "If I loved him as much as I said in those letters, wouldn't I have sent them . . . or a telegram he could not refuse?"

"You did send them, and they were refused. You spent $200 for one day in Arizona to see Lew—"

"To return his chain . . . to see Lew . . . to see Jack."

She reminds Hugi that she got a hug and a kiss from Jack Lenta—not from Lew. She couldn't call Lew, because he and his wife had an unlisted number. She couldn't call Jack that night, because he was married—so she'd called Steve. She'd purchased a bottle of Jim Beam on the way from the airport. Her memory has cleared; she now recalls intercourse in the living room of Steve's place—and that she was moaning and calling Lew's name during the sex act. Her moaning had awakened Steve's roommate.

"Was this a rape—or some sort of sex crime?" Hugi asks.

"Yeah—that's a good way to put it."

"You got up in the morning, and had Steve drive you to the post office?"

"Yeah."

"You didn't report it?"

"Ha! I'm often the victim of a crime with Steve—" She sighs at her interrogator's reasoning. "Mr. Hugi, you can believe what you want. I know what happened. Steve knows what happened."

Diane's tone grows more sarcastic with each question. Fred Hugi is another man trying to exert his *power* over her; beating him has become more important than convincing the jury.

She has forgotten the jury.

"Do you know the words to Duran Duran's 'Hungry Like the Wolf'?"

"No. Usually not. With New Wave music, you listen to the music."

"They all have the same theme?"

"I don't know."

"Your activities with the children really started in the first week in May, didn't they?"

"No—since April 4th."

"They didn't surface in the letters [to Lew]."

"Only because the letters were to Lew—for Lew. The kids surfaced because they were becoming more important to me than Lew. I was losing interest in Lew. I was running out of things to say to Lew. How many things can you say to patronize someone?"

Fred Hugi reads to her from the letter-diary.

"It was a lot of mush," Diane responds. "Something you write to a man. If I felt that mushy all the time, I wouldn't be able to deliver my mail straight."

Undaunted, Hugi reads more of the purple prose aloud.

Diane responds. She is rude; she is insolent. Lew's doubts about kids weren't the only problem. Until now, she hasn't bothered to mention Lew's other excuses. She ticks them off on her long fingers: "Nora's scoliosis . . . Nora's folks' money . . . his guilt about leaving Nora after four years.

"Mr. Hugi, *all* of my boyfriends are married. How can you say I couldn't be comfortable with a man that loves another woman?"

The press row glances at the female jurors—all married.

Diane seems bored as Hugi reads from the psychiatric evaluation done in Kentucky—the reports that indicated major psychopathology, anxiety, and depression. She brushes them away with her hand.

"Those tests were done in 1981. They were Steve's fault . . . It's true [the test results]. I faced the problems. I got a divorce—and then I got pregnant with a surrogate baby."

It has grown so hot in the courtroom. Muggy, airless, more confining than ever; the press bench is one solid gel of bodies—the disembodied hands struggling to take notes one hundred miles an hour. The press has never heard a murder defendant reveal herself so nakedly on the witness stand.

A battle of titans continues, a dialogue between masters of debate—one trained, the other instinctual.

Fred Hugi suggests to Diane that she must have felt desperate when she found herself in Oregon without Lew. Trapped again.

"Circumstances can't trap you—people trap you."

Hugi peppers her with rapid fire questions about the night of May 19.

"You went to see Heather? Why?"

To take the clipping, of course—about the free horses.

"Was it dark?"

"No, Mr. Hugi—it was light."

"Were your headlights on?"

"No."

"When you left, were they on?"

"Yes."

"You couldn't have just called her—to tell her about the free horses?"

"She didn't have a phone."

"So you leave—and it's dark?"

"Yes."

"At Marcola Road, you go sightseeing in the dark?"

"Yes."

"Where?"

"The Deerhorn—"

She talks with Cheryl. She pulls off to work on her checkbook.

"You decided—"

"I didn't *decide*. I just did."

"How much time passes when you're pulled over?"

"How should I know?"

"Is this a dream or did it happen?" Hugi can match her sarcasm when he wants to.

"It happened."

"How long?"

"I can't tell you because you'll make a fact of it."

"A half hour?"

"NO!"

"A minute?"

"It was more than a minute."

Again, she goes over her little conversation with Cheryl, there as they were pulled over to the side of Marcola Road, while she balanced her checkbook. Diane remembers that they talked about Cheryl's new kitten too.

"OK. You're not sightseeing when you leave there. You're going back to town?"

"Yes."

"Was the tape playing?"

"Probably. It was always playing."

"How were you feeling?"

"Fine."

"Not depressed?"

"Why would I be depressed?"

"You decide to turn on Old Mohawk—a secluded road?"

"Yes. The road didn't look secluded to me."

"You saw a man in the road?"

"Yes."

"You had your three children with you; it was dark enough to have your headlights on. Yet, you decided to stop the car. Why is that?"

Diane shakes her head wearily and rolls her eyes. This is all so ridiculous. Patiently, bored, she explains it to him again. If someone was hurt she didn't want anyone to pick up the injured party and injure him further. So she couldn't just roll down the window. She'd taken the keys for the children's safety. What if Cheryl had tried to climb up on the seat and hit the gear shift?

He wants more details, and she sighs with exasperation.

"My goodness, Mr. Hugi! That was a year ago!"

"Not a very significant event in your life?"

"Not before—"

OK. Take it again. Five of the jurors are taking notes.

Why hadn't she pushed the man back?

Because she'd been caught off guard. "I've had no reason to doubt anyone."

Diane's description of her entire life has been one long saga of rejection and betrayal, but now she says she has never had reason to doubt anyone.

She'd seen Christie shot, because the dome light was on. What details might she remember, even after a whole year?

". . . the eye contact and the bullet holes . . ."

"You slammed the door on him?"

"No, Mr. Hugi. I did not."

Diane's yellow eyes are blazing. She is enraged with Fred Hugi. How dare he insinuate that she didn't really try to save her children? He is just like Doug Welch and Kurt Wuest were in that interview so long ago now. Her hatred for Hugi is palpable.

"Go ahead," she hisses. "Ask me another question."

"And then, he—"

"He asked for the car again."

Wonderingly, Hugi asks, "A car with three gun-shot kids in it?"

"Who can make sense out of an insane man?"

"Person—"

"Man—"

"*Person*—"

"*Man.*"

Tell it again, Diane. The stranger hits her hand with his gun; she deflects the gun. He demands the car again, and she fakes throwing the keys over her left shoulder with her right hand. He looks in that direction. She pushes him. She leaps into the car and leaves.

She recalls that her arm was hit (shot) when he was three or four feet away, but she somehow managed to get the key in the ignition and drive off before he could reach her.

"You never saw him again?"

"No, thank you. I have not."

"You drove fast?"

"I don't know, Mr. Hugi."

"Fast enough—as you said—for the car door to slam shut?"

"I guess—"

She recites the drive to the hospital by rote. She has told it so many, many times. The injured mother comforting her dying children.

"At the stoplight, I saw the towel around my arm—"

"You took care of yourself," Hugi cuts in.

"I did *everything* for those kids to try to save them! If I passed out, they wouldn't have a chance."

She cannot recall any car behind her, any lights in the dozens of houses she'd passed. She'd seen only a white fence. She had thought only of getting to the hospital.

She had known immediately that she had some blank spots but the detectives had pushed her to come up with something. "I think the detectives were unfair because they wouldn't accept what I didn't know."

Hugi reminds Diane that none of the hospital personnel had seen her shed a tear.

"Isn't that funny? I only saw the doctors ten minutes that night, and the nurses fifteen. I don't imagine they saw much of anything."

"You feel the hospital was responsible for the children [Cheryl] dying?"

"I only found out *here* how Cheryl died. She died almost instantly. She had clots in her throat. When they cleaned that out, all the blood came up from her lungs. She had heart wounds, spleen. There was no blood on the car carpet."

Diane is near tears now—but the tears are of rage and frustration.

After lunch, the courtroom is packed tighter than it was for the morning session—if possible. Diane resumes the witness stand, her now-flat eyes fixed on Fred Hugi.

"You ever suffer head injuries?" he begins. The State's psychiatrist, Dr. George Suckow, needs this information so that he can validate—or dismiss—the possibility that Diane suffers from amnesia, repression, memory loss, and/or unconscious transference when Hugi calls him as a rebuttal witness.

"Yes. When Steve and I were married. In the living room—in 1975."

"*This* night?" Hugi asks, referring to May 19, 1983.

"Nope."

"Ever wake up in a different place and not know how you got there?"

"Nope."

". . . but you had memory problems from the time of the shooting until you got to the hospital?"

"No."

"Your memory bad in the hospital—?"

"Yes."

"When does it get better?"

"The next morning when I woke up—I still had gaps and holes in my memory."

No, she does not remember that she described the suspect differently to Dick Tracy and to Rob Charboneau.

Hugi pounds her with questions. How could the shooter know the children were there inside the car? Was he walking into the headlights? Could he see?

"I wasn't inside his head."

She cannot remember where the shooter stood—inside—outside—his arm through a window . . .

"Mr. Hugi, your people wanted everything to be exact."

"You were being pressured?"

"Yes."

"You faked throwing the keys—and then you said you lied. Which is true?"

"What I just said. I faked—"

"Why?"

"People were hassling me. Steve and others. I had a lot of self doubt— but I never doubted that I didn't shoot my children."

She has forgotten the trees, the white lines, the road itself—but inside her own body, she thought she was going fast. Yes, she'd told the detectives she'd never fired a handgun, never owned one, never "possessed" one. "That's true—they were Steve's."

". . . never *possessed*?"

"True."

"Never possessed?"

Diane calls for time-out. To her "possess" means to own. She does not want to talk about the .22 Ruger.

"It was *Steve's* gun; it was in my house."

Her arm had pained her terribly and acted "kooky, real weird." She hears that the detectives considered her wound a flesh wound. She shrugs her martyr's shrug.

"'I don't know who shot my kids,' you said," Hugi asked. "'I haven't the vaguest idea'?"

"True."

"'I do know,' you said."

"True."

"The suspect 'held my arm and called me a bitch'?"

"True."

"You said the yellow car tied in?"

"True."

"How does it tie in?"

"I don't know . . . everyone told me nothing made sense, *your people,* Steve, Lew. Even my dreams didn't make sense."

"Your parents told you that too?"

"Not my parents."

"You said, 'they' touched you—threatened to pluck your tattoo?"

"I said that."

"Why?"

"I believed it until I got some help."

"When did you decide to get help?"

"I didn't. My attorney did, 'cause I was on the verge of suicide. You listened to the tapes—they're idiotic. That woman was in trouble. Why didn't *you* get me help?"

"If you shot your own kids, would you have gone crazy?"

"I wouldn't do it, Mr. Hugi."

"Ever threaten Steve?"

"That depends on what you mean."

"His life?"

"No."

"Point a gun at him?"

"No—I'm the type of person that would cut off my nose to spite my face. I say lots of things to impress people that should never be said—that don't mean anything. I make my flip remarks . . . If I kept my mouth shut, a lot of times, I'd save people a lot of trouble—including myself."

Over objections, Fred Hugi points out that Polly Jamison's tests reveal that Diane is a deviant sociopath. Diane looks puzzled. She does not understand this term either.

"You told Detective Norenberg [a handwriting expert] that a trial is a play and that the best actors will win," Hugi reminds her. "You thought I would cut you off and not let you explain your answers?"

"Yes."

"Have I cut you off?"

"No. I appreciate that. Thank you."

Fred Hugi turns to Jim Jagger: "Your witness."

"When you said that you didn't care if they caught anyone," Jagger begins on redirect, "that you wanted it dropped, I called the sheriff's office and told them I was getting you to a psychologist?"

She nods indulgently. "Don't I always [say the wrong thing]?"

Hasn't Jagger always urged her to be honest with him from the beginning? Guilty or innocent? Hasn't he urged her not to talk so freely? Hasn't he said, "Do what you feel is right. We'll fly by the truth. Even if you're inconsistent, we'll deal with it later?"

Of course. She nods with a smile.

Jagger has more inconsistencies to deal with in Diane's myriad versions of the shootings than any lawyer might wish for in three trials. He stresses Diane's Baptist upbringing, the Good Samaritan story. Given her religious training, she had no alternative but to stop for the stranger.

Jagger tries to erase the picture of the promiscuous woman who prefers married men. He asks Diane to tell about the many men she has dated with whom she had no physical intimacy.

There was Scott; and Ray, who "certified your dog bites"; Rick who wanted to adopt her children; and Tim who played softball and video games with them. But then Lew had come along and he had "higher priority."

"Did you have priorities more important than men?" Jagger asks.

"My business, flying, and my kids."

Fred Hugi objects to the admission of Diane's second diary, the post-shooting diary. "The diary is totally self-serving . . . it's Diane Downs's world as she would like it to be."

At length, Judge Foote sustains Hugi's objections. Diane may refer to the diary to refresh her memory in court, but it will not be admitted.

Fred Hugi has a few more questions.

Diane assures him she has not been abusive to her kids for at least two years. Not since her divorce. "My life goes on spans—milestones."

"Did your plan to move to Oregon include Lew?"

"Initially, no . . ."

"You expected him to join you here?"

"Yes."

Diane scolds Hugi. "Christie's been in a lot of trouble, and you people are forgetting that. She's taking over a lot of Cheryl's personality, and that scares me really bad. She also woke up crying about wetting the bed, and she's *never* wet the bed—"

"You never recall grabbing Christie by the throat either?" Hugi spits out.

"NO!" Diane's throat blossoms pink.

Hugi walks away. He is done with her.

CHAPTER 42

I told my wife, "Look at that ugly creep!" Well, my wife drives down the road—all she sees is the white line . . . He was on drugs, I figured . . . His eyes were so big. I seen lots of 'em at Sisters—or right here on the Mall . . .

—Jim-Bob McCoin, witness for the defense

The bulk of the defense's case rests on Diane's shoulders. In four and a half days on the stand, she has given testimony even beyond the scope of questioning by her own attorney and Fred Hugi.

The gallery waits expectantly for more—but Jagger has no big guns waiting in the wings for the defense. No surprise witnesses.

There is John Hulce, the elderly gentleman who spotted an old yellow car days after the shooting, and Basil Wilson, who saw a tramp with the green and blue bag in the country club. Wilson wears a white cashmere sweater with the country club emblem over his heart as he explains that "all hippies look alike" so he cannot really describe the bum with the bicycle who had the audacity to wander into a private club.

The defense deserves points for variety. Jagger next calls two witnesses who describe themselves as "chicken farmers": Jim-Bob McCoin and Norm Hilliard, who contacted Jagger some weeks after the shooting. He referred them to Roy Pond, who found that they shared an address on the same street—but six blocks away—from the Wes and Willadene Frederickson residence in Springfield.

It is late in the day when their names are called, and they have apparently imbibed freely to brace themselves for the ordeal of testifying. Alcoholic fumes waft through the courtroom as each makes his way to the stand. Hilliard and McCoin visited Marcola Road that May night, although they had never crossed the threshold of the Springfield Country Club—and had no desire to. Norman Preston Hilliard, thirty, and his good friend, Jim-Bob McCoin, were, as they phrased it, taking care of some "game chickens" out at a friend's house between the golf course and the Mohawk Store.

Since cock fighting is illegal in Oregon, it is prudent for Norm and Jim-Bob to downplay their errand that evening. A two-car caravan left the chicken coops for Springfield about a quarter past nine. Andy Waldron, a friend, drove Hilliard; Jim-Bob and his wife followed in their own vehicle.

Hilliard recalls, "We was due for dinner at Jim-Bob's mother's house at 9:30, and we got there at 9:25."

As they approached the bridge over the Mohawk River (just at the intersection of Marcola and Sunderman roads) Hilliard had seen a man near the bridge, hitchhiking. He recalls that he had a steady look at him;

the man was wearing an army fatigue jacket, blue jeans, and was carrying a "sky-blue" bag. His round face was unshaven, and he had "deep, deep, dark eyes." The man's hair had been medium brown with bangs combed down, cut below his ears and above his shoulders—"shaggy, wind-blown"—five feet, ten inches, and about one hundred ninety-five pounds.

"We was going about forty to forty-five miles an hour. I heard about the shooting the next morning and didn't give it no thought until I saw the second composite. I compared it to my wife and children—if that happened to them—and I called her lawyer."

Hilliard has difficulty remembering his contact with Detective Pond. "Something I'll need to remember in my life, I'll keep notes. I never thought it would come to this that a man has to remember every *minute* to be that perzact!"

Jim-Bob McCoin figures he saw the man at the bridge "between 9:20 and 9:25—I never pack a watch—I break 'em." The man was on the north side of the road, headed toward Springfield. He had hair a little past his ears, looked like he hadn't shaved in six weeks, and wore a green army fatigue jacket and blue jeans. Jim-Bob remembers the stranger as fat and chunky, under five feet eight."

The witness jerks his thumb at Judge Foote, drawing guffaws, as he suggests that the stranger looks something like "this guy here." Courtroom protocol is foreign to McCoin. He apparently doesn't know that Foote is the judge. Since Foote stands way over six feet and is no way "fat and chunky," it seems a flawed comparison.

Neither has seen "no yellow car."

Their descriptions of the man don't quite mesh, but both say he wore an army fatigue jacket. Diane has described a man in a Levi jacket. The man they saw on the bridge was walking toward Springfield. It is conceivable that he might have veered off to the right when he came to the Mohawk Road.

This is the sort of suspect that Wes had looked for so assiduously—a wild drug-mad tramp seen out in the country only a half hour before his family was shot. No one has seen the man since. If he is the same man Basil Wilson saw earlier, he had gained weight and lost his bicycle . . .

Why on earth would Diane Downs—with her three little children in the car—have stopped for such a wild-looking stranger? Even as a Good Samaritan?

As McCoin leaves the stand, he swaggers out of the courtroom and hits both doors as if he is leaving an old-time western saloon. Only one door opens, and he spins out of control, around the post holding the cordon that keeps the crowd back. There is a crash in the hall.

Someone giggles, and Judge Foote raps for order.

"Call Willadene Frederickson!"

Diffidently, Willadene approaches to be sworn. She looks very nice, like a matron dressed up in her navy blue suit with a red and white striped tie for a spring Sunday at church.

Diane turns in her chair and smiles—a little wistful smile. She looks for the moment like a child whose mommy had shown up in the nick of time to save her. She has scorned Willadene as wishy-washy so often, but her *mother* is here.

Her father is not.

Willadene smiles back at Diane, placing her hand on the Bible. Willadene recalls to Jim Jagger that Diane arrived in Springfield on Easter Sunday, 1983. "We left Oregon for Arizona ten days before. We had a pick-up, and Diane had two cars. Katherine drove the white Ford Fiesta back."

Willadene *had* seen a microwave and a small television in the trunk of Diane's Nissan. She saw a rifle case on a little ledge at the back of the trunk, and a "cloth item. I moved it. It felt like a gun—"

Willadene saw only a portion of the gun; she sighs as she attempts to draw it on the blackboard. "I don't know a thing about guns but I saw a cylinder and it wasn't flat."

Willadene wipes tears from her eyes as she recalls the night of May 19, 1983. She describes her daughter as "hysterical—crying when I got there. Her eyes were red, her face was red, and tears were running down her face."

Now, Willadene sobs as she remembers her lost grandchildren and struggles to regain her composure.

Jim Jagger questions her about her family—how they were during the growing-up years. "Who was the enforcer of rules when you were raising kids?"

"I'd say pretty much both—he was head of the household."

What had they told their children about crying?

"We taught them not to be crybabies—to knock it off. We taught them to be tough."

"Does your husband cry?"

"No—my husband doesn't cry."

"Does Diane cry?"

"She tries to be tough like her father . . ."

Willadene feels that Diane held back her tears much of the time in the hospital that night to protect her parents.

"When was the last time you saw Christie?"

"I haven't seen Christie since October, 1983."

Direct examination was over. Willadene steels herself, drawing in and bracing for Fred Hugi's questions.

Hugi is not confrontive; there is sympathy in the courtroom for this woman.

Willadene is not sure just when the call came from the hospital—perhaps at 10:20 or 10:25. She and Wes had to get dressed, and they beat the police to the hospital by five minutes.

Yes, the towel around Diane's arm was one of hers. No, there had never been any mistreatment of Diane as she grew up.

Willadene told Hugi that she felt the hospital personnel had lied to them about the children's condition.

"Was your husband a good parent to Diane?"

"Yes. My husband was strict, but he treated all the children the same."

"Were you a good parent?"

"Yes."

"Did you 'seal yourself off from her'—so that she couldn't talk with you?"

Hugi's question, quoting some of Diane's earlier testimony, catches Willadene off guard. She glances quickly at the prosecutor in surprise.

". . . No."

"Did you take your husband's side? No matter what?"

"No matter what?" she repeats. "I took my husband's side most of the time. I was raised to believe the husband was the head of the household—but we listened to both sides. Parent *and* child."

"Was there physical discipline?"

"He spanked the children occasionally. He was not out of line."

"No more questions."

Willadene steps gratefully down from the witness stand. The logical next witness is Wes Frederickson.

He has not been called to testify. At the Springfield post office, the window between his office and the lobby—always open before—has been closed since the publicity started.

The defense now presents its own expert on blood patterns: Bart Reid, a criminalist who once worked for the Oregon State Crime Lab, now in private practice. Reid had observed as Jagger and Mary Ann Vaughan—Reid's associate—performed tests with fresh blood.

Using type O blood—drawn from a most accommodating Vaughan—Jagger and Vaughan stomped and splashed and sprayed it on a rocker panel from a new Nissan.

Reid testifies that there were only twenty-five or thirty spatters on the panel of Diane's car, and that high velocity could not be determined from so few spots "without a history." Reid has dipped a postal sweater in blood and experimented to see if the sweater's "whipping" cuff would leave the spatters that Pex termed back-spatter from a gunshot wound. He shows the jury "targets"—sheets of paper that he placed varying distances above the ground to catch blood as it dripped from the sweater.

Reid demonstrates four different blood-spatter experiments. As the drawn blood coagulated, the sweater was redipped, and dropped again and again above the rocker panel. The widths of blood spatter varied from four to twelve inches.

Bart Reid's testimony seems too scientific for the jury and much of the gallery and press row. And it backfires. What results from his lengthy time on the stand is a reminder that blood was shed, sprayed, spattered, and hemorrhaged in great profusion that night—not a wise picture to reinforce. On cross-examination by Fred Hugi, Reid begins to sound like a witness for the prosecution. Bart Reid admits he cannot disagree with Pex's findings.

Jim Pex had taken the rocker panel and all his blood-work back to El-
mira, New York, to confer with Dr. Herbert McDonnell. McDonnell is the
"grand-daddy expert" on blood patterns. McDonnell concurred completely with Pex's conclusions.

As Reid vacillates, Jim Jagger grins—a pained, rueful grin—and then
even he begins to look somber.

In the end, the defense bases its case largely on dreams. Dreams and human memory. Dr. Harold L. Hawkins of the University of Oregon, researcher in human perception and memory, consulting editor of the
Memory and Cognition Journal, takes the stand.

He explains that human memory has limitations; we perceive the
world around us and interpret it according to our individual frames of
reference. Human memory is not like a tape recorder. It diminishes with
time, and we hasten to fill the gaps between the bits and fragments we *do*
remember with our own details. Hawkins stresses that this reconstruction of memory is a basic human tendency—that we "fabricate" or "create" how it must have been, often unconsciously.

"Unconscious transference" becomes the buzz term for the defense.
Unconscious transference means that a subject places one event that has
happened within the same time frame of another event—even though
they may not have taken place concurrently.

We remember some information; we forget other input. Humans are
not infallible. A computer will spit back exactly what has gone into it; a
human mind will muddle it up with individual perception and extraneous information.

If the jury accepts the concept of unconscious transference, Diane's
continually changing stories of the shooting may be explained. And
Christie's testimony will be weakened.

Hugi objects; Foote sustains it. Hawkins is not allowed to testify that
Dr. Carl Peterson might have inadvertently placed the thought that her
mother had shot her in Christie's mind. While the jury is out of the courtroom, Hawkins discusses Christie's question: "If my mom shot me, Cheryl,
and Danny, I would want to go back to her, because it wouldn't happen
again. Maybe she just got really, really angry?"

And Peterson's answer, "But you don't think that she'd shoot at you anymore?"

In Dr. Hawkins's opinion, that response was tantamount to "taking a statement that is not an established fact, but treating it as if it were a fact."

But then, Jim Jagger did exactly that in his cross-examination of Christie as he led up to his crucial question, "You don't really know what has made you change from wondering to now thinking that's what happened. Right? Is that right?"

Diane's dreams have been brought into the testimony often, but no witness has been found to back up the defense's tentative theory that dreams too can be incorporated into unconscious transference. There is no research on such a phenomenon.

Sane humans may—and often do—mix up memories of factual events in their minds, fabricate, and become confused. But they do not mix up dreams and reality, fantasy and fact.

Not unless they do it deliberately.

Dr. Polly Jamison, Diane's therapist, is rumored to be the next—and last—witness for the defense. But Polly Jamison does not testify.

Susan Staffel, Christie's caseworker, testifies first in the State's rebuttal. Staffel made the decision to terminate Diane's visits with her children. "I have no axe to grind with Diane Downs; my only concern was—and is—the children." Yes, Christie had been brought to Fred Hugi's office to "practice" for court. "It's so difficult to testify in court— especially as emotional as this."

Christie's physical therapist from McKenzie–Willamette, Nancy Whitacre, explains that she worked with Christie to alleviate the catastrophic aftereffects of her stroke. When she began, Christie could not walk or use her right side.

Hugi asks Christie's response to this.

"It differed. She was very frustrated at first. As she gained function, she began to cooperate. In the middle of June, she'd hide and refuse all therapy. I'd have to chase her around. Later, she became *very* cooperative and she did more and more."

"What changed?"

"To my knowledge, she had learned she was going to a foster home and not home with her mother."

Hugi calls a final string of witnesses to confirm that there had been no plot to brainwash Christie or Danny: John Tracy, Christie's speech therapist; Dr. David Miller, Christie's pediatrician; Kim Morrison, Danny's evening nurse; Evelyn Slaven, the children's foster mother.

"Did you ever suggest to Christie that her mother shot her?"

Slaven bristles. "Absolutely not! In fact when Christie told Brenda that, she didn't believe her."

Evelyn, usually so calm, has good reason to be angry. For months—at Dr. Peterson's request—she forced herself to answer only "Oh," as Christie began to remember. She bent over backward to be neutral, even when she wanted so much to validate Christie.

The week runs itself out.

If Diane should have her baby over *this* weekend, the delay would halt the momentum building; now the atmosphere was like electricity in the air before a storm.

Jack Hamann, an investigative reporter from KING TV in Seattle, has wangled a jail interview Friday evening. Diane tells Hamann earnestly that she likes him—likes him enough to confide that she has miscalculated the due date of her baby. Actually, it is due within twenty-four hours!

"Are you still concerned about the State taking this baby away?"

"That's not really a problem." She smiles. "I'll just wait till they acquit me and then I'll have it."

By force of will, she intends to fight off whatever hormonal triggers might try to send her womb into contractions.

She sounds very strong; Hamann believes she can do it.

"Have you studied the jurors' faces?" he asks.

"I don't like to look at them."

"Why?"

"They don't interest me."

"Have you seen one of them that looks sympathetic?" he prods.

"No . . ."

True to her word, Diane is in court Monday morning, still pregnant, as Dr. George Suckow, the chief medical officer of the Marion–Polk–Linn County Unit of the Oregon State Hospital, refutes the unconscious transference theory.

"There is frequently no sense to it."

Conscious transference does, indeed, occur, Suckow says, but it is a most subjective concept. When there is no secondary gain from employing it, it is called "fiction." When there *is* secondary gain, it is called "lying."

The parade of witnesses is finished.

It is over, save for final arguments.

And the verdict.

This trial has gone on so long that it seemed it would never wind down to a true finish. It is the eleventh of June. Six weeks we have been together in Courtroom Number Three.

At 11:25, Fred Hugi stands for his final arguments. The weight he has lost is apparent. Twenty pounds certainly—or more. But there is a steely calm about him as he begins; his voice strong as he reads the charges. He speaks colloquially—"with ya," and "to ya."

"There's no doubt who did it . . . Mrs. Downs did it . . ."

Diane smirks and shakes her head.

"It sure would be nice if it was a bushy-haired stranger, because it would be easier for all of us to live with—"

Hugi lists again the changes in Diane's stories, the crime lab's physical evidence from the car, the apartment, the proximity, the blood spatters, the cartridge comparisons, the use of the .22 Ruger.

Her motive was clear: "Stress, the defection of Lew, money problems, past history."

Diane is the only suspect with the motive, the opportunity, the plan, and the .22 Ruger. And so much has been omitted in her testimony.

"She lied about owning the Ruger. That's left out. She would only say she 'possessed' it . . . When she learns the police have learned of a .22, it becomes necessary to explain how she gave the gun to Steve in Arizona— to have that connection so she can say, 'The gunman knew me.'"

Yes, Diane's hands had seemed free of gunshot residue. But Jim Pex had fired a similar Ruger seven times, waited a half hour for a swab test, sent it to the lab in Medford, and his tests came back "inconclusive." "Dust that falls off—and certainly if you wash it off—" Hugi suggests.

Diane's re-enactments of the shooting have placed the shooter's feet *outside* the car. But the wounds were all near-contact. Diane has said the stranger was only five feet eight inches tall.

"He'd have to have had arms like Wilt Chamberlain," Hugi says.

For perhaps the first time in trial, Diane Downs looks very, very serious. One by one by one, Fred Hugi is shredding her alibis, her explanations.

". . . so they say Tracy planted the bullet evidence. Why would Tracy plant it right at the outset? He doesn't know about the Ruger. He could have planted any other kind—that might be wrong."

Why indeed?

Suddenly, there is a ruckus at the back of the room. A large disheveled woman carrying a white plastic bag barges into the courtroom. Doug Welch and Ray Broderick leap up to assist her out.

"Why?" she bawls. "Maybe I know something?" She points at Broderick. "Ask him! He can tell you."

It is only the courthouse's resident "bag-lady"—so familiar to regulars that Hugi scarcely pauses in his summation.

"Christie related in quite some detail what for her must have been a nightmare like none of us have ever suffered. Her demeanor defied fabrication. You all watched it. Trust yourself. I submit that that child on the witness stand *relived* that experience . . . How could anyone *program* a nine-year-old to relate something that awful in that fashion—if it wasn't true?"

Hugi reminds the jury that Joe Inman followed the red Nissan after the shooting.

"He was at the scene where the casings were found one minute before he got to her car, and he didn't see anyone there and he didn't see any yellow car . . . He observed her driving was not erratic or unusual—just slow."

Diane had not asked for help; she had crept along until Inman passed her.

"Did she have shot-up kids in the car and the gun also? If she had gotten rid of the gun and the children were sufficiently communicative at that point where they were speaking—yelling—'Mom, you shot me!' or 'Why did you shoot me?' That wouldn't be very good to have Mr. Inman hear that either—if she stopped at that point..."

Hugi's voice was scathing as he went through the timetable of the shooting. It had taken Diane eighteen minutes to go eight-tenths of a mile.

"If she shoots the kids somewhere in a remote area, she can head into town and pull over on a secluded road. Then she stops after the kids are shot. She's got two things left to do: she's got to shoot herself. She's got to make it look like she was involved in this thing as a victim, and she's got to get rid of the gun... She puts her arm out, flinches the first time—she testified she doesn't like to hurt herself, doesn't like to feel pain—and she shoots... the second time and you've got the casings in the road..."

Diane has pulled over exactly where the river is closest to the road, the most opportune spot to throw the gun. She wraps her arm in the towel... But what if the kids aren't dead? She can't shoot again. She doesn't have the weapon anymore—so she goes s-l-o-w... At some point, the pace picks up.

"She arrives at the hospital. All the kids appear to be dead... Her main concern is which of the two girls died. Christie can identify her; Cheryl can't..."

Hugi explains why a twenty-five-minute trip took fifty minutes. "She has to scout out the spot, screw up the courage, tell the kids to go to sleep—and drive around and *hope* they go to sleep..."

Fred Hugi reviews the terrible scene at the McKenzie–Willamette ER, and the defendant's incongruously blithe remarks; he reads Christie's verbatim testimony.

"Dr. Peterson said that the way her memory came back was not unusual. He listed several faraway looks of terror in her face when she related this information... How would it feel if you were a nine-year-old child, and one day you went out for a ride with your mother and your brother and sister and then it got to be dark and the car pulled over and your mother came back with a gun and in front of your eyes murdered your sister, shot your brother, and then shot you? You would know how Christie felt. She was trapped in that car. There was *nowhere* for her to go.

She could just back up against the seat—the shot goes right through her chest and the second one comes out and goes into her hand into the same place..."

Dr. Peterson had given Christie permission to let the memories out in the open and to tell. But Christie had hoped for more. "I want my mom to tell the truth. Then I won't have to remember."

Again, we hear the frenetic sequence of Diane's life. Reconstructed in the voice of the man she detests, it sounds far less pathetic. Every facet of the case is in Hugi's mind—in perfect sequence. He is not overtly emotional, but he is unremitting.

Hugi reminds the jury that Christie told Dr. Peterson that her mother didn't love the family—only Lew. And, after the shootings, Christie said sadly, "Mom didn't even say 'I'm sorry.'"

He went as quickly as possible through Diane's affair with Lew. Told once, thrice, twenty times, even illicit sex palls.

"These are all [things], I submit—that border... on fantasy and certain delusional thinking—consistent with many things she'd done in her life, feeling that she is going to be a doctor, she's going to be a successful business woman, pilot, going to own a big house. And when, in reality, she's failed at everything she's ever set out to do in her life. She's failed in her marriage, failed in her relationships with men. She's never followed through and completed anything—just bounced around from one thing to the next and failed—and that's where we find her up here in Oregon with a pretty bleak outlook... She can't go back to Arizona."

Diane laughs suddenly. It is true; Diane *does* laugh when she takes a blow. The harder the blow, the merrier her laughter.

Diane whirls to whisper to Jim Jagger. But her attorney is listening to Hugi. Color, the true barometer of her feelings, creeps up her neck.

Hugi has left her no place to hide; Diane is pinned to her chair, as Christie had been pinned back against the seat—all of her failures paraded out in the light for the hushed room to examine.

"... letters that are just dripping with love for Lew and he's basically written her off and she knows it now... She's got a problem with the demand letter—the $7,700 demand letter from Denver that she's got to pay [for the burned trailer] . . . Her solution to that is to check into bankruptcy... get a fresh start... She's stranded here in Oregon. She's got three kids and her parents, and you know she's talked about how she gets on with them.

"... What's interesting then is to read her child abuse paper where she talks about just that situation—about how you get in a situation where the stress is too great, and you lash out at your children because there's no one else. And if you look at that child abuse paper, you see it's almost a cry for help or a prophecy of things to come in her life ..."

Diane's expression is one of amazement. She is dumbfounded that Hugi should connect the shooting to her paper. It is apparent that she has never noticed the parallels before.

Fred Hugi has not raised his voice until now. His examples all spring from Diane's life. She has talked so much, given so many interviews while he watched her on television, unable to respond. Downs's quotes are easy to come by; Hugi uses her own words to blast her.

"When she feels trapped, she suppresses her hostility and anger and then lashes out. That's a common pattern that she's developed over her life ... You read that child abuse paper and you look at her diary entries on May 16, 1983: *'I am so trapped, I love you.'*

"... she has no impulse control. *It's like driving an automobile without brakes* ..."

As Fred Hugi talks, Diane shakes her head more and more forcefully. She is truly astonished by his conclusions.

It is 4:14. Hugi has finished his closing arguments.

Jim Jagger faces the jury with a friendly grin at 10:37 on Tuesday morning. He announces that he has scrapped his original presentation overnight. No more chronology. He will address the particular issues.

He asks for no emotion, for no speculation from the jurors—only that they listen to "cold hard facts."

Seven points: Tracy and the bullets; Diane's statements at the hospital; her statements in June and July; Christie; the gun—related to Steve and Lew; blood spatter evidence; and Joe Inman.

Can he really reduce them all to cold hard facts that prove Diane innocent—the injured party and not the killer?

Fred Hugi sits quietly, his expression one of the mongoose watching the snake.

"There never was—never will be—a time lapse," Jagger says with assurance. "That approach is like selling used cars—I'm gonna talk about the person really responsible—using the exhibits and the facts."

Jim Jagger is shooting his scattergun. He is here and there and everywhere. It is, Hugi knows, a time-honored and effective courtroom technique. Keep the jury off balance with a torrent of questions. Razzle-dazzle 'em. Hugi and Broderick believe that Jagger has only to raise a twenty percent doubt to make it an equal push between his case and theirs. Theirs is the heaviest burden.

Jagger agrees that Diane has "helped to paint a bad picture by some of the things she's done in the past. She's made a lot of people dislike her . . ."

Diane nods her head, and chuckles.

It's impossible to dislike Jagger. He forgives Fred Hugi for his objections, admits he himself talks too fast, uses too much body language. He draws on an easel—wild, swirling lines apparently meant to demonstrate a point. But then he moves on, and we forget that his drawings make no more sense than Johnny Carson's old routine: "Take the Slosson Cutoff—" He chalks in his points in capital letters.

Jagger blames the hospital personnel and the police for drawing the battle lines that first night—a largely male group who had observed Diane and decided "how a woman should react." That behavior colored the whole case from there on out. All of her behavior can be explained by her background . . .

" . . . Her reaction throughout is to comply . . . Steve Downs raped her. He raped her in more than one way . . . She reacts more like a male would— a stereotyped male . . ."

Jagger telegraphs important information before he submits it. One piece of evidence deemed "BIGGER THAN LIFE" on his easel is her blue plaid shirt. "There's blood all over the ceiling thirty-two inches above the seat . . ."

But only a fleck or two on Diane's shirt.

Jagger works rapidly—talking about blood types, blood spatter, blow-back, exit wounds, entrance wounds, positions in the car, small irregularities in testimony. As he covers so much territory, Jagger stops often to remind the jurors to ignore their "emotionality." Easier said than done.

Why *had* Christie said, "Mom did it"? She was simply confused.

Jagger explains: stress and leading questions and suggestions and unconscious transference. "Children are more susceptible."

Jim Jagger uses the term "We" constantly. He and the jury are as one. "We are tired," he comments.

True. "We" all are.

Diane looks blank—almost woebegone. Why? This is *her* attorney, fighting for *her*. Is it perhaps because she is silenced? Jagger talks; she can talk no longer. She strokes her abdomen with the points of her long fingernails.

Christie's picture was wrong, according to Jagger—and it seems important to him that the shooter holds the gun in the left hand. The picture had no plaid shirt. And what Christie drew seems to be a revolver, not an automatic pistol.

Jagger re-accuses Dick Tracy of tampering with the evidence, of planting bullets hither and thither to make a case.

"I submit to you that a witness who is false in part of his statements may be lying about others—"

Diane nods sagely. Fortunately, Tracy is not in the courtroom. He would not suffer this repetition kindly.

Again and again, Jim Jagger reminds the jurors that they must come to a moral certainty—that they have to be sure before they convict anyone.

Why did the authorities take so long to make an arrest? "I suggest to you that was because there was still some doubt ... there's something else there—maybe something we didn't even know about ..."

He reads medical records. If he reads them all, we *will* be in this courtroom until Christmas.

But five o'clock comes first.

Jim Jagger has explanations for the alleged time lapse.

"Joe Inman came upon the Nissan eight-tenths of a mile away from the scene. He followed her two-tenths of a mile. He saw her for less than two city blocks. She was driving slower *before* and *after* Inman saw her. She did three things—tried to get Christie to roll over; she wrapped the towel around her arm, and she opened the window ..."

Jagger's reconstruction sounds logical. Diane has raced away from the shooter, only to hear that her children are alive! She slows down to help Christie. The smells in the little car are overwhelming, and Diane has to get air to help her kids. Maybe she grabs the towel at that point to wrap around her arm.

The defense attorney shouts, claps his hands together as he paces and bounces before the jurors. Why drive slow? Why not sit there and park? But her kids were gasping.

"Because she couldn't stand sitting along a dark road alone with dying kids."

Jim Jagger figures that Diane never even saw Joe Inman.

And now "TRIPLE STAR MATERIAL!"

"A short while later, she's going fast—the kids are ALIVE and gasping! What good did it do her to get to the hospital with one dead and two gasping and still alive? Why not stay out there long enough for them to die? She would only get Mr. Lewiston if *none* of them was alive."

It is a salient point. Diane had repeated it often in her early press conferences. If she was guilty, why drive the victims to the hospital while they were alive? And why kill only one? Lew had made it clear he didn't want to raise *any* children.

Jim Jagger rearranges the time chart. He adds a few minutes here, a few minutes there—until he has shaved the prosecution's twenty-five-minute gap to less than ten.

Heather Plourd and her neighbor might have been off a few minutes on the time Diane left.

9:45 to 9:47 Diane left (extra two minutes).

9:47 to 9:55 to the north end of Sunderman (add one minute).

9:55 to 10:01 to the pull-out. Cheryl and Mom talk. Diane balances checkbook (add five or six more minutes).

Jagger allows two minutes for the shootings.

10:12 to 10:15 Diane leaves after shooting, and drives eight-tenths of a mile before Inman sees her. She's slowing down to save her kids.

10:15 to 10:18 She still takes care of the kids, going slow.

10:19 to 10:29 She's driving to the hospital. Arrives. Nobody notices the clock right away because they're too busy. So let's take away a minute.

Fred Hugi, sitting quietly, is sweating blood inside. With a dull, leaden feeling, he wonders if he is losing it. Jagger's own words seem to energize him as he prances before the jury. Key phrases leap out.

Triumphant, Jagger approaches a finish. "Now, there is no time gap there which would be a time gap when you take from people's testimony, you know, the worst of all possible worlds, but I suggest to you what we have done. I talked about each of these and indicated things that were left out, wrong assumptions that were made. I suggest to you that there was no time losses at all. In fact, actually things fit in—in fact, actually about perfectly when you think and walk through the events that happened."

Jagger attempts to demolish the State's motive: an obsessive love for Lew. "It *is* bizarre. It *is* ridiculous. She's not naive . . . Why would she sacrifice her children for a man among *many* men?"

Lew has become an "arrogant, undependable, unreliable, scoundrel." Even if she didn't already have a new assortment of men to choose from, Diane would never have considered marrying him, Jagger announces, unless they had a "contract."

He dismisses Kurt Wuest and Doug Welch as men who lied to his client, who played "mindgames" with her, and then compounded their malicious intent by telling her right in the middle of her testimony that they were taking her unborn child away from her.

Jagger is winding up to a resounding finish.

"That man . . . has never been found . . . and I submit that gun, whatever make, year, etc. . . . walked away with him . . ."

"What happened to Diane Downs, the lady they messed with from beginning to end? They've taken her child away. I'll tell you what happened."

Jagger explains that as far back as June 4, Diane made references in her diary about reality—and unreality. At first, she had guilt, and then she got phone calls from other people terrorized by CSD. The fear. Confusion. Panic. Face scratching. Aloneness. No one fighting for you. Depressed. Suicidal . . . "All these things overlapping . . ."

"The person who killed Cheryl, that shot Christie and Danny and Diane Downs, was crazy. Had to be. Was drugged, must have been because it doesn't make any sense . . . what they're doing is messing with your [Diane's] mind. They can't do that anymore. You've heard all the facts. Allegations were made. Sometimes they were just mere allegations which were made without any suggestions, just with hope that you'd hear them and wonder and be suspicious. Thank God for afterthoughts . . ."

Jagger urges the jurors to put themselves in Diane's place. "I suggest to you that you have an honest hesitation and that if you're putting your own money on the table—in your own affairs—that you would hesitate to put it out in front of you. And, I would suggest your hesitation which would be pretty well founded. Real well founded . . . The only decision is whether or not—is that it's proven or not proven beyond a reasonable doubt . . . It's a serious decision. One that has serious consequences. Mistakes are sometimes made . . .

"On behalf of my client, we ask you—we *request* that you return a verdict of Not Guilty and not based upon emotion, not based upon some feelings . . . What I ask you to do is go back and think about the facts. The emotion is real misleading. It really can [sic]."

Jagger apologizes for his eight-hour final arguments. Typed later by a court reporter, they fill almost two hundred pages. On paper, Jagger rambles. To the ear, Jagger's arguments work—as he accentuates particular words and phrases.

Behind the press row, a spectator murmurs, "Hallelujah Brother! Come forward, and be bathed in the blood of the lamb! He's better than the Reverend Jimmy Swaggart!"

But Jim Jagger has not named the real killer as he promised. Did the jurors pick up on that?

It is 3:20 P.M. on Wednesday, June 13. The jury has brought their suitcases this morning. They will take them home again, for one more day.

Fred Hugi begins his rebuttal, his last chance to speak; he is convinced that Jagger has neatly cut out his twenty percent wedge of doubt. They may have lost it all.

Hugi has to reverse that. No one is going to hurry him now.

He points out that this is not a divorce trial; it doesn't matter what the ex-Mrs. Downs thinks of Mr. Downs.

"This is a very serious trial about three little children, two of them are with us still and both of them are permanently disabled now. Maybe we ought to come back to reality now, and let's look at . . . who did this to the children?

"In order to find that the defendant is not guilty, you've got to find that Christie is not truthful—discount her. You've got to find that all of these items dealing with the firearms tests are not accurate—that Detective Tracy came in here and committed a number of crimes, dummied up the evidence, and that the police—other police officers—were in the conspiracy with him . . . That Lew is in on it because he talks about a gun that he never saw. Steve Downs is in on it because he's not telling us about a gun that he got back. You've got to find that . . . the hospital people were—and are—telling lies anytime there is conflict with what Mrs. Downs recalls. You've got to find that Mr. Pex doesn't know what he's doing in the tests he performed . . ."

The two dozen tapes—"Does it seem to be a person who's nervous? A person under stress? I don't think so . . ."

It takes so long, this reweaving of the stitches in the fabric of the case Jim Jagger has ripped out. Hugi does it. He could have done it in his sleep. He knows where all the thin spots are.

And now he picks up the orange and pinky-purple beach towel that Judy Patterson unwrapped from Diane's arm on May 19, 1983.

Paul Alton has folded this towel in so many ways, trying to make the stains fit. It is obviously blood *seepage*, but he had to find which layer has been next to the skin, and which next, and next . . .

Alton has broken the code.

As the jury watches, Hugi folds the towel in half end-to-end, making a smaller rectangle. Next, he folds this rectangle opposite corner to opposite corner to form a triangle.

The blood spots match up. He shows the jury that the darkest stain is in the first layer that touched Diane's arm, and each layer up has less. All the perimeters match.

"What a nice neat pattern for someone to wrap themselves with . . ."

This is why Diane lost no blood in the car. How extraordinary that she should grab frantically for something to wrap around her arm, and come up with a perfect triangular bandage . . .

Hugi suggests that Diane prepared that towel-bandage beforehand, laid her arm in her lap atop the towel, shot herself, and then wrapped the ends neatly around her injured arm and tucked them in. Even as her children gasped for air, she had taken great care to protect herself.

The bloody towel—its puzzle broken—is a devastating visual blow for the defense.

It is more than Jagger can stand, even during closing arguments. He cries out that Hugi is bringing improper material into rebuttal.

Judge Foote overrules him. "You did argue that—that she wrapped the towel while she was driving. I think he can rebut that."

Fred Hugi has come up with a word that describes Diane Downs's attitude toward children: *fungible*.

According to the *American Heritage Dictionary,* "fungible" means: "Being of such a nature or kind that one unit or part may be exchanged or substituted for another equivalent unit or part in the discharging of an obligation."

Hugi has found the word chillingly apt. An aborted child can be replaced with a new pregnancy: Danny for Carrie. Cheryl is dead, but even now, Diane is growing Charity Lynn to replace her. Just as a mother cat or a sow counts her litter, needing only to come up with the same number, is it possible that Diane can destroy and replace her children at will, content that the numbers come out even?

Fred Hugi thinks so.

He likens her to a volcano, exploding under the pressure of stress.

The day ends with more words about blood. And the next day begins with it. We are awash in it, our minds and souls drenched with red. Fred Hugi talks on, his voice still quite soft, empty of emotion, dogged as a marathon runner nearing the tape.

He explains to the jury that the long wait to arrest was for Christie—so that she could learn to speak again. And feel safe enough to peel the layers from her memory.

Hugi dismisses Jagger's revised time chart peremptorily.

"The re-enactment by Mr. Jagger . . . is just wishful thinking, not based on any facts—just trying to reconstruct the evidence in a light that's most favorable to him—that he can live with. Problem is, he can't. Mrs. Downs took too much time to do this. To do the shooting and to wait before going to the hospital. Now, she may have used that time, taken some time to ditch the gun. It could be she may have also taken some time to make sure that, when she got to the hospital, that the kids were not in a state to say, 'My mommy shot me'—that they were sufficiently close to death where that wouldn't happen. She couldn't wait out there an hour—two hours . . . couldn't bring them in *cold* . . ."

Fred Hugi is dissecting Diane Downs. Is it wise? She sits before him, her maternity top actually shifting as the unborn baby kicks. Will the female jurors, in the last analysis, think it too much, his relentless pounding on a pregnant woman?

Or will they remember that this child too may be "fungible"?

". . . What she is good at is one night stands and affairs where there are no commitments required on her part. No—no real feeling, genuine feeling. She's quick to express 'deep concerns'—she's very good at that—expressing *deep* love, *deep* feelings, *deep* emotions, but she's never able to show it. It's just not there . . . Nobody is as selfish a person . . . She cares for no one but herself . . . We're told that she's such a 'Good Samaritan.' Quite the contrary. Quite the contrary. Diane comes first.

". . . When you listen to Mrs. Downs on tape, you notice that she sounds as believable on those tapes as she does in court. She's able to project this same story, the same degree of feeling in whatever she's telling—and that's her problem. You get that with an accomplished liar, and people that are used to it do it all the time . . . You've seen that here. She, in her mind, reconciles everything. There's an explanation for everything. She never admits that she's done anything wrong, no matter if you pin her down. It's just denial, denial, denial."

Hugi suggests that Diane's affairs are only a way of expressing her hatred. "Why do you suppose she preys on married men—there's a lot of men in the world . . . whether in Eugene or Chandler. Why did she try to juggle three, four, five, or more sexual partners in the air at the same time? Is she a person who's into giving love? Seeking love? Does love have *any* place in her emotions? Does it exist for her at all? She loves herself . . ."

It is 2:18 on this sunny, Thursday afternoon. Fred Hugi's voice, so long steady and flat, is full of rage. The contrast is shocking.

"We're talking about a child who's not here anymore—for what? For

Diane Downs's warped sense of values. Danny won't walk. Christie won't have her arm and her mind to use the way it was ... Look, lady. For once, you're not gonna lie your way out of this situation. It just doesn't cut it. You're a murderer—a cold-blooded, cruel, vicious, murderer!"

It is very quiet as Hugi returns to his chair.

Judge Foote instructs the jury that they must not be biased as they debate whether Elizabeth Diane Downs is guilty or not guilty of murder, two counts of attempted murder, and two counts of assault with intent to cause serious physical injury—beyond a reasonable doubt—convinced beyond a moral certainty.

Diane is gray-white. As Foote reads his instructions, she rubs, jiggles, and pats her belly with her left hand—as if it is a lucky charm. Diane— who has smiled for six and a half weeks—smiles only once during the instructions, as Judge Foote reminds the jurors not to put the cartridges into the .22 rifle when they examine it.

CHAPTER 43

"I wanted to understand how a mother could kill her child ... and I wanted to see her get what she deserves."

"I'm a mother. No mother would be alive if someone went after her kids. She'd die trying to save them. No mother would stop for a stranger—or, if she did, she'd give him her car willingly, if she could take her kids out safely."

"No one believes she's innocent—except in Marcola where they're still afraid a bushy-haired stranger is loose!"

"I'm a little embarrassed to be here, a little ashamed—but it's my town; something like this is so unusual that I thought I should come."

"She's innocent. They're crucifying her."

—Members of the gallery, waiting for the verdict, June 14, 1984

It is 2:37 P.M. The courtroom has been cleared and locked. But most of the spectators cannot bring themselves to leave the building. Claudia Langan—who signed the indictment as foreman of the grand jury—stays and so does Evelyn Slaven, and most of the gallery, and all of the press. The corridor lights are dimmed, leaving the long benches in shadow.

At least three dozen women have attended the entire trial. They line up to call home on the lone phone and instruct children to put TV dinners in, husbands to go out for supper. In the faint light they knit, read papers, and even nap on the long benches, silhouettes in reflected light.

The press corps moves through the double doors to the roof of the third floor. There is a grubby "garden" out here—a giant wooden box full of gray cans holding Oregon grape bushes, which seem to have been forgotten and are not thriving.

Downtown Eugene is spread out below, cushioned by the green hills. Sound carries strangely; sirens and the faint clink-clank of flag halyards in the wind have equal volume up on the roof.

The television cameramen are familiar with this rooftop oasis. They have set up their "stingers" days ago. They must have a direct-line-of-sight to transmit their signals. Some aim toward a truck with a micro-dish up on the Coburg Hills north of town; others point toward Skinner's Butte. From the hills, they sight on a relay station south of Salem, and then on to Portland, and then one hundred seventy-five miles north to Seattle. Live television.

The stingers look like giant mosquitoes or deadly weapons aimed in three directions, poised for the moment a verdict comes in.

Inside, in the corridor next to the elevators, a dozen cameras balance on their sticks on the legal side of the silver duct tape on the floor.

As the afternoon lengthens, the wind picks up. The verdict does not come by suppertime. The sun is disappearing, the wind is inhospitable, and still there is no sign of verdict.

At 10:15 the jury retires for the night, and a startled gaggle of press check back into the Hilton Hotel.

There are five pregnant women in the Lane County Jail. Usually, they have their babies at Sacred Heart Hospital. Rumor has it that Diane will deliver there too. No one knows for sure. Captain Ben Sunderland, director of the Adult Corrections Division, will make that decision. Publicity may force him to send her somewhere else.

Diane has no one to talk to, and she cannot write letters or start another journal. She has been denied pens or pencils for a week—ever since she commented obliquely to Chris Rosage, "Maybe I won't even *have* this baby . . ."

Surely the verdict will come on Friday. It would have been precipitous for the jury to come back in the first half-day—after a six-week trial. They have so much evidence to look at.

Fred Hugi can be seen occasionally ducking in and out of the DA's office. Jim Jagger turns his face toward the sun as he sits on the low stone wall in front of the courthouse. He grins and waves when we walk by. Doug Welch paces around the courthouse. Welch is edgy; Ray Broderick appears confident.

Doug Welch is worried about the long jury deliberation. He blames himself because this is his first homicide case. If he'd been a seasoned pro, his interrogation would have borne fruit. If the verdict should come back "Not Guilty," Doug Welch will be devastated.

Ten hours. Twenty hours. The court-watchers still wait in the darkened corridor outside the courtroom.

The verdict that seemed imminent no longer does. An almost palpable sense of unrest moves through those who wait. The press corps is subdued. Anybody who has ever covered a trial knows that the longer a jury stays out, the more likely they are to acquit.

It looks as if Diane Downs is going to be found innocent.

At 10:40, the jury sends word that they are ready to retire for the night. They have been out twenty-two hours.

The press has found Diane unofficially guilty since the day Christie testified.

"What if she isn't?" somebody asks in the dark lounge. "What if we only want her to be guilty because she has a rotten personality?"

It is a sobering thought. Is that what the jury is wrestling with?

The courthouse is locked Saturday. The press finds a way in; the civilian spectators are turned away, disappointed. The third day of deliberation is baking hot. Eighth and Oak streets are quiet until a jackhammer breaks the silence, and a compressor somewhere starts to hum.

Fred Hugi is home—out in the coolness of his trees and the breeze off the McKenzie River, working around his place. He has no particular plans to come into Eugene. After more than a year of tension, he is very relaxed. Jagger's final arguments only temporarily unnerved Hugi. He senses he has done what he set out to do. "When it was all over—after closing arguments—I looked at the jury. At that point in time—whether because of my final argument, or more likely, in spite of it—I saw six or seven jurors who wouldn't have voted Not Guilty if you held a gun to *their* heads. I knew the *worst* that could happen was a hung jury."

Back in Eugene, the jurors have not asked a single question of Judge Foote. They can acquit Diane of murder by voting ten to twelve, but to *convict,* all twelve must agree. Perhaps it is the unanimous vote on a murder conviction that's holding them up . . .

At 1:00 P.M. on Saturday, there is a ripple of excitement. The court clerk has been spotted in the hallway. But she is only carrying in four large pizzas for the jurors' lunch.

At least they have agreed on something.

Fred Hugi watches TV; the White Sox play the Oakland A's.

At 4:45 P.M., the jury sends word out. But it is not a verdict. They ask Judge Foote for a legal definition of "reasonable doubt."

For the third day, the five o'clock news for seven channels goes out: "There is no verdict yet in the jury deliberations in the Diane Downs case . . ."

No verdict. No baby. Everyone waiting is caught in some stasis of time.

Midnight, Saturday. Thirty-six hours. The jurors have not retired, nor have they sent any more messages. Fred Hugi has spent the evening watching another ball game.

The media fully expects an acquittal. The story leads will be "Why?"— why the jury believed Diane Downs and not Fred Hugi. And how soon will Diane Downs regain custody of Danny and Christie? With the new baby, she will have three children again.

And then, at 12:20 A.M., the lights suddenly go on in one of the courtrooms.

The verdict is in.

The principals reach the courthouse quickly—Fred Hugi from up along the river, Diane from jail. How the public knew is anybody's guess. Almost a hundred people wait in the line that has formed outside the courtroom. The cameramen stand ready.

Diane, accompanied as always by Chris Rosage, sweeps in. She is wearing the royal blue dress with the white seagulls, and she looks wonderful. Her hair is done; she has been allowed makeup. At almost 1:00 A.M., after waiting more than three full days, Diane walks head up—proud. And smiling. Rosage and Jagger hurry her past the press cameras.

Paula Krogdahl is here—for the first time—standing with Doug Welch.

Inside the courtroom, Diane continues to smile, as if she knows that she is about to be freed. Jim Jagger seems nervous for the first time; he actually wrings his hands. Fred Hugi looks as calm as anyone has ever seen him.

There are three uniformed sheriff's officers in the courtroom, and one in mufti. A demonstration, even an attack, is not outside the realm of possibility.

A door creaks and everyone jumps, but it is only Judge Foote. He warns that there is to be no demonstration of any kind when the verdict is announced.

Diane bites her lip. A gesture new to her.

Judge foreman Daniel Bendt—the tall, young engineer—stands to say that they have reached a verdict.

For an instant, no one breathes.

And then Judge Foote reads the verdicts aloud:

Guilty of attempted murder in the first degree.

Guilty of a second count of attempted murder in the first degree.

Guilty of first degree assault.

Guilty of first degree assault.

Guilty of murder.

For a beat, no one moves. Then a reporter—a kid who hasn't been here until tonight—breaks and runs for the door and crashes through it. He will be the first to the phone, the first to break a scoop others have earned.

Diane is white as paper and finally she, too, trembles. But she will not break. Not in front of the crowd.

Judge Foote orders a pre-sentence investigation and remands Diane for sentencing.

The spell is broken. Reporters race for the basement where Diane must pass through the sally port on her way back to jail. Diane and Chris Rosage emerge down below, hurrying toward the light so they can move through it and escape the cameras. It is too late.

Sandy Poole, a Portland reporter, watches Diane the moment before she must walk out into the photographers' strobes.

"She pulled herself up and arranged a smile on her face. Chris was crying but Diane managed to keep that smile."

Jack Hamann calls out, "What was going through your mind when you heard the verdict?"

"I don't know," Diane answers flatly. "What am I supposed to think?"

"Were the verdicts a surprise?"

"Obviously . . ."

Diane smiles until the doors of the jail wagon close behind her. Only then does she cry.

At 1:10 A.M., Jim Jagger answers reporters' questions. No, he was not surprised at the verdict; he knew that the jurors had voted to convict Diane of the four lesser charges rather early in their deliberations, that there had been only one holdout in the voting to convict her of murder. Yes, certainly, he had warned Diane that it wasn't going to be good.

Upstairs in Judge Greg Foote's chambers, Foote had ordered champagne and strawberries to be shared when the trial was finally over. It was not a celebration party; rather, it was Foote's way of rewarding his staff for their support over the long haul. Foote, his secretary, Marj McElhose, his law clerk, Sharon Roe, and his reporter, Kay Cates, and her fiancé, gathered to mark the end of something that had consumed their lives for a solid year. Greg Foote knew that Diane's sentencing loomed ahead, but for now there was respite, and he was mightily grateful to his staff for sticking with the case with as much dedication as he himself felt.

Fred Hugi would have been invited, but he had already ducked out of the courthouse. He had spotted Anne Bradley headed his way, and even though he likes Bradley, he had no comments for the press. Hugi headed into the night, back up along the river toward home.

The reading of the verdict had been basically ceremonial for him. Jim Jagger had already called Hugi with tentative congratulations on the lesser charges, saying, "I'm still hoping for a holdout."

And, indeed there had been one. Rumors later mentioned one juror and then another as the one who'd balked. No one would ever know for sure; the jurors kept the answer to themselves. The question that kept coming up before a unanimous decision could be reached had been: "If the case was so strong, why did the State have to wait for Christie to remember?" One of the questions Hugi suspected might come up.

Still, Fred Hugi had remained confident that the jurors would ultimately be unanimous on the murder charge.

And he'd been right.

Hugi was tired—but tired the way he felt at the end of a long run. The tension that had walked with him for more than a year was gone. He had begun the trial over one hundred seventy-five pounds. He now weighed one hundred sixty.

Judge Foote and his staff left the courthouse and went out for a late meal. The news of the verdict had hit the news at 1:00 A.M. Cars were honking along the streets, almost as if a war had ended. As Foote and his group walked into the Electric Station, diners in the restaurant stood up and applauded.

It was June 17, 1984, almost two o'clock in the morning. The sky was clear. The moon was seven-eighths full.

It was Father's Day.

CHAPTER 44

Ten days later—on June 27—Doug Welch and Chris Rosage drove Diane to Sacred Heart Hospital in Eugene. Her labor was induced at 4:30 that afternoon, and throughout that warm evening Diane's contractions accelerated. Chris stayed with her; if she had not, Diane would have been alone in her labor. Wes and Willadene were not there, nor any of the rest of her family.

Welch waited in the hallway. He heard Diane cry out only a few times. Women in other labor rooms screamed and moaned, and some cursed their husbands—but not Diane. She was stoic in her pain.

At Diane's request, Chris Rosage went into the delivery room with her. It was a far, far cry from the joyous scene at Jennifer's birth in Louisville two years earlier. There were no grateful parents crying with her.

Amy Elizabeth Downs was born at 10:06 P.M. She weighed eight pounds, five ounces and she was twenty and one-half inches long. Diane had reconsidered her choice of "Charity Lynn" after hearing Hugi describe her babies as "fungible." Amy Elizabeth was a lovely baby who looked to Diane much like Christie had at birth. She had almond-shaped eyes and long slender fingers.

Diane was allowed to hold her baby for a long time. She even let Welch hold her. Perhaps the birth experience had mitigated Diane's animosity toward Welch. More likely, Fred Hugi had proved to be so much more savage an enemy that Welch didn't seem so bad anymore.

Within a few hours Diane was back in her jail cell, emptied of love and the baby who had helped her through the bad months and the tedious trial.

In the morning, she wrote to Matt Jensen. The letter, forwarded through a long series of addresses, reached him days later. By that time, he had read of the birth in clippings sent from Oregon. Diane blamed Jensen for the loss of her baby girl.

"She is perfectly formed and healthy. I will not tell you where she is because you will not be allowed to see her. I don't know if the news media has learned of her birth yet, so I wanted to let you know myself. I guess what I really want is to spread my pain and loss to you. You may not even care, but I do. She is such a beautiful child and I will miss her greatly. Will you?"

Matt Jensen had already signed a document releasing any claim to the child. However, he had balked at being designated the biological father because he could not be sure. He asked that the document be changed to read, "I believe that I *could* be the biological father" before he signed.

Jensen knew he had been selected solely for insemination. He wished the baby well, and he hoped that she would be happy and safe. But he felt no connection to her.

Diane would write to him again, urging him to take the baby, so that Willadene could take care of her until she got out of prison: "Why did you let her go? . . . How can you just let her be adopted? Don't you know all the insecurities Amy will face as she grows up? She'll wonder why her mom and dad deserted her. She'll think she was unloved and unwanted. How can you say you wish that on your own child? What are you going to say in twenty-one years when she shows up on your doorstep and says, 'Daddy, didn't you love me?'

"You wouldn't even have to raise her . . . My parents [Amy's grandma] would have been more than happy to care for their new granddaughter for the next few years that I have to be away. I'm not gonna be gone that long, ya know!"

He didn't answer any of her letters.

He didn't know her.

Diane Downs took her place with the grotesques of the 1980s. On July 17 the tabloid the *Weekly World News* printed a full-page picture of her; "*Kids Cramped Her Style* . . . so the fiendish mom shot them!"

It was a long way from what she had once pictured: her picture on the cover of *People* or *Time*.

As Diane waited for sentencing, her days took on a sameness. Her cell was nine and a half by ten feet, with a bunk, a toilet, a sink, and one small window high up for light. Breakfast call in the Lane County Correctional

Center came at six, and lights out at 11:30 P.M. There was little to do but read and write letters.

Two months after the birth of Amy Elizabeth—on August 28—Diane appeared before Judge Foote again, this time for sentencing.

Both Fred Hugi and Jim Jagger spoke, and Dr. George Suckow testified about his psychiatric examination of Diane. Dr. Suckow's testimony was most important. Under Oregon law, a murder conviction brings a life sentence—but there is no mandatory minimum *unless* the convicted is declared a Dangerous Offender."

In Suckow's opinion, Diane's personality disorders qualified her. Dr. Suckow diagnosed Diane as having not one but *three* disorders: Narcissistic, Histrionic, and Antisocial.

Most laymen have difficulty understanding the term: personality disorder. All of us have personality *traits*—the way we relate, perceive, and think about ourselves and our environments. Trouble begins if our personality traits become inflexible and unworkable, blunting our social lives, interfering with our ability to function, to enjoy, to interact happily with others. If that happens, those traits or quirks become personality disorders. Those with personality disorders usually show manifestations by adolescence—or even earlier—and they continue into adulthood, although they may become less apparent as we age.

Even professionals refer frequently to definitions in the psychiatrists' bible, *DSM-III* (*Diagnostic and Statistical Manual of Mental Disorders*), to differentiate one personality disorder from another. And there is still a great deal of overlapping.

The fine points on all three disorders—Histrionic, Narcissistic, and Antisocial—as outlined in the *DSM* might well have been written about Diane Downs:

> 301.50 *Histrionic Personality Disorder:* The essential feature is
> a Personality Disorder in which there are overly dramatic, re-
> active, and intensely expressed behavior and characteristic
> disturbances in interpersonal relationships. Individuals with

this disorder are lively and dramatic and are always drawing attention to themselves. They are prone to exaggeration and often act out a role, such as the "victim" or the "princess" . . .

According to *DSM-III*, the diagnosis as a histrionic will often find the patient "craving for activity and excitement . . . exaggerated expression of emotion . . . irrational angry outbursts or tantrums . . . incessant drawing of attention to one's self."

301.70: *Antisocial Personality Disorder:* The essential feature is a Personality Disorder in which there is a history of continuous and chronic antisocial behavior in which the rights of others are violated, persistence into adult life of a pattern of antisocial behavior that began before the age of 15 . . .

Some of the myriad manifestations of the antisocial personality disorder beyond the age of 18 are "lack of ability to function as a responsible parent . . . inability to maintain enduring attachment to a sexual partner . . . irritability and aggressiveness as indicated by repeated fights or assault . . . including spouse or child beating . . . impulsivity . . . disregard for the truth . . . "conning" others for personal profit . . . recklessness . . . recurrent speeding . . .

301.81 *Narcissistic Personality Disorder:* The essential feature is . . . a grandiose sense of self-importance or uniqueness; preoccupation with fantasies of unlimited success; exhibitionistic need for constant attention and admiration; characteristic responses to threats to self-esteem; and characteristic disturbances in interpersonal relationships, such as feelings of entitlement, interpersonal exploitiveness, relationships that alternate between the extremes of overidealization and devaluation, and lack of empathy . . . Fantasies involving unrealistic goals may involve achieving unlimited ability, power, wealth, brilliance, beauty, or ideal love . . . In response to criticism, defeat, or disappointment, there is either a cool indifference or marked feelings of rage, inferiority, shame, humiliation, or *emptiness*.

Diane fits them all, in one slot or another. Despite her miles of tape and pages of words of explanation, Diane Downs remains an enigma. Her crimes are incomprehensible to the conscience-driven person—her behavior outrageous. But Diane Downs is not insane—neither legally or medically. She suffers from the personality disorders described in the *DSM-III.*

She always will.

Insanity can be cured. Personality disorders are so inextricably entwined in the heart and mind and soul that it is well-nigh impossible to excise them. It would be much less difficult to eradicate Diane's giant rose tattoo than it would be to change her perception of herself and others.

Psychiatrists who examined her before she was accepted into the surrogate mother program had come up with findings similar to Suckow's. She had not changed.

Nor will she.

The narcissist loves only himself. The histrionic is always "on stage." The sociopath (antisocial personality) has no conscience. And all three love mischief, excitement, and trouble.

Psychosis—insanity—is relatively easy to diagnose. Most psychoses can be cured or alleviated with aggressive therapy. Given the option, it is preferable to be "crazy." Crazy gets better; consciences don't grow back, and narcissists and histrionics never learn to give up center stage or their beloved mirrors.

Sometime in her past, perhaps when others failed her, when her frail ego faltered, Diane Downs turned inward. She perceived that no one liked her, or had enough time for her. She fell in love with her own image. "I thought I was the nicest person I knew."

The narcissist expects special favors of others without responding in kind. Diane seems to have felt this sense of "entitlement" since she was a child.

When Diane could not manipulate people to do what she wanted, she reacted with indignation and rage. Four-year-olds scream for ice cream; adults learn that you don't always get what you want. Diane Downs never did.

Diane's interpersonal relationships were the most destructive of all.

What she wanted mattered; what someone else might want or need did not. Whatever means she employed to attain what she wanted—lying, cheating, wheedling, seduction, manipulation . . . even murder—were entirely justifiable in her mind. Continually, she sought someone to take care of *her,* to make *her* life wonderful. Her course was unrealistic and pregnant with disappointment, but she never varied. Even with Christie and Cheryl and Danny. Their assignment had been to love her totally, to make her feel needed—but then to stay away when she wanted to be with one of her men.

For all of her life, Diane has searched for "pure love." "Heart love." But she can offer nothing in return. Diane Downs's hunger for unconditional love is akin to a trick pitcher that seems eternally to be half-empty—even though a steady stream of fluid pours into it.

The term "histrionic" derives from the Latin word for actor: "histrio." Anyone who has seen Diane Downs on the witness stand, on television, or at a press conference will nod at the second diagnosis. She is on stage *wherever* she is. Her life is a continuous performance. If it takes slitting her wrists or firing a gun through the floor to get someone's attention, she will do it.

Diane Downs is a sociopath—an antisocial personality—perhaps the most familiar psychiatric term to most of us. She has not the slightest concern for the rights of others. A brilliant mind with no conscience to guide it, the antisocial personality has been likened to a blank television screen, to a computer, or a robot. It mimics "real" people, giving back only what it must to receive gratification.

The sociopath breaks hearts and minds and lives, and is disastrous as a parent. It was never programmed to be a caretaker.

A sociopath's children are like puppies or kittens brought home on the spur of the moment: dispensable, expendable, and all too often, "fungible."

"Mrs. Downs claims innocence," Dr. Suckow wrote, after examining her. "And shows no remorse. She regards the children with no empathy and as objects or possessions. Feelings she has for them are superficial and only extend to how they are part of her and her life."

Recent research into the problem shows that three percent of all American males are considered antisocial, while only one percent of women are. Interestingly, little boys tend to show sociopathic traits early in childhood, while girls with antisocial personality disorders rarely exhibit symptoms before the onset of puberty.

Studies show that a familial pattern has emerged; it is particularly common to find that both male and female sociopaths have fathers with the same personality disorder.

All three of the personality disorders attributed to Diane Downs carry with them frequent bouts of depression. And that is hardly surprising. Since the narcissist, the histrionic, and the sociopath demand so much from others, and give so little back, relationships cannot survive.

They cannot love. They do not even understand love—and yet they seek "love" unceasingly.

Diane Downs is brilliant, but there is linkage missing in her ability to reason. She can go from A to C, but the circuitry of her mind appears to be missing B. She doesn't understand that if she says one thing and does exactly the opposite, the disparity between the two becomes apparent. She continues to believe that she can do whatever she wants because she has only to "explain" it. Her thinking is like an ostrich's. The giant bird believes if it puts its head in the sand, it becomes invisible.

It is a far easier task to place Diane within the parameters of certain personality disorders than it is to pinpoint why she is the way she is. Diane claims sexual abuse at the hands of her father. In open court, she has accused him of subjecting her to a year or more of night terrors. He has not denied it.

It is impossible to be sure one way or the other; Diane Downs has out-and-out lied about so many aspects of her life. Other events are misperceived.

And sometimes she tells the truth.

Diane recalls emotional abuse, lecturing, and lack of emotional support. She felt trapped, denigrated, unimportant. She learned to hide inside herself, to shut the world out behind a black wall of nothingness. Her screams were inside. She remembers her first "blacking out" at the age of sixteen; it is likely that the phenomenon began much earlier.

It is impossible to know if Diane's psychopathology is inborn or the result of abuse. Studies show that sexually abused children learn to disassociate themselves from their bodies. They deal with the abuse by going away someplace—in their heads. It is the only way they can escape. Betrayed by an adult whose role should have been that of a protector, they learn to feel nothing at all.

If one does not feel, one cannot be hurt. Nor can one feel anything for anyone else.

As the abused child reaches puberty and adulthood, he often uses his/her body to get what he wants. The majority of prostitutes—both male and female—were sexually abused as children. They have long since learned to allow others to use their bodies while they have "checked out" with their emotions.

It is a kind of little death.

Diane Downs is sexually promiscuous. She may have seduced men for reasons that were not in the least sexual. She may have learned to offer her body to protect her mind.

Did Diane Downs *ever* feel love or compassion? Or is it possible that the baby girl born in August of 1955 was, like the title of the bestselling novel that month . . . a "bad seed"?

Diane's memory of being different, of being unhappy, stretches back to her first awareness. She may have been *born* needing too much, demanding too much. Insatiable.

More than one rational forensic psychiatrist has said flatly, "Some children are simply born evil. They start out evil, and they remain evil."

Evil. Always Diane's favorite epithet. She is quite conversant with the parameters of evil.

In the end, students of the so-called criminal personality, researchers into the deepest, ebony-shaded deeds of human endeavor, admit that there is so much they do not know. The most unlikely killers commit the most heinous crimes.

If it *is* abuse that has made a monster, do we blame the monster or the abuser? Or both? Although we cannot risk letting the monster out to destroy other lives, we can, perhaps, learn from case histories.

Diane's suggestion to "stop the cycle" was to eliminate an entire generation. As Fred Hugi pointed out, she almost did . . .

Attempted murder and assault in the first degree are Class A felonies in Oregon, and carry a twenty-year maximum with a possible ten-year minimum mandatory. A Dangerous Offender status *demands* a thirty-year maximum and a fifteen-year minimum.

Diane—svelte and lovely in a lavender sundress topped by a bolero—rose to speak to Judge Foote before he administered sentence. Her voice was tremulous, dramatic, and choked with tears.

"I would like to say that I came before this Court, was tried, was found guilty—because I am a law-abiding citizen. I'll do my time . . . for this man. I care about the community. They can't let their guard down. The killers are still out there.

"I love my kids. Christie's my best friend. Danny cried for Mommy in the hospital. I carried a little girl for nine months—and only held her for four hours. Most important, Cheryl died . . . I will serve my time, and then I'll find that killer and bring him in . . ."

Foote gazed down on her silently. And then he pronounced sentence on Diane. He spoke with surprising venom.

He stressed first that if Diane should ever make money from writing a book about herself, much of it would go to pay fines to be levied by the court for the cost of the investigation and trial.

Foote praised the heroism of the medical team at McKenzie-Willamette. "Those people did the best that could be done. They should be commended. The death of a child is one of life's greatest tragedies . . . what might have been . . .

"When it comes intentionally . . . at the hands of a parent—it's just—an outrage. I don't apologize for the times I've reacted with emotion. The court grieves for Cheryl and feels sorrow for Christie and Danny . . . anger . . . frustration. I don't apologize for that. That's ironic, perhaps, since the defendant lacks those emotions."

Foote said that it was his intellect—his reason—that told him Diane had objectified the children to enable her to rid herself of them "like useless baggage."

He had fought his own battles with reason and emotion. His reason told him "she should never be in a position of freedom. She doesn't *deserve* to be free—that's emotion."

Foote said he knew all too well that a judge can never be sure of what the corrections department, or the parole board, might do. "I lose all control of the case then. I have to try to pre-suppose what they'll do."

With his present power Foote handed down his sentence, each word flung at the woman who stood before him—a woman who was so beautiful, who looked so soft and frail, but whom he clearly saw only as a monster.

To guard against some future parole board forgetting the enormity of her crimes, Foote decreed that the sentences would run consecutively:

> For Murder: Life plus five years minimum because she had used a firearm; for Attempted Murder, counts two and four— thirty years, with a fifteen-year minimum (the mandatory five-year firearm charge would run concurrently); for Assault in the First Degree, counts three and five—twenty years, with a ten-year minimum (with the mandatory five-years firearm concurrent sentence).

Gregory Foote had just sentenced Diane to life plus fifty years in prison, with a twenty-five-year mandatory minimum. He leaned toward Diane and said, "The Court hopes the defendant will never again be free. I've come as close to that as possible."

Diane had expected to go up to Salem to the Oregon Women's Correctional Center; she hadn't expected that her sentence would be so overwhelming.

She simply refused to believe it. She would find some way to change it.

Diane was anxious to leave the jail in Eugene and get on with this next milestone of her life, but she was leery of arriving at prison alone. She had made one woman friend in the Lane County Jail—a woman named Billie Jo—and Diane planned for Billie Jo to accompany her to Salem.

Diane had given Willadene a long list of things to bring: clothes, her bathing suit, her tennis racket, her makeup—all her "must haves for prison."

Her plans started to go awry when Billie Jo's commitment papers hadn't come through on August 31. Diane was scheduled to be transported to "the joint" that day. She would be alone—except for Chris Rosage who drove the van, and Doug Welch.

Diane was livid. In a fit of temper, she tore up a handful of letters she'd intended to mail. When Rosage and Welch arrived at the jail at 2:00 P.M., they were met in the sally port by a corrections officer who cautioned, "Stand by. Look out. Diane is in a foul mood today—I've never seen it before; nobody here has ever seen her act this way before."

Diane had written Randy Woodfield to watch for her entrance into prison. "I'll be the one with the wiggle and the jiggle." It is doubtful that Randy could even see the walk into the women's facility from his cell, but Diane had prepared meticulously anyway.

Doug Welch's mouth almost dropped open when Diane walked out of the holding room in the jail. The pregnant defendant and the slender woman who had appeared at sentencing three days before had gone through yet another metamorphosis. This was a woman who had dressed for sexual trolling.

"She came out of the holding room strutting her stuff, exaggerated hip movement, long confident strides. She was angry, and nobody in the area escaped her wrath."

Even Welch—who had always been Diane's least favorite cop—had only seen her so furious once before—during the hardball interview the previous summer.

Diane's hair had been cut very, very short on the sides, with a lock of hair falling over her forehead, the characteristic punk-rocker wisp of hair at the back of the neck. Her naturally brown hair had grown out. There were only a few streaks of blonde left.

She wore skintight Levi's, so tight that every mound, cleft and tuck was accentuated. Her jeans were tucked into the wildest pair of boots Welch had ever seen: shiny black leather with six-inch, spiked heels. The boots came up over the knee and were cut in the back into a V—probably to allow the leg to bend. Above this, Diane wore a short-sleeved sheer white blouse cut low in front. Her bra did nothing to support the breasts that jiggled with every furious stride.

Yes, the prisoners in the state penitentiary would remember Diane

Downs's arrival. She looked mean, she looked bad, and she looked sexy. She did not look like a devout Baptist or a grieving mother.

Chris Rosage moved to put the "belly-chains" on her prisoner, and as she patted Diane down, she commented quietly that she'd "never seen boots like that before."

Diane, who usually liked Chris, snapped, "Well, it's just because you don't run with my kind of people."

Diane caught Welch studying her outfit, particularly the boots.

"What's wrong, Doug? Haven't you ever seen boots like these before?"

"Only on Bat Girl," he answered mildly.

As Chris adjusted the belly-chains, Diane turned to Welch. "What are you going to do when the truth comes out, Doug?"

"Oh—probably just read about it," he answered.

At seven minutes after two, the trio walked to the Ford prisoner's van and Diane was placed in the rear compartment. The belly-chains allowed her cuffed hands only slight movement. Her rage seemed to have diminished. She sat quietly on a bench which ran along the side of the van and stared out the rear window as they pulled out of Eugene, passed Springfield, and then gathered speed along I-5 going north.

Friday, August 31, was a gray day with spates of hard rain. Diane, who loved sunshine, would see only clouds and rain during the hour's drive to prison—her first prolonged time outside since her arrest six months before.

And, most probably, her last.

Welch studied her, and she turned to catch his eyes. She forced a resigned smile.

"Are you scared, Diane?" he asked.

"What do you think?"

When he glanced back later, he saw that Diane had wriggled until she was on her back, her legs spread obscenely wide, her bare midriff exposed. She stared into his eyes, and it dawned on him that she was attempting to seduce him. For God's sake, why? Maybe because he was the last male she would see before prison?

He looked away, toward the road ahead.

They pulled through the main prison gates at one minute to three.

Diane sat up and looked around. "Well, Diane, this is it," Welch said. "Here's your new home."

She gave him a sarcastic smile. "Thank you."

The guard in the tower requested credentials. Chris Rosage responded, "We're from Lane County. We have one female prisoner."

They drove through, past the men's sector.

Diane said suddenly, "Ya know, you're OK, Doug."

"How can you say that after calling me names for fifteen months?"

"I can't believe anyone can be as bad as you've acted. What's your sign?"

"Cancer—but I don't think we're compatible."

Weapons secured, they drove on slowly to the Women's Center, located next to the Oregon State Penitentiary.

They headed down the long narrow sidewalk that leads to the intake area. Welch, following Diane and Chris up the walk, heard a voice yelling at him, someone banging on a window. He turned to see a plump black woman in her thirties.

"Is *that* 'Lizbet Diane Downs?"

He nodded. In the intake area, they were greeted by two pleasant-looking women who logged Diane's personal property, and began to fill out forms.

Welch felt Diane's eyes on him again. He returned her gaze.

"You've lost some hair during all of this, Doug—or maybe I've just never looked at you before."

"I probably have."

"Well, smile, Doug—don't look so sad."

"Oh, I'm not," he taunted her, aware that she was drawing him into one of her sarcastic games. "I'm elated—I'm thrilled."

"Hmm. I know you are."

Diane's belly-chains were removed, and Rosage and Welch turned to leave. When Welch reached the threshold, he turned and looked back at Diane.

She was leaning with her back against the wall, staring at the floor. Her smile was gone.

The deputies walked back down the sidewalk toward the gate, and the same woman banged on the window and called to them again.

"Hey! Hey—was that *really* 'Lizbet Diane Downs?"

Again, Welch nodded.

"Y'am mo beat her up. Y'am mo kick her ass . . ."

Behind Chris Rosage and Doug Welch, the door to intake slammed shut. Diane was alone now with the other women prisoners. For a moment there, as she'd stood leaning against the wall, she had looked again like the little girl who waited desperately outside the schoolroom for recess to be over.

CHAPTER 45

Fred Hugi got a phone call in the first part of November, 1984; it was like a nightmare that had come back full blown. Diane had been in the penitentiary for three months when Chandler Police sergeant Ed Sweitzer called the Lane County DA's office with news that would prove appalling.

The missing gun had been found. A .22 Ruger pistol, a semi-automatic bearing the serial number listed for the gun thought to have been in Diane's possession—#14-76187—had been recovered in a narcotics raid by Sergeant John Hansen of the Perris California Police Department. When Hansen punched the serial numbers into the National Crime Information Center computer network, he came up with a hit citing a warrant for the gun out of Chandler.

Paul Alton flew to Chandler once again, and subsequently to Perris, California. The narcotics dealer had obtained the weapon from a Perris acquaintance. That man told Alton that he had acquired the .22 in Phoenix around Christmas of 1981!

But how could that be? Steve Downs and Lew Lewiston both swore that Diane took the gun with her when she left Arizona in April, 1983 . . .

Assuming that someone had misremembered dates, Alton had the

.22 test-fired and all the components—shell casings, bullets, etc.—
shipped to Jim Pex.

*Pex found no similarities between these bullets and casings and those
found at the death site on Old Mohawk Road.*

This gun they had sought for so long was not the murder weapon! This
gun could not have been the gun Steve Downs had owned.

Alton couldn't believe it. There had to be some explanation.

He traced the .22 with serial number #14-76187 from the Sturm-Ruger
Company in Southport, Connecticut, to Arizona Hardware in Phoenix,
and then to the Chandler Gun Shop owned by Fred Barton. Barton's records showed he acquired it on January 24, 1978.

Billy Proctor, Steve Downs's friend, said he'd purchased the gun six
days later. It had disappeared during a time when Steve and his best
friend were living with him. Proctor was convinced that either Stan Post
or Steve had stolen it from him.

Billy Proctor was seriously ill with cancer. But he agreed to meet with
Paul Alton. How could that gun have ended up in Perris, California, Alton
wondered.

Proctor shook his head, pondering the question. Suddenly, a memory
dawned.

"I bought that gun—that gun they've got in California—but I only had
it for one day. That first gun."

"*First* gun?" Alton echoed.

"Yeah. I wanted a .22 Ruger like that—but I wanted one with target
sights. I took it up to Mesa, and traded up for a Ruger with adjustable
sights. I bought a vinyl case and two extra clips for the second gun."

Proctor had completely forgotten that he'd traded the gun he bought
at the Chandler Gun Shop after only a day. Alton asked him if he had any
receipts or papers that might show the serial number of the second gun.

Proctor called back a half hour later. He had found an old gun box.
"There's a .38 inside, but I can see where I wrote the serial number of that
other Ruger on the box. It says, 'Ruger automatic: Serial #14-57485.'"

"That's the gun Steve stole from your house?"

"Yeah. I'm sorry—but I completely forgot about the first gun. I had it
such a short time, and that's the one listed at the gun shop. The one
Downs had is the one I got in Mesa the next day."

Kathy Austin, of the Chandler Police Department, started now to trace the new gun from its original point of origin. It too had come from Sturm-Ruger originally. It went first to a wholesaler in Massachusetts and then was shipped on November 1, 1977, to a loan company in Mesa, Arizona.

Austin called the loan company/jewelry store. Their records verified Billy Proctor's memory. "The gun was sold to William R. Proctor on February 1, 1978. He traded in another Ruger—the one with the original serial number you were looking for: #14-76187."

Paul Alton worked his way through all the owners of the "wrong" gun and satisfied himself that it had never, ever been in either Steve or Diane Downs's hands. Steve had stolen the *second* Ruger that Billy Proctor had purchased—the gun with the adjustable sights that Stan Post had described. And Diane had taken that second gun from Steve.

Nothing had changed then. The gun that had been used on the night of May 19 was still missing. It was still a .22 semi-automatic Ruger manufactured by Sturm-Ruger Company. But the serial number had been wrong. The missing gun bears the number: #14-57485.

AFTERWORD

At the Women's Correctional Center, Diane—whose case had been deemed Project 100 by the Lane County Sheriff's Office—was, coincidentally, given a similar prison number. She was now #0100W.

Diane continued to grant interviews throughout the fall of 1984. Reporters had merely to ask for an audience with her at the prison in Salem. She still protested her innocence, but she was remarkably cheerful. As long as the glow of the media warmed her, Diane functioned quite well.

She told a reporter from the *Cottage Grove Sentinel* that she much preferred the Oregon State Women's Correction center to the Lane County Jail. She bragged that she had scored higher on the IQ section of the routine entrance diagnostic tests than any woman who had come to the women's prison in five years.

"Personally, I think I'll probably do pretty well in college here ..."

Diane planned to get a "state grant" to finance her college education. "I want to be a teacher . . . I think probably something like family development—or something along those lines."

The institution did offer college credit courses in all manner of subjects—from creative writing to plumbing, but prisoners had to *earn* the right to attend. Diane was a long way from that.

She could wait. In prison, Diane was allowed outside to walk on the grass, and she even had a sunburn. The sun had always cheered her.

The woman who needed male admiration to validate her existence was locked up with eighty-three females. Diane was not popular with her peers, but no one had attacked her physically. There was a verbal exchange or two, notes slipped under her cell door.

Half of her correspondence in the Lane County Jail in Eugene had been from convicts, and Diane continued to write to "the guys." She had an enthusiastic following among the male prisoners. Mailcall always meant a stack of letters for her. Randy Woodfield, who had hinted at—and then denied to the media—his formal engagement to Diane, continued to write, but she grew tired of him.

Diane's first assignment was the kitchen crew, which meant getting up at five to cook and wash dishes.

She had a single cell initially, but was moved to share a double with a woman convicted of poisoning her children. Diane tacked up pictures of Christie and Danny, and the newborn shots of Amy Elizabeth. There were no pictures of Cheryl.

She found prison boring, but she was, for the most part, a compliant prisoner. She was written up by a guard who claimed she was in the yard facing the men's section—nude from the waist down. The demerit was eventually removed.

Diane found that many of the other prisoners had "turned off their minds. It's really sad, but they are like walking vegetables." She read murder mysteries and love stories, but said she didn't watch soap operas.

Diane insisted for months that she would be free in five to seven years.

And then she said confidently that she would be out of prison in six months to two years, convinced her appeal would be successful.

In the meantime, Diane planned to take philosophy and psychology in prison college classes. By January, 1985, she had changed her career ambitions; she had decided to become a counselor for teen-agers, to help them cope with the "rigors of growing up in a mean, tough world." She was initially granted permission to attend college classes, but that was withdrawn. She was—and is—considered an escape risk.

When the Oregon State Parole Board met in the spring of 1985 to consider Diane's minimum sentence, they were succinct. She will not be considered for parole until 2009. When she is fifty-four years old, a decade after the turn of the century, the parole board will again ponder each year a decision to hear her petition for parole.

The board had listened well to Judge Gregory Foote's comments.

Exactly a year after Chris Rosage and Doug Welch drove Diane Downs to the Oregon State Prison, she grudgingly granted a television interview; she explained that she no longer trusted the media.

The woman on the screen in September, 1985, had once more changed in appearance. It has always been so. Through each phase of Diane's life, she has melted into her surroundings, assuming a kind of protective coloration. The color of her hair, its length, her make-up and attire, are only partially responsible for the continual transformation. It is as if Diane Downs has no idea who she really is; she is like heated wax conforming to the shape of the container it fills.

After that first year in prison, she appeared the complete convict—no longer delicate, clearly fifteen pounds heavier on starchy prison fare. But it was more than that. There was a hardness about Diane, some subtle loss of femininity. The deep circles beneath her eyes and the skin pallor so evident at her trial were gone. She looked to be blooming with health, very tan, and without make-up. Her cheeks were round, her jawline strong. The television camera caught her eyes squinting into the sun. Hard eyes. She looked for all the world like the female truck driver she once was.

Her hair was straight, long, and brown, but she tossed it from her brow with the same impatient shake of her head. She continued to smile broadly as she spoke of tragedy and loss.

In the fall of 1986, after *two* full years in prison, Diane faced the cameras yet again. Mary Starett from KATU TV in Portland prevailed upon Diane to skip one of the college classes that she is now permitted to attend. She would grant an interview, Diane stressed imperiously, if she were the *only* convict filmed. She would not participate in a group discussion of how women coped in prison.

The face that flashed across Portland screens is delicately lovely. Diane now looks like a homecoming princess, a decade younger than her actual age—as if being incarcerated offers a beauty regime far superior to the Golden Door or any other posh spa. Yes, she says softly, she had been so depressed at first that she didn't bother with her hair or use makeup, but her hope of a new trial in the year ahead has cheered her.

Her external regeneration is complete. Her cosmetics have been applied with a skilled hand, her huge eyes edged with silver blue and kohl, her high cheekbones blushed pink. Her eyebrows have been plucked away almost entirely. Diane's hair is ash-blond and curls to her shoulders. Her nails are long, and exquisitely manicured.

Either Diane has had elocution lessons, or she has learned from her earlier television interviews. She speaks more slowly. She pauses at sentence breaks. There is a studied calmness about her that was never there before, as she urges educational opportunities for prisoners and expounds on the need for rehabilitation. After all, all of them will one day be out among the populace again, she warns. Without rehabilitation and education. "We'll go out and be the same—or worse."

Diane blames her conviction on "past press," declaring that the jury never really looked at the evidence. She explains that her sister convicts have long since accepted her "because I'm just me; I'm just a little girl—they can see I'm no threat."

And yet, behind her newly demure media-facade, Diane Downs continues to behave bizarrely. This last fall, she prevailed upon one of her attorneys to bring her Cheryl's autopsy photographs, which she insisted she needed to help prepare her appeal. In her cell, she studied them for a long time, then horrified fellow prisoners and guards by insisting that they look at her dead daughter's image.

One guard demurred forcefully, but Diane pushed the photos into her field of vision. The woman ran from the corridor, vomiting. That guard set about getting the pictures away from Diane. It was not easy; Diane wanted to keep them.

Nevertheless, prison becomes Diane. Perhaps she feels somehow safer locked up—even as she predicts that she will soon be free.

This woman whose life has been one long rebellion against rules and control has come at last to a place where her every waking moment is governed by rules, where she is under the control of others.

Prison.

Fred Hugi, in his final arguments, described Diane as "the truck without brakes." She has brakes now.

For the moment.

Diane predicts that the day will come when she will be reunited with her living children. She plans to put an ad in the paper when Christie is eighteen, urging her to come home. She expects to be out of prison by then. She laments that the presents, poems, pictures, and letters she sends the children are returned unopened.

Diane's announcement that she intends to collaborate on a book to tell "the real story" has sparked a special bill in the Oregon legislature to prevent Diane (and other convicted felons) from profiting by writing about her crimes.

Above everything else, Diane yearns to be pregnant again. Her worst fear is that "female problems" may force her to have a hysterectomy. There is a deeper sense of urgency in her drive to conceive. Aware of her propensity for seeking out and seducing genetically superior males, prison authorities keep a close eye on Diane.

She considers herself "married" to a prisoner named Frank, although the prison "marriage" is hampered because Diane cannot actually be with her "husband," and because she was sent to the "hole" (isolation) for three months.

Diane wrote to another male prisoner, asking him to correspond with a female prisoner who Diane considered a rival for Frank's affection:

> ... *it's obvious this girl is either bored, or has a death wish—*
> *and since I sorta wanta stay outta seg, I'll choose to believe she's*
> *bored. I can't think of any other reason she wants to hit on* my

*"husband" . . . I am asking if you would like a pen pal that spe-
cializes in the filthiest smut around? Of course you would. You're
a healthy, red-blooded American convict . . . Please don't ever tell
Frank I wrote to you and turned you on to this 'lil morsel, cuz
he'd be mad at me for "manipulating" this whole thing—when,
in fact—I have no desire to manipulate anything . . .*

*. . . I love Frank with all I have . . . this man really has my
heart . . .*

Diane has acclimated.

Still, if she *could* only have a fetus growing in her womb again, her spirits
would soar. Children represent an almost mythic—and elusive—goal to
Diane. "Kids are neat—innocent, young, pure. Grown-ups are tainted
somehow."

Locked away in prison, perhaps forever, Diane is still seeking pure
love, long after she destroyed the purest love she ever had.

The children Diane sought to destroy found themselves, at long last, surrounded by love. In September, 1985, all legal connections between Danny
and Christie and their "natural mother" were severed. They would spend
three healing years in the Slavens' home.

Evelyn Slaven had taped all of Diane's appearances on television, and
she showed Christie selected segments long after the trial was over.
Christie watched, becoming more and more indignant.

"She's lying," Christie cried. "She's telling great big lies. Are people going to believe her instead of me?"

Evelyn, pleased that Christie finally felt free to express anger, assured
her, "*You're* the one they believed, Christie."

As much as she trusts Evelyn, Christie never called her "Mother." "I
doubt that Christie will ever again want to call anyone 'Mom,' 'Mommy,'
or 'Mother,'" Evelyn Slaven says. "Those, sadly, are *bad* words, frightening
words to her. 'Moms' hurt you."

Christie moved up to middle school, starting seventh grade in the fall
of 1986. Her right arm is still partially paralyzed; since she is left-handed,
she doesn't exercise it enough. She works very hard to do as well in school

as she did before her stroke. She once got straight A's; she is back up to B pluses. The keen intelligence is there, but she must move through an "extra loop" before she answers questions. If she feels secure, she will say nothing until the answer comes. If she feels pressured, she may give a wrong answer first—to buy time. But she *always* knows the answers.

Danny remains paralyzed from the chest down. He usually crawls using his hands, his palms turned outward, his legs dragging behind. He can navigate upright in a rig called a "podium," which holds him rigid below the waist. By wriggling his shoulders, he moves with amazing speed.

On a trampoline or in a pool, Danny seems the bubbly, fully coordinated child he was once. Among the pictures the children sent to Judge Gregory Foote the Halloween after the trial, there are several of Danny laughing on a trampoline.

Ray Slaven had "a really good feeling the first year that there was a possibility he might be able to recoup some of his losses. He was so determined—but it didn't happen. He doesn't really concentrate anymore on things he can't do; he works on what he can do. Like turning on a light. When he got to that point, that was a big deal! He's real spirited."

For Christie and Danny, Diane became, gradually, only someone they knew once. Evelyn Slaven noted that they continued to feel responsible for Diane for a long time.

"I told them that she was OK. That she was up in prison, and probably she'd get to go to school soon—that they didn't have to worry about her any longer—because she had her own life. They were relieved. It took Christie, of course, the longest to let go.

"Finally, they didn't ask about her anymore at all."

Christie and Danny were quickly "mainstreamed" at school. Danny lasted only three days in kindergarten before it was clear he was beyond it. He was skipped into the grades. He loves to study, and is especially fascinated with calculators, computers—anything having to do with numbers. At six, he cannot yet understand all the ramifications of what has happened to him.

Christie volunteered to be manager of the volleyball team and, last spring, of softball. She is still a bit uncoordinated to actually play, but with supportive peers, her shyness is thawing. She finished the last school year as "first chair" in the school band, playing the French horn.

Christie and Danny spent many, many weekends with Joanne and Fred Hugi—quiet pleasant times, according to Hugi, "doing things that are fun." Christie and Danny had become a part of Fred Hugi's very private life; the bonds formed on the morning of May 20, 1983, were irrevocable. Together with the Slavens, Fred and Joanne Hugi are responsible for helping Christie and Danny understand what it is like to be loved, to be children.

Christie and Danny see *no one* they had known before May 19, 1983. They have literally stepped into a new, kinder world.

After the verdict, returning with Sue Staffel from a visit with the children at the Slavens, his car window open, Hugi recalls tensing when he heard the raucous strains of "Hungry Like the Wolf" coming from a tape deck in another car. His jaw set and his stomach roiled . . . and then he relaxed and smiled at Staffel: "They're playing our song."

The "she-wolf" was locked up. The kids were safe. The song no longer represented tragedy to Hugi; it represented justice. Even so, Fred Hugi remembers that Diane came within a hair's breadth of being acquitted. If all the children had died, and if Diane had not had the rifle on her closet shelf with the identical cartridges in it, he believes she would have walked away . . . free.

Amy Elizabeth has been adopted.

Steve Downs still lives in Chandler. He regrets that the State of Oregon's recently restored death penalty is not retroactive. "There are not too many people who have done worse than she has. I'm no angel, but she really needs to be eliminated from off this earth."

He does not see or write to his children.

Doug Welch and Kurt Wuest are still with the Lane County Sheriff's Office, again as detectives. Their career fortunes remain dependent on the voters' yeas or nays on budget levies.

Dick Tracy has retired and is now a private investigator.

Paul Alton has retired.

Louis Hince has retired.

Gregory Foote retains his judgeship.

District Attorney Pat Horton is now in private law practice.

Ray Broderick continues to work as an investigator for the Lane County District Attorney's Office. Across his office from the wall that holds his ever-changing collection of cartoons, there is his poignant sketch of Cheryl Downs, and next to it—a frame containing twelve scraps of lined yellow paper, smoothed out where they were crumpled. The jurors' final twelve "Guilties."

Pierce Brooks spent almost a year at FBI headquarters in Quantico, Virginia, as project director for VI-CAP, where he set up the Violent Criminal Apprehension Program to track and trap serial murderers—the realization for Brooks of a longtime dream.

Paula Krogdahl passed the Oregon Bar Exam; she is married, working as an assistant district attorney in Salem, Oregon; she is a new mother.

Lew Lewiston continues to carry the mail in Chandler; he is happily married to Nora. Together, they burned all of Diane's letters, pictures, cards, and poems. They have bought a new home. Lew no longer drinks or smokes.

Willadene Frederickson visits her daughter in prison, faithfully each week. Wes Frederickson is still the postmaster of Springfield, Oregon.

On a time continuum, Diane's case is about halfway through the court system. Fred Hugi will not completely relax until the Oregon Supreme Court affirms her sentence. His estimated date for that is probably 1989 or 1990.

On Palomino Street in Chandler, nobody remembers Diane Downs's name. Her charred trailer has been repaired and cleaned up; the new owners cut away the bougainvillea she planted and put in stone-cast burros. In Oregon, the Little Mohawk is clear and cold still, the white painted stripes across the road have worn away, the fields of white flowers are back. It has all healed over.

Only Cheryl is gone forever.

———

"I'm just a person," Diane Downs once said fervently to Dana Tims of the *Oregonian*. "Just a little girl. I'm not different from anybody else. People think the system has a lot of flaws as far as letting people out too soon. They don't. They lock these people away for a long, long time—especially if they are in for murder.

"Chances are you will never get out . . ."

Christie remembers Diane telling her in the hospital that she must not tell. But, when it was all over, when her mother had been kept away from her for such a long time that she finally began to feel a little bit safe, Christie asked a question about something she couldn't understand. One question she needed an answer for.

She asked it often.

"Why didn't anybody hear us screaming? We were screaming and screaming. Why didn't anybody hear us—?"

Someone did. The cycle is over.

POSTSCRIPT

Christie and Danny share a home today with two people who love them and are committed to giving them a serene and happy future. Since the summer of 1986, they have lived with Joanne and Fred Hugi.

UPDATE: 1988

PART ONE

There are some stories that never end; Diane Downs's saga may well be one of them. As long as Diane is alive, the most a biographer can hope to do is keep abreast of the schemes and changes Diane's busy mind churns out.

When Diane granted her interview to Portland's KATU in the fall of 1986, she fully expected to be involved in a new trial by the following summer. She appeared supremely confident, but when she was asked to speculate on the odds that she would go free, she shyly ducked her head and said softly, "I can't predict the future. . . ."

Privately, she believed she could; she had simply mastered a studied humility on camera. She was now given to phrases such as: "I cannot speak for others—I don't have that right," and "I don't know what they want of me—to give me back my children. I just don't know what they want."

Diane had learned to speak softly, and with great reticence. She was no longer the transparent, verbose woman who talked without thinking. She had acclimated to her surroundings, but in a most tentative fashion. Of the 126 women who were serving time in the Oregon Women's Correctional Center, Diane chose to converse with a half dozen at most.

By the time she ended her second year behind walls, Diane Downs was neither actively liked nor disliked by her peers. The number of threatening notes that had been slipped under her door, of comments murmured in the rec room or dining hall, of clumsily deliberate stumbles knocking her against corridor walls, had diminished and then stopped.

"I wouldn't let them break me to the point I'd go to my room and cry," she explained defiantly. As always, her emotional survival depended upon a superior facade.

Diane laughed as she posed for KPTV's cameras and flipped fried potatoes on a huge grill in the prison kitchen. Lars Larson, one of her media confidants of the old days, had come from Portland with his camera crew to interview her. As always, the cameras pleased Diane. She was clearly in charge of the filming session.

"I'll tell you what"—she smiled, not at the photographer but directly into the lens—"*I'll* hold the camera, and *you* can fry potatoes."

Love songs blared over the kitchen's sound system. Young women locked away from men stirred gallon vats of food, and Diane flipped the same potatoes again and again for the camera. "See Diane Downs fry potatoes," she scoffed. "She *should* be going to college—but she's got to earn her whole dollar a day. . . ."

Diane's most faithful visitor was her mother. Willadene Frederickson made the hour-plus trip up to Salem at least three evenings a month, and usually more often. Diane's brother Paul came often too, and Wes Frederickson sometimes accompanied Willadene—particularly for holiday visits.

Visitors waiting to see other prisoners recall Diane as a smiling, friendly woman who seemed particularly fascinated by the children who came along to visit. She seemed nothing like the notorious "child-killer" they had read about, and yet something made them reach a hand out protectively as Diane stooped to peer into their little ones' faces.

"She asked questions about my little girl's 'potty-training' and things like that," one visitor recalled. "She seemed really nice, like any young mother you'd meet who wanted to compare notes."

Each visitor was allowed to take a dollar in change to be used in the snack machines in the visiting room. Prisoners were not permitted to stockpile money, a precaution against the possibility that they might escape.

But there were ways around the rules. Figuring out ways to bend the rules is a major preoccupation in any prison. A number of prisoners had contrived to hide hundreds of dollars in tightly rolled bills inserted deep into their vaginas.

Diane had one frequent visitor outside her family: Richard Cone, thirty-six, her official biographer. Cone, an Albany, Oregon, man, was working with Diane on a book—*Conspiracy of Silence*: Diane's story of her innocence and of the "real killer" who she maintained was still free. It was a first book for both, and written without a publisher's contract. Diane and Cone had pressed on with their collaboration even after the "Slayer's Act" (or Son of Sam Statute) ruling by the Oregon legislature.

Temporarily stymied, Cone announced that he would argue before an administrative hearing in Salem that his book contained no first-person descriptions by Diane of the shootings. Without that firsthand account, Cone contended that the book did not violate the law enacted to prevent convicted felons from profiting from accounts of their crimes.

His arguments to the legislature and vehement letters to editors of Oregon papers fell on deaf ears, but Cone and Diane continued to visit often, talking of manuevers that would expose the corrupt system that Diane insisted had placed her in prison.

Cone's marriage broke up, and he moved to a duplex on Trade Street S.E. in Salem—partially to facilitate work on his book about Diane, and also to work as an aide at the Fairview Training Center (for the Developmentally Disabled) outside Salem.

Cone visited Diane on January 25, February 1, February 7, February 8, May 9, and June 6 of 1987.

Anxious to stay in the public eye, Diane never refused a media visit, but the requests for an audience with Diane Downs grew sparser. Infamy, like fame itself, rapidly dims in the minds of the public as new crimes supersede the old.

The spring of 1987 was a bad time for Diane. She learned that there would be no new trial to look forward to. Both the Oregon Supreme Court and the Oregon Court of Appeals had turned down her request for a new trial, and both had done so "without comment." She heard about the final turn-down while she was in the dining hall.

"What can you do? Let it devastate you? That would let them win. I won't let them do it," she vowed, and she lifted her chin and smiled more widely.

Now Diane was on her own. The State would no longer provide funds for attorneys for further appeals.

The four-year anniversary of the shooting on Old Mohawk Road was on May 19, and the birthdays of Diane's last two baby girls passed by. She didn't know where they were. She didn't know what their new names were.

At least Diane had won her battle to attend college, and she went to class eagerly four days a week, even though she went in handcuffs. She took general studies at first, and found she liked political science and history most, but Diane was looking forward to studying more psychology and working in a master's program. She confided to one reporter that she longed to run for public office one day, as the country certainly seemed in need of sound leadership.

Diane much preferred to talk to the teachers and prison personnel than to her sister convicts. Some guards termed her an "apple polisher" ... and worse. "She just hangs on their every word, as if she thinks they're wonderful. It's all a bunch of B.S.," one guard snorted.

Diane also "brushed up" on her conversational Spanish, although she had little use for the language in an Oregon prison.

Diane jumped at the chance for a phone interview with Elouise Schumacher of the *Seattle Times*. That spring of 1987, Schumacher, who had covered Diane's trial in 1984, listened for hours, her fingers flying over her word processor's keys, as Diane's familiar voice spilled over the phone lines.

> [In prison] when you go to school, you don't work. You study. In winter, we sit around and be bored a lot. In the summer, I go out and lay in the sun. I'm in a double cell—I have to be ... I'm a real private person. I like being alone. There's no place to be alone in here. The worst part is, quite frankly, it's like being treated like a retarded three-year-old. We're not allowed to think for ourselves and feel. That's insane. ...

Diane was enraged about *Small Sacrifices*. The book had not reflected her feelings, she told Schumacher, but she still "had faith. One of these days, someday, somewhere [the real killer will be found]. I just don't think it's possible for someone to commit murder and not say anything. I just have faith it will all come together one of these days—

"I have too much faith. I believe that, deep down, everyone's a nice guy . . . cuz I'm a die-hard optimist. . . ."

Still, Diane was furious about the hardcover jacket of *Small Sacrifices,* the golden unicorn with a splash of red behind it. "Don't they *know* what unicorns *mean* to me?"

Diane Downs was no longer the only surrogate mother who had hit the headlines. Asked her opinion of Mary Beth Whitehead's refusal to turn her baby over to the natural father and his wife, Diane said she was pleased that Whitehead had lost her bid to keep the baby girl she'd delivered.

> I think the parents should have the child. I believe anyone who enters into an agreement should stick by that agreement. I understand feelings of motherhood. I see her [Whitehead's] point of view—but she has no compassion for other people. She promised them for nine months that they would have the baby. That's cruel . . . I had doubts when she [Diane's surrogate baby] was born . . . I think about her a lot . . . I'm human. I can't predict what's going to happen in the future—when all my kids are grown up. All I ever wanted to do was grow up and be a Mom. I did it well. . . .

Again and again, Diane's thoughts focused on her children. She bemoaned the fact that Fred Hugi had never responded to her requests for prison visits from Christie and Danny, that all her gifts to them—including a stuffed unicorn—were returned. Elouise Schumacher felt a chill when Diane described the first thing she would do when she was free.

"I'll probably show up on the D.A.'s doorstep and ask if I can come in and hug my kids. . . ."

Initially, Diane had confided to Lars Larson that she was pleased about the fact that Christie and Danny were living with the man who sent her to prison. That was good, she explained, because now Christie would have Fred Hugi's ear when she finally told the "truth" about the shaggy-haired gunman. Diane insisted, however, that she thought Christie was physically—but not emotionally—safe in her new home.

It was a common theme for Diane, the importance of emotional safety. Quite probably she was talking about the little girl she herself once was, left far behind in Arizona but still buried inside the adult Diane beneath layers of bravado. Oddly, Diane continued to insist that *she* had always provided both physical and emotional security for her own children.

Diane's said her biggest worry about Christie and Danny was their need to know that "Mommy's all right. They're little; they need to know *I'm* O.K."

I. I. I. . . . The world continued to revolve around her as she shone—not the brightest star but the *only* star.

Diane Downs and Randy Woodfield were the best known of the convicts who filed across the stage in graduation ceremonies at the Oregon State Penitentiary in June, 1987. Diane wore a leaf-green cap and gown over a lacy white blouse; her hair was blonde and swept away from her face; rose-colored earrings failed to offset the pallor of her skin. As she accepted her diploma, her associate of arts degree in general studies, she did not smile for the photographers. She stared straight ahead, her eyes fixed on something no one else could see. Her eyes were as green as her gown on graduation day—those strange eyes Japanese legend calls *San paku*, "eyes of death." The pupils, surrounded by wide expanses of white, reflected each color they focused on.

Diane knew her first parole hearing was set for a date well into the twenty-first century. She was thirty-one years old, and she had every reason to expect she would be locked up until she was almost sixty.

What good would it do her to have a master's degree or even a doctorate?

July 11, 1987, was a gray Saturday in the Northwest, a rare cloudy day in a summer that would bring the first drought to Oregon and Washington in almost a century.

The 8 A.M. count at the Oregon Women's Correctional Center in Salem was 126 prisoners. There were prisoners sentenced for drug offenses and for murder and everything in between. The state budget did not allow for category segregation of female inmates; the whole correctional center was designated *medium* security, a situation that made it dicey at times for guards. Joan Palmateer, security manager, had long yearned for a beefed-up security setup; there had been four successful escapes in the past decade, but the escapes hadn't been newsworthy enough to merit more than three-inch articles on back pages of local papers.

Two eighteen-foot-high fences, topped with razor wire, kept female prisoners inside. The outer fence was equipped with an alarm that was a little *too* sensitive. A strong wind or a bird lighting on the outer fence could trigger the alarm, and as with the boy who cried wolf too often, the sound of the fence alarm was no longer as urgent-sounding as it might be.

On July 11, Supervising Sergeant Greg Reed was the officer in charge, and Junko Smith was the control officer. Corporal Tina Turner-Morfitt was overseeing the first floor, and Kathie Dowden was on the second floor. Officer Lisa Skeen was scheduled to arrive at 8:30. Patti Byrd was the volunteer officer, and Richard Ladeby was heading the kitchen crew. Dr. T. Lovelace, a dentist, and his assistant were in the women's prison that Saturday morning to treat prisoners with dental problems.

Compared to the rest of the week, Saturday morning was a lazy time during which prisoners could choose to sleep in the cells they called their "houses." Diane Downs invariably slept late on weekends, but on July 11 Guard Patti Byrd noted that Diane was up and dressed early. It was only 8:25 and Diane seemed anxious to get out into the recreation yard, waiting impatiently for the yard gate to be opened at 8:30.

Byrd smiled and opened the gate, and Diane brushed past her and headed for her favorite picnic table in the corner of the yard. A few feet beyond the table the perimeter fence meets the inner fence. Guards had grown used to seeing Diane Downs lying on a bench there, her neck cradled on a towel, her face turned up to catch the sun.

There wasn't much sun to catch on July 11. But the air was mild, and prisoners could see grass and trees through the steel mesh fence. Diane, who hated sharing a cell, could at least be alone out in the yard.

Prisoners Louise Seifer and Gretchen Schumacher (no relation to Elouise Schumacher) sat with their elbows on one of the other tables, their backs to Diane. Gretchen and Diane were close and constant companions, and Louise, a "short-timer," talked to Diane once in a while because she felt a little sorry for her.

As Diane walked by the two women prisoners, she said sotto voce, "I'm going now. . . ."

They didn't turn around. They didn't really believe her, but if she was crazy enough to try for it, they didn't want to see it happen. What you don't see, you can't tell later—and a "snitch" is the lowest form of life in prison.

Diane was wearing gray 501 jeans and a polyester blouse. The blouse was shiny dark blue, striped with paler blue, and short-sleeved. Perhaps she had chosen it by accident, perhaps deliberately. This was the blouse that had been brand-new when Diane wore it in her long interview with Anne Bradley Jaeger in December of 1983, a blouse that became familiar to thousands when Jaeger's documentary on Diane aired.

The blue blouse was old now, and too large. Diane's weight, always fluctuating, was down, and she was quite thin. She did not look thin on that Saturday morning, however; she looked strangely bulky. In prison parlance, Diane was "double-dressed." Two layers of clothing, not against the cold but so that the runner can shed layers as a lizard sheds its skin, changing its outward appearance.

Diane wore three pairs of panties, two bras, two blouses, two pairs of socks, white tennis shoes. Hidden beneath the towel she carried were a pair of beige gloves with leather palms and a two-toned gray stocking cap—clothing hardly conducive to a suntan, but most helpful for a woman who was about to take her leave of prison walls.

Louise Seifer turned for an instant to watch Diane and saw her head to her favorite picnic table near the fence. Louise turned away and stared straight ahead, her back tensing.

Louise heard a noise, a clanging, and a snapping back, as if someone had gone over the fence. Instantly, the speaker system boomed, "Check Zone One."

Unable to resist another peek, Louise darted a glance toward the men's penitentiary and caught a flash of someone—it *was* Diane Downs— on the outside of the fence. She saw an Oregon State Penitentiary guard up on the wall, and she was sure he must see Diane.

Louise flung herself on the ground and pressed her cheek close to the grass. She expected the guard to shoot at Diane, and she didn't want to see it—or get caught in crossfire. But there was no sound. Louise was baffled. The guard had to have seen Diane.

Nothing.

Louise sat back up.

Diane had done it. Diane Downs was on the other side of the fence, on the free side.

It was 8:40 A.M.

Two hundred miles north of Salem, my phone rang at 9:05 A.M.

"It may only be a rumor—all we have is what we just picked up on the Salem police scanner. But it looks like she's out. She's escaped—"

I knew the voice. It was Lars Larson. And I knew who "she" had to be. Diane Downs. There was no way that Diane Downs could be out of prison. Bad joke.

Only it wasn't a joke. Within ten minutes, Larson called back. He was sure that his source was correct that Diane was loose. Nobody knew how yet, or where she might be, or if she had had help.

I made two calls, while already the "call waiting" tone on my phone beeped continually. Larson's scoop had hit the AP wires, and anyone who had a radio or television on knew that the "child-killer" was out. But not everyone listened to the media early on a Saturday morning.

First I called Anne Bradley Jaeger at home in Eugene. We would divide up the two vital calls to be made. She would know how to find Fred Hugi and verify that he knew that Diane *might* be outside the walls of the Oregon Women's Correctional Center. I didn't really believe it yet, nor did Jaeger—nor did Fred Hugi when Anne Jaeger called him. But if it was remotely possible that Diane had made it outside the prison yard, there were two families who had to be ready. The Oregon Women's Correctional Center was only an hour and a half by car from Springfield—and from Christie and Danny.

And what had Diane said to Elouise Schumacher only a month before? "When I get out, I'll probably show up on the DA's doorstep and ask if I can come in and hug my kids."

The second obvious targets would be Lew and Nora Lewiston. I dialed their number in Chandler, heard it ring eight times, and then Nora's voice answered. "I don't want to scare you," I began. "But it looks as though Diane may have escaped from prison."

There was only a gasp on the other end of the line.

"She doesn't know where you live now," I said. "She has no idea where your new house is."

"No, she doesn't," Nora Lewiston said tightly. "But she sure knows where the post office is, and Lew's out on his route. I'm leaving now and I'm going to find him."

The sequence of events at the Oregon Women's Correctional Center had happened so rapidly and so smoothly that they seemed choreographed by a clever mind beforehand.

Just as Patti Byrd let Diane into the recreation yard, a tremendous crash had sounded from the multipurpose recreation area inside the women's prison. Sergeant Greg Reed and Kathie Dowden rushed to the room and saw that a piano had fallen on one of the inmates.

The woman, whose job it was to clean the recreation room, was known in the prison as "Killer Bea." Now, "Killer Bea" lay screaming and wailing for help with her right leg crushed beneath the heavy piano. Reed and Dowden enlisted the help of the watching inmates, lifted the piano, and sent Bea off to the infirmary.

No one knew why the piano happened to fall, or how. It had never fallen before. But it seemed that things were not as bad as they'd looked at first. Bea would have some bruises, but she was more frightened than hurt.

Five minutes had passed since Diane Downs sauntered out into the recreation yard. There are women prisoners who say that Diane came back from the yard once, just long enough to peek into the rec room and see the flurry of activity around the piano. Some swear they saw her face in the doorway, and then she was gone.

When the fence alarm in Zone I sounded once at 8:40, Officer Lisa Skeen walked out of the kitchen sally port and scanned the section of fence. Rich Ladeby stepped out of the kitchen back door too. Neither saw anything unusual. No bird sat on the mesh fence, and the fence wasn't shaking.

Skeen and Ladeby shrugged. It was the same old problem. The alarm system was more a nuisance than a warning device. An errant gust of wind or a swallow pausing to rest set the thing off.

Junko Smith, in Control Center 1, notified Tower 9 in the Oregon State Penitentiary that the alarm had sounded, and then he attempted to check the suspect area with the camera system.

At 8:43, Lisa Skeen went to Control Center 2 and cleared the zone alarm.

The prison band was tuning up for practice over in the penitentiary, the sound carrying over to the women's facility. It was a typical Saturday morning, except for "Killer Bea's" mishap. Rich Ladeby soon forgot the fence alarm as he gave instructions for lunch preparation. Lisa Skeen went back to her guard duties.

Louise and Gretchen and a few other prisoners remained in the recreation yard, talking quietly, tapping their feet to the band next door.

It was five minutes to nine when prison nurse JoAnne Bowlin arrived for work. She parked in the front lot. Bowlin reached over to grab her purse, and her eye caught some movement at the northwest corner of the parking lot. Looking closer, she thought she could see a figure lying prone under a 1965 white Chevrolet pick-up.

Bowlin got out of her car, still looking toward the truck. Suddenly, she saw a woman crawl out from beneath the white Chevy and walk rapidly across the parking lot toward State Street.

It looked like Diane Downs. It couldn't be—but it sure looked like her. The woman wore blue jeans and had something wrapped around her head, a turban or a scarf maybe.

Bowlin was tempted to run after the woman, but if it was Diane, she wouldn't be able to handle her alone. It was against prison policy to confront an escapee without backup, and JoAnne Bowlin had a barely healed shoulder injury that would put her at a disadvantage in a struggle.

Bowlin stared after the woman as she ran toward a wooded area across State Street, and then the prison nurse whirled and ran into the prison office. She spoke to Lisa Skeen in a low voice.

"I think Diane Downs just escaped—or else I just saw her twin out in the parking lot!"

Skeen ran to S14B, Diane's cell. Only Diane's roommate was there.

Supervising sergeant Greg Reed immediately announced an emergency count, ordering all inmates to their cells. Even though Diane was not popular with the other inmates, their voices buzzed now, wondering if Diane "had made it." If she had, she had done more than get away. She had beaten the system.

The recreation yard was cleared. There were only three women still sitting at the picnic tables—Louise Seifer, Gretchen Schumacher, and another woman. Not Diane Downs. Diane was not in the yard.

At 8:00 A.M., the count had been 126 female prisoners.

At 9:10 A.M., the count was 125.

Reed, fearing that one of the most dangerous prisoners in the women's prison was gone, had already notified the Salem Police Department and prison superintendent Robert Schiedler and assistant superintendent Sonia Hoyt.

Now, the official count over, it was definite. The missing prisoner *was* Diane Downs.

Kathie Dowden searched Diane's cellmate and then returned her to the general population. The cell itself was dead-bolted until investigators could go over it for some clue that might lead them to Diane Downs.

The only obvious signs she had left behind were a towel lying on the picnic table, where the perimeter fence met the inner fence, and, beneath the white pick-up truck a discarded blouse, torn and shredded from the razor wire atop the fences—the blue blouse worn so many years ago for the interview in which Diane was so animatedly triumphant, positive she would never even be arrested.

The razor wire itself was squashed flat where the fences met, where it had not been strung as thickly. For a woman as athletic as Diane was, a run at the fence, up and over, and a drop down the other side had been a cinch. JoAnne Bowlin said the woman running across the parking lot wasn't even limping.

The Oregon State Police were notified. An APB (All Points Bulletin) went out over the wires of the thirteen western states' law enforcement teletypes.

Somewhat belatedly, in the aftermath of an "impossible escape," Fred Hugi received his *official* notification that Diane Downs was on the loose.

It was five minutes to ten. If Diane *was* heading toward his home to see her children, and if she had had help escaping and a car waiting, she could be coming up Fred Hugi's driveway within the next ten minutes.

Fortunately, Hugi had been notified by our unofficial phone network, and he was in no danger of being caught off guard by the woman he had sent to prison almost three years earlier.

Hugi kept his .45 close by. He would never allow Diane to harm Christie and Danny again, even if it meant he had to sleep with one eye open the rest of his life.

Diane Downs was free, all right. It was verified. But where was she?

PART TWO

Both the Oregon State Police and the Salem Police Department began a search shortly after 9 A.M. that Saturday morning. Oregon State Police lieutenant Edward Croucher directed all Salem troopers to the area around the prison. Croucher and Senior Trooper Wayne Moreland were airborne in the state police's Super Cub surveying streets and alleys below by 9:21.

"Felony Flats" they called the area. Those blocks around the Oregon State Penitentiary, filled with the sometimes ramshackle houses and apartments occupied by parolees, the halfway houses, the families who had moved to be close to someone they loved who was inside the walls. More than other neighborhoods, this one might view an escapee as one who needed shelter and a helping hand.

At 10:20, Sergeant Mel Whitenberger of the Salem Police Department notified the state police of a report called in by a Salem family. Detective

Merle Hart of the state police arrived at Salem headquarters to be briefed. Hart, along with Detective Sergeant Jim Reed, would be in charge of the hunt for Diane Downs.

Glenda Hawkins, thirty-nine, had called police at ten minutes after nine. "I think I might have just given a ride to Diane Downs—but she's supposed to be in prison, isn't she?"

Glenda and Charles Hawkins, forty-two, and four of their seven children were returning from nearby campgrounds after saying goodbye to relatives, and their eyes were drawn to a slender young woman at the side of the road. It was July and she looked peculiar in her stocking cap and gloves.

The family was driving north on Airport Road, a stone's throw from the rear entrance of the state police parking lot, when this very agitated woman ran directly into their lane and forced their van to stop.

"She stood right in front of the van," Charles Hawkins told police. "She didn't give us any choice."

She had seemed frantic as she ran in and out of the road, and then around to the driver's window, "My boyfriend's hurt—he's just around the corner," she cried.

Before the Hawkinses could react, the woman jumped into the front seat and directed Hawkins west on State Street. First she asked to get out at the Plaid Pantry (a convenience store), and then she asked to be let off at the "pizza parlor."

"You must mean Sybil's Omelettes," Glenda Hawkins said. "There isn't any pizza place around here."

"Yes." The woman nodded. "That's it."

Odd. She didn't really seem to know where she was going. The woman hopped out at the corner of 24th S.E. and State Streets, and walked rapidly away from the van. The Hawkinses saw no "injured boyfriend," and wondered why their passenger hadn't asked them to call an ambulance or paramedics to help him.

Bemused and more than a little suspicious, they hurried home and quickly thumbed through a newspaper with a review of *Small Sacrifices*. They wanted to compare the face they'd just seen with an image of Diane Downs. A small picture of Diane accompanied the piece.

"That *was* her!" Glenda Hawkins said, and her oldest daughter agreed.

It would take someone with Diane's bravado to escape from prison and then hitchhike right in back of the Oregon State Police station. Merle Hart believed that the Hawkinses supposition was correct. They had given a ride to the infamous Diane Downs.

Had Diane arranged to meet someone on the corner of 24th and State? Why had she asked to go first to one store and then another, and finally agreed to a third? Hart didn't miss the fact that both "Plaid Pantry" and "pizza parlor" had the initials "P.P." It might mean something—but what? Diane didn't know her way around Salem. From what the investigators could gather, she had never been there before the day Doug Welch and Chris Rosage drove her to prison in the police van.

Nevertheless, she was gone. Blocks away from the prison now, swallowed up in the maze of streets that constituted Felony Flats. Police considered using dogs to track her, but there were so many people in the area that it would have been futile—too many scents to confuse the bloodhounds. The state police plane overhead made passes back and forth, looking for a running woman in a stocking cap, and saw no one who matched the description.

When night fell, depression settled over the searchers. Under cover of darkness, Diane Downs could go just about wherever she wanted. She might be huddled in the trunk of a car, smiling to herself as she was spirited farther and farther from the Oregon Women's Correctional Center.

The most persistent rumor circulating on that first day of Diane Downs's escape was that she had been picked up by a car waiting near the prison and sped to a downtown Salem street corner, where another car/truck had been waiting to pick her up. If that version was true, Diane could well have been out of Marion County by the time the prison count verified that she was gone.

Where would she go? Her priorities in the past suggested a possible agenda that would send her first to a safe hiding place. She would "lay low" as they used to say in B gangster movies. Next—and possibly concurrently—I believed Diane would attempt to become pregnant again. That way, even if she should be recaptured, she would have "someone inside to talk to" again. Since her first conception, she had never gone so long without being pregnant. Third, I thought she would try to see Christie and Danny—if only for a moment or so—just to prove that she *could* do it.

After that, revenge would be a belated goal, but one that could not be ignored.

Fred Hugi was torn with indecision. Should he stay at home and guard his family, or should he go up to Salem and join the hunt for Diane? Should they buy an attack dog? Maybe he should just pack up Joanne and the children and take them someplace far away until Diane was recaptured. But he hated to do that; Christie and Danny had just settled into a life without upheavals. Why should they have to leave this place where they had felt so safe?

In the end, the Hugi family stayed put, refusing to let fear drive them out of their home. Christie and Danny were guarded all the time, although they didn't know it. When Danny had a campout picnic planned with his class, the outing went on as scheduled, but Doug Welch went along, watching.

Sometimes it seemed to Fred Hugi that he was once again involved in a solitary fight to save the kids. Did anyone else realize how dangerous Diane Downs was? Did anyone really care that she was walking around loose? The low point would come for him when the Lane County Commissioners refused to approve a $1,000 reward for information leading to Diane's arrest!

In Chandler, Arizona, Lew and Nora Lewiston tried to go ahead with their lives as if they too weren't constantly looking over their shoulders. They had built a huge room onto their new home so that Nora could operate a day-care center. From early each weekday morning until suppertime, their house was filled with the shouts and giggles of more than a dozen toddlers. Nora loved kids, and she loved her new business. Diane's escape threatened all of that.

Nora was frank with the parents of her charges; she told them that the headlines about the Diane Downs escape in Oregon could have reverberations in Chandler, and that it was possible Diane might even try to find the Lewistons' home.

"The parents were really nice," Nora recalls. "Only one mother kept her child home."

Representatives of the S.W.A.T. (Special Weapons and Tactics) Team of the Chandler Police Department came to talk with Lew and Nora as soon as the APB on Diane's escape went out. It was frightening—especially for Nora Lewiston—to see how seriously the Chandler police looked at the situation. If the *police* thought Diane was on her way to Chandler, maybe that meant she *was* headed back to see Lew again. Or to kill Lew. Or to kill them both.

The nightmare was beginning all over again.

Chandler, Arizona, was indeed one of the places police considered Diane was most likely to run to. She had been brushing up on conversational Spanish in prison; she might well be heading for Mexico. And Chandler was along the way.

A desert-born girl sick of rain, soured on the Northwest, would almost naturally head south.

"We had a plan to follow," Nora Lewiston remembers. "The S.W.A.T. team told us that if Diane somehow got in here, they would 'blow' the front door—but for us not to panic because that would mean they were coming in the back way. . . ."

As days passed with no word of Diane's whereabouts, the waiting grew tenser. An escapee who had made it for twenty-four hours had passed the critical period. Good as gone.

It was no way to live for either the Hugis or the Lewistons.

I had bad moments too. If Diane was bitter about Lew and Nora, she was enraged with me over this book. Since publication, I had seen her video image a dozen times—Diane spitting fire, furious that I had had the temerity to criticize her shortcomings as a mother, and aghast that I had concluded she was guilty of murder. On those television shows, where a live—or "almost-live"—interview with the infamous Diane Downs was a coup, Diane reversed herself on almost everything she had said in the past; she denied even her courtroom testimony. She insisted her childhood had been happy, blighted only occasionally by "things like the weather or something."

As to her alleged motive for murder—Lew—Diane had turned toward the camera and said vehemently, "I dare any of those women on the jury to see him naked—and tell me I would shoot my own children for him. He had a sunken chest and a pot belly. . . ."

Yes, Diane was angry with me. Prison authorities warned me that I must be on guard; Diane had raged to them for hours, castigating "that book." More than the male killers I have written about, Diane seemed dangerous. Not only was she smarter than they were, she was totally unpredictable. What if she had picked revenge over freedom? She could have run north instead of south. She might have only pretended to brush up on Spanish when all the time she'd been planning to run to Canada—via Seattle. Canada was a thousand miles closer to Salem than Mexico was, and there are so many tiny hamlets edging the border into British Columbia, easier exits from the United States than the borders of Arizona or California.

Seattle police called to say that they were watching my house, and that all I had to do was dial 911 if Diane showed up, and they would respond at once.

Were we all jumping at shadows? With a face as recognizable as Diane Downs's had become, it seemed impossible for her to remain free for long.

Officers Kathie Dowden and D. Verdieck inventoried the possessions Diane had left behind. Several items listed on her property list were missing. Three gold chains, six pairs of earrings, and several rings were among the items missing. The jewelry wasn't really valuable—but could be negotiable on the outside. No one could estimate just how much cash Diane might have secreted on her person.

Detectives Hart and Ken Pecyna checked Diane's visitors' roster in prison. Her only visitors of late had been her family and Richard Cono, her biographer. The whereabouts of Wes, Willadene, and Paul Frederickson were quickly established. They had been in Springfield that morning. Court orders were obtained to put "pen registers" on the Frederickson phone—on the chance that Diane might call from wherever she was hiding. If she did, the call could be traced immediately.

Hart and Pecyna next checked all the public telephone booths along State Street from 24th Street to 17th Street, jotting down the numbers so that they could check with the phone company and establish who had been called from those public phones during the hours after Diane's escape.

None of the numbers proved helpful.

Hart and Pecyna were most interested, however, when they saw how many times Richard Cone had visited Diane in prison—the last visit being only a month before her escape. They were more intrigued when they discovered that Cone's current Salem address was only a quarter mile from where Diane was last seen by the Hawkins family.

When Pecyna rechecked the phone booths on State Street, he located a booth at the Circle K Store that had pages torn from the phone book. The map of Salem was missing from the book, as well as part of page 32, the part that had contained Cone's name, address, and phone number.

It could be coincidence. And it was unlikely that Diane had not already known that information about her biographer.

Still.

When Hart and Pecyna went to Cone's duplex, they found a newspaper on the porch and mail in the mailbox. Neighbors said that Cone had been away for a few days.

Richard Cone called Merle Hart at 10:30 that first Saturday night. He said he had no idea where Diane was, but that he would be glad to be interviewed if it would help. Pecyna interviewed Cone the next morning at the Fairview Training Center, where Cone was working the 6 A.M. to 2:30 P.M. shift in one of the "cottages."

Cone told Ken Pecyna that it was true he had a contract with Diane to write her book. Because of their professional relationship and because of their many "close conversations," Cone felt that he and Diane had become good friends. Downs had told him the previous summer that she could escape anytime she wanted to—and she had mentioned "going over the fence."

"I told her to contact me if she escaped—so I could interview her," Cone said. "And then I told her I'd turn her in."

Cone said Diane had also told him that if she escaped, she would head for California to look for the shaggy-haired stranger, the "real killer." She had also told him she would try to get her children back.

"Once she decides she will focus her energy and thoughts on something, she will do very good. . . ."

Richard Cone said he had been in Portland at the time of the escape. He had left Salem at 3:30 Friday afternoon (June 10) and driven to Portland to the home of a woman friend. He had arrived back at his Trade Street S.E. duplex apartment a little after 9:30 on Saturday night.

His apartment had been empty when he returned, and there was no indication that anyone had been there.

Oregon State detectives checked out Richard Cone's whereabouts on Friday and Saturday, and found that he had been where he said he had been in his statement. There was no reason to think he had assisted Diane in her escape.

Then who?

Sightings of "Diane Downs" poured into state police headquarters in Salem as WANTED bulletins were posted all over Oregon and Washington.

WANTED

DOWNS, ELIZABETH DIANE

WF, DOB 08-07-55, 31 YEARS OF AGE, 5'6"

LIGHT BROWN AND GREEN

SCARS: 5" SURGICAL SCAR ON INSIDE OF LEFT FOREARM

2" SURGICAL SCAR ON BACK OF LEFT FOREARM

5" SURGICAL SCAR ON LEFT HIP

EACH EAR PIERCED ONCE

DEEP CROWS FEET AT CORNERS OF BOTH EYES

FINGERPRINT CLASSIFICATION 20 M IT -00 5 L 1R 100 5

WARRANT: ESCAPE, NO BAIL, LEDS WANT W031130047

DOWNS WAS CONVICTED OF THE MURDER OF ONE OF HER CHILDREN, AND THE ATTEMPTED MURDER OF HER TWO OTHER CHILDREN. ON JULY 11, 1987, SHE ESCAPED FROM THE OREGON WOMEN'S CORRECTIONAL INSTITUTION. CONSIDERED DANGEROUS.

PLEASE NOTIFY DETECTIVE SERGEANT JIM REED OR DETECTIVE MERLE HART, OREGON STATE POLICE—SALEM, TELEPHONE (503) 378-2593

The pictures chosen for her wanted posters showed two sides of Diane. In one, she posed demurely in a lace blouse and smiled softly. Visible in the background is the eighteen-foot fence she would one day scale in her escape. The other picture shows the somber Diane at her graduation two years later, her face marked with blemishes and her eyes surrounded by deep lines.

Doug Welch, in his office in Eugene, looked at the WANTED poster and grimaced, "They don't show who she really is—what she looks like. To do that, they'd have to have a dozen photographs—and then they wouldn't have all the different Dianes."

And all over the Northwest citizens saw different "Dianes," who might or might not be the real thing.

One man reported a very pregnant red-haired woman hitchhiking alongside the northbound lanes of I-5 in Portland. "Her hair was red, but her face looked just like Diane Downs's!"

In a way, that would have been the ultimate disguise for Diane: a pregnant woman, her "baby" a rolled towel. Diane's hair had been golden blonde, ash blonde, light brown, and dark brown since she entered prison. It might be any color by now.

An elderly woman in a trailer park in Vancouver, Washington, called police to report a young woman who had suddenly appeared in a neighbor's mobile home. "I think it's her—that Downs woman."

On July 14, Merle Hart took a statement from a businesswoman.

> At 2:10 P.M. today, I left the back of [her business] to go to Albany. I was headed towards my car when I saw a woman to my right, who was taking big strides, walking towards me. The woman asked me if they had caught Elizabeth Diane Downs. I said I did not know. She asked me if I knew where she was and I did not want to get close to her. She was walking away from me when she said that Downs wanted to go back to prison. I thought the woman looked like Downs. The woman was wearing blue shorts with a blue and white striped blouse that was tied up in front. She was wearing white tennis shoes. Her hair was blonde and longer than mine. I did not see the woman's eyes. She was headed towards Court Street, towards Willamette University when I last saw her.

On July 19, a young Salem woman called police. Shortly after midnight, she and two companions had seen "Diane Downs" hitchhiking south on South Commercial Street. The hitchhiker had worn faded jeans and a yellow and white horizontally striped shirt. Her hair was short and blonde.

"We drove by, going thirty miles an hour, and she looked right at me. It was her all right."

The caller and both her girlfriends picked Diane's picture from a police montage. The girl who'd been driving said, "She looked straight at us and kind of smirked as we went by."

For the Oregon State Police, the hunt was supremely frustrating. Another caller on July 19 described *another* female hitchhiker heading south on South Commercial. She had light brown hair, shoulder length, and wore red shorts. She had been picked up by someone in a small white truck.

"As I went past her, I thought she looked kind of familiar. And then I realized it was possibly Diane Downs."

The calls continued to flood in, recently paroled inmates from the Oregon Women's Correctional Center were screened, and specific phones continued to be monitored. But as the days passed, and then a week passed, it seemed painfully clear that Diane must be far, far away. Local sightings seemed unlikely.

Diane might be in Mexico City, or Madrid, or New York City. Or some little town in Indiana or Montana. Perhaps she had even had a lover waiting somewhere for her, some man, perhaps, whom she had met through a Lonely Hearts column and exchanged letters with. She wrote such seductive letters.

Was it possible that Diane could become someone else, take on a new identity as other infamous escapees had? Could she marry again, and start a new family? Could Diane Downs ever be content with a quiet life, a "normal" life—the kind of life she said she missed so much? Perhaps. For a while.

But then she would grow cold without the spotlight. She would have to surface again. She couldn't possibly survive in complete anonymity. Even her freedom wasn't worth that much.

It might take six months. A year. Maybe even two years. In the meantime, lives would be put on hold. Fear—caution—a sense of constant awareness, would affect so many people until Diane Downs was once again behind bars.

The Downs escape stayed on front pages for a long time. In Washington, D.C., Oliver North testified and made his own headlines—but he never nudged Diane Downs off center stage in the Northwest.

Back at the Oregon Women's Correctional Center, Diane's cell—S14B— was searched and re-searched. And then, on July 15, Oregon State Police detective Loren Glover looked closely at a clipboard that held a thin stack of prison stationery. Clean. White. But when Glover held the board up and tilted it toward the light, he could make out the faintest of indentations on the top sheet. Glover couldn't decipher what had been written on the sheets that had once been above it; it was probably some aimless scribbling.

Tests at the Oregon State Police Documents Section failed to enhance the impressions enough for them to be legible.

One more try. Detective Glover packaged the single sheet of paper carefully and sent it by overnight mail to the FBI's Document Section for processing with a device called ESDA: Electrostatic Detection Apparatus. With black metal filings, magnetism, and more advanced forensic science procedures, the ESDA can sometimes bring out markings invisible to the naked eye or even to a microscope.

The procedure took days. It was July 20 when FBI supervising special agent Chuck Perrotta of the Document Section called Oregon State Police sergeant Jim Reed. Perrotta described a straight-line map he'd raised from the thin sheet of white paper. There was a square with the letters "P.I." or "P.P." inside. There was an address there too, and the words "You are here" inside another larger square on the map.

Reed recognized the configuration of streets. Felony Flats. "P.P." might be the Plaid Pantry. The address was 2262 State Street S.E., two blocks from where Diane had hopped out of the Hawkins's van more than a week ago.

Reed ordered immediate surveillance of the house at 2262 State Street. He determined from utility records that the owner of record was a man named Robert Stephens, thirty-two. Several different men were observed going in and out of the rundown home, but the surveillance team never saw a woman there.

That didn't mean there was not a woman there now, or that one hadn't been hidden inside for some time. Determined to find out the reason that Diane had had a map leading to Stephens's house in her cell, Jim Reed obtained a search warrant for that house.

At 3:06 P.M. on July 21, Merle Hart and Jim Reed, accompanied by five state police officers and two Salem Police Department sergeants, knocked on the door of 2262 State Street. Robert Stephens answered and gave verbal consent to search the house; he insisted, however, that he was alone in the house.

"Are you sure?" Merle Hart asked.

"Just me."

The search soon revealed Jim Sinclair, one of Stephens's roomers, on the landing at the top of the stairs.

Sinclair seemed nervous. Reed and Hart looked beyond him and saw that there was a bedroom they had not yet searched; it was upstairs and on the west side of the house. The door was closed.

"Is there anyone else in the house?" Hart asked.

Sinclair hesitated for a moment. "Yes, there are two more."

"Is one of them a woman?" Hart pressed.

Sinclair's shoulders slumped. "Yes . . . Downs."

Jim Sinclair was handed down the stairs to waiting troopers. Merle Hart and Jim Reed ordered the occupants behind the closed bedroom door to come out.

The door remained closed, and there were no sounds from inside. Hart stood aside and reached out, quickly turning the knob and pushing the door open.

"Come out here!"

For moments, there was no movement inside. Sweat trickled down the shirt collars of the state police detectives and the troopers poised on the stairs. There were no windows. No air there. And very little, if any, room to retreat if the couple in the room came out with weapons.

Suddenly, there was someone in the doorway. An extremely tall man with dark hair and a bushy moustache walked out, his hands in front of him to show he was unarmed.

It was Wayne Seifer, husband of Diane's prison acquaintance Louise Seifer.

Merle Hart continued to speak quietly to Diane, who stayed in the little bedroom at the top of the stairs. Despite orders, she would not come out. They waited, listening to Hart instruct Diane that she had nowhere left to go. She must come out.

And then she was there in the doorway. Her hands too were empty. She looked very thin, and she wore only a man's T-shirt and a pair of men's brown and white boxer shorts. She wore no makeup, and her hair was a little damp, as if she had just taken a shower.

Diane grinned at them, a half rueful, half triumphant little grin. She looked down the stairs at Seifer as his hands were being cuffed, and her eyes were tender.

Seifer, thirty-six, looked back at Diane and murmured, "This is what I get for being a nice guy—"

Diane was allowed to dress in her own clothing—the jeans she'd worn in her escape and a pink cotton shirt. It was obvious that she wore no bra as she was led, still smiling, out to the state police car. She was so thin that the cartilage in her neck showed clearly in ridged circles as she lifted her head proudly. The skin beneath her eyes was smudged with dark circles.

But still, just as a uniformed arm reached out to keep her head from bumping the car roof as she was ushered inside, she turned and smiled at the cameras. Once again, Diane was in the center of dozens of cameras— television and print media cameras catching her every expression.

Diane was taken first to the Salem State Police Office, where she gave a statement to Ken Pecyna. The men who'd shared the house on State Street with her gave their own statements individually.

Behind the mass exodus into the strobe lights of waiting newspeople, a search of the bedroom Diane had occupied began. Merle Hart and three troopers found a Daisy BB gun, not recently fired. There were numerous newspapers, most of them containing stories about Diane's escape.

Left behind were two gold necklaces: one with a cross, and the other— the little gold bar melted down from Cheryl Lynn's twin-heart necklace, Cheryl's name beginning to wear away a little now.

A grocery sack in the bedroom held the rest of Diane's possessions:

(1) pair of beige gloves with leather palms

(1) light- and dark-gray stocking hat

(1) pair of white socks, with two pink stripes

(1) white bra, size 36C

(1) flesh-pink bra, size 36C

(1) pair blue-green underpants, size M

(1) picture of Downs and three other people

(1) gold-colored ring, opal stone

(1) gold-colored wedding band

(1) pair gold-colored earrings, with small clear stone

(1) pair of tweezers

(1) business card (attorney)

(1) key, with S14A stamped on it

(1) cash register token

(1) blue Correctional Services address book

Back at the Oregon Women's Correctional Center, Louise Seifer watched television incredulously. But she said nothing to anyone around her. She watched her "old man" Wayne being led out of the old house, his wrists cuffed, and bit her lip. He was the best man she ever had, and even though they were estranged, she still loved him.

Diane smiled at Ken Pecyna and state police officer Cynthia Kok as she discussed her escape.

I escaped Saturday, July 11, 1987. Since that time, I have stayed at the address I was arrested at. . . . The reason I escaped was because I was trying to go find the person who I thought killed my children. His name is Samasan Timchuck. I know he is an Indian. His grandmother lives in Marcola. His father lives in Wyoming. His last address I knew of was in California. I wanted to find him and look at his face. I'm not sure what I would have done, but I would not have killed him.

I had thought of escaping a lot. Actually it was a bad time to escape because Sgt. Reed [Greg] was on duty at O.W.C.C. He can run. The thoughts of my kids being with the person who put me in prison and my mother not being in good health, I felt, brought me to leaving also. This was an ongoing concern. I also had no purpose in just sitting there because of finishing school. I had time on my hands.

I had watched the routine of the tower guard and knew he would be watching the men's prison. I heard the band in the men's prison tuning up to play. I knew I could scale the fence in 30 seconds...

Diane described how she had double-dressed, and how she had watched the employees in the women's prison to see where they were. She had not seen Lisa Skeen. "If I had seen her, I would not have tried to go."

After I went over the other side, I went straight for the sergeant's pick-up ... I hid underneath ... I had looked around and knew what direction I was going. I heard them call out, "Zone One," and so I waited for them to clear the area ... I never heard them clear the zone, so I pulled off my blue blouse and put on my cap. I got up and quickly went toward State Street ... across a bridge ... across a field, and over to Airport Road. I started walking and was going to hitch a ride. I knew the public didn't know I had escaped. I saw a small sporty cop car go by. I assumed at this time the police were looking for me. I flagged down the first private car that came by ... I knew the cons had talked about the Plaid Pantry a lot. I lied to those people....

Diane walked west after she got out of the van. She found the house on State Street. Diane would not admit, however, that she knew who lived there. She insisted she'd just dropped in, and encountered men "who looked like convicts."

She said the occupants had led her to Wayne Seifer, who said she could stay for a few days. She was nervous until she found there was no phone in the house. But she felt the men were interested in her "as a female."

> ... I didn't want any problems, so I played up to Wayne. Wayne responded and hugged me. It felt good to be human again. I didn't feel any more hate, like I did before I escaped. We had sex shortly after.

Diane said that she had told the men in the house she preferred not to give her name. But the second night, they had had beer and she had admitted who she was.

> ... I stayed upstairs most of the time I was in the house for eleven days ... Bob, Wayne, and Jim had talked about how I had better leave. I'm not sure what was going on in their heads. I assume that they were afraid of getting in trouble. This is because people have a tendency to self preserve. I had no deals for money. I had no money ...

Diane had never been popular at O.W.C.C., but a standing ovation was planned for her return. She had escaped and she had stayed out for eleven days. The prisoners sent the word down the line that she was coming back in, and they were prepared to cheer and clap.

Word got to the superintendent, and a "lockdown" was ordered. Diane came back to prison to a hushed silence instead of a roaring crowd. She was led to an isolation cell.

Diane had gambled and lost. She was now locked up in a tiny cell with a steel door behind another barred door. She could talk to no one, and she could wear only a nightgown, robe, and slippers. She could read one book a day.

All the wonderful tales she might have shared with her prison friends would have to go untold.

The public was probably most shocked to learn that Diane Downs had been less than a half mile from the women's prison ever since her escape. All the time the huge dragnet for her grew until it covered the western half of the United States, she had been holed up in a tiny bedroom with a stranger.

Wayne Seifer, Robert Stephens, and Jim Sinclair were jailed overnight and charged with hindering prosecution. Released, they were voluble with the press.

Jim Sinclair, who had discussed religion for hours with Diane, said, "Basically, what it was, was she was a human being. She said she was in trouble; we tried to help her. I guess the law wouldn't look at it that way...."

Robert Stephens said he learned early on who Diane was and that she was in prison for murder, but that it hadn't worried him. "She is a very nice person who is vibrant and frisky.... She seems the type who could bring a lot of joy to people on the outside.... Maybe I should feel sorry or repentant, but I don't think I did anything that wrong. All I did was help a person who needed it."

Wayne Seifer, an aide at a halfway house for mental patients and a part-time worker at a golf course, felt more deeply about the eleven days he spent with Diane. He had fallen in love with her.

In a way, Wayne resembled all the men Diane had loved in the past. He was tall, dark, moustached—a kind of easygoing guy. Technically, he was still married, but he and Louise had had a lot of problems. And Louise was, after all, locked up in prison.

Seifer said Diane had stayed in his room, and he had brought home "happy movies" to watch on the VCR. She asked for "health food—tacos and sandwiches."

After the first night—when they made love—they slept together each night. He recalled having sexual intercourse with her only about a half dozen times.

Seifer felt protective toward this slender blonde woman who had come to his home asking for help. "I just said, 'I'll take care of you and when you feel you have to leave, you have to leave.' But I warned her that the one time she went out the door, 'You're not coming back.'"

Diane had gone out the door, albeit not willingly. In prison, in her isolation cell, she longed for Seifer, who Diane declares is her one perfect love. Seifer told reporters that he loved Diane too, and that he found her "the most honest woman I have ever known."

To help Diane, Seifer hired two private investigators to find the "real killer."

The imminent engagement of Diane Downs to Wayne Seifer was too much for Louise Seifer, Wayne's legal wife. She watched the television coverage of the romance and fled sobbing from the recreation room to her cell.

Two days after Diane was recaptured, Louise agreed to talk to Detective Terry Crawford.

Louise had written to Wayne sometime in June, she recalled, addressing her letter to the group home where he worked. His return letter had the State Street address on it. About a week before Diane's escape, Louise said she had talked to Diane about Wayne and how much she wanted a reconciliation with him.

Diane had said her main goal was to escape. She said she had $3,000 and that she would give half to Louise if Louise helped her find someone on the outside who would help with her escape. It was just prison talk, and Louise didn't believe Diane—especially because Diane said she was going out through a window, which was impossible. Diane said she had a way to do it.

On the Friday evening before the escape, Louise said Diane had come up to her in the TV room and said, "Draw me a map."

"She didn't say what, as I knew what she meant. I used the state writing paper they give us. It was on Downs's clipboard. It was a map from the penitentiary down State Street to 22nd Street. It had 2262 State Street on it, and 'You are here' depicting the penitentiary. I think I put the initials 'P.P.' on it, which I think meant Plaid Pantry.... Downs looked at the map. She started to tear it up. I took it from her hand and tore it up and then put it in the garbage."

Louise Seifer looked down and sighed. "She told me not to worry as she wouldn't sleep with my old man...."

Diane's promises, especially about men, are written on the wind. And now, everywhere Louise turned, she had to watch or read about her "old man's" affair with Diane Downs. Wayne was saying he wanted to marry Diane as soon as possible to some reporters, but he'd told the Associated Press that he wouldn't absolutely confirm he'd proposed.

It was just as well that Diane was not out in the general population.

The big question loomed. Was Diane pregnant? She had had ample opportunity. Prison officials would not comment.

Diane appeared, shackled, for arraignment on escape charges, and she looked radiant. Her skin was pink and healthy-looking, and she had definitely put on weight. She smiled both at the cameras and at the state troopers who guarded her.

Diane pleaded "Not Guilty" to escape, a rather odd plea since there were dozens of witnesses who could attest to the fact that she had left prison without permission and that she had been found a half mile away, barely clad, in a man's bedroom. But then Claude Dallas, an infamous Idaho murderer, escaped from prison there a few years ago, was free for many months, and was found "*Not Guilty.*"

Diane was not as persuasive. Although officials surmised she was risking only an additional year in prison by escaping, she was found guilty and sentenced to an additional *five* years in prison on November 23.

How much would it really matter? It would mean she would be eligible for parole in 2014, instead of 2009.

Infinitely more disappointing than her sentence was the news that she was not pregnant.

Alone in her isolation cell, Diane had nothing to do but read and think. She became concerned when she read Letters to the Editor in Salem papers, and picked up the only pen she was allowed, an orange felt tip, and wrote to the *Salem Statesman-Journal*.

She complained about her psychiatric evaluation (Dr. George Suckow) and said that five professionals had found her nice and normal. (These would have been the psychologists who examined her for the surrogate clinic, and, of course, they did not find her as she recalled.)

"I was also surprised," Diane wrote, "to read a letter from a woman who is thankful she doesn't have to worry about Diane Downs jumping out of the shrubbery when she retrieves her morning paper. Sure—I can understand why she might have reason to fear me. After all, I was once a Sunday School teacher and homeroom mother. I've done some really scary things in my life, like bake brownies for the school bake sale, and help a classroom full of second-graders paste red, yellow, and orange strips of construction paper on their turkeys....

"But, of course, no one ever writes about those things. No one wants to think about the fact that maybe—just maybe—Diane Downs didn't shoot her children. Because if that's the case, then someone might have to do something, and that might involve standing up against public opinion. It's much easier to believe that justice was done and forget about the woman in the cage. . . . Why can't anyone say anything nice anymore?"

If Diane were to stay in the Oregon Women's Correctional Center, she would do "hard time." Isolation. No privileges, or very few. She was now a danger not only outside but inside. She would be a firebrand if let out in the general population. She would, however, not be likely to escape again. The publicity surrounding Diane Downs's leap for freedom has brought the women's facility the security it has long needed. Razor wire bales top all fences, and they are designed to collapse and trap any escapee who makes the top of a fence, cutting her painfully if she tries to struggle. Concrete piers have been sunk yards deep all around the base of the fences.

Fred Hugi, among others, argued vociferously for Diane's transfer to another facility. Given her intelligence and her ingenuity, he did not trust even the beefed-up security measures. He no longer wanted Diane only an hour and a half up the road. Hugi contacted everyone he knew who had some clout with the governor of Oregon and lobbied steadily to have Diane sent somewhere else.

There was little argument that he was right. But where could they send Diane? Oregon officials wanted her in a maximum-security facility, and they wanted her some distance away from Oregon.

She was not the kind of prisoner welcomed with open arms into any prison situation. Nevertheless, a deal was struck in November. And with it, a strange closing of a circle. Fred Hugi had come from New Jersey in his late teens and young adulthood. He had hunted on the ground where the Clinton Correctional Institution for Women now stands.

And it was Clinton that finally agreed to accept Diane Downs—but only after Oregon promised to accept *two* difficult New Jersey prisoners.

Within days of her sentencing for escape in Oregon, Diane Downs left Oregon, perhaps forever. Accompanied by security manager Joan Palmateer and a male guard, Diane boarded a commercial airplane for a night flight. She had no idea where she was going, and, indeed, did not know her destination was Clinton until they arrived and she was admitted.

Nevertheless, Diane talked through the night, a steady patter, all the way across America. It had been so long since she had had a real chance to talk to someone.

Clinton is entirely maximum security. It is as safe a place to incarcerate Diane Downs as could be found. And yet Fred Hugi is haunted sometimes by the memory of a woman named Joanne Chesimard, a member of the Black Liberation Army. Chesimard was found guilty of the murder of a New Jersey state trooper on May 2, 1973. She was sentenced to life in prison in 1977.

On November 2, 1979, Joanne Chesimard escaped from the Clinton Correctional Institution for Women. She is still at large.

ACKNOWLEDGMENTS

In the three years I have worked on this book, I have been most fortunate to have been offered the intelligence, empathy, sympathy, inspiration, support, and recollections of so many people. I am more grateful than I can say to:

Sheriff Dave Burks, Dick Tracy, Kurt Wuest, Doug Welch, Jon Peckels, and Bill Kennedy of the Lane County Sheriff's Office; Lt. Jerry Smith, Springfield Police Department; Jim Pex, Oregon State Police Crime Laboratory; Ray Broderick, Paul Alton, Paula Krogdahl, Lane County District Attorney's Office.

Judge Gregory G. Foote, Lane County Circuit Court.

Shelby Day, Judy Patterson, Jan Goldberg Temple, Carleen Elbridge, McKenzie-Williamette Hospital.

Nancy and Billy McCoy, Evelyn and Ray Slaven, Claudia Langan, Eugene, Oregon; Edison A. Barlow; Charlene and Robert Knickerbocker, Chandler, Arizona; Maureen and Bill Woodcock, Donna Anders, Ann Combs, Barbara Easton, Jennie Everson, Betty Fredericksen, Bill and Shirley Hickman, Gerry Brittingham, Andy Rule, S. Bruce Sherles, James Jones, Diane and Alan Espy, Dr. Peter J. Modde, Seattle, Washington; Laura Harris, Battleground, Washington; Mike Rule, Pullman, Washington; Dick Reed, Camas, Washington.

Press: Elouise Schumacher, Betty Udeson, *Seattle Times*; Rick Attig, *Springfield News*; Dave Angier, Dee Dixon, KGW; Maureen Shine, KMTR; Sandy Poole, Henry Zinman, Paddy Kean, Mary Starett, KATU; Ross Hamilton, Kathleen Monje, Dana Tims, the *Oregonian*; Jack Hamann, Diana Wilmar, KING; Sally Hodgkinson, UPI; Ken Koopman, *Cottage Grove Sentinel*; Eric Mason, KOIN; Ann Portal, Eugene *Register-Guard*, with special thanks to Anne Bradley Jaeger of KEZI, who shared her insights regarding the videotape of her exclusive interview with Diane Downs, and to Lars Larson, KVAL.

I wish to express my particular gratitude to Enes and Jana Smith of the Eugene Police Department; and to Mildred Yoacham, my favorite and most dogged researcher; Sophie M. Stackhouse, my favorite critic; Leslie M. Rule, my trial assistant; Frederick Noonan, my copy editor; Michaela Hamilton, my astute and encouraging editor throughout this long and sometimes discouraging three-year project; Joan and Joe Foley, my first, last, and always literary agents; and, finally, to my friend Pierce R. Brooks, the man responsible for my writing this book, with my highest respect and admiration for his contributions to his fellow man.

ABOUT THE AUTHOR

Ann Rule wrote thirty-five *New York Times* bestsellers. Her first bestseller, *The Stranger Beside Me*, was about her personal relationship with infamous serial killer Ted Bundy. A former Seattle police officer, she used her firsthand expertise in all her books. For more than three decades, she was a powerful advocate for victims of violent crime. She lived near Seattle and passed away in 2015.